BRIEF ENCOUNTERS

Emily Coleman
and Betty Edwards

DOUBLEDAY & COMPANY, INC.
GARDEN CITY, NEW YORK
1979

Library of Congress Cataloging in Publication Data

Coleman, Emily.
    Brief encounters.

    Bibliography
        1. Interpersonal relations. 2. Etiquette for
men. 3. Etiquette for women. 4. Men—Sexual
behavior. 5. Women—Sexual behavior. 6. Intimacy
(Psychology)   I. Edwards, Betty, joint author.
II. Title.
HM132.C56   158'.2
ISBN: 0-385-12174-1
Library of Congress Catalog Card Number 77-16908

Acknowledgments

We are grateful to our editor, Sally Arteseros, who encouraged us during the difficult times, cheered us during the good times and maintained her enthusiasm for the book even when ours sometimes faltered.

We are also indebted to the countless men and women who shared their personal experiences with us and to the many authorities on human relationships who granted us interviews. While it would be impossible to list everyone who has contributed to this book individually, there were some who were particularly helpful to us:

Dr. Bruce Bernstein, psychologist, who, many years ago, sparked Emily's interest in exploring the value of short-term relationships and encouraged her to design the first Brief Encounter workshop.

Madelyn Hathaway, psychodrama instructor, who helped us train some men and women to become "gentle aggressors" and who helped them put this training into actual practice.

Dr. Adele and Sam Scheele, social engineers, who sparked our own creativity by describing some of the techniques they have used in their own work in helping men and women work, play and live together more pleasurably and effectively.

Dr. Barry F. Singer, Associate Professor of Psychology at California State University at Long Beach, and Joel Springer, Ph.D. candidate at the University of Minnesota and marriage and family counselor, who not only spent much time talking with us about their work in the area of male-female relationships but who also granted us access to their research material.

Dr. Roger Coleman, Ray Cooper, Dr. Keith Tombrink and Hans VanderMeyden, who made many helpful suggestions about the book and who also helped by simply being themselves.

To Keith Tombrink, my beloved, who is at the heart of my Tender Circle.

Emily Coleman

To my friend, the late Joanne Norris, who gave me far more than she ever knew.

Betty Edwards

Contents

Contents

PART I

1

Brief Encounters and Short-Term Alliances:
Why you have had, are having and will continue to have them

The only relationships we seem to value are those that last, if not forever, at least for a long, long time. And leaving any kind of long-term relationship—whether with a person, a job, a place or an idea—is often seen as a failure. How often have you made or heard statements like these:

> Joe and Phyllis got a divorce just one month before their twentieth anniversary. What a shock! That's one marriage I sure thought would succeed.

> How can you just walk away from me (or your job, our house, the Democratic party, the Elks) after all these years?

> Harry just wasted all that time he spent studying medicine. Now he's decided to become a sculptor.

We are afraid to become involved in relationships that don't appear to show any promise of going on for a long, long time. We tell ourselves or others:

> Why waste time with him/her? There's no future in it.

I haven't bothered to make any friends in this town because I'm only going to be here six months.

Even wanting to make changes in an existing long-term relationship can bring the tearful or hostile accusation: "You've
changed. You used to *be, feel, think, do* . . ." Clearly we want our
relationships to stay the same—and to go on and on. As in the old
marathon dances of the 1930s, we pick as winners, not those who
dance the best, but those who endure the longest.

We give a gold watch to those who retire after forty years on
the same job, a big party for those who have been married twenty-
five or fifty years, certificates or plaques to people who have been a
member of any organization for five or ten or fifteen years. A
"best friend" may be called that simply because we have known
him since fifth grade. Time, stability, permanence—to many these
are the ultimate criteria of a worthwhile relationship.

And yet the reality for most of us, whether we are married or
single, young or old, male or female, is that fewer and fewer of our
relationships are lasting for a very long time. Even people who
seem to epitomize stability—those who are happily married, involved in a committed long-term relationship or surrounded by a
huge and loving family—experience an almost constant flow of
other people in and out of their lives. More and more of us are
finding it necessary to say "hello" and "goodbye" more rapidly
than ever before even though a lot of times we don't like such
short relationships. Here are some of the reasons why.

We Americans are a mobile group. You may be required to
move to hold on to your job, because your spouse has been promoted, because you want to move "up" to a better neighborhood
or can no longer afford your present one or because you are a victim of the typical American wanderlust and simply want to move
on to someplace different. Whatever the reasons, by the mid-
seventies close to 36 million Americans were changing their place
of residence during a single year.

And we change jobs just as readily. Not only do young people
try out and quit many jobs—baby-sitter, box boy, service station
attendant, salesperson, parking valet—before settling on a career,
it has become increasingly common for adults to move from one
firm to another. Or if they stay with the same firm, to move a
number of times to different departments or even cities. It is no

longer unusual for persons to change from one career to an entirely different one several times in their lifetime or even to have two careers at the same time.

Geographical and job mobility combined with ease of transportation move a lot of people into and out of our lives at a rapid rate. Recent studies by social psychologist Stanley Milgram indicate that most Americans are acquainted with from 500 to 2,500 people, and though some of these will remain in your life for a long time, most won't. You can no longer take it for granted your marriage partner will be one who remains. The average marriage now lasts but seven years. And in a country where there is now one divorce for every two marriages in our so-called "average" communities and almost twice that in a number of our major urban cities and coastal areas, movie stars and wealthy playboys are by no means the only ones who can lay claim to two, three or even more ex-mates.

Obviously, millions of Americans are not staying in the same place, on the same job or with the same person forever and yet few people feel entirely comfortable with the reality of a life that conflicts so sharply with the values they have been taught. It is difficult to accept the fact that we are not going to stay with many things—places, jobs or people forever—not even those we care for very deeply.

It is the purpose of this book to help you come to terms with that social reality and to show you how to make the most of relationships that may not last forever or even for a very long time. Whether you call them temporary, transitory or short-term, relationships of this nature are here to stay. You are undoubtedly having them now whether you realize it or not. And short-term relationships are neither inherently superior nor inferior to long-term ones. It's just that they are a fact of life in this rapidly changing world and that to feel emotionally fulfilled—or perhaps even to survive—all of us need to develop a different goal for relationships than duration. In addition, short-term relationships can be a source of joy, enrichment and satisfaction *if* you acquire the attitudes and skills to do two things:

1. Enjoy to the utmost whatever moments are spent with another person—no matter how few these may be.
2. Make agreements with others to get more—much

more—of what people can give one another to enrich their experience of life *right now* instead of being limited by concerns about what might happen tomorrow.

What keeps people from doing these two things and valuing relationships for what they are—no matter how long they last—is that we tend to use the words "short-term" and "long-term" as value judgments, with short-term meaning inferior and long-term meaning superior. Thus, many people think that a man and a woman who have been going together for a year and a half are having a long-term relationship and that is "good" because it looks as though it is going to last. However, if they get married and stay married for only five years, that is a short-term relationship and "bad" because it didn't last.

However, when you look back on your life, probably many things you thought were long-term at the time—a job, a home, a love affair, a friendship—now seem like short-term aspects of your life. And there are probably some short-term relationships you had—knowing they wouldn't last—that you valued because of the circumstances surrounding them, circumstances that forced you to take a different attitude toward the relationship. It may have been a friendship you developed with someone during the course of a work project, knowing you would not have contact after the project was completed because of time and distance. It may have been the love affair you had on a trip knowing it wouldn't last "forever" because he or she lived on the opposite coast.

Thus, if someone were to ask, "How long is a short-term relationship?" that question could not be answered in terms of days, weeks, months or years. Each person's answer would depend upon what kind of relationship was being considered, his expectations of its permanence and the circumstances surrounding it.

We aren't suggesting that people have no concern about the duration of a relationship, think only of today and not make promises to each other. In fact, to have good short-term relationships, people must make clearer, firmer, more responsible promises. However, these promises should center around the present and immediate future and not on some illusory "forever." And the duration of a relationship must not be our only or even our primary yardstick. When it is, we can't appreciate life's moments.

And life is made up of moments—moments of tenderness, of laughter, of devilishness, of hope, of insight, of success. The quality of our lives is based on how much we live for *now*—on how many moments we allow ourselves to experience.

Unfortunately, we tend to forget many of our special moments since we have no ceremonies, gold watches or certificates to mark them. But you can recall and cherish them and learn how to have more of them. You can especially enrich your life by learning how to share some special moments with other people—special moments we call *brief encounters.*

Brief encounters are short periods of time when people are so close to one another that they can almost hear the other's heart beat, sense the other's thoughts and feel the other's joy and pain. Each person "encounters" the other in a vitalizing way—exposing facets of himself (beliefs, experiences, feelings) not ordinarily exposed—and is heard and seen and understood by the other.

The amount of time people spend together isn't the important thing about a brief encounter—nor where it takes place—nor how long they have known each other. It can take place when people stand together in line for fifteen minutes and never see each other again. It can take place on a cross-continent airplane ride when seatmates completely lose a sense of time because they are so taken with one another. It can take place when people sitting in the living room they've shared for twenty years suddenly see and hear each other as if for the first time.

Nor is the desire to repeat a particular brief encounter necessary for the experience to be significant. Many times, like climbing the Pyramids, it's something you wouldn't want to have missed but you wouldn't necessarily want to do it again. And a brief encounter can be disturbing—can shake you up—by making you think about things you never thought about before and by making you feel things you never felt before.

You have probably had dozens—maybe hundreds—of brief encounters, but you may have difficulty recognizing their importance if you accept the common belief that only time can bring in-depth encounters. Perhaps you have pushed the memories of brief encounters back into the dark corners of your mind, but they are there. Sometimes a song, or the scent of a certain perfume, or a snapshot or letter you discover as you clean out a desk drawer can bring joy or pain or wistfulness—and the memory of a brief encounter you savor in secret believing no one else would understand.

In the "Brief Encounters" workshops Emily has given for hundreds of men and women (to help them learn the importance of short-term relationships and how to get more out of them), there has never been a person who could not recall at least one particularly significant brief encounter.

Kathleen remembered an encounter that brightened her outlook during an unpleasant period of her life. She and her husband had moved to a new town and, even before the unpacking was finished, he had left on an extended business trip. One cold and gloomy rainy day she was cooped up with a sick daughter and feeling sorry for herself. She had too much to do and no friends or neighbors to talk to. She resented the move and her husband's absence and was convinced she would never again have the kind of friends she had in the old home town. Her resentment increased when she realized she would have to leave her ten-year-old alone while she went to the store for her prescription.

Trudging along the wet sidewalk to the corner drugstore, she began to enjoy the exhilaration of the wind and rain on her face. As she opened the door to the drugstore—glowing and flushed from the exercise and the elements—a man coming out of the door paused, looked at her and exclaimed, "My God, you're beautiful." She got the medicine and floated home, her resentment gone, convinced that people were O.K. after all and maybe even as nice here as in her former town.

Tom, another workshop participant, told of a brief encounter, one that lasted only thirty minutes, but that taught him a valuable lesson. It was a time of considerable pressure in forty-five-year-old Tom's life. His job required more of his time than usual, his teen-age children were undergoing the typical teen-age traumas and he and his wife were in the midst of a marital crisis. Then, just as he felt he could hardly handle the problems he was having, his mother had a severe heart attack. Although she recovered, the illness left her shaky, frightened and feeling terribly alone.

On his way to visit her one afternoon, a visit sandwiched between a business conference and a trip to the marriage counselor, Tom dashed into a cafeteria for a quick lunch. He happened to sit across a table from a bright-looking little old lady. In the course of making "small talk," Tom found himself suddenly opening up to the old woman and telling her of the anxiety and guilt he felt about his mother—about the fact that he spent all the time he could possibly spare with her but that it just didn't seem to be enough. Tom thought the old lady would praise him for his sacrifice in finding time every single day to visit his mother, no matter what it was costing him in job and family pressures and nervous strain to his system.

To his surprise, she gave him a lecture which went something like this:

> You just can't give in to those old people who want to be twenty again and healthy. They can drain you dry so you'll end up feeling old and miserable along with them. Your mother is old and sickly, and she has to face that fact. You can't make her happy; she has to do that for herself. And, in fact, you may be weighing her down with the burden of your pity.

Tom left the cafeteria feeling better about his mother—and about the rest of his life—than he had in a long time. He saw that he had been hurting his mother by his unconscious demand on her to recover, to not be sick, to, in effect, get well and get off his back. He realized he couldn't solve anyone else's problems, not his children's nor his wife's. A lot of his anxiety and guilt had come from taking too much responsibility for others.

Brief encounters like these are the punctuation of life, the experiences that give emphasis and meaning to what otherwise might make no sense at all. However, for a brief encounter to grow from a significant moment to a meaningful relationship it is necessary for the parties involved to make agreements with one another, to develop an acknowledged alliance.

Alliances, in fact, give form and purpose to all sorts of relationships not only those that grow out of brief encounters; acquaintanceships can develop into short-term relationships, and long-term relationships can gain stability and enrichment through the use of alliances. An alliance is a contract people make to do something to, for or with each other in exchange for something returned. Unlike a brief encounter, alliances don't just happen. Since they require the cooperation of all participants, they have to be consciously and deliberately "made."

People have always made alliances with one another. But the alliances we have paid the most attention to in the past either were long-term ones that served more to limit and confine a partner than to give pleasure or encourage growth (i.e., "Love, honor and obey until death do us part") or have been for the purpose of linking people together to fight a common enemy or achieve a common goal. Wars, vendettas and elections all depend upon alliances being made by people who don't care much about good things happening to each other; they just want bad things to happen to somebody else.

The kind of alliances that are important today are short-term ones between people concerned with one another's pleasure and personal development. It takes these temporary alliances to assure that people get what they want and need and to keep relationships up to date, since everyone's wants and needs change with time and circumstance.

A temporary alliance is a contract between people who care about one another made for the purpose of giving and getting something that is wanted or needed at that particular time (but not necessarily forever). It can be a contract to listen to one another's troubles without criticizing or giving advice. It can be a contract to be devilish together—to eat hot-fudge sundaes, jaywalk, shop for unnecessary clothes, use profane words and laugh a lot. It can be a contract just to have oodles of playful, lusty sex but not to talk of problems or have heavy discussions. Or it can be a contract for people to teach each other something of value—something intellectual or something very practical and mundane. There are many reasons for making short-term alliances.

It is not the degree of caring or the depth of involvement that characterizes a temporary alliance. Caring is important, but it can vary from casual friendship to passionate love. What is essential is that both partners feel good about what they agree to do. And the rewards of their alliance are in the present or the foreseeable future.

Temporary alliances can have definite limits—in duration or scope or both. Or they can have no perceivable limits but the partners recognize that they are bound to require changes from time to time and so don't expect them to go on forever as is.

An alliance limited in duration was made by Harry and Sally. When Harry met Sally, his wife had been ill for several years and was unable to give him much affection or intellectual stimulation.

Sally had just gotten a divorce, feared a long-term commitment and felt the need to live alone. Yet she wanted the warmth, comfort and sexual pleasure available in an ongoing relationship. Together Harry and Sally worked out a plan whereby they could see each other discreetly once or twice a week with the idea that they would discontinue their alliance when she wanted more involvement than he could offer or when his wife recovered.

An alliance limited in scope—but with no limits on its duration —was made by Nancy and Evelyn, residents of an apartment building. Both of them—single career women in their late twenties—were a little overawed at the impersonality of the huge apartment complex in which they lived and unsure about how to meet the many available and eligible males who also lived in the complex. They formed an alliance to give each other emotional support as well as practical help in enlarging their limited social circles.

They made a firm commitment, which could not be lightly broken (particularly not for a last-minute date with a male), to spend a long evening together once a week. During this evening, they prepared dinner together, ate well and leisurely and discussed whatever was concerning either of them at the moment—jobs, friends, men, redecorating, etc. In addition, each one was committed to organizing some sort of small social event—a dinner, brunch, party—every other month as a way of bringing more interesting men and women into both of their lives.

Temporary alliances are important to long-term relationships as well as short-term ones. Two people, by making a number of alliances with one another, one after the other, can turn a short-term relationship into a long-term one. The authors of this book started their relationship with a brief encounter when Betty (in the role of free-lance magazine writer) went to interview Emily (in the role of authority on male-female relationships). During the interview the roles dissolved and the people behind them emerged. We talked all afternoon, during dinner and into the wee small hours of the morning, discovering in the process that we had many things in common, including a desire to write books on human relationships. A few days later we developed an alliance to write a book together and started working on outlines.

During the period of our first alliance, we merged our personal and social lives so closely we became each other's "primary person." A primary person (to Betty's way of thinking) is one who brings you chicken soup when you are sick, whom you can call at three in the morning in an emergency and who will bail you out of jail. To Emily's way of thinking, a primary person is the one you think of first of all when you have a triumph or defeat to share—the person you can depend upon to appreciate your joy or to comfort you. During this phase, we laughed a lot, cried a lot, "therapied" each other and gave some terrific parties together. But when we signed our first book contract and settled down to actually write a book, the terms of our alliance changed. Because we spent all day, every day, writing and because of the stresses of our creative collaboration, we found it necessary to see less of each other socially. The professional relationship—creative, exciting, demanding—became the focus of the alliance.

Our alliance changed again when Emily got a new primary person in her life—a man—who became her lover as well as her business partner. She had less time for writing, while Betty, who had taken a leave of absence from her full-time teaching job, had more.

We've made no "forever" promises to each other. Our professional alliance could end when we finish this book. Our personal alliance could end whenever it is no longer satisfying or growth-producing or simply when circumstances take us away from each other. All we know is that we are sharing something good today, something we expect and hope will go on, but something we can let go of when we have to—with love and gratitude.

While everyone is capable of experiencing joyous and enriching brief encounters and temporary alliances, many people avoid them because of the belief in one or more of the following myths:

Myth No. 1. *Short-term relationships will hinder your long-term ones.* People who have a close primary bond with a member of the opposite sex often fear that the relationship will be threatened if they have relationships of any depth with other people. Therefore, many couples deliberately or unconsciously shut out other people with their "just we two" attitude. But it is unrealistic to expect another person, even the most loving spouse, to be able to fulfill all your needs. And to marry or move in with someone with the idea that you are going to be suddenly "fulfilled" in every way is to burden your relationship with an impossible weight.

While the majority of people expect to get their sexual and

emotional needs fulfilled in a long-term committed relationship, they have many other needs their partner may not have the time, energy, inclination or ability to fulfill. One partner may desire to participate in more social or sports activities than the other; one partner may want and need someone to hold long intellectual discussions with; and both partners need friends with whom to share their joys and troubles.

When you get your needs and wants filled through auxiliary brief encounters and temporary alliances, you are more likely to enjoy your ongoing relationship. You will not resent your partner because he can't give you everything you need and want; you will not expect more from him than he can give; and you will not make him feel guilty or inadequate because he does not have the ability to fulfill all your needs.

Myth No. 2. *Short-term relationships make you shallow.* Shallow people "kiss and tell." They flaunt their short-term relationships, brag about how many affairs they have had and how they "love 'em and leave 'em." When others, already prejudiced against short-term relationships, see this sort of behavior, they accept it as proof that short-term relationships must be shallow and meaningless.

Certainly short-term relationships can be shallow and empty. So can a long-term partnership or even a fifty-year-long marriage. The length of a relationship doesn't determine its worth any more than the length of a person's alliances indicates his character. There are as many, if not more, unmotivated, insensitive, irresponsible, selfish clods performing like robots in shallow but enduring relationships with mates, children and friends as there are unmotivated, insensitive, irresponsible, selfish clods flip-flopping from bed to bed, job to job or bar to bar.

Myth No. 3. *People who have many short-term relationships are using others and that is bad.* People must use other people in order to grow. We can't grow alone. And we have but two choices —grow and survive or stagnate and die. People also must be used by others in order to feel useful—to feel worthwhile and to validate their own existence. Believing that you are helpful to others is what makes the difference between merely existing and really living. All of us, like silver goblets, shine and glow when used frequently, tarnish when left on the shelf.

However, people do not flourish when abused by others—when they are treated as interchangeable "things" and then callously "discarded" when their usefulness is over. And yet, when an alliance is no longer mutually satisfying, when people outgrow each other, or when circumstances force one or the other to move on, the relationship can be ended with kindness and compassion and without making the person who is being left behind feel he has been cast aside as worthless.

Sometimes just the way a goodbye is handled can make a person feel he has been valued or can make him feel he has been coldheartedly discarded. Far from suggesting an "easy come, easy go" attitude, we are suggesting people learn to develop sensitivity and skill so that when a parting does become necessary, they will be sure they are not abusing others.

If short-term relationships won't harm you just because they are short-term, can they help you? The answer is unequivocally: *Yes, Yes, Yes.* Learning to enjoy the short-term relationships you are now having, appreciate the ones you have had and deliberately seek out more and better ones in the future can enhance your life in many ways. In this book we will present new opportunities for your pleasure and personal development and show you how to take advantage of them. Here are some of the specific ways this book can help you:

1. *In building an emotionally fulfilling life even if you don't have a one-and-only.*

As long as anyone living today can remember, we've been told through subtle and not so subtle means by parents, teachers, social and religious customs, laws, songs and advertisements, that being half of a heterosexual couple is the *only* way to be. However, there are times in a person's life when circumstances prevent him from making a long-term commitment, the right person isn't available or a mate just isn't wanted. Most persons feel that it is just natural and normal to be emotionally malnourished and to feel lonely at these times. This is not true, but believing it is true can make it happen.

Taking it for granted that a long-term mate is required to fill a person's needs for affection, companionship, fun and sex can cause him to overlook the many people all around who could give him much of what he wants right now. Getting rid of the idea that the only relationship that can really satisfy is one with a member of the opposite sex—one that must last forever—allows a person to look at everyone with new eyes. It permits the formation of more emotionally rewarding friendships with people of the same sex and encourages a person to take pleasure in whatever someone of the opposite sex has to offer *now*, instead of being disgruntled that he or she can't or won't guarantee everything that is wanted *forever*.

Not only does getting rid of this cultural one-and-only myth permit the discovery of wonderful, helpful others, it also reveals more options and brings contentment with the options available.

If you want a long-term monogamous relationship, you'll be better able to wait for the right person to come along if your needs are being fulfilled each day. You won't be as apt to rush in and grab somebody who is not right for you and sign a lifetime contract just because you are starved for human contact.

On the other hand, if you decide never to have one monogamous relationship or if you simply are unable ever to find one intensely satisfying love, it doesn't mean you have to live your life as a second-class citizen emotionally. You can build a supportive network of friends. In this book, we'll give you a blueprint for a constellation of attachments that will permit you to thrive whether or not you have a one-and-only—and some new tools for building this supportive network.

2. *In showing you how to use others (without abusing them) to develop new facets of your personality, to develop a rich inner life and become more effective as an individual.*

The relationships that we have with others literally shape us as human beings. Every person with whom we have had close contact becomes a part of us. As Dr. Herbert Otto, internationally known leader in the human potential movement, says in his course "Developing Personal Potential," "You become what you are through interpersonal relationships and you will become what you can be through them also."

You can't possibly learn from family members or through study or experience all that you need to learn to get along in these times of rapid change and a knowledge explosion. You must learn—and learn quickly—from the people you meet. That person sitting next to you in the airplane or across the room from you at a party may have just the information you need. To live well, even to exist, we need to learn about computers, income tax changes, communicable diseases, Medicare forms, condominiums, aerosol cans, steel belted radials and the nutrients and contaminants in food. You must discover who knows what and get them to share their knowledge with you.

In addition, in order to discover the many *yous* there are, you need contact with others who are not in the same socio-economic bracket, who dress, think, talk and act quite differently from you. By sampling a wide variety of people with a wide variety of interests, you not only bring new knowledge and excitement into your life but you become a more fascinating person. We'll show you how you can use brief encounters and short-term alliances with a wide variety of other people—teachers, friends, students, playmates, co-workers, neighbors, relatives—to become a more creative and effective *whole* person.

3. *In showing you how to end relationships that don't last forever with the minimum trauma for all concerned.*

In the past, most people gave little or no thought as to how to end a relationship with grace, tact and finesse and move on. *There was no need.* Meaningful relationships were supposed to go on as long as the people involved in them lived. But since people didn't live as long in the past, forever just wasn't as long as it is today.

Let's take a new look at Romeo and Juliet. Can you imagine what might have happened if they had lived today and been able to get married? After twenty-five years of looking at one another over the breakfast table, they would have been bored. And they would have had a lot of problems because her mother couldn't come over for a visit as long as she was married to *him* and his father wouldn't lend him money to build up his business as long as he was married to *her.*

But Romeo and Juliet didn't live long enough for their relationship to die. Before vitamins, modern sanitation, vaccination and antibiotics, life was short. During the Middle Ages, the average life expectancy was somewhere between twenty-one and twenty-eight years. Had they lived, Romeo would have been an old man at thirty-five and Juliet would have lost most of her babies before they were five years old—had she not died giving birth to them.

Yesterday's attitudes and skills aren't enough for coping with life today—not when most women can expect to live until they are seventy-five and men until they are sixty-seven. "Forever" becomes somewhat more ominous when it could mean fifty years of a tedious, unrewarding marital relationship or sixty years of increasing boredom during a "lifetime" friendship. Our lives are considerably different but no less difficult than those of people in the past. Where they had to learn to deal with the death of their loved ones, we have to learn to deal with the fact that many significant people in our lives—mates, friends, relatives—are going to stay alive and that many of our relationships will die before we do.

Today we must learn to say goodbye to relationships that have died—to develop rituals and techniques for bringing about closure. If we don't, we'll carry around as excess baggage a load of "unfinished business" that will keep us from moving on and living our lives as fully as we can. Whether it is the massive loss we feel when a significant figure goes out of our lives or the more constant but smaller losses we feel as people move in and out of our lives, we must all learn to say goodbye with skill and compassion.

In this book we aren't going to pretend that goodbyes don't hurt—to give you a formula guaranteed to make parting no more than a momentary pang. Both of the authors, because of divorce, death and changes, have felt personal losses far too deeply for that. But we have learned from our losses and want to pass that knowledge on. There are ways to make your losses easier to bear; there are attitudes and skills to be developed that help you cope with the pain that partings can bring, that help you "let go" with less grief, regret and anger and move on to new relationships sooner.

4. *In revealing how to deal with the stresses caused by the ever-increasing people-turnover in your life.*

As you reap the benefits of brief encounters and temporary alliances, you may find that at times you are in danger of becoming "over-peopled"—having more people in your life than you can comfortably handle in terms of time and energy. The truth is that you simply may not have the time or inclination to have a relationship with all the people who are interested in having one with you. Or you may want to concentrate on one or a few relationships for a while, or on a work project, and need to back away temporarily from some alliances you have already established.

In this book, we show you how to "unpeople," to put some relationships on hold and, in a kind and caring way, change the terms of others. This is a necessary skill today because the enormous changes going on—in jobs, residences, life styles, knowledge, relationships—cause all of us to show signs of stress behavior now and then. And research has shown that people sometimes get physically ill when there are more changes in their lives than they can cope with. While there are no definitive studies to prove how many relationships humans can tolerate or how fast they can get in and out of them without physical or psychological disease, learning to "unpeople" at times can help you control the amount of stress in your life.

Learning to make the most of short-term relationships will not always be easy. You'll have to change attitudes you've had for a long time and develop many new interrelating skills. But changing your attitudes can be exciting and learning new skills can be fun— especially if you talk some friends into joining you in trying some of the behavior we suggest.

Supportive friends of the same and of the opposite sex—friends who also want to learn to make the most of relationships that may not last forever—can applaud your successes, chuckle at your escapades, commiserate over your moments of embarrassment or rejection and give you feedback on what it is about your behavior that may be helping or hindering you in your attempts to form new kinds of relationships.

Whether you use this book alone or with the help of friends, we have provided a specific assignment for you at the end of this chapter as well as suggestions and techniques within almost every chapter. The assignment will help you become aware of your present attitudes, relationships and behavior and the suggestions and techniques within each chapter will provide you with specific behavior you can try out at parties, at work, in elevators, on the street—wherever there are people with whom you might want to have brief encounters or short-term alliances.

While *Brief Encounters* is a consciousness-raising book, it is also a guide. To get the most from it, do the assignments and try as many of the suggestions as seem safe and feasible to you—and some that don't. You can gain insights, fun and new friends to help you lead a more adventurous, meaningful life. The assignment at the end of this chapter will help you take a closer look at the kind of relationships you are having *right now*. So get going, and whether you have a brief encounter, temporary alliance or long-term relationship with this book, we hope the "moments" you spend with it will be happy and beneficial ones.

ASSIGNMENT

1. List several relationships that you now have which you consider short-term.
    a. Why do you consider them short-term?
    b. What needs do they fill for you?
    c. Do you consider them satisfying? Why or why not?
2. List several relationships you consider long-term.
    a. Why do you consider them long-term?
    b. What needs do they fill for you?
    c. Do you consider them satisfying? Why or why not?

People, People Everywhere:
Why aren't you meeting them?

Brief encounters, and short-term alliances have to begin some-where, sometime, with someone. People meet in a variety of ways. A meeting can be ever so casual at a gathering of some sort—social, political, educational, religious or business. Or formal—an intro-duction arranged by a mutual friend. Or purposeful—a calculated and successful pickup in a bar or on a street corner. Or it can even be accidental—an unlikely crossing of the paths of strangers that occurs frequently in the movies but less often in real life.

What happens at that first meeting is significant. It can deter-mine if there will be more than one meeting and even influence the tone of the relationship from then on.

What makes the difference is whether you actually make con-tact with that other person—whether you acknowledge his exist-ence as a person or whether you just use him as a "social module" —an entity who happens to be sharing a seat with you on a train, lighting your cigarette at a party or waiting on you at a store. Though it takes awareness to make contact, it doesn't take any more time than *not* making contact does. In fact, contact—that feeling of having made a momentary connection with another warm, alive human being—can occur in the twinkling of an eye, before any words are spoken, as when two strangers gently touch each other in passing—with their eyes, and smiles or gestures.

You can never be sure when that feeling of having made con-tact will occur. You can acutely feel the absence of it, and try your best to get it and yet not be able to go past that social distance that prevents the people you meet from connecting with you. You can seek contact, be ready for it and if you're lucky, find someone else who also is seeking it. Or it may come as a complete surprise when during an introduction you desultorily take a stranger's hand, look into his or her eyes and realize with a start that he is really looking at—*and seeing*—you.

The purpose of this chapter and of the three that follow is to help you learn how to meet strangers and make contact with them, to enjoy the contact itself, no matter how fleeting, and to be open to whatever might come out of that contact.

There are several good reasons why everyone—married or single, young or old, rich or poor—needs to learn to meet others easily and make effective contact. Everyone needs to know that he is not alone in a cold, hostile world. Everyone needs frequent reassurance that all around are a lot of warm human beings who have something in common with him. Everyone needs the feeling of being supported by a network of non-constricting connections.

Some people need new connections more than others. For example, anyone who has just moved, had a job change or gotten a divorce is likely to be extremely conscious of the need to make friends and sooner or later will be motivated to seek new contacts. But even those who on the surface seem to have their "people-needs" met, who are married, have children and a wide circle of friends, may suffer from overwhelming loneliness at times. Those around them may move, may become less available for contact, may desire a different sort of contact or may leave emotionally. Though surrounded by people, a person can feel desperately alone if he lacks the skills to meet and replace those who have moved on—to turn strangers into friends, lovers, husbands, wives, roommates.

This kind of loneliness frequently stems from an inability to connect with the people who are around. According to psychiatrist Allan Fromme in *The Ability to Love*, "True loneliness is a basic sense of unconnectedness with people. It is in essence the denial of satisfaction of a deep need that we all share, the need to form relationships, to become attached, to love and be loved in some way."

The loneliness we are referring to, so common in our culture, is not the same as being alone. Everyone needs to be alone at times, have solitude in order to think and dream and create. And everyone is lonely now and then when going through periods of intense personal growth or change. But chronic loneliness is unnecessary, unproductive and sad. It happens when people—in ways they don't even realize—cut themselves off from contact with others and with themselves. Though they may try to communicate, they find themselves, like a phone with technical problems, chronically disconnected.

Learning to really connect with others can help to ease some of the chronic excessive loneliness and boredom that is prevalent in our society. Here is why:

It is easy to feel that you are "out of it," that you live in an alien, hostile world of people who aren't "your kind," who don't understand you and who are out to get you. Many times we limit our friends and acquaintances to those who make about the same amount of money that we do, who have similar jobs, are in our age bracket and have the same marital status, in an effort to surround ourselves with those who seem "our kind" so we can relax a bit.

Actually, every person you see has something in common with you no matter how different he or she may appear. It's a fact that all human beings have feelings in common. But it is more than sharing similar feelings that connects us. When you come out from behind your façade and find ways to slip behind the façade of those around you, some of the many links between you will emerge. You discover the ways in which you are connected to others in a vast web of humanness that makes you feel supported, respected and reinforced.

It can be both surprising and comforting to discover that you share a mutual friend with someone who seems quite alien to you. Or perhaps you have gone to the same school at different times or lived in the same city. Or you do the same kind of work or want to. Or you have similar tastes in food or music, have similar hang-ups or aspirations.

One of the reasons men and women enjoy themselves so much and find so many interesting people at the Friday-night "People-Samplers" Emily and her partner, Dr. Keith Tombrink, hold for their Man-Woman Institute is that participants are encouraged to look for things they have in common with other people. As people enter, they are grouped with three or four others they don't already know and are encouraged to talk together with the purpose of discovering what they have in common. An excited buzz soon fills the room as a hundred or so former "strangers" find out they aren't strangers after all.

Next time you find yourself with people who don't seem to be "your kind" and you are feeling out of it or bored you can liven up things by doing a little behavioral science research on your own, by testing the theory that if you put *any two people* together and get them *talking about themselves,* sooner or later they'll discover they have something in common. You can tell strangers about this theory and ask them to help you test its validity. Or you can keep it in mind as you talk to those you don't know very well and it will help you steer clear of the meaningless party "chit-chat" we all indulge in far too often, and direct the conversation along more personal "contact-making" lines.

Here is how to go about it:

> Look around and pick one or two other people—people you don't know already—and start talking with them. Talk in any way you want but with the idea in mind to try to discover what you have in common. Here are some suggestions:
>
> 1. Ask questions you wouldn't ordinarily ask.
> 2. Volunteer information you wouldn't ordinarily volunteer.
>
> After you've made a number of discoveries (and you will) tell your new friends what you particularly like about them or let them know your first impressions of them—what you thought about them when you first saw them. Or you can explore in more depth some of the subjects that came up as you sought similarities.

If you try this exercise, you'll discover how easy it can be to make contact with strangers. Why, then, don't more people do it? After all, there is no scarcity of people with whom to have brief encounters and relationships. People are everywhere—crowded together on city streets, jammed together in recreation areas, uncomfortably close in restaurants, movies, theaters and clogging the highways and skies with public and private vehicles.

The first and most important reason is that we simply do not know how. Until now, people-meeting skills have not been that important to us and so they have not been incorporated into our educative process—either through our formal schooling, through the informal but even more important education we receive from family and friends, or through the skills and attitudes we pick up by just being a member of society. In the past we didn't have a continuous stream of people running through our lives; in fact, the life of a young man or woman was molded toward only one significant meeting—that of his or her future spouse.

Society was geared to make that meeting possible. Matchmaking relatives, friends, townspeople were all on the lookout to help eligible people connect, and there were plenty of acceptable places for young people to meet—church socials, dances, picnics, coming-out parties, balls. Everyone had a stake in getting people married, in maintaining the economic and social basis for traditional family life.

There was less confusion then as to just who was eligible as a potential spouse. The only "acceptable" mates were of one's own class—meaning a similar economic status and preferably cultural background. Though that limited choice, it also limited the need to get out and meet a lot of people of the opposite sex. In fact, anyone who did have a lot of contact with the opposite sex was definitely suspect and, if female, beyond the pale.

When a woman married, she didn't need to make new friends. If she stayed in her home town she had her female relatives and girlhood chums. In any case, her husband's social circle became her own. Men—then as now—tended to make their friends on the basis of their work. Married couples just didn't need the ability to meet people and make new friends as much as they do today.

Those who didn't marry had less choice than today. They were social misfits and if past a certain age (an 1895 etiquette book refers to girls over twenty-five as "elderly girls") were not expected to be seeking mates. Their life style, and thus their social contacts, were preselected for them. Women might live with married relatives as unofficial baby-sitters and household helpers or work in certain careers (the stereotype of the "old maid" schoolteacher was all too real). Men could play the role of indulgent uncle, town eccentric or society bachelor (if rich enough), but even then they didn't have to worry about meeting women for their sexual needs—they went to prostitutes for that. There was nothing like today's "singles scene" where unmarried men and women from eighteen to eighty must screen many people of the opposite sex—with few guidelines on "proper behavior" or how to do it—in order to meet the "right" person or persons for them.

Americans have always been mobile but in the past when they moved, they frequently traveled in groups both for protection and because it tended to be cheaper. On the long journeys West by covered wagon or train, people had a chance to make friends with their fellow travelers and many towns were founded by groups of men and women who had come West together. For those pioneers who settled the lonely prairies the family was still a source of economic and social cooperation and frequently included several generations; family members could rely on each other to ease the loneliness of the new environment.

Today the pace of moving around has accelerated and change is part and parcel of our society. People are always new to something these days—to a home, a job, a neighborhood, single life, ideas. And rarely do they have the support of a group of others to help them adjust to this newness. Corporation families are regularly uprooted and sent halfway across the country to areas where they don't know anybody and have to establish new ties. Many men and women—because of a divorce, breakup of a relationship, loss of a job or simply from a desire to improve their lives—choose to make a fresh start in some new place by themselves.

Fewer people today live in small towns; they want the variety, privacy and convenience of the city but the price they pay is often loneliness. Ralph Keyes, author of *We, the Lonely People: Searching for Community,* believes that with all its faults the small town provided something very important. Everyone was known to other people by sight and by name. Today even the small mamma-poppa stores that used to make city neighborhoods more homey are disappearing under the competition from supermarkets, franchises and chain stores. Keyes calls these small stores "human contact points" in the impersonality of the city and stresses that as they disappear former customers feel the loss:

> Each lost contact—druggist, butcher, bartender, beautician or barber—may not mean much by itself. But as one mounts on another, each of us feels a little more alone. Who knows me? By name, by face, by history and quirk?

Most of us are not known where we live. There is a different clerk at the supermarket every time, a different teller at the bank. If we live in the suburbs, there are few ways to make contact with others. Except for the shopping centers—which are closed at night after nine o'clock—there is no one out and about to talk with. Even walking at night can be a suspicious act and in some places, like Beverly Hills, the police may stop and question you if you do take a late-night walk. Cities are dangerous and isolating places and their inhabitants are suspicious and frightened and hardly in a mood to attempt meeting strangers.

But we just aren't prepared for this sense of unconnectedness and isolation that seems to suddenly descend upon us as adults. Allan Fromme points out in *The Ability to Love* that children are nurtured in groups in our society—the family, the neighborhood, Sunday school, the Scouts, dance class, Little League, and the groups that develop in school. At college everyone—even the "fiercest nonconformist"—joins some kind of group.

But on graduation these groups suddenly shatter as young people take jobs, marry, travel—never to re-form in the same natural way. And the young person no longer has an automatic framework in which to meet people. As Fromme says:

> For most of those who return to a home in the city, as well as those who leave home to make life in a city, there is literally no group, no neighborhood, no community of human scale into which they can fit themselves. The city is too large to be a community in itself, and city dwellers are too mobile, or too jealous of their privacy in crowded quarters, to make a friendly community of their apartment house or block or neighborhood.

Because of the design of our cities and suburbs, it is very difficult for people to interact in a natural way with those who are different in age, race, economic or marital status. We have suburbs for those who are married and have families, singles complexes for the unmarried, retirement "villages" for the elderly and special neighborhoods for the poor and racial minorities. These divisions set up barriers between people and they have been extended to our social organizations in a greater degree than ever before. As the price of meeting someone you must clearly identify and label yourself. Which group do you want?

A singles hiking club for those between twenty-five and fifty-five.

A square-dancing group for retired people.

A photography group for couples only.

and so on—

However, even though our traditional way of life is being disrupted by all these factors, sociologists, psychologists and other students of human behavior have paid remarkably little attention to the ways we make contact with strangers and the need —in light of changing conditions—to develop new social rituals which would help strangers meet and make contact. And yet it is our present social rituals—those automatic little courtesies we extend to each other as part and parcel of our everyday life ("Hello," "How are you," "Nice day, isn't it," "Thank you")—that to a very large degree determine how, when and where we meet people. According to sociologist Erving Goffman, in his book *Relations in Public*, all short interactions between individuals consist almost entirely of these social rituals—the way we greet and say goodbye to people, the way we apologize when we step on a stranger's toe or perform an elaborate charade of nonchalance for the benefit of onlookers when we trip on the sidewalk, the way we offer someone a light or ask directions.

These rituals enable us to interact more comfortably with strangers when we are in public and save us the necessity of deciding what to do in every situation. But they do not make it easy for us to make emotional contact with strangers and in fact most social rituals prevent us from making this sort of contact with those we don't already know.

Most of our rituals are very arbitrary about what constitutes proper *contact* with a stranger. In our society, touching—which is one way to become aware of your connections to another— is rarely condoned in public with intimates, much less with strangers. In fact, in a study of couples sitting in cafés in four different cities psychologist Sydney Jourard discovered that couples in Paris touched 110 times during an hour's conversation, couples in Puerto Rico 180 times, couples in London not at all and couples in the United States once or twice—and those were just little pats compared to the caressing, squeezing, tickling, rubbing that went on with the Parisian and Puerto Rican couples.

However, Dr. Leonard Zunin, psychiatrist, lecturer and author of *Contact: The First Four Minutes,* points out that we do have an acceptable social ritual whereby a strange man and woman not only may touch but may even hug each other—and that is at a dance. In that context, without any preliminaries, a man can go up to a strange woman and ask, "May I have this dance?" and if she agrees (which she can do nonverbally by merely standing up or moving toward the dance floor), he is permitted to take her in his arms. However, he must keep within the rules of the social ritual even then:

1. The music must be playing.
2. He must keep his feet moving.
3. He must hold her in the approved dance position.
4. When the music stops, he must stop hugging her immediately and not touch her from then on.

Obviously, if a man were to attempt to touch a woman in such a way in the supermarket or even if he were to say to her, "May I hold your hand for a moment? It will be ten minutes before we are waited on anyhow," he would most likely get into some sort of trouble—maybe even arrested. Even attempting to make conversation with a stranger at a supermarket is not part of our accepted social ritual. According to Dr. Zunin:

> Our culture has fallen short in building in rituals that fill in the horrendous distance between smiling at a stranger in a supermarket and hugging him at a dance. It is acceptable to smile at a stranger in a supermarket or ask a question. Not much more. There is nothing between that limited interaction and the socially accepted ritual of touching a stranger at a dance. The gap between is massive. This is part of the reason we have a lot of loneliness in our society and a lot of difficulty.

Whether we call these rituals etiquette or manners or courtesy, they are vitally important to the way we interact with people we know and with people we don't know. There is a common core of beliefs—a set of basic values—underlying our social rituals that have come down to us as part of our Western heritage. These rituals have been transmitted to us through centuries of usage and have been recorded in etiquette books from the fifteenth century on. Although some rituals have changed in the light of changing conditions (men seldom tip their hats to ladies anymore since they don't wear hats) and although some rituals now seem ridiculous to us (like the need for women to have chaperones), most individuals still try today to act in public in a manner consistent with our long-established, basic rituals. The style may be, as Gerald Carson says in *The Polite Americans*, different, but the intent is the same:

> Today's off-hand manners run from casual to sloppy. But appearances, to the extent that they suggest there aren't any standards at all, are deceptive. There always are standards. The fact that a young man does not call upon his fair lady bearing a nosegay or a slender volume of sentimental verses does not support the inference that he is lacking in devotion. All that has changed is the style. He does bring his offering. It is a fluffy, stuffed animal for her collection or the latest hit record.

So even in this age of people who seem to be questioning all the rules—the age of the *Playboy* and *Cosmo* girl, the age of encounter, the age of do-your-own-thing—most of us are still relating to others, at least in public, according to the same basic rules that have been in operation for centuries. And the most basic of all the rules is:

Don't trust strangers. We have not traditionally been either charitable or trusting to strangers in our society—with some exceptions. We are very helpful as individuals and as a society to those strangers who are clearly weaker than we are. We will give money and aid to victims of floods and hurricanes and always to the sick, but not as readily to strangers who don't seem as weak or who even seem threatening—like racial minorities in our cities.

It is easier to suspect people who do not seem one's "own kind" of a tendency toward sexual "immorality" and physical violence—people of a different religion, race, language or cultural tradition. Thus, in America the most feared "strangers" have been the immigrants who began coming to this country in great waves starting in the 1840s. As they began swarming in—first the Irish, then the Germans, then the Italians, Eastern Europeans, Jews, Mexicans, Puerto Ricans, and so on—the native stock of predominantly Anglo-Saxon origin felt threatened and feared the loss of their economic status and cultural traditions.

We labeled and stereotyped whole groups of strangers—the Irish were "Potato mouths," the Germans seemed to all have a red nose, a tipsy gait and drink a lot of beer, the Italians were "wops" who made a lot of noise and drank wine, and so it went. As each group of strangers became accepted and trusted and thus not quite strangers anymore, this wholesale mistrust extended to the next group of unassimilated immigrants.

Therefore, we have always had a sort of double standard for strangers—automatic mistrust of those who have not yet become our kind and a cautious acceptance of those strangers who seem to be "our kind" and who have the right *credentials*. Thus, in the past a stranger often gained acceptance into a particular social circle by carrying letters of introduction from a mutual friend to one of the town's social leaders. But giving a letter of introduction was serious business, as this quote from an 1895 etiquette book, *The Ladies' Home Manual of Physical Culture and Beauty*, reveals:

> To enter a society to which one is a stranger, some introduction is required. Going to a strange district, one carries letters of introduction. A man presents you to his friend, and vouches for your social position and good conduct. He introduces you to others. The Texan gentleman had a very proper idea of the responsibilities of an introduction when he said: "Mr. A, this is my friend, Mr. B; if he steals anything, I'm responsible."

The same etiquette book acknowledged that it was permissible for strangers to enter into conversations with each other if they were guests of a mutual acquaintance at a dance or dinner party since that automatically constituted an introduction. And, according to *Vogue's Book of Etiquette* written in 1925, it was O.K. to talk to a stranger you might meet in someone's home because "if the hostess were late for dinner, as some have been known to be, and one or two people arrived in the drawing-room before she came down, they would be lacking in both good sense and good breeding if they sat glowering at each other in silence until she appeared."

These same rules still prevail whether we are consciously aware of them or not; we still feel free to enter into conversation only with the strangers we meet through a mutual acquaintance, and when we go to a new town or want to move up into a new social status, we must let the others know somehow we are the right kind of person before we are accepted. However, letters of introduction are obsolete and we haven't yet developed a friend-guarantee card that we can carry in our wallets.

One way an individual can break through the mistrust of strangers in a new town is to join some sort of organization—preferably a national one. Membership in such organizations constitutes an automatic introduction to strangers and serves as a letter of introduction for newcomers to a community.

However, outside of the people we meet through acquaintances or at meetings of the organizations we join, everyone else is a stranger—and *off limits*. The general rule in middle-class society is that unacquainted persons do not strike up a conversation in public for other than socially acceptable reasons like asking directions. So people out in public, either as individuals or with other people, are effectively "sealed off" from the others all around them. It is no wonder so many feel isolated in the midst of crowds—particularly at periods in their lives when their people-supply has been depleted. Unless there is a wide variety of organizations to join (and they happen to be "joiners") or unless they have a friend willing to introduce them to others, there are literally no strangers to whom it is socially acceptable to speak in the places they habitually go—the laundromat, the supermarket, the drugstore, the restaurants, the movies.

However, there are two notable exceptions to the rule that people can't speak to strangers in public. When traveling, Americans tend to be very gregarious and not at all like the Englishmen in the satirical story who were cast away together on a desert island for years but never spoke because they had not been introduced. In fact, it is sometimes considered rude not to talk to fellow guests at hotels and resorts or to fellow travelers on trains and planes.

The second exception to the "don't speak to strangers" rule is at bars or other places where alcohol is being served. Although the atmosphere might be subdued and reserved at first, the noise level goes up in direct proportion to the amount of alcohol consumed and so do the smiles and hellos strangers give each other. But people aren't really making contact; it is the alcohol that is having all that fun.

Women are even more suspicious of strangers than men because ever since they were little girls, they have had drilled into them warnings against strangers. Although young children can be molested and require protection, these early admonitions continue to influence women long after they are grown. Strangers—especially male strangers—are seen as wily seducers, as people out to take advantage of them or even as potential rapists. This distrust of male strangers coupled with the chronic war of the sexes serves to keep men and women from trusting each other enough to make genuine contact when they do meet. In Chapters 4 and 5 we'll look more fully at why this female attitude is no longer appropriate and how women can—safely—make contact with male strangers.

A second basic thread that runs through many of our social rituals and one that also keeps us from making contact with strangers is that *a person should not call attention to himself in public.* Our social rituals are based on middle-class morality and they strongly emphasize being respectable, proper, genteel, restrained—particularly around strangers. This behavioral ideal has been strongly emphasized in every etiquette, courtesy, manners or conduct book written in the last four centuries. Here are just a few samples:

> Propriety should govern all street behavior. Polite people never do anything on the street to attract attention; they should neither talk in a loud, boisterous manner, nor laugh uproariously. (*Ladies' Home Manual*, 1895.)

> Don't talk or laugh loudly in the street or in public places. (*Vogue's Book of Etiquette*, 1925.)

> Not to attract attention to oneself in public is one of the cardinal principles of etiquette. (Emily Post, *Etiquette*, 1960.)

The result of this taboo against any sort of spontaneous activity is that our cities and suburbs are quiet in terms of human noise. The only noise that we consider acceptable—or unavoidable—is machine noise. So the horns blare, sirens scream, jackhammers blast and garbage cans clang but our cities—unlike many European and Latin ones—do not pulsate with laughter and talk and children's play and music.

Clearly many of the social rituals that have developed in this country tend to conflict with human feelings. We do not trust our humanness; we do not accept ourselves as we are; we try to stifle expressions of our pleasures and passions and grief.

Sociologist Philip Slater, in *The Pursuit of Loneliness*, deals with the conflict between human feelings and social rituals that is so prevalent in this society. He believes that for many—the older generation in particular—social rituals have a "validity which takes priority over human events." The film *The Graduate* was shocking to many because of the scene where the hero interrupts a wedding to cry out his pain and his love for the prospective bride. He literally drags her away physically while being pursued by the outraged guests. But few of us would dare interrupt such an event —no matter how urgent our personal needs. The behavior of people—even in potentially dangerous situations—leads Slater to conclude that many people "would quietly die rather than 'make a scene.'"

Our distancing social rituals are further reinforced by our body language. Julius Fast, author of *Body Language*, says that in public we "mask" ourselves through facial expressions, gestures and body movements to conform to what is proper, accepted or expected. At the same time, as Fast points out in *Body Language*, we have an opposite need to drop our masks—to "transmit wildly and freely, to tell the world who we are and what we want, to cry out in the wilderness and be answered . . ." Unfortunately, our masks sometimes get so rigid that they can change from protective and privacy-gaining devices to crippling ones. Then we are unable to transmit the right "message" to those we would like to make contact with.

Body language is learned; it varies from culture to culture. Children assimilate it consciously and unconsciously in the process of growing up. Here are some of the unwritten rules of body language we seem to have been born just "knowing"—rules that reinforce our distrust of strangers and our own natures:

> Do not sit next to someone in a public place—a subway, park bench, theater—unless all the other seats are occupied.

> Do not stare at another person in public or maintain prolonged eye contact. If male, do not gaze into another man's eyes intently unless you intend to fight or become

intimate. If female, do not maintain eye contact with a man unless you are willing to be approached. If someone catches you staring, you must immediately look away.

Do not touch a stranger in public, and try to maintain an acceptable social distance from him—four to seven feet if possible. If you must get closer or even touch him due to crowding, tense your body so it will be clear you are not enjoying the contact.

In elevators position yourself away from other people if possible against the side or back of the elevator facing the door and do not look at or talk to anyone.

If you break any of these rules, you can expect some interesting reactions. Dr. Zunin sometimes deliberately violates body-language taboos as a way of making contact with people. In a public place—like a park—where there are lots of empty seats, he will sit down next to someone instead of taking one of the empty seats. In his book, *Contact*, he tells what happens:

This kind of exercise is part of the practice of *stepping out of role*, which is not only fun at times, but can be very useful in teaching you more about yourself and others. I have an excuse when I step out of role because I am always "researching modes of contact." I may sit beside someone for a few minutes, and then turn and explain my ploy, asking for their comments. In hundreds of such incidents, I've never had anyone refuse to level with me. They tell me how they felt when I sat down, and this approach has led to some fascinating conversations.

Clearly our body language is "distancing" and it is hard to break through a stranger's mask even if you wish to make contact. As an experiment we asked some of our friends to try smiling at strangers in public. According to our volunteer "researchers," they had difficulty in even catching a person's eye to smile at him. When they did smile at strangers, about half of them smiled back. But the other half responded with suspicion, fright, aloofness or a look that seemed to say, "What's wrong with you, you creep?"

Nowhere is this slightly "paranoid" attitude toward strangers more apparent than in New York City, where the normal social rituals and body language have been distorted in ways that usually make contact not only impossible but downright dangerous.

Since New Yorkers can't avoid violating each other's space in crowded subways, they simply pretend no one else is there. As a result, the subways are filled with people who regard each other as non-persons. It maintains their privacy but it also leads to a lot of inhumanity.

While the causes of crime and violence in New York are too complicated to discuss here, it seems reasonable to assume that this treatment of each other as non-humans certainly contributes to human loneliness, frustration and maybe even a tendency to want to let everyone know that one is really a *person* through some sort of attention-getting device like violence or threatened violence.

Julius Fast says in *Body Language* that New Yorkers are not vicious—just shy and frightened. He reminds us of the first Great Power Blackout when New Yorkers let their masks drop and helped each other through the crisis. We believe that that is exactly what we all need to do now—let our masks drop and begin to trust each other. As individuals and as a society we are in crisis. The loneliness, alienation and apathy that millions of Americans feel—that makes them behave in violent and inhumane ways to each other—results largely from a lack of contact and connectedness to other people.

We must look more closely at the role our social rituals play in keeping us from meeting, making contact with and really relating on a deep level to others. We need to become consciously aware of why we act the way we do toward others and the effect of our actions upon relationships. We need to deliberately develop new rituals to help strangers make contact, to find space for contact in existing rituals, to socially give ourselves "permission" to violate or fragment distancing rituals and to learn to overcome the assumptions and fear of rejection that keep us from daring to do these things. And we need to learn the skills that will help us accomplish this in a style that is sensitive and warm—a style that does not violate other people's rights or privacy.

But most of all we need to develop a new attitude toward meeting and making contact with those we don't already know—the same attitude that unknowingly we take along as part of our bag-

gage when we go on a trip. We need to become full-time travelers
through life—as Nancy did after a recent trip to London. On her
trip Nancy fell in love with London and its inhabitants and the
feeling was mutual. She was wined by Englishmen, dined by English couples, and she participated in some hilarious pub crawling
with Englishwomen. She felt so at home that she even developed
a fantasy about moving to London permanently. But it seemed
that everyone she met in London had the same fantasy about
Southern California.

"Why in the world are you here in this drab city when you
could be lying in the sun at the beach or looking at movie stars?"
they asked her. Then they would add, "I've always wanted to go
to California. I think it is the most exciting place in the world to
live."

Nancy realized that her newfound zest and ability to attract
strangers didn't come from the city of London; it came from her
attitude. She was more approachable because she wanted to get to
know what the English people were like; she was more willing to
"fragment" the rules—partly because she wasn't totally sure of
them and partly because she knew that as a "foreigner" her mistakes would be charming rather than offensive; and she was more
adventurous because she thought she might never return and she
didn't want to miss a thing.

If you—like a traveler to a strange land—live your daily life with
the attitude "I may never be here again," you too will want to get
acquainted with the natives and will be less likely to worry about
breaking rules. You will take advantage of what is going on in the
here and now with the people that are in the *here and now* with
you. You may find them friendlier and more approachable than
you imagined.

Dr. Zunin refers to this attitude of living in the *now* and being
willing to reach out and make contact with others—with all
the attendant risks—as "adventuring through life." Adventuring
through life, says Zunin, has to do with an attitude:

> An attitude of just being fascinated with how our species
> works as you walk down the street versus the attitude of
> "Oh God, I'm going to try this new thing and it is going
> to be so difficult." What is your orientation on meeting

strangers? Is it exciting to break the ritual or a burden? And what does that say about how you live your life?

In the next chapter we are going to tell you just how to go about "adventuring through life" and make real contact with all those wonderful others in the world. But before you learn new ways to meet people, we want you to take a look at the kind of contact you are making right now with strangers.

ASSIGNMENT

Answer these questions in writing or discuss your answers with a friend. It will give you some insights into your present behavior and perhaps some clues as to why you may or may not be meeting new people.

1. Are you both approaching and approachable?
   a. Think of a time when a stranger approached you. How did you respond? Why? What kind of a mood were you in at the time? How were you dressed?
   b. Think of a time when you approached a stranger. How did he respond? How were you feeling? What was it about that person that made it possible for you to approach him? How did that make you feel?
2. What sort of people tend to approach you?
   a. What do they look like?
   b. What qualities do they have?
3. What sort of people do you approach?
   a. What do they look like?
   b. What qualities do they have?
4. Do the kind of people approach you that you want to approach you?
5. Do you approach the kind of people you want to?
6. For several weeks keep a log of the people who approach you in public, at parties and so on. Notice how they did it and how you reacted.

3

How to Talk with Practically Anybody, Anywhere, Anytime

Dr. Adele and Sam Scheele are "social engineering" consultants who design techniques for government agencies, schools and industry—techniques that help people work, play and live together more pleasurably and effectively. This vivacious and creative young couple (whose headquarters are in Los Angeles) have turned both their professional and personal lives into an adventure. Wherever they go, they seem to take along built-in fun and an ability to make immediate contact with other people. One night they went out to eat and were seated at the last available table in a crowded restaurant, a table for four. Just then, another couple came in, and knowing they were in for a long wait, Sam called over to them, "Why don't you join us?" The couple, very embarrassed, didn't think it quite proper to say "yes" and yet apparently were unable to say "no." Cautiously they sat down with the Scheeles but were reluctant to give their names or any details about themselves. Sensing that the unconventionality of the situation made them uncomfortable, Adele, in her bubbly way, suggested that they all make up a name, profession and life story for themselves, just for the evening. As the four of them concocted fanciful stories about themselves, the tenseness evaporated and they laughed and chattered like old friends.

The Scheeles have developed a social skill that is much needed today—the ability to break through social barriers and make contact. Recognizing the need for this ability, Sam and Adele originated a course called "Getting in Touch with Reality." It was presented by the University of California Extension Division and taught many men and women to orchestrate creative interaction with others. The purpose of this chapter is to show you how to "orchestrate creative interaction with others" so that you can have pleasurable first-meetings with more of those wonderful "others" all around you.

First, though, let's look at the things that might keep you from even trying to make that first-meeting come about. There are four common fears that often stand in the way of strangers making connections with one another—particularly in public: 1. the fear of being hurt; 2. the fear of being impolite; 3. the fear of being trapped; and 4. the fear of being rejected.

THE FEAR OF BEING HURT

When most people are approached in public by strangers, their first reaction tends to be wary—perhaps the stranger is going to try to sell them something, swindle them, beg for money or even find out who they are and where they live and rob or rape them later. The authors, who have been divorced for a combined total of fifteen years, have made it their practice to go freely out into the world and explore places and people. Our family and friends chide us for our attitude toward strangers, calling us idealistic, naïve or uninformed. Many of them refuse to take walks at night, go out or travel alone or talk with people they don't know. Yet despite the risks they think we are taking, we have had few unpleasant experiences and no hurtful ones. However, the pleasure and nourishment we—and many others like us—have gotten from strangers has never made headlines.

We are not going to deny that there are times when attempting to talk with strangers is not a good idea—when they, for example, refuse to make eye contact with you, when they are belligerent or drunk, when they are in "gangs" or when you encounter them in isolated parking lots, on poorly lighted and deserted streets or in high-crime areas. There is even some risk in making contact in well-lighted public places where there are plenty of other people around.

But the risk has been exaggerated in the mass media and the response of many people to these "scare" stories only makes the situation worse. Dorothy Samuel, television broadcaster and free-lance writer, suggests in her book *Safe Passage in City Streets* that the best way to get safety on the streets is to get people on the streets. "Busy people," she says, "happy people, socializing people. People who are not fearful. Anyone who has roamed Union Square in San Francisco at night, or Fisherman's Wharf or Chinatown, knows that city streets can be festivals, that strangers can greet each other, that laughter can ring in the air." Ms. Samuel believes the fear of violence at the hands of strangers we encounter in public is out of proportion to the risk.

The best way to lessen your fear of physical harm from strangers is to develop a greater understanding of people—particularly those in stress—and the ability to cope with a potentially dangerous situation when it arises. We aren't talking about becoming an expert at self-defense or about purchasing some sort of weapon. Few of us, male or female, have the ability to physically fend off someone who is "psyched up" to commit a crime. Even modern police forces now train their staffs to use force only as a last resort and to rely on psychological "weapons" when it is at all possible. The way you perceive people has a strong influence on how they will actually behave toward you. When you are in a situation where you aren't sure of someone's intentions, calmness and a matter-of-fact atti-tude can make a difference because that person may not be sure of what he is going to do either. If you respond with fear or hostility or treat him like an "animal," he may act like one. On the other hand, if you are able to treat him like a human being but one that you aren't going to let intimidate you or take advantage of you, he may behave in an entirely different manner.

THE FEAR OF BEING IMPOLITE

All of us learn, sometimes directly and sometimes indirectly in the process of growing up, what is considered permissible behavior in public. As we mentioned in the preceding chapter, these "correct" ways of behaving have not changed as fast as our way of life. However, we are still controlled by them—largely because we rarely examine our beliefs about what is proper and the price we are paying at a particular time for trying to be polite.

Social psychologist Stanley Milgram has found that when people violate established customs, it creates a tremendous anxiety. You have probably felt this sort of anxiety when you were forced by circumstances to do something in public you wouldn't ordinarily do—like ask a stranger for a dime to make a phone call, ask someone for a ride because your car broke down, ask the bus driver to stop because you were going to be sick.

Milgram himself experienced the effect of going against a social ritual that most people adhere to without even thinking about it. As research for a study he was making on the behavior of people in subways, he went up to a stranger and asked for his seat without giving any reason at all as to why he wanted it. Even before he asked, he felt intense anxiety just in anticipation of what might happen. Then, although the man gave up his seat without fuss or questioning, as soon as Milgram was seated, he felt overwhelmed by the need to show the man that he really had a reason to ask for the seat. Writing in *Psychology Today*, Milgram says of the experience, "My head sank between my knees, and I could feel my face blanching. I was not role-playing."

While you probably won't want to repeat Milgram's experiment, you will find it necessary occasionally to go against propriety if you intend to make contact with strangers (since even speaking to strangers is, in many cases, not quite "proper"). The best thing to do is just accept the fact that you are going to be nervous if you are more friendly than usual to a stranger or if one is friendly to you for no apparent reason. However, act as if it doesn't bother you and take action in spite of it.

THE FEAR OF BEING TRAPPED

Nobody likes to feel trapped—that he can't get away from somebody or that he has to go along with what another person wants to do when he isn't comfortable with it. But nobody likes to back away from a conversation with another friendly person either, or to turn down a request he might make. It is the fear of having but two choices—feeling trapped or having to say "no" that many times keeps us from reaching out. If we start talking with someone we don't know, he might turn out to be offensive in some way or a bore and we'll not be able to get away. Or else he'll expect us to do something we don't want to do.

In fact, it is the fear of having to say "no" later that keeps many people from saying "yes" now. Thus, improving your ability to say "no" and feeling entitled to say it is a way of preparing yourself to make contact with interesting strangers. Developing the attitude that it is O.K. not to talk with someone who wants to talk with you or to stop after you've started or to decline an invitation just because you don't want to accept it is one that is necessary for sheer survival. If you try to make yourself available to everybody who wants you and to do what they want you to do, you'll exhaust yourself. You must set limits for yourself and take charge of your own destiny. You'll be more comfortable when people approach you and you'll be able to approach them more often, in a spirit of adventure, if you know you can decline or back away with tact and finesse. Here are some tips for saying "no" to someone who indicates he wants something you don't want to give.

1. Be firm but kind. As you refuse a person's request, look him directly in the eye. It may be difficult or painful for you to do this (you may be embarrassed, frightened, reluctant to hurt or even physically repelled by his appearance) but it will make him feel better. By looking at him, you are acknowledging his humanness and his right to have asked. If you avoid looking at him, he is likely to feel that he is being dismissed as worthless.

2. Watch for his reaction and respond appropriately. If he seems hurt, give reassurance. Say something like "Please don't be upset by my turn-down. I'm certain you'll find other people whose company you can enjoy." If he makes an insulting or slurring remark (and this will seldom happen if you are kind but firm), do not lash back or apologize. Request firmly that he stop. "Please don't insult me. I didn't mean to insult you but only to turn down your offer." If he seems to want to challenge you, don't let yourself get caught in an argument. If he should say with defiance, "Why not?" a good way to reply is to smile graciously

and say, "Because I don't care to." Not wanting to do something is the only reason nobody can argue with. Be aware if you give a reason for your refusal, you may be inviting further attempts at persuasion: "Of course you have time to sit down and have a drink with me."

3. Be specific about what you are refusing. If you do not want further contact at all, let the person who asks know it with a simple statement that is kind but that doesn't invite further conversation. Your message should imply, "Thanks but no thanks." It is especially helpful to turn someone down in a way that allows him to have the last word, a polite word. This makes him feel that he has the upper hand, that he has gotten something for his effort, that he has lost none of his dignity by asking. "I'd rather not, but thanks for asking," can allow a person to say, "You're welcome," and walk away feeling good, encouraged to try again with someone else.

Sometimes a person you think you might like asks for something at a time that is not convenient. When this happens, make it clear that you are not turning *him* down but only his request for contact *at that time*. Make some kind of statement that clearly suggests, "Not now but later." To be good at turning someone down, you must be skilled at more than saying "no" in a pleasant manner. You must be prepared to suggest alternatives as to what you'd like. "I'd like to sit here quietly for a while but could you come back later?" is almost certain to get you what you want—no contact at the moment but the opportunity to get to know the person later.

If a person you'd like contact with suggests an activity you don't like, your reply should suggest you might be open to something else. "I don't want a drink but could we just talk?"

A word of caution: Don't refuse an invitation or an offer of contact just because you aren't certain of what you want. Instead of giving a flat refusal, you can say, "I don't know. Before I can make up my mind, I need more information." (Or to know more about you or what will be expected of me.) Or "Could I think about it and let you know later?"

THE FEAR OF REJECTION

Nobody likes to be turned down when he reaches out to make friendly contact, but many people are virtually immobilized by the fear they will be rejected. While some people believe that you must first learn to accept yourself totally before you can make successful contact with others, we disagree. Although liking yourself a lot is important, you can't wait until you are always comfortable with all aspects of yourself before you reach out or you'll never reach out. Being completely happy with ourselves is something that most of us experience just now and then for brief periods. You have to work on it all the time. And one way of building self-esteem is through getting involved with others. If many people seem to like being with you when they've known you but a short time, you'll find it easier to like yourself.

Because of soft spots in our self-esteem, all of us fail to speak to others sometimes because we assume in advance they won't like us and we fail to check our assumptions out. Have you ever looked at someone—someone you thought you might like—and said to yourself, "He or she certainly wouldn't like me," and then avoided trying to make contact? What you are doing is assuming that because he has certain characteristics you admire (e.g., youth, good looks, money, fame, talent) he is different from and "better" than you. Rather than attempt to make contact, you, in effect, reject him before he can reject you. Many times two people who are attracted to one another completely ignore one another because each is afraid the other is "too good" and would reject him.

When we are afraid of rejection we tend not only to see some people as "too good" but others as unacceptable. It is easy in a new situation with people you don't know to say to yourself:

They are all losers (or phonies or clods or neurotics).

They are all too old (or too young, too rich, too poor, too conservative, too far-out).

What you are doing is convincing yourself that they aren't "your kind" as an excuse for not trying to find out what anyone is really like. You are afraid to take a chance.

When you find yourself not reaching out to people because you think there is something wrong with a whole group of them, focus in on several, one at a time. Ask yourself: Exactly what is wrong with him or her? What is he too old (or young, bright, dumb, pushy, passive) for? And in what ways would that seriously affect me? Then take action to test if your assumptions are true.

Here is an exercise you can do in a social situation that will help you discover some of the assumptions about other people (and yourself) that may be keeping you from asking a stranger for something—even a few moments of conversation.

ASSIGNMENT

Look around and pick out a person that you think you would like but that might not like you—i.e., one you assume would turn away if you reached out in a friendly way. Then carefully think through the answers to these questions:

What wouldn't he like about you? (For example, your clothes aren't good enough; you aren't smart enough; you are too fat, too skinny, etc.) Be aware that the things you think would make people reject you represent your judgment of yourself. They are attributes and qualities you don't like.

Think through what you could do to salvage the situation if the person you like were to rebuff you.

Now pick out a person you think you wouldn't like—i.e., one you assume you wouldn't enjoy being with. Then carefully think through the answers to these questions:

What do you think would happen if you went over and started talking to him? (He would bore you or monopolize the conversation or make a pass, etc.)

Think through what you could do if you were to find yourself in the situation you anticipate with the person you don't care for.

Approach each of these people. Try to get to know what they are really like. Let them know some of your positive qualities. As you interact, carefully observe what is happening as though you were a *spectator at a spectacle*. Be aware of what is happening and also of what you are thinking and feeling.

Later think about how many of your assumptions were right, how many wrong. Did you enjoy yourself? Did others enjoy you?

If you do this exercise a number of times, you'll learn that some of your assumptions aren't true. However, sooner or later, you are going to get rejected. Someone you reach out to is going to rebuff you, and it is going to hurt.

What is it that goes on in our heads that makes a "no" from a stranger painful? You can discover what it is by listening to what goes through your mind after you've been turned down. There are two different significant sentences and two different reasons but it all adds up to the same conclusion: "It is hopeless."

The next time you reach out with a friendly overture toward someone and are turned down—when you smile or wave and he doesn't smile or wave back, when you invite her to dance or dine or talk with you and she declines—if it hurts a lot, see if you are saying to yourself either "I shouldn't have asked" or "He shouldn't have refused." That word "shouldn't" is a clue that you've concluded that the world is not as it should be.

When you hear yourself saying, "I shouldn't have asked," chances are you are taking someone's refusal to interact with you as the rejection of you as a person. The thought that lies beneath is "There must be something wrong with me or he wouldn't have refused." If you try to tune in on what is going on in your mind at that moment, you'll probably discover that you are calling yourself names; "I'm too old, too ugly, too tall, a klutz," or something else very negative.

On the other hand, when you hear yourself saying, "He shouldn't have refused," you are taking someone's refusal to interact as an indication of his worthlessness. The thought that lies beneath is, "If he were brighter, kinder, more knowledgeable, or more something, he wouldn't have refused my friendly overture." If you carefully tune in to your mind at that moment, you may find you are whispering in your own ear a gloomy message: "It will always be like this. I'll always be turned down. People (or men or women) are no damn good. I am doomed to loneliness."

When we interpret rejection as an indication of the worthlessness of ourselves or others, a turndown even from someone we don't know and who doesn't know us can sometimes be so painful that it keeps us from trying to breach the social barriers for a long time afterwards. A woman in one of Emily's workshops told of an incident that occurred when she moved into a new neighborhood and was anxious to make friends with her neighbors. One morning she saw the lady across the street watering her lawn. Since they had never met, she went outside and waved a friendly "hello." The lady totally ignored her. A day or two later, she once again waved to her neighbor and, once again, she was ignored. Chagrined, she decided it was just an unfriendly neighborhood and began avoiding contacts with all neighbors. However, one afternoon she ran into that particular nieghbor at the library and they began talking. "By the way," the lady remarked, "if I ever pass you without speaking to you, don't get upset. I don't have very good vision and without my glasses I can't see anyone." Emily's student realized how close she had come to being a recluse in her own neighborhood because of what she saw as rejection by one person.

COPING WITH REJECTION

If you are a sensitive human being who cares about other human beings, you can't help but be deeply disappointed by them sometimes. However, with new attitudes and skills you can decrease the number of occasions on which you get turned down and lessen the severity of your pain. You can also learn to handle rejection in better ways when it happens and not let it depress you or keep you from reaching out again. Here is how:

1. *Realize that rejection will be more likely in some circumstances than others.* In our society, where we tend to be suspicious of those who are not our "own kind," you are more likely to be rejected if you go into a group that is different from you in age, economic status, etc. For example, if you are the only comparative "nobody" in a group of status-seeking celebrities or an older per-

son at a beach frequented by teen-agers, you may feel out of place and they may even overtly let you know they think so too. However, if you don't let the hostile feelings make you hostile, too, there is frequently someone there who will be receptive to you. In almost every group situation, no matter how negative it might seem, there is usually a little haven somewhere. You can discover it and overcome that initial rejection if it is important to you and you are willing to invest a little time.

Psychodrama instructor and role-training consultant Madelyn Hathaway encountered this sort of rejection when she was working with a group of senior citizens at a community center. The men accepted her but their wives rejected her because they felt she, being younger and livelier, was a threat. But Ms. Hathaway made friends with one woman who was from her home state and who reminded her of her mother, and the woman became, in effect, a bridge to cross over to friendship with the other women.

Ms. Hathaway has made a study of why people choose other people in a group and found they pick them for two reasons: (1) they are like themselves and (2) they can meet their needs. If you are in a group of people unlike yourself, the best way to become accepted is to find a way to meet their needs. Ms. Hathaway once joined a rock choir at a local church composed of singers ranging in age from eighteen to twenty. The first few times she went, their rejection of an "old lady" was an almost tangible thing and she felt like running home. But she stuck it out, was friendly and satisfied the needs of the group by being a good singer. In about three months she was a well-liked group member.

2. *If you are rejected, deal with the emotional blow that you have just had.* Whether it is a minor disappointment or a deep hurt, rejection usually takes your breath away. The first thing to do is take a few breaths and tune in on your body. It helps to concentrate for a few moments on the feelings in a particular part of your body. Though it may sound like an odd thing to do, tell your feet to become aware of how they feel in your shoes, or your arm to become aware of how the arm of the chair feels against it, or your wrist to pay attention to the way the watch band encircles it. Silly as this may seem, it really works and it is physiologically and psychologically valid. What you are doing is temporarily disengaging your mind that is causing you trouble by repeating those "shouldn'ts."

When you are breathing well again and have become aware of your bodily feelings, it is time to call your mind back into action and decide what to do. Give yourself a pat on the back for having tried. Emily tells her students that if they aren't getting soundly rejected at least three times a week they aren't trying enough new things. They aren't finding out what they can get away with. And remind yourself that it is not *you* that is being refused but rather the gift you are offering—the gift of interaction.

A person may not want your gift at the moment; he may not want it ever; he may not care for it in the form you are offering it. It helps to think of the feelings you have when someone refuses your offer of a cup of coffee. They may refuse because they don't ever drink beverages that contain caffeine, because they don't want a stimulant right then or because they don't like to drink coffee served in a mug. Just as people have their own reasons for refusing a cup of coffee, they have their own reasons for refusing our overtures. If it was possible to understand all that is going on in their minds, we wouldn't take it personally.

When you have been rejected and feel bad, physical contact or stimulation can be helpful. If someone is nearby whom you can ask for a hug or a pat, do so, but if nobody is available you can stroke yourself. One way of doing this is to get something to eat or drink and, very slowly, concentrate on enjoying the sensations of each mouthful. Another way is to slowly and lovingly stroke a part of your body such as your forehead or arm to give yourself comfort. Brushing your hair, washing your face or reapplying fresh makeup can help.

If you are at a party or gathering with a friend or spouse, it is sometimes helpful to go to them for support. Tell them you are feeling a little hurt because you were rejected and ask them to give you a compliment, to assure you that you are a worthwhile person. Let them know this is no time for advice such as "For Pete's sake, Harry, if you weren't so aggressive people wouldn't reject you." You just need to be told that you are O.K.

3. *Remind yourself this rejection is not necessarily a closed door. You have alternatives.* Sometimes when you have made a request and have been refused, you might, instead of backing away, want to ask additional questions to clarify the refusal. Perhaps the person is refusing what you've offered and not you. He might accept something else as a means of making contact (e.g., an offer to

sit and talk rather than dance). Or maybe he just doesn't want what you are offering at that moment (e.g., he might like a dance later but is engrossed with someone else now). One man we interviewed expressed great indignation at the fact that a woman refused his offer to dance one night, saying she wanted to smoke a cigarette. His sense of self-esteem suffered because it seemed to him she put a cigarette above him. We suggested that he could have said something like "How about it? When you finish that cigarette will you dance with me?" or "May I sit down and talk with you while you are smoking your cigarette?" Or if he could say it in a light tone, it is permissible and in good form to say, "I'm not sure whether you really want that cigarette right now and will dance with me later or whether you'd rather not dance with me at all. Would you please tell me which?" The point is to make sure your request for clarification doesn't come over as an attempt to pressure someone (which may make him resentful) or as a self-pitying ploy (which could make him feel guilty).

Sometimes when you've been turned down, you can recoup by telling of your disappointment in a light, sharing manner, not as an accusation. ("Darn it, I was afraid you'd refuse. I've been watching you for some time and it really took a lot of courage to walk over here.") Or you can give additional information that might cause a person to change his mind. ("I think you are missing something good. I'm a real fun person to dance with.")

4. *If you are frequently rejected or frequently shattered by that rejection, take a look at yourself.* It could be that there is something in your behavior that is offensive to others. There are two things you can do. One is to ask some of your friends to observe you and give you some helpful hints and suggestions. However, ask them to do this in a positive, caring way. The other is to examine your own thinking processes to see if there is a "hidden agenda" behind your attempts at promoting interaction. If you have unrealistic expectations of what a person can do for you, people will sometimes sense this and back away. If you approach a man at a party with a sense of urgency, with the thought that you must make contact so that he can give you a job, his refusal to talk or join you in a drink could upset you greatly. If you feel compelled to find a mate or someone to have sex with you, the refusal of a prospective partner for a dance might be very upsetting. If your expectations are limited merely to making contact with

that person at that moment, it should be quite easy to shrug and say "So what" if he doesn't want contact.

Just recognizing the common fears about making contact in public and learning better ways to cope with them is a big help in regard to talking with strangers. But it's not enough to make first meetings as good as they need to be. The way we spend time the first time we are with a person is very important. What happens during that first meeting determines to a large extent if there will be another meeting and sets the tone for any subsequent relationship.

There are four phases to a satisfying first meeting: overtures, small talk, getting personal and closing. Following are some ways to be more effective in each phase:

MAKING AN OVERTURE BY LOOKING

Though there are a number of ways two people can show their interest in one another, the most common first way is non-verbal—by looking. However, most people don't realize the messages they send by the way they look at others and frequently send looks that make contact difficult. Here are what some of those looks are like:

> The look that ignores the existence of people. You can look at a person without really seeing him; we most commonly do this to waiters and salespeople but we also often look at strangers like this. And it turns them into non-people for us.

> The stare. When you stare at someone, you also turn him into a non-person because you are visually examining him without letting him see anything about you. Your expression becomes hard and he becomes like a butterfly on a pin.

> The look of disdain or disgust. Sometimes when we see people who are different from us, in race or age or clothing and hairstyle, we assume they are less human than we are and give them a "you are repulsive" look.

> The look that ignores the whole person. If you are only in-

terested in one aspect of another person—as someone to have sex with, as someone to take you to dinner—you are reducing him to a single function and turning him into an object to be used for your pleasure rather than seeing him as a person with feelings and wishes of his own.

The best way to look at someone if you are interested in making contact is with an attitude of friendly exploration, a look that says, "I see you and you are O.K." To have this look on your face requires that the right thoughts go on in your mind. A smile can be a non-verbal overture but only if it is sincere. To look at people in a way that will disarm them and build trust, you must pay attention to what is going on in your mind.

People differ greatly as to what they think when they first look at strangers. Those who get along best with others usually notice what they like about people before noticing what they don't like. Though it is easy because of our cultural distrust of strangers to get in the habit of noticing nothing but drawbacks, it is possible to train ourselves so we notice people's good points first. And everybody has lots of them. When we look at people as though we knew they had a number of attractive physical features and personality assets and we are taking note of them, the expression on our faces becomes accepting. We send out friendly overtures. People like us better when they feel that we are not criticizing them.

Next time you are in public, try one or more of these ways of looking as a first step to making contact.

1. Take time to look carefully at the people all around you. Examine a number of them from head to toe while making a mental note of what you like. Become aware of their physical attributes—hair, eyes, height, shape, the style and color co-ordination of their clothes—and of the personality assets you think they have—i.e., they seem lively, intelligent, methodical, direct. Skip over what you don't like and concentrate only on what you do like. If you catch their attention, hold onto their gaze and send a mental message of "I like what I see."

2. Allow your look to be an exaggerated response to the way others are looking at you. If someone smiles a little at you, smile a lot. If you see someone frowning, wrinkle your brow, look them in the eye and frown hard back.

3. Look someone in the eye while quietly doing something pro-

vocative to evoke a response. Raise and lower your eyebrows rapidly a few times, wink, wrinkle your nose.

Any one of these three ways of looking will lay the groundwork for the next step, which is speaking.

SMALL TALK

The most reliable way to begin a conversation with a stranger is to start off with small talk, something that will get his attention but will keep a friendly distance between you until he has had a chance to build up enough trust to let his guard down, to let you into his "psychological space." Each person has a zone of privacy that must be entered to reach him. However, if you enter it brusquely, indifferently or too quickly, you can make him feel that his territory has been invaded. When this zone is violated, you will be rebuffed. This can happen if you narrow the physical space between you too fast—if you move close or touch him—or if you make personal remarks too soon.

Think of your attempt to make contact as exploratory—as putting out sensitive but intriguing verbal feelers toward something very delicate in order to see what will happen. Whatever your approach, it should allow a person to realize he has choices—to move closer, to back away, to respond, to not respond. Vary your approach according to the other person's personality and mood. Though some words and phrases are better than others and can be used frequently, a pat "line" just won't work. Try being cautious and dignified with someone who seems closed or rigid, reassuring with someone who seems nervous or troubled and adventurous and playful with someone who seems warm or open.

It can be helpful to comment on the beauty of the surroundings, an item in the newspaper, something that is going on in your immediate environment or even the weather. However, don't continue impersonal chitchat too long or your companion will get bored and will tune you out. And if you are standing in line or in an elevator, he'll get away before you can get below the superficial level. If you want to make a connection, you must get personal.

GETTING PERSONAL

One of the best and quickest ways to get personal is to let a person know some of your feelings. Express emotion but in an upbeat way. People are tired of hearing gripes and don't want to get involved with others who think this world is a miserable place and that nobody ever does anything right any more and that there's nothing to be done about it.

Try letting someone know what you are happy about. "I just came from the hospital where my sister had a baby. We're delighted it is a boy." Or about some vulnerability you are experiencing. "I felt a little uncomfortable about taking the initiative in talking with you. I hope it is O.K. It's a new skill I'm learning." Or what you're concerned about right now. "I'm new in town and don't know anybody. How about you?"

One thing that helps people become comfortable with and interested in strangers is to discover they have something in common. That is one of the reasons expressing feelings is so important. It creates a bond when people are aware they have similar feelings.

The fact that they have had common experiences, that parts of their life stories are similar, can be another bond: to discover they both were raised on farms, or went to Hawaii for a vacation, or have been divorced. And a good way to prepare yourself to quickly reveal a number of things that can form bonds and make you seem like an interesting and worthwhile person is to become familiar with your life story by writing your autobiography.

Writing your autobiography may sound like a tremendous task but it isn't. You don't need to write a book about yourself—just three short sketches. You need to be able to give a one-minute biographical sketch, a five-minute one and a ten-minute one. Now, nobody is going to stand by and listen to you tell the story of your life for ten minutes or five or even one. You will have to talk about yourself in bits and pieces but you'll find it of considerable help to have the information right on the tip of your tongue and to know the kind of picture you will create in the mind of the listener.

Think back on the critical incidents in your life that made you the kind of person you are. Jot down key words and phrases to jog your memory and give the sequence you want. Concentrate on bits of information that will create a picture of you that will help people understand you better. Telling someone you went to a Catholic school tells him a lot about the attitudes you were exposed to as a girl. Saying your father had a dry-cleaning store reveals you did not have a background of wealth and privilege.

A helpful thing to do is to encourage three or four of your friends to prepare autobiographies and then to get together and practice on one another. Give each other suggestions as to which facts to include and which to leave out and on gestures and tone of voice. You'll be surprised how much you'll learn about your friends—even those you've known for years—if you do this. Also this will give you the opportunity to talk about yourself out loud, without notes, with an interested audience, so that when you do meet strangers, you'll be prepared.

Another good way to get personal quickly is to tell people hunches you have about what they are like in ways you can't possibly know about. However, instead of relying on the hackneyed, "I'll bet you are a Libra," bring up something most people will find easier to talk about—i.e., their hobbies, where they are from, occupation. Phrase your guesses like compliments. For example, "You look as if you play tennis. Do you?" or "Your accent sounds Australian. Is that where you are from?" or "Your beard makes you look like a psychiatrist. Are you one?"

Avoid making guesses as to a person's sex life, financial situation or age. These are touchy subjects in an early conversation though they can be fascinating subjects at a party when a "Silent Impressions" Questionnaire is used as an ice-breaker.

Telling people your hunches about them is such a good way of getting people to talk about themselves that Emily designed a "Silent Impressions" Questionnaire for use in her Brief Encounters workshops. It helps people become aware of how much they think they can tell about a person just by looking at him and how much they can really tell. And, at a party, it helps strangers break through small talk and get acquainted quickly. Here is the questionnaire.

Silent-impressions questionnaire

1. In what area of the country or world was this person raised?
2. In what city does he/she live now?
3. What is his/her level of education? In what fields?

4. What kind of work does he/she do?
5. What is his/her approximate yearly income?
6. What kind of home does he/she live in? Describe—e.g., house or apartment, formal or informal, casual or meticulous, etc.
7. What are his/her political values—liberal, conservative or reactionary?
8. What are his/her hobbies and interests?
9. What kinds of music does he/she like?
10. What kinds of sports interest him/her? As a participant or observer?
11. How old is he/she?
12. What is his/her marital status—divorced, widowed, separated, never married? How many times married?
13. Does he/she tend to be monogamous in relationships or have a few or many sexual companions?
14. What do you think he/she would like about you?
15. What do you think he/she would not like about you?

Here is how to use the questionnaire at a social gathering where there are a number of strangers.

1. Ask each person to choose (by mutual consent) a partner he has never met before. (If some guests have met, don't worry about it, they will still learn a lot of new things about each other.) The partners are to sit near to one another but not talk.
2. Give each person a copy of the questionnaire and ask him to fill it out quickly (in about five minutes) on the basis of hunches and not lengthy reasoning. Encourage people to look one another over carefully during this period but to remain silent.
3. At the end of five minutes, ask each person to share as many of his answers as he wants to with his partner, allowing his partner to correct, verify or amplify as seems appropriate.
4. After a half or three quarters of an hour, ask people to gather in a large group and share what they discovered about themselves and each other during this exercise. Then ask them to mingle with others and to continue sharing fantasies and biographical facts and feelings.

Conversation will just flow after people answer this Questionnaire. So much has been brought to the surface to talk about and so much of the worry about being too personal has vanished. People love testing their hunches and it is amazing how often they will be right if they take the time to really "tune in" on the other person.

In getting personal through talking about your feelings, life story and first impressions, try to achieve a balance in your conversation—a balance between your talking and your companion talking, a balance between sharing and gentle questioning. Some people are good at talking about themselves—their experiences, opinions, responses, etc.—but forget to take a breath, ask some questions and listen to the other person. Others are good at asking questions, listening, taking things in but fail to hold up their end when it comes to talking about themselves. When there is a conversational balance, both parties will be more comfortable.

CLOSING

At some place during that first meeting with a stranger there comes a moment of decision. You realize either that this person doesn't interest you very much and you'd like to break off the connection or that you'd like to continue. And sometimes the conversation will be broken by circumstances unless somebody does or says something and quickly. You may have started talking while standing in a long line and now there are only one or two people in front of you. You may have met someone going down in the elevator and now the light goes on to show that your next stop is the lobby. Sometimes you have more time—for instance, when you have enjoyed talking with the person who sat next to you at a dinner party and now have the rest of the evening ahead of you, or you like the person who is your seatmate on a train or airplane.

Whether you have to do it quickly or have a longer time to plan your strategy, it is necessary at some point to ask for something that will give you further contact or to make it very plain that if the other person were to ask, you would accept. As you come to the end of line you've been standing in, you might want to say to your companion, "I'd like to talk to you further.

Can we go somewhere and sit down and continue our conversation?" As the elevator nears the lobby floor, you could say, "I've enjoyed our few minutes together; do you have time to join me for a cup of coffee?" At a party you might want to say, "I'd really like to see you again. Could you and your wife come over for a simple and early dinner on Tuesday?"

The point is to be direct, be specific, ask for exactly what you want and don't be afraid to ask. You can't expect your companion to read your mind. Closing is probably the most critical stage in the meeting phase of a relationship. This is the place where connections that have been enjoyable and could be continued are dropped—not by choice but by default. Just as a salesman, although he is friendly, sensitive to his client's needs, and knows how to present his product to its best advantage, is not going to be a success unless he completes the last step—asking for the order—a person will not be a success in interpersonal relationships unless he develops the skill of asking for what he wants.

Also, the style of asking is important. Requests must sound like requests and not like demands. If, as you ask, you make certain to imply, "Will you . . . ?" or "May I . . . ?" it will sound as though you do not intend to impose. Such behavior makes a person feel that you respect his "psychological space" and thus he can often be more comfortable in doing what you have suggested.

A word of caution: Don't suggest future contact unless you really want it. Instead, say something like "Thanks for the time we've spent together" without saying or implying, "I'd like to see you again." You can be gracious without being dishonest.

There are certain phrases that it is probably best *not* to use. They have been used so frequently to avoid the embarrassment of saying goodbye that they are confusing. Don't count on such phrases as "I hope we see each other again soon," or "We must get together sometime," or "Drop in and see me anytime," to get you further contact. You must be a lot more direct and specific.

NEW RITUALS

All of the above suggestions are "safe" ones—ones that fit within the bounds of established social behavior. All we have done is find some "elbow room" in them in order for you to make contact. But if you feel a little daring, you might enjoy creating some new social rituals yourself, ones that will help you make contact more quickly. Who knows, maybe one that you devise will catch on and become popular. To get you started, here are some ideas we have found helpful. We hope you will try them.

1. *Have personal cards printed.* In this country we have a tradition of business cards but they are usually for the purpose of gaining new business contacts. Though some people use them for personal contacts, this can be quite confusing. If someone thinks you are soliciting business when what you really want is further social contact, your friendly overture will be overlooked. Using business cards this way can also put people off. If your position is an important one or the name of your firm is impressive, a person can feel inferior and that you wouldn't be interested in him. Or he may think you are deliberately trying to "one-up" him. Personal cards must be much more informal than business cards to be effective.

One innovative woman we know has designed an unusual personal card. In the center, printed below her name in the space where a person's title ordinarily appears, it says "Human Being." Below that, in the corner where it is customary to list one's business activities, it says, "Ideas, Feelings and Experiences Shared." She passes these out freely and they are most effective. They say much more about her than is written on the card. They say she is warm, open, friendly and creative and very much interested in other people.

When you have a personal card, it is easy and graceful, as part of the goodbye ritual, to say something like, "It's really been interesting talking with you. Let me give you my card." It puts no obligation on another person but he then knows how to make contact with you if he would like to. And if the person you are giving your card to is of the opposite sex, it adds a feeling of dignity to the encounter that it is not possible to get when you write your number on a scrap of paper or matchbook and hand it over. Through the use of a personal card, you are saying, in the simplest way possible, "This is who I am. Feel free to call me if you'd like to get together sometime."

2. *Develop your own "hang-out."* When you were in high school or college, chances are you had a "hang-out." Whether it

was a coffee shop, a drugstore, a drive-in or a beer bar, the purpose
was the same—to provide you with a place where you could always
run into your friends and easily meet new ones, a place where you
weren't required to do anything more than *be there* and a place
where the very fact you were there showed you "belonged." For a
variety of reasons most of us give up our hang-outs after we supposedly "grow up." We claim we don't have time; our lovers or
spouses object to the time we spend away from them; there just
aren't any suitable hang-outs around except for bars, which generally are considered strictly male hang-outs or pickup places for singles. Or, more often than not, it simply doesn't occur to us that a
"hang-out" is what we need.

However, Ralph Keyes, author of *We, the Lonely People*, believes you don't outgrow your need for a hang-out. In fact, according to Keyes, "The people who are beyond 'hanging-out,' well-to-
do, urbane, years out of school—may be the ones who need most
to hang-out." We suggest that, as part of taking charge of your
own reality, you develop your own hang-out—a place where you
feel comfortable about spending a little time, where you are
known by face or name and where you find it easy to make contact with people you don't know.

While we are convinced everyone can benefit from having a
hang-out (even married people), the *type* of hang-out that suits
each person best will vary according to the time he has to spend
and his particular life style. And don't make the excuse that, since
you don't like bars, you just can't find a hang-out. Almost every
shopping center has suitable hang-outs. Small specialty shops—pet
stores, health-food shops, book stores, plant stores, card and stationery stores, gift shops, delicatessens and bakeries with a few
tables and chairs, small restaurants—all make good hang-outs.

The main thing is that you really enjoy being there browsing
through the merchandise, talking with the clerks and other customers, lingering over a purchase or a cup of coffee. If you go in
on a regular basis and usually make some sort of small purchase,
the clerks will soon recognize you and say "hello." You'll feel at
home enough to enjoy a much-needed sense of "community," you
can talk to them about something that interests you (plants, pets,
whatever) and you can meet others who share your interests. Park
recreation centers, libraries, museums, also make good hang-outs if
you truly enjoy the activities going on there.

Because people enjoy the camaraderie of eating and drinking with others, bars and restaurants have always been traditional hang-outs—but more often they have been exclusively masculine hang-outs. This situation is changing today and many small neighborhood bars make an attempt to provide an atmosphere where women not only are welcome but will not be "hassled." If you are a woman who would like to use a restaurant or bar for a hang-out, these tips by Amy Gross from an article in the July-August 1975 *New Woman* should be helpful. Says Ms. Gross, "Choose one or two places *in your neighborhood* for your five o'clock drink and Saturday morning breakfast. If you are comfortable there, you will *look* comfortable there and therefore approachable. And if you don't like the approach, you can discourage it easily. After all, being a regular at this place, you're among friends."

Although she is directing her remarks to single women interested in meeting men for future partners, the tips make sense for married women and for single or married men who just want to meet people or even just get out of the house for a while. "Don't just sip your drink and leave," adds Ms. Gross. "Take your newspaper, open your mail, write your letters there." If enough people want to develop the social ritual of personal "hang-outs," more places will attempt to meet this need. We've already heard of several restaurants that have a big round table where people eating alone can be seated with other "un-coupled diners" if they wish.

3. *Use a "pickup" card.* When Emily was presenting a program several years ago at a national convention of the Association of Humanistic Psychology, she invented a "pickup" letter to make it easier for the convention participants to meet each other. The AHP members were so delighted with the ease of getting acquainted through this letter that, emboldened, they began presenting it to other people they saw in restaurants, bars, stores and even walking down the street. As a result, they had some terrific conversations and in some cases started new friendships. The letter is short enough to fit on a small card and reads as follows:

Hello, my name is _____

You are an interesting-looking person, and I would like very much to meet you. Will you please give me ten minutes of your time so we can get acquainted? I'll keep track of the time, and I promise to leave at the end of ten minutes unless you want me to stay longer.

I hope you'll take a chance. It could be the start of a nice friendship for both of us.

In a Man-Woman Institute Singlelife Seminar called "Meeting That Special Person," cards with this message printed on them are given to participants along with these instructions: Approach a stranger that you think you'd like to know better, smile in a warm, friendly way, hand him/her this card and say, "Excuse me, I'm taking a class to help me get acquainted with people in new ways. Will you please take a minute to read this?"

This card is good for making contact with members of the opposite sex because it helps create a "safe" environment: It lets them know exactly what you want and that you will leave in a few minutes if they so desire. However, it can be used for meeting people of the same sex as well.

You can easily make such a device for yourself by printing or typing a similar message on a 3×5 index card. If you are artistic, add some color or designs to make it attractive. Be certain it is easy to read and clean and neat. Carry it with you at all times. You can never tell when you might want to use it. You can say, as you hand someone the card, "I've just read a book that encourages people to try new ways to get acquainted. Will you please take a minute to read this?"

Though it may sound difficult, almost impossible, to walk up to a perfect stranger and hand him this card and then stand there silently waiting while he reads it, it isn't. Making up your mind to do it may be difficult, for you can imagine all sorts of terrible things that *might* happen. They won't. It is just the fear of strangers that has been bred into you that makes you imagine horrible things. We are so certain this card will work that we make this guarantee: Use it ten times and you will meet at least three interesting people and have two unusual experiences. And nothing will happen to you that you can't easily cope with.

If this card does not live up to its guarantee, let us know and we will write you up as an unusual research statistic. (Write us also to tell good things that happen; we like to hear about them as well.) If you should have trouble using this card or doing any of the other things we suggest, tell yourself that you are doing them as part of a research assignment on human behavior. It will make doing them a lot easier. Our friends love it when we ask them to try new ways of making contact as a means of gathering research data. They feel authorized to try things they want to try anyway.

ASSIGNMENT

With all of these suggestions, you may feel swamped and not know where to begin. Here is what to do first. Start this very day trying to catch the gaze of friendly-looking strangers. Try to hold it for five seconds. As you do, concentrate on sending a quick, friendly nonverbal message. You can make up your own or here are some suggestions:

You're great, just as you are!
You seem like a very friendly person.
I like what I see.

Bear in mind that many other people have read this book too. So from now on, when anyone looks into your eyes, assume he is sending you a friendly message. Savor it. If many people do this every day—send friendly messages with their eyes and take time to enjoy the ones they get from others—we can, just by this simple technique, change our views of a stranger from someone who might hurt us to someone who might give us something good if we will allow it.

4

Gentle Aggression

The "pickup"—a public meeting between a man and a woman—is still not completely respectable. It smacks of cheap, quick sex. Even many young people, supposedly freed by the sexual revolution and the women's liberation movement, seem to share the view of Emily Post, who describes a pickup as a "public kind of encounter which is *never* correct. A gentleman," she adds, "may not use a lunch counter, bus or retrieved glove as the basis for an introduction to a young woman; the traditionally correct formal introduction, made by a mutual friend, is still necessary."

Though this advice sounds quaint and archaic, when we suggested to a young friend of ours (who was complaining that she never met any men) that she try some of the suggestions in Chapter 3, she exclaimed indignantly, "I couldn't just go up to a strange man and start talking to him. He'll think I'm trying to pick him up and that I want to go to bed with him." And her reaction is not unusual.

We still hold ourselves back from much simple friendly human interaction with members of the opposite sex by the worry of "Will he/she think I'm making a pass?"

In fact, according to Dr. Barry Singer, associate professor of psychology at California State University at Long Beach and instructor of a course on dating, "Among college students the old barriers and the old roles are as rigid as they ever were. The male is still expected to initiate contact but he can only do this in certain socially approved places—in class, at a dance or party, maybe at a singles bar. It is still frowned upon for him to approach a girl he doesn't know who, for example, is sitting under a tree on the campus or browsing in the library."

In spite of assertiveness training and other motivating activities that have made many campuses a bastion of women's liberation, when it comes to initiating contact with men, even the most outspoken feminists hold back. Though a few try it out, sometimes shyly and sometimes with belligerence, at the first rejection most of them scurry back to their more traditional "waiting" role. As a rule, college students don't really enjoy going by themselves to the places where they might meet people in "acceptable" ways—i.e., college dances or parties. They feel hemmed in and inadequate because of stereotypes and rigid role expectations. Though some do attend alone on the lookout for a partner, even more—on campuses throughout the nation—simply do not date at all. Meeting and dating is too much of a hassle. Others, according to Dr. Singer, cope with this problem by going steady or getting married.

Actually, underneath much of our present male-female ways of relating the same basic assumption prevails that governs Emily Post's advice—relationships between men and women are sexy. According to this assumption, the only reason a man and woman might want to meet would be for the purpose of sex. This assumption has led to a lot of manipulative behavior between men and women and has tended to turn their getting-acquainted behavior patterns into a power struggle—one centering on sex and money.

The strategy behind the struggle goes like this: Women have been taught they must get a husband—a protector and provider who will take care of them and all their needs—in order to be "real women." But they must go about achieving their most important life goal indirectly because to go after a man directly is "unladylike," "pushy" or, even worse, "aggressive." Therefore, a woman learns to play manipulative games to interest a man in being her lifetime provider. And her chief commodity of exchange is sex. Whether she uses the promise of sex in the future as a lure or "gives in" because she feels she must, to get her man, she is taught not to consider her own sexual feelings and needs.

Men, on the other hand, believe that a "real man" aggressively goes after what he wants, which, he has been taught, when it comes to women, is sex. Since men are also taught that tenderness is unmanly, many concentrate their efforts on, not a search for love or friendship, but getting sex. Convinced (by a thousand "nos" and the fact that women don't take the initiative in asking for sex any more than they do in asking for initial contact) that their sexual needs are greater than women's, men believe they must have a commodity to exchange for the one wanted. The commodity most men use is money—money to buy her time and attention while he makes his sexual "pitch."

Each person learns to judge his or her value by how willing the other sex is to give its chief commodity. Women believe that if men spend money on them, they are worthwhile, particularly if they don't give sex in return. Men believe that if they get sex, they are worthwhile, particularly if they don't have to spend much money to get it. Though men and women are not usually conscious of the intricacies of their money-sex negotiations, the cost of this exchange is high to both—not only in self-esteem but also in their development as full human beings. He has to expend a lot of time and energy in order to be able to provide the money and take the major responsibility for their relationship—and this can be taxing to his health. She does not have the opportunity to take responsibility for her own relationships and sex life.

The sort of interchange that limits a man to the "asking" role and a woman to the "yes" or "no" role cheats both sexes—of a wide choice of potential partners and good feelings. He doesn't get a chance to know many of the women who might find him attractive—women he either hasn't noticed or is afraid to approach. He misses out on the good feelings that come from being asked, from being wanted by others. She doesn't get a chance to know the men she finds attractive who don't ask her. And she can never experience the feeling of power that comes from knowing who you want, going after him in a direct and up-front manner and being successful.

Our goal in this chapter is to help men and women meet and have equal, honest, esteem-building relationships whether these last a few minutes or a lifetime and whether the possibility of sex is or isn't a factor. And because the "pickup" (i.e., public encounter) is the major way many people are able to get together in our mobile and rapidly changing society, we want to defuse the sexual connotations that underlie it and turn it into a more open and exploratory approach—one similar to the British "chat-up."

In an English pub, the interaction between men and women is considerably different from that in an American bar. Maybe it is the courteous low-key nature of the British or maybe it is the informal structure of the pubs which allows people to get acquainted in an easy and spontaneous way over ale and darts. Whatever it is, when men and women do have a drink together or engage in a conversation, there is no sense of obligation on either part or an assumption that the interaction is inevitably going to lead to sex. The opportunity to chat with another person and get to know him a little better is a source of pleasure in itself.

Sometimes this attitude carries over outside of the pub. Betty discovered the difference between the British "chat-up" and the American-style "pickup" when she was sitting in Hyde Park in London and an Englishman sat down beside her. He began talking in an easy and relaxed way, asking where she was from, telling her a little about himself. Though worried about his intentions, she talked with him because he was attractive and gentle and she was lonely. Soon the conversation deepened, and he shared some of his feelings, particularly his sadness that he had just broken up with his fiancée. Betty then shared with him some of her apprehension about being alone in a strange city. They talked and walked through the park for several hours, holding hands and giving each other warmth and comfort. At the end of their time together, both expressed how much it had meant to them and parted—forever. To all external appearances this was a "pickup"— yet what went on between them was not a sexual negotiation, for neither paid for, sold or gave up anything. Instead, as a result of mutual sharing, both gained. Afterward, they felt better about themselves, each other and the world in general.

It is that feeling that such a conversation can't happen that often keeps it from happening. Certainly the kind of brief encounter we just described is rare but primarily because people don't see it as a possibility. Actually the potential for all kinds of fascinating supportive interaction between men and women is there if both sexes will develop the attitudes and skills to take advantage of it—if they will become gentle aggressors.

WHAT IS GENTLE AGGRESSION?

"Gentle aggression" is androgynous behavior—a blending of traditional sex roles—that de-escalates the war between the sexes and puts both on the same team. It is a new sort of role for both men and women—one that encourages men to be more gentle by toning down their sexual aggression and that encourages women to be more assertive instead of manipulative. Gentle aggression is a role that neither limits people to certain specific "right" behavior on the basis of gender nor recasts the old power struggle in a new form. We do not advocate role reversal with the woman becoming not just assertive but aggressively and hostilely "macho" and the man becoming passive and resentful. Nor is the new role we endorse a part of the sexual freedom backlash in which people pressure each other for sex under the guise that sexual liberation is "in." What we advocate for both sexes is role expansion. (A role simply refers to a way of behaving in a particular social position—mother, father, teacher, student, male, female, etc.) It requires that both sexes pick their own values and goals rather than those that men and women are supposed to have, and that they add new social skills to their present repertoire of behavior, dropping others that keep them from living their values and reaching their goals.

Gentle aggression, although promoted for both men and women, is not based on a belief that there are no differences between the sexes. Nor does it take the chemistry out of male-female interaction. It is far more conducive to romance than the old-fashioned behavior patterns that are many times a cover-up for fear, frustration and hostility. The assumptions beneath this role are that interactions between men and women do not always hinge on the possibility of sex nor does either sex have to feel one-up on the other for the meeting to be successful. These assumptions free people to have not only more interchanges with members of the opposite sex but more truly friendly interchanges. They permit men and women, single or married, to talk with many members of the opposite sex, to enjoy some time together with no other purpose than just that. They also permit those who are looking for partners to sift through many potential dates or mates, with no need to hurry, simply for the pleasure of having a number of enriching and memorable "brief encounters" while seeking the one who will best fill their needs. Such assumptions, because they result in honest communication and compassion, also set a better base for short-term alliances or long-term relationships that might develop from these encounters.

PRIVILEGES AND RESPONSIBILITIES OF THE GENTLE AGGRESSOR

Men and women who regard each other as objects to manipulate in a power struggle—who view each other with suspicion, who see the other sex as having all the advantages—will not be honest or gentle with each other. The dictionary defines "gentle" as meaning tender, kind, compassionate, and there simply isn't enough of that quality in relationships between men and women today. When the traditional roles were more sharply defined and fewer people were questioning them, there was perhaps more gentleness between the sexes, but the gentleness of the male was often the condescension of a stronger person to a weaker and the gentleness of the female was often merely passivity. With the advent of women's liberation and the sexual revolution, some of this surface behavior has changed but not the underlying power struggle.

Today some men have decided that if women want equality, men need no longer be "gentlemen," and they have thrown out a lot of their old "chivalrous" behavior—with its built-in gentleness. One woman, trying to break out of the old male-female roles and be assertive, approached a man she didn't know at a dance and asked him to dance. He looked at her coldly and said, "If I'd have wanted to dance with you, I'd have asked you."

On the other hand, some women, perhaps deciding they can get power of their own only by putting men down, have started treating men in unkind and abrasive ways and so they have lost a lot of their gentleness. One young and highly attractive man went up to a young woman sitting at a table at a singles bar with some girl friends and asked her to dance. She looked him up and down as thoroughly as if she were inspecting a horse she wanted to buy and then, smiling triumphantly at her friends, she drawled, "No, I really don't think so." The young man was so shaken by the experience that he had to go home.

Much of this lack of concern for the feelings of others comes from the fact that each sex envies the other for its supposed "special privileges" and chafes at what it sees as its own restrictions. This resentment takes a heavy toll because if a person mistrusts men and women in general he cannot deeply love one particular man or one particular woman. Even if he claims that particular person is "special" or "different," his lack of respect for their sex denies the very essence of that person's being—his or her very humanness.

If you find that you often make generalizations about the opposite sex that show hostility (and envy, guilt and resentment are masks for hostile feelings), watch out for hostility in your behavior. You can be certain you are sometimes thoughtless and cruel if you say (or even think):

Men are only interested in one thing: sex.

Women are only interested in one thing: money.

Men have it made. They get to go after what they want. (Or get to decide what should be done, tell others what to do, etc.)

Women have it made. All they have to do is sit there and wait to be asked. (Or lie there and be made love to, etc.)

Gentle aggression is based on the idea of respect for yourself and members of your sex as well as for the opposite sex. The way to get and to show this respect is to provide yourself with the privileges usually accorded the opposite sex while at the same time accepting the responsibilities that go along with those privileges. In addition, those who want to be gentle aggressors must realize that since they will be stepping out of the traditional male or female role and behaving in unexpected ways, people are apt to find their behavior surprising. While many will welcome it as delightfully refreshing, others may at times be thrown off balance. However, the important thing is that such behavior will provide more payoffs than setbacks.

The need for new behavior becomes more apparent when we

take a look at what is typical male and female behavior in two areas: social and sexual conduct. Let's talk about women's behavior first and take a look at what they must do to get more of the privileges men have and yet not overlook the accompanying responsibilities.

Though more and more women are finding a place for themselves in the world of work, very few seem fully aware that it is their world, too, when it comes to social and sexual opportunities and responsibilities. In the first place, they have simply not learned the social skills necessary to get along in today's world. In the past when women's place was clearly in the home, a woman learned the appropriate skills for the expectation. She learned how to keep house and rear children and pour tea and dismiss servants, but she didn't learn how to pay the check at a restaurant, have a peaceful drink in a bar on a hot day without being hassled, how to let a man know she was or wasn't interested in talking with him in public. She didn't have to know how to do the latter things because she was "sheltered." The price she paid for being protected was also being treated like a helpless child in many other ways.

Because of the women's liberation emphasis on taking their rightful place in the work world, some women have taken on the responsibility of earning their own living, *but* few have gone out into the social world and taken full advantage of their opportunities. Socially, many women are still as crippled as if they had bound feet. Many are reluctant to drive on the freeway, to dine alone, to go to a museum, a play, a concert alone—to go almost anywhere in public without the company of a male. We know far too many women like this. There is Beth, a divorcee, who is worldly and sophisticated. Every winter she goes to Aspen to ski, every spring she goes to the Golden Door to regain her slender figure and every summer she entertains lavishly in her oceanfront home. But she cannot go to dinner by herself because she is worried that people will think she can't "get" a man and because she doesn't know how to order the right wine, tip, and so on. Then there is Joanne, a married woman who flirts with other men at parties; she knows her husband is in the other room to back her up if her "flirting" gets her into trouble. But she wouldn't dream of going to a bar or restaurant alone because she thinks men might try to pick her up, and she doesn't have the social skills to cope with that situation.

The handling of money in a social situation in mixed company is also an area in which most women lack experience. They could profit from an examination of their behavior and the attitudes toward men that underlie it. Even women executives who handle budgets for large corporations seem to assume when they are out on other than company business that if there is a man in the crowd, he will buy the drinks or pay for the dinner. Such assumptions, though they follow logically from growing up in a world where men had the money and the power and women weren't permitted to have either, must be thrown out. If a woman doesn't want to feel bought and paid for, she is going to have to take responsibility for herself financially when in the company of men just as she would do if in the company of women.

Another reason women are inexperienced socially is that they simply don't feel they have the right to be out in public—especially at night—unless they are half of a couple. This belief deprives millions of women of the many social opportunities available to them. Joan K. Davidson remarked on this phenomenon—a phenomenon she calls the "Couple Assumption"—in an April 7, 1977, New York *Times* article: "Without force of law—but with all the unfathomable power of folklore—it effectively excludes thousands of New Yorkers from fully enjoying the city's wealth of arts, impedes the healthy growth of audiences, and subtly contributes to the general unhappiness. It could be called the Couple Assumption—the implicit belief that audiences at cultural events will arrange themselves in serried ranks of neatly balanced pairs, and that lone people, especially women alone, will stay away."

We challenge the "Couple Assumption," and we encourage women to learn the skills that will enable them to go places alone and handle any situation that may arise. Having these skills not only will give a woman confidence but will make her feel like a complete person—not just half of a couple. The more experience a woman has in taking care of herself in the world, the better she can avoid a potentially unpleasant or dangerous situation. Such skills frequently prevent having to use a "rape whistle" to keep from being taken advantage of. Perhaps even more important in the long run, knowing she can take care of herself allows a woman to see men in a kinder light—less as hostile strangers who might do her harm and more like people she feels free to interact with.

The second area in which women need considerable encouragement and training involves sexual conduct. Most women are still shirking the responsibility for their own sexual fulfillment in spite of the opportunities available to them. And these opportunities are just about unlimited thanks to the sexual revolution. It is now widely understood and accepted that women, too, not only have a sex drive but also have the capacity to enjoy a wide variety of sexual experiences.

But for a woman, asking for sex is particularly scary because it is such a switch from the traditional female role. Because of her nervousness and lack of practice in asking, her request often comes out as a demand. A sexual demand affects men in much the same way it does women—it makes them feel less than equal and as though they are an object whose only function is to satisfy someone else's needs. Because women have been brought up to believe men always want sex, they usually fail to see the need to take his feelings into account. They discount his need for tender "wooing," and many times unknowingly subject him to emotional rape.

Women who do take the initiative usually do so only with men they are sure are interested in having sex with them; frequently they reserve their overtures for men who have previously asked them. The kind of sexual behavior we advocate involves a woman making the first sexual overture when she wants sex even though she isn't sure whether or not he does. In seeking the privileges of the opposite sex, she must not repeat its mistakes. She must be more honest and more communicative than men usually are when they initiate sex. A woman needs to be aware of what her sexual request means to her and how it will affect him—is she letting him know she loves him, attempting to start a sexual relationship or just seeking pleasure for the moment? Since his response will be influenced by her intent, she must be sensitive to his feelings and let him know hers. After all, the sexual revolution is meaningless if it just encourages women to treat men as ever-ready studs. New abilities need to be developed by both women and men who want to get relationships off to a good start.

A large part of taking sexual responsibility involves learning how to take a sexual refusal gracefully. For most men, the word "no" is something that they have been accustomed to hearing most of their lives from the opposite sex. But women seem to believe (since it is so hard for them to ask and since a man is supposed to be always horny) that once they offer, a man is bound to say "yes." When he doesn't, a woman may fall apart, believing something must be wrong with her or he wouldn't have refused or, if not, then something must certainly be wrong with him.

Many times women who are refused, particularly when the refusal is not done in a kind way, say, "I'll never ask a man to go to bed again" (or to dance or to do whatever they asked for that was refused). They forget that men get turned down all the time and that nobody likes being turned down. Men aren't born with an automatic ability to take refusals in their stride; they've just had more experience. On the other hand, they haven't had as much experience at refusing sex. Consequently, they are sometimes clumsy, insensitive, even cruel in the way they say "no." Later we'll give some ideas on how both sexes can ask for and refuse sex in assertive but kind ways.

Just as a woman needs to learn to ask for sex she also needs to learn better ways to say "no." Because of the new sexual ethics, the art of saying "no" is more important than ever to a woman. She no longer has the backing of the "double standard" to reinforce her decision not to have sex. "A nice girl doesn't" is no longer a good reason. Her only guideline now is what feels right to her and what she wants. She must constantly re-examine her feelings and thoughts, however, because she is so unaccustomed to paying attention to what she wants that she can easily go along with sexual experiences that she doesn't really want while calling herself "sexually liberated." A woman cheats herself of the privileges she's entitled to when she goes to bed with a man merely to ensure another date, or because she believes that everyone else is doing it so "why not?" or because she is afraid that he'll think she is sexually inhibited if she doesn't. Today, according to Dr. Manuel J. Smith, author of *When I Say No, I Feel Guilty,* "many single women feel that sexual relations in dating situations are their admission tickets into a relationship with men; they are paying a price for not being lonely instead of mutually sharing something both exciting and tender."

There are important things for women to remember that will allow them to feel comfortable and confident while picking up or being picked up by men: (1) they are adult human beings, complete in and of themselves and capable of taking good care of themselves; (2) they and men are entitled to want sex or not want sex and the best sex is possible only when both want it; (3) they are able to assume their own financial obligations, and it is not a male's job to do that for them.

Men, too, need education in social and sexual behavior. Though many times it is assumed that men "just naturally" are knowledgeable and confident in these areas, it just isn't so. They have been trained for the old-fashioned roles of father-protector and sexual aggressor, and while such behavior is O.K. sometimes, when it is automatic it prevents much friendly and honest interaction between the sexes.

Through gentle aggression a man can expand his role and in doing so experience some of the privileges—and responsibilities—inherent in the female role. To have the privilege of a woman's companionship as an equal and feel comfortable, he must learn that (1) he doesn't always have to pay and (2) he doesn't always have to offer sex or even want it.

Men need to learn to assert their right not to automatically go along with the cultural assumption that they should *always* pay when they go out with a woman. We aren't suggesting that the man should never pay or that men and women should *always* go dutch; we aren't interested in imposing new "rules" to take the place of the old. What we are interested in is that men and women share the responsibility for their interaction more—deciding where to go and what to do and who will pay. In Chapter 9 we'll be more specific as to how a man and woman can work out the money issue equitably; now we merely want to point out how the assumptions about and use of money affects the possibility of a friendly public meeting between a man and a woman.

Money has tended to be the male's major weapon in the power struggle between men and women, and both sexes have been damaged by the manipulative use of money to gain power in a relationship. It encourages women to be "gold diggers"—to use or withhold their sex for financial gain. It has encouraged men to view women as sexual objects—as things who not only could be bought but had to be. And it has made many men feel that their only value to women is the money they spend. As one recently divorced man put it, "I guess I have resentments about women because it doesn't seem my relationships have been reciprocal. When I have paid, it has been taken for granted that that was my role. I was rarely thanked. I need to know my only value is not my paycheck. I guess a woman feels if a guy doesn't spend much on her she isn't worth much. I have the same kind of feeling. I'd like to be called sometime and have someone say, 'How about dinner? I'd like to take you to a great restaurant.' If that happened even just now and then I could feel my only value was not that I could pay for things and she could feel her only value wasn't sex. I'd like to know somebody liked me just for me."

And the money game leads to situations like the one described to us by Gary, another bachelor friend who has been in the singles "game" for a long time. Gary was out at a bar one night when two attractive young women came in and started talking with him. He bought them drinks and they invited him to come over to a different bar at a nearby hotel where they were meeting some friends. He followed them over and joined them at a table with four or five other people, including several men. One of the women gave Gary a big "come-on"—rubbing his leg, blowing in his ear and gently suggesting, "Why don't you buy another round, honey?" Gary paid for the party but she went home with one of the other men—who turned out to be her long-time boy friend.

"Don't get me wrong," explains Gary. "I don't expect a woman to jump into bed with me because I've bought her a few drinks or dinner. In fact, if I ask someone to be my guest, I'm not expecting anything more and I don't think most men are either. However, a lot of women seem to interpret a straight invitation to a glass of wine or a meal as a sexual come-on. But it burns me when a woman plays me for a sucker, which, unfortunately, has happened to me more than once. The woman used her sexuality to get me to pay for her party and it rankles me that I was worked over and fell for it."

A man need not feel he must always be expected to perform sexually in order to be a "real man." One of the opportunities available to him through gentle aggression is discovering that he can still be a sexual being even if he doesn't want sex all the time or with everyone. Dr. Keith Tombrink, Emily's partner in the Man-Woman Institute, says that for many men, seeking sex is just their way of getting a woman to say, "I care about you." According to Dr. Tombrink, "Most men really want a woman to care about them and be tender but hardly any men will admit that."

We found this to be true when we interviewed men for this

book. At first, they would say, "Of course the reason I try to pick up a woman is so I can have sex," but later in the interview, when they trusted us more and were more relaxed, some different thoughts emerged. Jack, a divorced man of thirty-two, told us that frequently he feels he is expected to be "on the prowl" in certain places such as a singles bar. In fact, says Jack, the mere act of entering the bar is an ego threat. It is as if he is putting himself on the line "to score" and no matter what his intentions are at the beginning of the evening, he ends up wanting to find a sexual partner. This is especially true if he is with a male friend who is "hustling" a woman. Then he gets "really competitive." Adds Jack, "I end up drinking too much, which is part of easing the inhibitions and anxiety. Then I have to contend with a hangover, and I probably didn't even get laid—but I was out until two or three in the morning in the hopes of it. I get caught up in this sort of behavior even though I know the chances of a good sexual happening in such circumstances are slim."

Not only is it harmful to a man to seek out the symbol—i.e., sex —of something he wants even more—i.e., contact and caring—but it is harmful to him emotionally to let women use him sexually when that isn't what he really wants at the time. Because of the sexual revolution, some women are demanding sexual fulfillment and their demands (even if they aren't verbal) make many men feel like withdrawing from the sexual arena. And psychiatrists and psychologists report that more and more men are troubled with impotency and other sexual problems because of their uncertainty about their sexual "role" these days.

The fact that a number of men are unable or unwilling to become sexually involved is the other side of the coin from always being interested in sex. Men have had the fantasy that they never could get enough sex—that life would be perfect if only they could find a lusty woman who wanted it as much as they did. Now that more and more women are coming on lusty and wanting sex as much—sometimes even more—than men do, men feel threatened. What is threatening is not just the sexual demand but the loss of their fantasy of how perfect life could be *if only* women were different. However, we believe, the withdrawing from sex is for many men just a stage they have to go through as they learn to change their sexual attitudes and develop new relating skills.

Men as well as women need to learn to get in touch with their own sexual feelings and wants. While the tendency has been for women not to seek sex when they wanted it, and not even to recognize that they wanted it, men have been brought up to seek sex when they don't really want it. They have denied the gentle side of their nature. Thus men need to learn to seek tenderness—soft words, pats, hugs and non-erotic, affectionate stroking—rather than sex when that is what they want. But, of course, they must first learn that they can still be very masculine and yet be soft, sensitive and vulnerable.

A skill that many men need is the ability to say "no" to unwanted sex. A young friend of ours learned this the hard way. He is a gorgeous young man who just loves women and sex, and women reciprocate. In fact, women were always coming over to his apartment to go to bed with him. For a long time, he was flattered and attempted to accommodate all his eager young guests. But when he started going to graduate school and his studies began to suffer, it was a different matter. Suddenly one night he realized that he'd rather be studying than making love. So he told the young lady involved that it wasn't that sex with her didn't interest him—it was just that, at the moment, his studies interested him more. But as he says, "It was the most difficult thing I ever did in my life because I was afraid she would think I wasn't masculine."

HOW TO BEHAVE LIKE A GENTLE AGGRESSOR: ESTABLISH CLEAR SOCIAL SIGNALS

All of us, all of the time, are using "social signals" to tell members of the opposite sex something. We can't help it. The way we dress, our facial expressions, gestures, manners and mannerisms, the way we make eye contact, move and position ourselves, and, of course, our words, give clues as to whether we are available, what we are available for and who we are interested in. Problems arise when our social signals aren't clear, when they don't say what we'd really like to say or when they seem designed to keep another person in line by making him or her uncomfortable.

When social signals become automatic, they tend to do all these things.

Most of the social signals traditional in public places are nothing more than habits based on whether you are a man or a woman and on the idea that a "pickup" implies sex. Habitual signals are often dishonest. For example, it is traditional for a man to look in a speculative, interested way at a woman he finds attractive who is approaching him on the street. It is equally traditional for her to lower her eyes and not look directly at him. In reality, he may have no interest at all in making contact with her but may be living up to the behavior expected of a "red-blooded male." On the other hand, she might be very interested in making contact with him but she doesn't dare appear forward by signaling her interest.

Habitual signals are often ambiguous or exploitive. They not only often fail to get us what we want but often get us what we don't want instead. After her divorce, Emily soon discovered the inadequacy of her usual social signals. She found herself continually sought out by men she didn't care for and ignored by the ones she liked. Through examining her behavior and her thoughts, she came to realize that when a man she found attractive looked at her, she immediately looked away because she didn't want to appear "unfeminine" and aggressive. However, if her eyes caught the eyes of a man she didn't think attractive, she would continue to look at him and smile because she felt sorry for him. She had to go through quite a retraining process in order to stop acting "nice" (and phony!) and learn to become a gentle aggressor.

The social signals of the gentle aggressor are honest and direct but also kind. He tries to send a clear message to whatever group of people he is with that he is available for contact, and he also takes the initiative to send messages to particular individuals he is interested in. Letting people know you are available for contact does not mean that you are available to everybody for anything they want; it merely means that it is O.K. to approach you, that you are approachable. It would be great if there were a way to indicate availability through some kind of universal signal, like holding an index finger straight up in the air or wearing a badge of a certain shape or color, but there isn't. We have to learn to do it in other ways, and the most obvious ones are the way we dress, the way we hold and move our bodies and where we stand or sit when in a place where there are other people.

The way a person dresses is a much more important means of communication than most people realize. If you wear sunshiny colors, you are sending out a message of warmth that helps indicate you are available for contact—to everyone. At a party, you will find it more difficult to hide in a corner like a hermit than if you wear somber colors. Color and style of clothing can be a big help in contacting people when that is what you want and avoiding contacts when that is what you wish. When the authors take a plane for business reasons, we usually wear clothes that are brown or black or beige because, on the way, we want to be alone to concentrate on the presentation we will be giving, and on the trip back, we want to relax without the stimulation of conversation. However, when we travel for pleasure, we wear bright colors, loud prints and sometimes even kookie clothes. Then we want attention and we want it from people who like "characters."

Clothing should be worn that is in keeping with your surroundings, your personality, and that will stimulate the kind of people you want to meet to be attracted to you. Men wearing business suits will be apt to attract women with middle-class values, women who are interested in traditional relationships. Men wearing beads or an earring, a dashiki or a robe, will probably attract less conventional women.

A word of warning: Don't draw attention to a facet of yourself you don't want to be noticed. If a woman wears a low-cut dress, she is inviting men to look at her breasts. There is nothing wrong with her wanting to show them off. It can be fun for her to display and for them to look. However, she should not be insulted if a man shows interest in them and if he shows much interest in her sexuality and overlooks her brain. She should be comfortable with her sexuality and with both accepting and declining sexual invitations if the message she sends out for everyone to see is "I am a sexy woman." And she should be prepared to have to put out a bit of effort to let a man know she has other sides to her personality. But it's that way with any message we send out with our clothing. We are all complex creatures and it is impossible to make all of our many facets obvious at first glance. We must make choices as to what we want to reveal and when and be prepared to supply additional information and to correct misconceptions graciously.

Besides sending out messages about our availability by the way we dress, we also send them out by means of our body language—the way we hold and move our bodies. A woman who stands and walks with her spine straight and inflexible may be doing so because she has a rigid, unyielding personality or because she is in an unfamiliar and frightening situation or because she hurt her back while skiing, but she is sending out the message: "Warning; I am inflexible." In the same way, a man who stands with his arms folded across his chest and a stern expression on his face may be cold or may be painfully shy, but the message he is sending out is: "Stay away. I want to be by myself."

Many men seem to adopt this posture at bars and at singles events. Frequently, these men long to talk with a woman, or anyone for that matter, but are paralyzed into inaction. Unfortunately, they appear self-sufficient, cold and disinterested—enough to keep most people away. It would be helpful if they could get a different expression on their faces, relax their arms and stand in a place where they were more easily accessible, but sometimes they can't. However, a gentle aggressor need not be put off by such "stay away" demeanor, as we shall discuss later. A gentle aggressor knows that while it is a good idea to try to send out a direct and honest message with social signals, none of us can do it all the time. We sometimes need others to see underneath our surface message, to sense the scariness it covers and to reach out to us in spite of our "stay away" message.

Sometimes the way we position ourselves in the environment sends out a false message that can keep others from knowing we are available for contact. Many times single women who want very much to meet men but who are at the same time afraid of what might happen if they do, will fairly shout their unavailability —and without saying a word. You see them at singles bars and dances, two or three together huddled around a table in a dark corner focusing all their attention on one another, never looking up to try to make eye contact with anyone else. And then they go home, wondering what is wrong with them, or with men, that none were attracted to them. They don't seem to realize that the way they positioned themselves clearly stated: "No men wanted here."

One newly divorced woman, Gerry, was introduced to singles bars by a never-married friend who was very knowledgeable about good ways of getting acquainted with men. She and her friend had one drink at a small table in the back of the room, and Gerry was prepared to stay there and talk to her friend for the rest of the evening. However, her friend wouldn't allow it. She put forth some good advice: "Sitting here drinking with me all evening won't get you any new men friends. What you need to do is go to the ladies' room, fill your glass with water and then go over near the bar and stand all by yourself, sipping your drink and looking and smiling at everyone. If you are easy to get to and nobody has to buy you a drink to get your attention, pretty soon someone will talk with you and you'll relax. After that, it will be a lot easier to pick out the ones you want to talk with and be more specific with your smiles."

To sum up, gentle aggression starts with showing your availability through social signals, and it is necessary to pay careful attention to your clothes, body language and positioning in order to let others know if and when you are available. However, it is unrealistic to expect all the people you like to approach you. It is necessary for each person, female and male, to deliberately pick out the individuals he or she wants to contact and send direct messages to indicate his or her interest.

Tips for women

Here are some suggestions a woman can take to let a man know: "I am interested and I want to have contact with you."

1. Make eye contact with a man you are interested in, and smile. Because it is traditional for women to avoid looking men directly in the eye, a direct look and a smile is a very powerful invitation to a man. It lets him know it will be "safe" for him to approach you—that at least you are interested in getting to know him better—and that you won't give him the "cold shoulder" if he comes over to you. It sounds simple but listen to what men have to say about this technique:

> If I look at a woman and she smiles back, that is 80 percent of the battle.

> A woman doesn't have to be verbally inviting to get me to talk to her. All she has to do is smile.

> It is just amazing the impact a warm smile has on me.

2. Ask a man to dance with you. Most men will accept because they are flattered to be asked. If you do get turned down, don't give up; ask another. Remember men don't get accepted every time. It does happen that sometimes a man will be rude to a woman who takes the initiative, but it is very rare. If it happens, don't take it personally and give up asking. Don't let any one person's refusal rob you of your power to reach out for who you want and to make many men feel great.

3. Offer to buy a man a drink. Most men have never had the pleasure of being treated to a drink by a woman. Though it seems like a simple thing, this act can have great significance to both parties. It is an indication to a man that a woman thinks he is so attractive that she is willing to spend money on him in order to get a little time to talk with him. A man rarely gets such a compliment. The act serves also to remind the woman herself that she is able to pay her way with money and doesn't have to buy her way with sexual favors or passive acquiescence. It breaks through the conventional male-female "roles" and helps people contact each other as individuals with equal rights.

4. Refuse the offer of a man you don't know who offers to buy you a drink when you know what he really wants is to talk with you and try to get to know you better. Tell him, "No, thanks, I don't want you to buy me a drink but I would like you to sit down and talk with me for a few minutes so that we can get to know one another a little better." A woman who lets a man know that she values him and not just his money makes a lasting impression. All men like this kind of aggression. It is only belligerent aggression that turns them off.

Just as women need to relinquish their passivity to become gentle aggressors, men need to intensify their gentleness. They must learn to behave in ways that keep them from being seen as too pushy or as only interested in sex. Many times the reason a man gets turned down by women is that he invades their psychological space too abruptly. Men have learned to carefully check a woman out, to watch her and think about her before approaching her. In places where singles gather, a man may sit back and wait, watch and cruise for two or three hours in order to feel comfortable before going up to a woman. She, on the other hand, may not have even seen the man until he suddenly appears, seemingly out of nowhere, in front of her. To have a stranger suddenly asking her for something—a dance, her name, to buy her a drink—is startling to a woman especially if she is nervous about being in a situation which makes her seem available as a "pickup" (a scary word to most women).

The fact that women are startled is one reason they are sometimes rude to men who approach them. One man complained that women frequently give him a "vacuous stare" when he says "hello" to them. As he says, "It is disconcerting to me to say a friendly 'hello' and get a look of mystified astonishment, followed by a complete ignoring of my presence."

Tips for men

For this man and other men who want to get acquainted with more women and to be turned down graciously when they are turned down, we offer these suggestions for making contact:

1. Make sure a woman sees you before making your approach. A woman who is "invaded" doesn't feel kindly toward her invader. Here is what one woman says of a recent experience. "I was sitting at the bar quietly listening to the music and not talking to anyone. I had just gotten there and was getting my bearings before I attempted to make contact with anyone. Suddenly, somebody begins thumping me on the back—almost making me spill my drink. I turn around and this guy is grinning like a fool, saying, 'Care to dance?' Of course, I didn't care to dance after that approach."

2. Ask to share a certain specific amount of time and state exactly how you'd like to spend that time. One reason dancing is so popular is that it permits a man and a woman to be together for a limited amount of time—the length of a dance—and then to separate easily unless both want more time together. A successful approach brings these safety factors into a first meeting. Here is one way to show a woman you respect her right to own her own time.

Walk up to her and say something like: "You look like a very interesting person to me. Could I please have five (or ten) minutes of your time to talk with you and see what we have in common. I will leave at the end of that time if you want me to." If she agrees, keep careful track of the time. If, when the time agreed upon is up, and you've decided you'd like to know her better, announce that you are going to leave unless she specifically asks you to stay. And then say goodbye and leave, but do so slowly so that she has time to decide whether to say goodbye or to ask you to stay. If, when the time is up, you've decided you do *not* want more contact, thank her for talking with you, say goodbye and leave. Such an approach gives the conversation direction and makes it more meaningful. It also permits both parties a dignified exit if it is wanted.

3. Make initial contact in a series of small steps that show you want contact with her but that you are willing to wait until she is ready. Just as a good lover uses a slow pace and sensitivity to his partner's moods, so does a gentle aggressor. He realizes that women need time—time to look at him, get a sense of him, think about him. And contrary to male folklore, women do not appreciate a blatantly sexual approach, though many put up with it thinking "men are like that." It is inappropriate to come on too fast, too sexy or too pushy with a stranger. Since many women have not learned how to assertively say "no" to a demand, this sort of approach sometimes appears to be successful but the subsequent interaction is not likely to be satisfying to either.

One of our favorite "gentle aggressors" has made an art of approaching women in public at a slow, deliberate pace and he not only succeeds in meeting the women he wants but also in establishing many warm and caring relationships, some that do and some that don't involve sex. This is how he does it. "I realize that women are afraid of being overwhelmed when they go out. It is hard enough for a lot of them just to go out alone much less to have to contend with a lot of male pushiness. Therefore, I'll stand or sit where I can catch a woman's eye and when I do, I smile. A lot of times she'll look away really fast but later on I'll catch her sneaking looks at me. Then I'll laugh and she laughs too and we've already established a rapport. Sometimes I might tap my glass to ask if she wants a drink and if she nods 'yes,' I'll send one over. But I never follow the drink until she's had plenty of time to look at me and smile at me. By the time we do start talking, a lot of barriers are already down."

SEX TALK FOR GENTLE AGGRESSORS

Establish what you would like from the other person in regard to sex as soon as you can do so without making him feel that is all that you want from him, that you do not value him as a person. It is impossible to pick an amount of time that a man and a woman must know each other before discussing the possibility of sex. Sometimes it is O.K. an hour after meeting; sometimes it is appropriate on the first date or the third; sometimes they must know each other a number of months or even a year or more before bringing up the subject. However, the sooner sexual expectations are made clear and an agreement is reached, the sooner both parties can relax and be themselves and not worry about giving the wrong impression or being taken advantage of. However, extreme care should be taken in discussing sexual expectations. They have a powerful effect on a person's feelings of self-worth. The way you let your sexual expectations become known is as important as when.

Following are some indirect allusions to sex made at an initial meeting that should never have been made. Such statements make a person feel that his value consists in his being a cog that might fit into someone else's wheel, that his wishes, his individuality, are not important.

"You and I are going to have breakfast together tomorrow" was one man's opening remark to a woman he met at a party. Though he meant it to be a compliment, an opening gambit, she felt that if she even stood and talked with him she was tacitly agreeing to that statement. So she left.

That man was certainly not acting like a gentle aggressor in the way he let his sexual wishes be known. Neither was the woman we heard say to a man she had met no more than fifteen minutes before, "Do you want children?" When he replied that he didn't, she turned on her heel and left—presumably to find a better potential husband and father.

Though a person's willingness to fit in with your sexual wishes should not be the only factor when considering him or her as a potential friend, it is an important one. It is reasonable and necessary to think about your sexual feelings and expectations and to want to discover his or hers. Such a discussion can help you decide if you want to see that person again; if so, under what circumstances, and what will be expected of you.

If you have decided you want to have sex with someone or even if you don't, if you believe he or she wants to have sex with you, you should talk about it. It is O.K. for either a man or a woman to bring up the subject. (Women, in particular, need to be encouraged to bring up the subject. They are apt to turn over the responsibility for initiating or even talking about sex to the man just as they turn over the responsibility of paying for things.) Whoever brings it up should express his feelings and wishes directly but gently and then ask the other person to say what he wants. Don't ask another person to say what he wants until you've laid yourself on the line first, but *do* ask. Don't assume you know and proceed accordingly. Sex is an important human activity and deserves a great deal of sensitive dignified discussion. We must learn to talk about it to prevent psychological rape. Sexual activity carries a heavy emotional load to all of us. It means different things to different people, even different things to the same person at different times. Action without sufficient discussion can lead to people feeling used and abused.

Here are some suggestions for ways of introducing the subject of sex early in a relationship:

> I am attracted to you. I'm having romantic and sexual fantasies about you and I'd like to get to know you well enough to resolve them one way or another. How do you feel about me?

> I'm turned on to you sexually, and I'd like to go to bed with you whenever you feel the same way. Would you like to have sex with me sometime?

Both of these statements show interest without being pushy or apologetic. They permit the other person to express the desire for a platonic relationship without offending or to express an interest in sex without agreeing to it right now.

Learning to decline a request for sex in a way that is gently aggressive is as important as learning to ask for it. Though because you are the sex you are or have the personality or status you have, you may use one skill much more than the other, everyone can profit from developing both skills. Sometimes people you want sex with simply won't ask for it, and sometimes those you don't want it with will ask. Life is like that.

There are many ways to say "no" but the best ways—those that get you what you want and let the other person know how you feel without insulting him—are honest, kind and indicative. Let's discuss honesty first, for honesty is the cornerstone of all good interactions between people.

The reason most often given for being evasive or even telling lies when saying "no" is: "If I'm honest, I'll hurt his feelings." What you must remember is that being honest does not mean you have to be *brutally* frank. You can be honest without being cruel. You don't have to tell someone he is ugly. You can tell him you are not attracted to him. When you become adept at telling the "sweet truth," you don't have to worry about getting caught in a web of deception and you won't find yourself doing what you don't want to do rather than risk hurting someone else.

The second factor to emphasize in saying "no" is kindness. It is fairly easy to learn to say kind words that are also honest. The difficulty lies in expressing your wishes, your feelings, your opinions in a way that shows you believe it is O.K. for the other person to have wishes, feelings and opinions that may differ a great deal from yours. It is usually helpful to make "I" statements, to actually use the pronoun "I" in your refusal. However, care must be taken that your phraseology and your tone convey the notion that the reason for your refusal is that the suggestion runs counter to what you want or think is right or appropriate and not that it runs counter to some universal or "correct" value system.

The third point to make in refusing an offer of sex is to indicate in your reply what you want, expect or hope for in regard to sex in the future. A refusal can be firm and yet not flat. A refusal that is indicative tells a person whether you don't want to see him or to have him ask for sex ever again or if you'd like to see him but not for sex or if you don't know what you want. A refusal that is honest, kind and indicative will make the person who hears it feel like saying, "Thank you for letting me know," before walking away, changing the subject or opening up a discussion.

Exactly what you decided to say will depend upon whether you don't want sex because (1) you aren't sexually attracted; (2) you are attracted but have some other reason for refusing; (3) you aren't sure about your attraction or your wants, or both.

Here are some examples of phrases that are honest, kind and indicative but that vary as to feelings and wants. Though you probably won't want to use them verbatim, by studying them you can be prepared when the occasion arises to express your own sentiments in a way that you are certain is gently aggressive.

> I don't find myself sufficiently attracted to you to want to date you, but thanks for asking.

> I don't care to now, but I'd like to keep the option open in case I change my mind. I enjoy your company.

> I'm flattered that you are sexually attracted to me. Though I'm fond of you, going to bed isn't the kind of relationship I want. Could we do other things together instead?

> I find myself sexually attracted to you, but not yet comfortable with the idea of having sex with you. I might be when I feel I know you better.

> I am sexually attracted to you, but you are married and I don't want to have sex with someone who is married.

> I am sexually attracted to you, but we have different ideas about commitments in sexual relationships, so I'll have to decline.

Two more points in regard to sex that will improve your ability to have exciting brief encounters and rewarding short-term alliances are these: Though it is not usually easy to discuss your sexual feelings honestly with somebody when you don't want sex and he or she does, if you will do it anyhow, you will feel freer to have other kinds of contact with him or her. When it is out in the open where you stand with each other in regard to sex, you can usually pat, hug and talk freely. This is much more desirable than making a habit of closing off contact when one of you isn't sexually interested or else doesn't know how to say "no" without offending. The second point is this: When you give a reason for not wanting to go to bed with someone, make sure it is the real reason. Otherwise, you may get caught up in your lie. If you tell someone you aren't sexually interested because he is married and he says he is in the process of getting a divorce, you'll be in an awkward position if that was just an excuse. But if you mean it, this new information can make a difference in your decision.

HOW TO DEAL WITH NON-GENTLE AGGRESSORS

Annette, a sophisticated divorcee we know, argued with us about our theory that men and women can talk on an honest basis, saying, "You just don't find many men around who act like gentle aggressors. The ones who need to change the most are the ones who won't read this book. So what good does it do me to change?"

We pointed out to Annette that it wasn't necessary for men to change their behavior prior to meeting her. We guaranteed that many times their behavior would improve if she started acting toward them in a different way. The idea is, of course, that behavior is reciprocal. You can change another person's behavior—if you don't withdraw, strike out or lecture, but instead let him know you want to be friendly but have limits.

When you learn a new behavioral skill (or any other skill, like bridge or karate, for that matter) it is unrealistic to expect all those you meet to be as skilled as you are. And you will certainly miss a lot of brief encounters and short-term alliances if you back away from everybody who isn't as good at relating to people as you are. One requirement for achieving status in the art and skill of gentle aggression (the equivalent of a master in bridge or a black belt in karate) is to learn to cope with non-gentle aggressors in ways that are gently aggressive—and it can be done.

Here is an example of an offensively aggressive approach that many women will recognize. Jan, a slim, blond, recently divorced woman of forty-two, on her first night out as a single, was sitting at a table in a disco with her brother-in-law and sister. A man approached her, leaned over and started the following conversation:

MAN: Planning on staying a little while?
JAN: A little while.

MAN: Well, we could have a good time together.

JAN: Is that so?

MAN: Yes, first we could dance and then later on we could make love. I'll give you the best time you ever had.

Jan got very upset at the implicit demand in this approach, gave him a haughty "no" and vowed she'd never again put herself in a position to be approached like that. She did what a lot of people do—she decided on the basis of one or a few negative experiences to give up.

How foolish! Certainly such an approach can be upsetting, but it won't help anything to give up either your hope or your power just because somebody else behaves like a clod or a boor. Nor do you have to behave like a clod or a boor because he does.

In this case, the chances are that the man didn't realize the effect his approach would have or he certainly wouldn't have used it. Or maybe somebody refused him in an unkind way or approached him in an unacceptable way that caused him to feel hurt or angry or scared—to put up his guard. (Many times when a person feels defensive, he acts offensive.) Whatever his reason, it is impossible to determine on the basis of one such interchange whether or not a person would be interesting to know.

Jan would have felt better for sure and she might have discovered a new potential friend if she had responded with gentle aggression. There are ways that would have let him know what she wanted, acknowledged his right to want what he wanted, permitted her to keep on interacting with him for a bit longer and thus give him a chance to correct the bad impression he had made.

Here are some statements Jan could have used that might have changed his behavior and his expectations or permitted him to move away without feeling he had been slapped in the face.

I'm not interested in going to bed with you tonight but I am interested in dancing. Care to dance?

I don't know you well enough to decide what I would enjoy doing with you. Why don't you sit down and tell me about yourself.

You seem to be offering me a package deal. If you need a quick decision, my answer will have to be "no, thanks."

In each case, she would be letting him know, but in a kind way, that his conditions were too limiting and that he must broaden them if he wanted some of her time and attention. She would be gently asserting her right to her own pace and wants.

While women rarely demand sex in this abrupt verbal manner, they do sometimes make unreasonable demands on men they have just met. By their attitude, they demand that a man give them his attention or spend money on them—or else feel like an idiot or cheapskate. A man friend told of being at a party on board a yacht when a woman came up to him and said, "You are the only one here who interests me." Her manner implied a possessive "You're mine" attitude. She assumed he would just naturally want to spend time with her and proceeded to follow him wherever he went for the rest of the evening.

The question is: How can a man cope with a demanding woman he barely knows other than by trying to ditch her or by being deliberately rude and telling her off? The answer: The same way a woman can cope with a man who expects of her what she is not willing to give. Let a person know what you want but in a way that acknowledges his right to want what he wants.

In the previous example, for instance, the man could have kept himself from feeling trapped if he had said:

> That is very flattering. However, I think you have some expectations of me right now that I might not care to fill. Would you please tell me what you want of me?

> I appreciate the compliment, but I don't know you well enough to know how much you interest me. Why don't we talk for a few minutes to see what we have in common?

One way women make demands on men they have just met is by acting as if they expect the man to buy them a drink or take them someplace. They seem to take it for granted that it is a man's role or duty or obligation.

When a woman makes such demands and a man feels he is being taken advantage of, it would be helpful if he could realize she is caught in a "sex-role rut." He might then be able to swallow his frustration and say, with much lightness and humor (and not in a needling, sarcastic way), "Gee, I'd like a drink, too. Why don't we flip a coin to see who pays?" Or he might say, "I'm a terrible driver. I really think we'd better go in your car." The idea is for him to behave in such a way that she gets the point that there are other ways to do things than the way she has in mind. Although there is no guarantee that she will get the point or will want to change even if he speaks up in a kind way, it is certain she won't change if he says nothing and won't want to change if his remark is hostile.

A gentle aggressor when put on the spot doesn't have to go along with the manipulation, or blast or retreat, he has another alternative; try something different.

A good time to try something different is when a person you are with monopolizes the conversation in such a way that you don't get to know one another by interacting. Sam, a rather quiet man, usually finds that women take over the conversation because it takes him a while to get warmed up verbally. He conspires in this verbal monopolization because many times he is more interested in them physically than in learning anything about them and is super-anxious not to offend. However, he frequently gets so saturated with the incessant talk that he loses any interest at all—even in the physical—and just wants to get away. Though he feels trapped and complains bitterly about gabby women and the difficulty of finding one to go to bed with, he has trapped himself by not acting like a gentle aggressor and salvaging the conversation and the interaction.

When you feel trapped by a verbal monopolizer, it is easier to cope with him without getting hostile if you remind yourself he may be talking for a variety of reasons. He might be nervous; he might be trying to impress you; he might have something he wants to get off his chest. Instead of stewing in annoyance at the constant stream of chatter, worrying that you're never going to get to say what you want, take action. Break in with a direct request delivered in a light, non-accusing way: "Hey, you've told me a lot about yourself and now I'd like a chance to reciprocate and tell you something about myself." Or: "Hey, you've had quite a while to talk. How about my having a turn now, O.K.?"

Recently Betty met a newly published author who monopolized their time together by continuously talking about his book. He even kept opening it to read certain passages to her. Though tempted to walk away from what seemed like a hopeless situation, she finally interrupted by saying, "Your book seems fascinating and I think a fascinating man must have written it. Why don't you put it away for a little while and let me get to know you."

Though he seemed startled by her interruption and there were a few seconds of heavy silence while he apparently thought about what she had said, he finally broke into a big grin, said, "Say, that's a good idea," and put his book away. They then started to talk *with* one another and established an entirely different tone for their interaction.

HOW TO LET SOMEONE KNOW YOU DO OR DO NOT WANT TO SEE HIM AGAIN

Because the "pickup" has been at best only a semi-respectable social ritual, there are no clear-cut rules for ending one. People are not likely to give much thought to bringing effective closure to something they don't think they should be doing anyway. The main problem appears, on the surface at least, to be a fairly simple one. The question a person must ask himself is this: "Do I or do I not want to see this person again?" If you do, it is up to you to ask for his or her phone number or offer yours. If you don't, it is up to you to convey in a straightforward but kind manner that you do not.

Many first meetings become an only meeting not because the persons involved don't want to or can't make arrangements for another meeting, but because neither says anything about doing it. Each waits for the other to make the first move. A woman may hold back, telling herself it is up to a man to make the first move; a man, if he really likes a woman, may fail to suggest a subsequent meeting for fear he will be rejected.

But that is not the only hazard to closure. Many men ask for a telephone number when they have no intention of calling it because they "don't want to hurt a woman's feelings." They don't seem to realize that they can hurt her feelings much more by building up her hopes and then not calling. They don't seem to realize how much time she can waste trying to be around the phone in case it should ring. And when it doesn't, she might blame herself for some inadequacy or wonder what she did or said that "turned him off" when he seemed so interested.

One gentle aggressor we know, who had taken the number of a woman at a party and then decided he didn't really want to see her again, called her and told her just that. He had had a very interesting conversation with her at the party, but on thinking about it later, realized they had very different life styles and values. Since he was looking for acquaintanceships that could blossom into relationships, he realized that it would be best not to pursue theirs. But conscious that she expected him to call, he had the courtesy to let her know his thinking and why he didn't want to have more contact.

Women use the similar excuse of "not wanting to hurt" for giving a man their number but then always being too busy to go out with him whenever he calls. Somehow they believe that when they say they are washing their hair, or have to go to a meeting, or have a previous engagement, or have a relative visiting—time after time after time until he finally gets the message that she doesn't want to see him again—that that is somehow being kinder than telling him directly. Or sometimes, using the excuse of "being polite," they give a fake phone number.

That happened to Paul one night at a singles bar. He was sitting at the bar when a beautiful young woman came in and sat down next to him. They began talking and she turned out to be a college student, studying fashion design. Since Paul was an artist, they had a lot in common and their conversation was lively and interesting. He suggested they get together again to continue the conversation and she agreed. She gave him her number and told him to call her. However, when he did, the number was the wrong one. He found her right number from information because she had given him her right name and called her, assuming she'd given the wrong number by mistake. Again she agreed to a date and promised to meet him for dinner at the same place they had met. You guessed it. She never showed up and a crestfallen Paul said, "That's the story of my life."

Though telling a social lie to get out of having to say "no" to someone is a very common practice, it can create problems for both parties. Besides, it is hurtful and it makes each sex resent and mistrust the other. A graceful closure is not brought about by saying nothing or by telling a "little white lie" but results from an act of gentle aggression.

Here are some suggestions for bringing graceful closure to an interaction with a stranger:

1. Make a gift of your phone number to someone you'd like to see again, and invite him or her to call you. Whether you are a man or a woman, it is both your obligation and your privilege to let your wishes for further contact be known. Emily ends all the programs she gives for singles by passing out a packet of small yellow slips to each participant. On the top of each slip is printed the sentence: "I'd like to know you better," followed by a space for name, address and phone number. Both men and women are encouraged to give these to people they have met whom they would like to have further contact with.

2. Convey the message that you like to talk on the phone as a means of getting to know people better. Whether giving out your phone number or asking for someone else's, suggest that the phone not be reserved just for making arrangements to go someplace but that it be used for friendly dialogue. Men and women seldom tell each other it's O.K. to call just to talk, and very often a phone call after a meeting is assumed to be a request for a date. Sometimes a man and a woman will make a date that turns out to be less than satisfactory, whereas if they had talked a time or two on the phone, it would have become apparent they didn't have enough in common to warrant a further meeting.

3. Be aware of the anxiety members of the opposite sex have about members of your sex and behave in a way to reduce that anxiety. Sometimes a woman is reluctant to give a man she has just met her phone number for fear that if it turns out she doesn't care for him, he will call repeatedly and pester her. Or sometimes she is afraid he may be married and is pretending not to be. A man can alleviate these anxieties by offering a woman his phone number and saying something like "I'd like to have further contact with you. Here is my phone number. I'd like it very much if you'd call me just to talk so we can get to know each other better. If you want to give me your phone number, you can, but it isn't necessary. I can wait for your call."

A woman who would like to see a man again can ask for his phone number, but since this kind of behavior is still unusual for a woman, she should let him know why she wants it. Since men sometimes suspect they are being asked to something just so they will pay, she can show that it is he and not his wallet she is interested in if she suggests, "I'd like to get together with you for a walk along the beach," or "I'd like to invite you to a party sometime," or "I'd like to take you out someplace," or "I'd like us to go out someplace together, dutch treat." This makes it easy for him to decide whether or not to give her his phone number or whether further dialogue is needed to clarify what she expects of him.

4. Don't be evasive but do be kind if you don't want or aren't sure if you want further contact. When someone asks for your phone number and you don't care to give it, a good reply is: "I don't care to give it to you but thank you for asking." Say it softly, give a big smile and turn away. Remember, you have a right not to have to explain your decision to anyone if you don't care to. If you have spent considerable time with a person at your first meeting and enjoyed the time together but not enough to want to see him again and you feel pretty certain he wants to see you again, it won't be easy to let your wishes be known. However, it must be done. Start out by complimenting him by saying what you have enjoyed—i.e., getting to know him, dancing with him, talking with him—and then conclude by telling him something that indicates that there is nothing wrong with him but that you do not care for further contact. You might want to say something like "I don't believe the chemistry is right between us," or "I don't find myself strongly enough attracted to want to have a continuing relationship with you." Naturally, he may be disappointed, but he will be less hurt than if you are dishonest or if you leave him dangling and say nothing.

If you aren't sure whether or not you want further contact, it is good form and quite kind to say just that and then to ask the other person how he feels and what he thinks might be done to help you make up your mind.

These are only a few suggestions but they are enough to indicate that bringing closure to contact with a person recently met is worth thinking about and to stimulate you to develop your own style of gentle aggression.

These gentle aggression suggestions we've been giving you in this chapter really work; they are not abstract theory. In the next chapter we'll tell you how a group of men and women tested our gentle aggression role in a very difficult arena—a singles bar.

5

Putting the Gentle Aggressor Role into Practice

You can't expect to make up your mind to become a gentle aggressor and be an instant success. But then, if you want to become proficient at horseback riding, you can't expect to slip into the saddle with grace and finesse the first time you mount. Practice is required for any new skill, whether it is bicycling, sculpturing, driving a car, dancing or relating.

However, practicing social skills has some hazards other skills don't. In the first place, you can't make your first attempts at trying new ways of getting acquainted, in private. In the second place, your success depends to a large extent on the response you get from others. If they don't happen to be in a receptive mood, you may feel like a failure though you may be exhibiting championship form. Because our culture is as it is, at most places where you might go to practice "pickups" you'll not get the encouragement, cooperation and suggestions for improvement from others that make learning fun and keep you practicing until you lose your amateur status. (The People Samplers and Singlelife Seminars of the Man-Woman Institute are an exception. One of the reasons unmarried people learn so fast and enjoy these programs so much is that Emily and her partner, Dr. Keith Tombrink, create an environment in which it is easy to validate and complement each other and offer feedback in a kind way.) However, you can turn any public place into one where you will be treated kindly by taking along your own backup team—a group of friends who are also interested in learning how to become gentle aggressors. No trained leader is required. All that is needed is good will among the participants and a willingness to experiment.

In order to show you just how easy and how much fun it is to develop a support team of "gentle aggressors," Betty Edwards, with the help of Madelyn Hathaway, Los Angeles-based psychodrama instructor and role-training consultant, taught four participants—two men and two women—to become gentle aggressors and helped them try out their new learning at a singles bar.

The participants selected for this project had not met before but were chosen because each had attitudes and a personality representative of a large segment of the single population. We would, of course, expect you to invite people you know and like to join you. All that we asked of prospective candidates was that they be interested in meeting people of the opposite sex, be willing to train a bit and to try something different. We had no trouble finding volunteers. Practically all the people we spoke with, disillusioned at the esteem-destroying games and manipulative behavior they had encountered as part of the meeting and dating process, were enlivened at the idea there might be a better way and intrigued by the experimental aspect of our project. We wanted both male and female participants so they could practice with and discover their impact on each other but also so they could discover the web of common feelings they had and develop a better understanding of the wishes and fears of the opposite sex. We recommend that you include members of both sexes in your backup team but don't include people who are sexually involved with one another. They are apt to be so interested in watching each other that they won't pay enough attention to making new contacts and will inhibit each other's honest reactions and comments. Don't hesitate to invite people you don't know very well as long as they seem warm and friendly and willing to experiment. You'll soon get to know them better. The number of team members we selected—four—was an arbitrary one chosen to provide some variety and yet keep the recording of reactions fairly simple. The most important aspect in building a backup team is the idea of focusing on a common goal and the way to reach it and then developing a camaraderie in the face of shared fears.

The remarks each participant made when accepting the invitation give an indication of their particular concerns. Beth is a petite, bubbly, very attractive twenty-eight-year-old who has never been married. She said, "Sure, I'll do it. What do I have to lose? It won't bother me if I goof during this project. After all, it's just an experiment. Gee, wouldn't it be just great if we could always think of life as one big research project and ourselves as experimenters always learning and trying new things. Then we wouldn't expect ourselves to always know the right thing to do and think it was the end of the world if we didn't."

Phyllis is forty-five, divorced for a year and a half after a twenty-year marriage. Five foot six and not really fat, she is certainly not slender either. Not that you can tell much about her figure in the ladies-luncheon type clothes she wears. A former suburban housewife, now a "displaced person," she said in response to our invitation, "I guess all anybody can do is experiment these days. There doesn't seem to be any right way anymore. Things have changed so much since before I was married, I can't believe it. Now I never know if a man I've just met is a 'swinger' who'll ask me to join him in a threesome or a traditional man who'll be shocked if I call him on the phone."

Pete, thirty-two, tall and slender, is a glib-talking, curly-haired, mustached bachelor. He exudes self-confidence and prides himself that he can approach any woman, any time, any place, and never be at a loss for words. Though he isn't seeking a committed relationship, he has been bothered by some of the reactions he's been getting recently. Said Pete, "I just about got hit the other day when I asked a woman sitting next to me in a bar if I could buy her a drink. She let me know in no uncertain terms it was useless to try to 'buy' her. All I wanted to do was be friendly. But I've also been called a cheapskate for not buying a woman a drink."

Steve, a long-time divorcee of forty-eight, is short, bright, serious and quiet. Very kind and also very shy, he has a long face and big watery brown eyes that give him a whipped-puppy demeanor. His remarks in response to our invitation seem to sum up the disillusionment of many singles: "I'll give it a try even though I'm not sure if it will do any good. I've had so many bad experiences that I've just about given up trying to meet people. It's easier to stay home."

Though we had no trouble finding volunteers willing to experiment with new behavior to help them make better contacts, when we explained we wanted them to try this new behavior out in a singles bar, we were met with vociferous objections. Single people, even those who sometimes patronize singles bars, tend to take a very negative view of them as desirable places in which to meet other people.

Steve and Pete almost backed out. They both characterized the women they met in singles bars as "losers." "And," added Steve, "I'm leery of developing friendships with women I meet at bars. Even if they seem nice, you can be sure they are out to get something for nothing or they wouldn't be there."

Our women volunteers made similar prejudgments about the men in singles bars. They believed the men were only interested in getting women into bed as rapidly as possible and for the least expenditure of money and time. "In fact," said Beth, "I think having to go to any kind of a singles place to meet someone is the pits. I don't want a man who has to meet women that way."

We assured our volunteers that they were not going to be expected to "score" or to find a mate but only to make meaningful friendly contact, and then we explained why we had deliberately chosen a singles bar for our field test. We believe that if a person can learn to filter through swarms of people—kindly but efficiently —in a singles bar, he'll probably be able to do this almost anywhere. We wanted to see if, in this difficult atmosphere, a person could manage to feel good about himself or herself while being sensitive to the feelings of others. We wanted to really challenge our theory that if a person played the role of a gentle aggressor and had a backup team, he could have a good time and learn a lot besides.

As part of their preparation for dealing with the handicaps and problems of this environment, we carefully discussed with our volunteers the necessary service provided by singles bars and also what made most people feel as they did about going to them.

Singles bars, despite the intense prejudice toward them, are one of the few places in our society designed for meeting others. People aren't there to do their laundry, shop for groceries, get educated or find spiritual enlightenment—and just incidentally to look around for available people. They go there for the specific purpose of meeting, being with and talking with others. By their action, they are saying, "I want contact." Considering our people-distancing social rituals and the lack of other socially structured ways for men and women to meet, they serve a vital and much-needed function for those who know how to use them. However, there is no doubt that they could stand a lot of improvement, for the behavior common there frequently creates as much loneliness as it assuages.

One of the problems is that most men and women don't have the attitudes and haven't learned the skills needed to have a good experience in a singles bar. They walk in with their old repertoire of social skills and expectations—ones they learned as part of the traditional male-female roles. And because of the underlying money-sex power struggle inherent in those roles, they bring into the bar with them an atmosphere of suspicion and hostility. John Godwin, who has studied hundreds of singles bars and events for his book *The Mating Trade*, says of most of them that "an element of barely suppressed belligerence permeates these assemblies, sometimes so strongly that the sexes seem to be circling each other in a sparring crouch. Not a stance conducive to romance."

Some of the belligerence stems from the fact that people resent having to go out and look for someone. Influenced by romantic novels and movies, they expect desirable people to just fall into their laps. They also expect a romantic relationship to spring into being rather than starting with an acquaintanceship and being painstakingly constructed in bits and pieces, the way it happens with really good relationships. Though people will search for a good job for months or years and expect to have to increase their work skills to get the job they want, they seem to feel that if they spend time looking for desirable people and trying to increase their repertoire of social skills, that means there is something wrong with them.

Many people simply will not go into a singles bar at all for fear of being surrounded by "losers" and of being seen as "looking for someone"—as if that were a sin. Most of those who do go feel extremely self-conscious. They fear this action will be interpreted as meaning, "I'm available, desperate and easy." Both men and women worry about what people will think they are available for. Both want attention and caring but are afraid they are going to be conned into paying too high a price. Women worry that men will think they are available for sex just because they are there. Men fear they are going to have to pay either with more money than they care to spend or by getting caught up in some sort of relationship with strings attached. As a result, both sexes when entering a singles bar put up their defenses. Some assume a super-cool façade that makes them seem above it all while others spew out charm and witticisms all over the place in order to appear "with it." Thus, it is difficult to get below the superficial level with them.

All of these feelings make people anxious in singles bars and our culture has not taught us how to deal well with anxiety. It has taught us to take a chemical to mask it. Therefore, a lot of people drink more at singles bars than they ordinarily would. Though this certainly helps them feel less anxious, it also cuts down on their ability to know their own feelings, to think clearly and to get a true picture of others.

Before arranging a "training" meeting for our gentle aggressors, we made certain they understood the gentle aggressor role and what would be expected of them. In forming your own team, you will find it helpful to get people you would like to work with to read not only this chapter but also Chapters 3 and 4.

At the initial get-together at Betty's house, we first served our team members a buffet dinner and suggested that they talk with one another and try to get acquainted as quickly as possible. Though they didn't know each other, the idea of working on this unusual project together made them eager to share thoughts, feelings and experiences. And so for about an hour they laughed and relaxed before Madelyn asked them to be quiet for a little while so she could tell them about role-training and have them try it out.

While it will be necessary for your group to have a leader, all that is required is a person who can organize and direct the activities. Our group had a bonus in that Madelyn has had years of experience as a role-training consultant and we planned to use the role-training as one of our major tools.

There is nothing at all complex about role-training. It has been in use for many years—by industry to train stockbrokers, salesmen and receptionists; by mental institutions and parole officers to prepare inmates for the outside world when they are ready to return to it; and by marriage counselors to help feuding spouses resolve conflict.

Actually, we all perform in many different roles in the course of our daily lives, and there is some sort of socially accepted guidelines to our behavior in these roles. We act one way as students, another as teachers. We act one way as parents to our children, another as children to our parents.

It is important to be familiar with a variety of roles, for many times staying in one makes life simpler. You feel secure and are able to accomplish what you want to accomplish without having to think about every little thing you do. However, it is equally important to be able to step out of a role at the drop of a hat—to be spontaneous—when some aspect of role-behavior doesn't work.

The problem is that in the course of learning to behave in particular roles people use a limited set of responses in social situations and tend to get locked into them. They either aren't aware of, don't learn or aren't comfortable with other behavior. It is easy to become rigid and lose social spontaneity—the ability to respond in many different ways to any given situation. This is particularly true of the traditional male and female roles where the reaction of men and women to social stimuli and to each other becomes almost predictable. As a result, male-female interactions take on the characteristics of ritualistic jousting—the battle of the sexes—instead of being alive and vibrant with the endless possibilities of human interaction.

The way we used the role-training technique was to have our participants act out their new gentle aggression roles in "scenes" structured to simulate reality—i.e., a pickup at a singles bar. Through the responses of the opposite sex, they could learn how they were coming across in this new role and through sometimes taking the role of the opposite sex, they could get a firsthand viewpoint of the problems and pressures of that sex.

As a sort of "warm-up" Betty asked the participants to think of and talk about an incident they could recall when they or someone else behaved in a gently aggressive way in a meeting situation. Beth remembered a time she was walking down a crowded street in San Francisco when a man came up and asked her if she knew where Market Street was. She gave him directions and walked on a half block or so. When she stopped to look in a shop window, he appeared beside her again and confessed, "I really know where Market Street is. I just wanted an excuse to talk to you." She laughed, he invited her for a cup of coffee and they spent a delightful evening together—having dinner, talking and walking. Beth says of the encounter, "The way he approached me was so honest—and sort of sweet, somehow. He let his vulnerability show, which disarmed me. It made me trust him."

Steve told of an experience he had some years ago of meeting a girl on a subway in New York City. She too was from out of town and not concerned about breaking the "don't talk to strangers" custom on subways. He was standing next to her hanging on to a strap and remarked, "If I had a seat, I'd offer it to you." They got to talking and he asked her—since they were both visitors to the city—if she'd like to do some sight-seeing with him. She said "yes" but added, "However, I am married and don't want to get involved in anything sexual. And I do have to catch a train at eleven tonight. But if those limits are O.K. with you, I think we can have fun together."

Said Steve, "It was great to have the bit about sex out in the open like that. Naturally I was disappointed but then I didn't have to worry if I should or shouldn't make a pass. And so we took off like a couple of kids. We rode the Fifth Avenue bus from one end to the other, went to the top of the Empire State Building and took the Staten Island ferry. We laughed, talked, held hands and had a great time. Then I took her to the station and that was it."

Steve felt that both of them had been gentle aggressors by coming on in a low-key minimum-expectation way and letting the other know their wishes in regard to sex.

It was pointed out that these successful interactions took place in a setting where pickups aren't ever sanctioned—in public in a big city—and that the gently aggressive nature of the first contact set a positive tone for what happened from then on. After a few more experiences were related, the participants seemed eager to try what they had been told they would do: see if they could act like gentle aggressors in the simulation of a bar scene.

If you decide to work with your friends, be sure not to skip this "warm-up" stage of sharing experiences. It builds bonds of trust and understanding between team members and creates the supportive mood necessary for the next step: the actual role training.

Madelyn moved the living-room furniture around to set the first scene—a singles bar with a dance floor and tables all around it. Steve and Pete and Phyllis were asked to act like single men standing at the edge of the dance floor. Beth was given the task of acting the gentle aggressor and making contact with the man she was most attracted to. Before she took any action, Madelyn had her do a soliloquy first, a very important procedure when using the role-training method. She was told to start talking out loud about her feelings in regard to taking the initiative and then to take action when she was ready.

This is how Beth expressed what was going on inside her: "Oh God, here I am. They are lined up over there and what do I do? Do I walk around in front of them and pick out one or do I wait here until they notice me? Well, I'm feeling pretty good about myself, so I am going to walk by with a smile on my face." (She walks by but keeps on going.) "Anyhow, I've done it and now I feel like a fool. What am I doing here? Look at all those other gorgeous girls. Who would want to talk to me anyhow? This is a terrible situation to be in. Wait a minute. What am I doing? Stop this. Be yourself and stop worrying about what others will think."

At this point, Beth took a deep breath, walked over to Pete, smiled and said, "Would you like to dance?"

PETE (coldly): No.
BETH (flustered): Why?
PETE: I don't feel like it.
BETH (angry): What's the matter? Do you have to do the big macho thing and be the one to ask?
PETE: I just don't want to dance.

The group burst out laughing because Beth and Pete—in their attempt to expand the traditional roles—had merely reversed them. This is understandable because Beth's only guideline for taking the initiative has been watching how men do it and Pete's only guideline in being approached has come from watching women.

The group critiqued Beth's approach. Unanimously they decided she had certainly not been gently aggressive. It was suggested that it would have been better if she had tried to establish eye contact and get return signals from Pete before speaking to him. It was pointed out that she came on very abruptly in that she immediately asked him to do something without any intervening warm-up period of small talk.

She was asked to repeat the same scene and to put herself in the mood of a gentle aggressor before taking any action. This time her soliloquy went like this: "I really feel like being out with people tonight. I'd like to talk with several interesting people and maybe dance. I am not worried about whether or not anyone thinks I'm here to get laid. I know why I'm here and I have a lot to offer because I'm an interesting person."

Beth strolls over to the men and stands as though watching the dancers, listening to the music. She catches Pete's eye (her target) and smiles. He smiles back.

BETH: Great band, isn't it?

PETE: Well, it is a little bit louder than I like it.

BETH: Oh—what kind of music do you prefer?

PETE: I like classical for listening but for dancing I guess this is O.K.

BETH: Would you be interested in dancing to this?

PETE: Sure.

Beth looks up at him, smiles broadly, slowly reaches out and takes his hand and leads him to the dance floor.

The group congratulated Beth for catching on so quickly and she, perspiring profusely, heaved a sigh of relief and flopped down on the floor to rest. Others joined her and a discussion ensued about the kinds of problems encountered in singles bars, a prelude necessary for selecting the next scene.

All members of our group agreed that their two main problems were getting acquainted with those they wanted to meet and avoiding entrapment by those they didn't want to be with. Phyllis requested the opportunity to try to be the gentle aggressor in a scene where she would be hassled by someone objectionable, a situation she frequently found herself in.

After much discussion, the group finally agreed on a scene to help Phyllis act out her predicament. It was set up as follows: a bar at which two men are seated with an empty stool between them. Pete offered to play the man who gives her trouble; Steve the one she wants to meet. The scene starts as she comes in the door. She is told to do a soliloquy as a gentle aggressor, to put herself in the mood before beginning any action. After her soliloquy, she stands at the door long enough to look around and orient herself. She then buys cigarettes from a machine to give herself more time to get accustomed to the darkness and get her bearings. Attracted to Steve and seeing an empty seat between him and Pete, she sits down on it. She pulls out a cigarette and starts to light it, but before she can do it, Pete bends over and blows out the match, saying, "Aw, come on now, honey, don't smoke that. It'll kill you. And we wouldn't want that. You must be the prettiest thing I've seen in ages. Tell you what. Why don't you have a drinkie with your ole buddy here."

PHYLLIS (gracious but aloof): No, thank you. I prefer to buy my own drink. (Orders one and asks bartender to light her cigarette.)

PETE: Well, you can at least talk to me. I'm lonely.

PHYLLIS: Right now, I'd like to just sit quietly and listen to the music and enjoy my drink.

PETE (Goes on with a variety of other comments—getting worse and worse.)

PHYLLIS (Shifts her position and makes it clear with body language that she doesn't want to talk to Pete. Turns toward Steve and smiles.): Hello.

STEVE (startled): Oh, hello.

PHYLLIS: I'm sorry to intrude on you but could I talk with you for a few minutes? The man next to me is coming on a little strong and if I start talking to you, he'll probably back off. He's had too much to drink and so there's no use my trying to talk to him. I know you probably want to be alone and I'll leave you alone in a few minutes.

STEVE: Hey, that's O.K. I'd just as soon have someone to talk with anyhow.

(They begin an animated conversation.)

Madelyn pointed out that Phyllis used gentle aggression to "crack" Steve without being hostile to the other man or letting him control her behavior.

Phyllis was exhilarated by the interaction and appeared more lively than she had all evening. She reported that the whole thing wasn't difficult at all because it had been set up so that she knew just what she wanted and what she didn't want. Someone in the group suggested that maybe the times she found herself being hassled were times she just couldn't make up her mind what she wanted.

Steve said he didn't have that problem in bars. He could always see somebody he'd like to meet, but by the time he got up enough nerve to reach out, they were either gone or somebody else was with them. The group decided Steve should try reaching out and they set the scene: There is a small table with two chairs at it. Beth, whom Steve finds attractive, is sitting in one of them sipping a drink. There is a half-finished drink in a glass in front of the other chair.

Steve's soliloquy goes like this: "Gee, but she's pretty. But she must be dumb or why would she come to a place like this? Or else maybe she's a lush. She does have two drinks on her table. Oh, she's not a lush. The other one belongs to her boy friend. He's a big boxer and very jealous and he's just gone to the toilet. Well, how do I know it's her boy friend's drink? It could belong to her mother. What does it matter whose drink it is? I'm a gentle aggressor and us gentle aggressors check things out. I've got to approach her, but what if she yells at me?" He tries to catch her eye, but she won't look up. Finally, he approaches timidly and says, "Excuse me, but could I please have some of the peanuts on your table? I didn't have time for dinner, and I'm very hungry."

BETH (disinterestedly): O.K., help yourself. (Hands him the bowl.) You can have them all.

STEVE (standing there with a puzzled look on his face and the bowl in his hands): Excuse me, again.

BETH: Yes?

STEVE: There are two chairs at your table.

BETH: So?

STEVE: Is somebody with you?

BETH: Yes, a girl friend. She's dancing right now, but she'll be back any minute.

STEVE: Since she'll be back any minute, would it be O.K. if I sat down and talked with you just until she got here, then I'll leave.

BETH: Oh, I guess so.

STEVE: While we are waiting why don't we play a little game and try to see how many things we have in common; that way we'll get to know each other quickly. (His speech becomes hurried.) Oh, I bet I know something we have in common. I think you are very pretty. I hope you think so, too, because you sure are.

BETH (flustered, but interested; really looks at him for the first time): Oh, well, I don't know. I guess, yes, sometimes I think I am kind of pretty, but not *very* pretty. But, I know something we have in common. We are both wearing blue. You have a blue shirt on and I'm wearing a blue dress.

In the discussion that followed this episode, Beth remarked that getting someone's attention by making her feel sorry for you as Steve did with his "I haven't had any dinner" approach isn't usually effective with her but that because he hung in there and kept trying even when she appeared disinterested, he finally got through to her. The timing of his compliment and his obvious sincerity as he expressed it were good aspects of his approach that were pointed out to him. After the discussion, the roles were reversed and Steve played the female at the table while Beth played the male who wanted to make contact, and then there was further discussion and suggestions were made to help both parties act like gentle aggressors whether they were approaching someone new or being approached.

As the evening wore on and each person had the opportunity to participate in several scenes and to watch and comment on even more, everyone's relating ability and spontaneity increased. Madelyn and Betty spoke less and less as the group members, discovering the validity of their own perceptions, freely shared their observations and suggestions. When it was time to quit, though it was late, no one wanted to stop and all looked forward to "D-day" and the field test at Big Daddy's disco, which was to take place two nights later.

Big Daddy's—a huge disco with three floors and three bands in Marina del Rey, California—had been chosen as our testing site mainly because its sophisticated atmosphere reeked with the status-seeking, performing, suspicion, veiled fear and hostility so prevalent in most places where singles go to meet. We felt that anyone who could go to Big Daddy's, not drink too much, carry out his assignment to attempt contact and come home feeling better than when he got there, would be able to attempt a pickup anywhere from a tennis court to an elevator.

Before leaving for Big Daddy's, the volunteers were asked to say how they were feeling. And last-minute advice and instructions were given. Phyllis was very nervous because she figured she was too old to be in such a youth-oriented place. Beth was worried at the prospect of being an aggressor—albeit a gentle one. It didn't seem right for a girl. Though we kept reminding her it was O.K. for a woman—and that she was a woman—she kept asking for reassurance and wanted to have all the instructions repeated. Steve and Pete acted more blasé—perhaps because the aggressor role was more familiar to them and they had been in this sort of milieu more often than the women. However, the feelings expressed were typical of the male-female roles. The women expressed, even exaggerated, their feelings while the men came across as logical and in control, the way men do most of the time even when they are paralyzed with fear.

The instructions given to the volunteers were these: To split up as soon as they were inside the building, to go their separate ways and take care of themselves but to remember that they were members of a team. If they wanted advice or reassurance, they were to contact another team member but to be careful not to interrupt if he or she seemed to have established a rapport with someone else.

Their purpose was to attempt to make at least two contacts using the tactics of a gentle aggressor. They were told to be aware of their thoughts and feelings and what triggered them, to observe themselves in whatever they did—to be "spectators at the spectacle."

They were cautioned to attempt contact only with people who genuinely interested them, for we wanted them to be sincere and honest. Success was to be measured not by making someone like them, by getting a date or by how many contacts they could make, but by what they learned about themselves and others as they tried out the role of the gentle aggressor.

Betty and Madelyn were to be there as observers, to give advice if it was needed and to nudge the participants a bit if they got off the track and became manipulative, phony, or allowed themselves to be taken advantage of.

At 9 P.M., all entered Big Daddy's. The music was blaring, the place was packed with strutting young flesh constantly on the move. No one stayed with anyone for very long, and when people were standing and talking together, their eyes were somewhere else.

Here are the experiences of our group members:

Beth went to the upstairs bar, and before she could order a

drink was overwhelmed by men. Some asked her to dance or to have a drink. Others kidded her, flattered her, showed off for her. She found herself talking to men she didn't want to talk to—just to be nice; dancing with men she didn't want to dance with—just to be friendly or because she felt sorry for them; allowing herself to be hugged and fondled by strangers—just because she didn't want to hurt anyone's feelings. Betty, who discovered her in her inundated state, reminded her that the role of the gentle aggressor involved choice and that she was to take the initiative and seek out men who interested her.

Emboldened by this support, Beth began making the "rounds" and learned new things about herself. As she said later, "It was very interesting because I had to think about what attracts me to men. At first I thought it was their physical appearance. I know there is a type that looks really good to me. But then I found out it wasn't so much how they looked but that they looked deep and interesting. But then some might look as if they had interesting stuff in them but it wasn't coming out. It was as if they had it but were keeping it all for themselves. I got into watching men's movements. I found myself really wanting to get more into someone who was open, lively, bubbly. It was a whole process of thinking about what I was really interested in."

Beth's first gentle aggression was with a young man named Roger. She approached him and started talking to him. At this point, she reported later, she learned a lot about the meeting process. As Beth said, "I think I'll be less critical of men who talk about nothing at the beginning. I can see where you haven't really got much to go on. It was hard for me to figure out what to say and keep trying to think of things to say. I guess up until now I've let the man carry that burden. Anyway, I started out talking about the place itself—mentioning the band—and then switched to more personal things—asking if he'd been there before."

Beth asked Roger to go downstairs where it was quieter so they could talk but then she discovered he was a conversation monopolizer. She didn't like him because his monologue nearly put her to sleep and she forgot to use gentle aggression to assert her right to talk. Even more than that, she thought he was chintzy because he didn't offer to buy her a drink. She slipped into the feminine role of expecting to be taken care of, got so bored listening that she lost all interest in trying to tell him about herself, and gave up.

She finally suggested they go upstairs again where the music was playing, and as soon as a man asked her to dance, she accepted, glad to get away.

Beth's next experience was more positive. Early in the evening she had spotted a man she liked but before she could approach him, he was gone. However, when she saw him later, she immediately walked over to him and said "hello"—something she never would have done before. He was glad she had taken the initiative, for he had been wanting to meet her but had been unable to find a time when she wasn't with other men. She found this man, Richard, easy to talk with and later made several observations she considered important. "You can't force relationships," said Beth. "You find it easy to talk with them or you don't. With Richard I did a lot of laughing even though we weren't talking about anything in particular. Our life styles were similar, so we had rapport. The next time I go out to meet men, I'm going to look for rapport rather than the looks. The key is the kind of rapport that makes you feel relaxed so you can laugh and joke. And you know what, I'm going to places where there is dancing and lots of different rooms because taking initiative, both in approaching and in getting rid of people, is a lot easier when you can move around from room to room."

Pete had some unusual experiences at Big Daddy's even though being at a singles bar and picking up women is nothing new to him. Pete has been giving women a line ever since he can remember. And they've been falling for it. His problem is that he sees so few women worth approaching. He likes the beauty-queen type, young and shapely, but then is disappointed when they can't talk with him about the ideas of Kierkegaard or Marx or Maslow. He said in the follow-up session, "That evening I felt more relaxed than I've ever felt before at those places. I guess it was because I didn't feel a compulsion to be 'on the make.' I was more willing to check women out and just get acquainted and see what would happen rather than feeling I had to make something happen." Pete's attitude change resulted in several interesting experiences for him. First, he began noticing women more just as people —not as sexual prospects. For example, he saw a girl and a guy standing near each other at the edge of the dance floor. It was obvious they were dying to meet each other but each was too shy to make an approach. Pete went up to the guy and started talking to him. Then he looked over at the girl and said, "Oh, hi!" as though he knew her, and after a few seconds asked, "Do you know Harry here?" When she said "No," he said, "I don't think I know your first name," and when she said it was Beverly, he introduced her to Harry. He stayed for just a minute or two while they got started talking and then excused himself and left.

The group members were quick to seize upon this incident and discuss how they could use it to help one another out. They decided that the next time they went out as a team (and they all wanted to try it again) they'd set it up so that if a member wanted to meet someone in particular, he or she could ask another member of the opposite sex to get acquainted and then introduce him.

But acting as a gentle aggressor in introducing two people to each other was not Pete's only experience. Not only did he find himself being more sensitive and kinder to women who didn't look like beauty queens; he found it paid off. Since the role he was to act out was one of exploration, not conquest, he tried something new when a woman of thirty-five or forty who didn't appeal to him physically came up and asked him to dance. Ordinarily, he would have turned her down, muttered something about being "too tired" and felt very uncomfortable. This time he thought, "What the hell, it's only for one dance. And maybe she's trying out a new role too and needs some encouragement. Besides, it will give me a chance to scout while I'm on the floor and see someone I might really like." Not only was the woman a good dancer; she knew how to talk. They continued their conversation over a drink and although he asked for her phone number from force of habit as he always does "to make women feel good," he said at the follow-up session that he thought he just might give her a call. He'd never been out with a woman older than he was before, and it might prove to be interesting.

Steve's view of the world and his way of interacting with women was considerably different from Pete's. He had always found it difficult to reach out because he knew nobody worthwhile would find him interesting. Actually, the only women he felt comfortable with were those he thought needed him and he felt sorry for. The helpful and cooperative side of his nature was well developed and he wanted to be sure to do his part in this project. This gave him the excuse he needed to make friendly overtures toward a woman he never would have had the nerve to approach before and to express some of the charm he didn't know he had.

Rather early in the evening, Steve was sitting at the bar having a drink, looking shyly at all the women he could see and trying to figure out the best way to approach one, when a lovely young woman sat down next to him. He looked at her and smiled in a way that let his double dose of delight show. He was delighted that she was so attractive and delighted that he didn't have to get up out of his seat and go find a woman. "Hi," he said, "I've been waiting for you all night. What took you so long?" He was surprised to hear these words come out of his mouth, for they sounded like something Pete might say.

The woman, Peggy, smiled broadly and, taking her cue from him, replied, "I'm very sorry I made you wait, but I had to finish my work before I could leave." He asked what work she was doing, found out she was a tax attorney, and since he is an accountant, they had a lot in common and were off to a running start.

After talking for some time, Steve said, "Why don't we get together sometime next week since we have so much to talk about." She agreed, gave him her phone number and they continued to talk. After about two hours, he broke away from her, but only long enough to seek out Madelyn and Betty and tell them what had happened and ask if it was O.K. for him not to try to make a second contact since he didn't want to leave his newfound friend. They congratulated him, said it was just fine with them and pointed out that he had really fulfilled his requirements anyway, for the way he approached them and asked for what he wanted was certainly representative of a gentle aggressor.

Phyllis was the one who had the most difficulty initiating contact as a gentle aggressor—partly because she had not been out as a single very much since her divorce and partly because she was painfully aware that she was older than most of the crowd and she didn't see anybody she thought was in her age bracket. Though she wasn't ever able to really take the initiative, she did repeat phrases in her mind trying to make herself comfortable—the way she had learned to do in a role-training soliloquy: "It is my world, too. It is O.K. for me to be here. I am O.K." She found herself a spot at the bar where she could watch the dancing and sat there sipping a tall cool drink, quietly thinking about all the recent changes in her life and feeling quite comfortable being by herself. After some time, a man who had been standing nearby with his back toward her, turned around and said softly, "Do you feel as uncomfortable here as I do?" A conversation ensued and she found out he was newly divorced and trying his wings in the singles world. She also found out that though he was a few years younger than she, her age didn't make any difference to him. They fell into a very natural conversation about how different the social scene was now from their before-marriage dating, and he asked her to dance. He also asked her for her phone number.

In the follow-up session to evaluate the evening's experience and their own roles as gentle aggressors, the reaction that all shared was that doing the whole thing with a group and as an experimental project made all the difference in the world. With a backup team and the right mind-set, it was much easier to lay themselves on the "line" where they might be rejected.

However, individual members learned different things and could see ways in which they could improve their meeting and relating style. Beth discovered that she had never had a chance to think about what she wanted in a man because they always approached her. "If I could approach men more openly—with the idea that I was just out to have a good time and to explore, to get acquainted well enough to know if I wanted to get acquainted better—I'd probably have to spend less time with each person. I'd be able to make the rounds quickly because I'd soon spot it if there was nothing there for me and move on."

Phyllis discovered that new social skills have to be developed one step at a time and going to a new environment and making yourself comfortable there is an important step. You don't have to expect yourself to reach out the first time around.

Phyllis also discovered that she was considerably bothered by her age, and that she thought her age alone made her undesirable. She discovered at Big Daddy's that that was not true. However, she learned that singles do tend to gather in age groups. Her team members gave her the names of other singles bars where the majority of the people are considerably older than they are at Big Daddy's. Two other things contributed to making her evening a success: the discovery that good things can happen to you if you hang in there and don't let your anxiety make you withdraw, and the fact that she is considerably stronger and more adaptable than she thought.

The most important thing Steve learned was that he is bright and charming and attractive to pretty, bright and charming women—at least to one of them. But as he put it, "If this one likes me, probably others do too, and I just have never bothered to take the chance of finding it out."

For Pete, the evening resulted in not trying so hard. The idea that he could go out for an evening and not "score" or meet anyone particularly significant and yet have a very good time was a real mind blower for him.

Because everybody not only learned a lot but had a very good time, all wanted to go someplace together again. We gave them a lot of encouragement to do it but also suggested a couple of other things for them to try that we believed would help them and others have more brief encounters and short-term alliances. We suggested that each of them become an organizer of a gentle aggressor backup group and that they each take responsibility for teaching the role-training method to several of their friends. We hoped in that way to spread learning, understanding and fun as quickly as possible.

PART II

6

The "We Process":
Making relationship contracts

The ability to make contact with new people is certainly one that must be developed in today's fast-moving society. But another skill may be even more important: the ability to build supportive and non-confining relationships—and quickly. Unfortunately, not many people have this ability. It is not an inborn one. Nor does our society teach us how to develop it or even that we should. And so, many people end up feeling lonely because they don't have enough relationships (at least, supportive ones) or because they are over-peopled—pulled in too many directions by too many people who want too many things.

It is easy to understand why so many people have problems with relationships. Few people spend much time thinking about what they want from a particular relationship and what they can realistically expect; even when they do, most don't know how to go about getting what it is they want and expect from others. The purpose of this chapter is to present a step-by-step plan that will help you develop supportive and non-confining relationships with new people and also improve your existing relationships—even those that have gone on for a long time.

First, we need to look at just what a relationship is. A relationship is the sum total of everything that goes on between two people once they have made contact. It includes the way they behave toward each other, what they say and do, and also their thoughts, feelings, ideas and fantasies about each other. Relationships differ in many ways. They can be based on the deepest of feelings or on nothing more than mutual interests. They can last but a little while or go on for a lifetime. Relationships can also vary greatly as to how meaningful they are—i.e., how much they contribute to an individual's emotional health and personal growth. They can be nourishing, or they can sap strength, energy, creativity and joy from either or both partners. Variations are endless.

But all relationships have one thing in common: they are made up of different stages. Even that minuscule relationship you have with the person you talk with while riding a bus home from work has a beginning, a middle and an end. And longer relationships can go through many phases. The young couple casually dating become the blissful newlyweds, then the proud parents of a baby, then the harried parents of several children, then doting grandparents, then a retired couple. The bond that holds them together, their relationship, changes as circumstances change. It is a living, flexible, growing thing, much like a green plant that pops out from a tiny seed and gradually becomes a huge vine. It is never the same for very long and it needs feeding and pruning— different kinds and amounts at different times.

However, when people don't have a mental picture of their relationships as living entities outside themselves, entities that, like plants, need shaping and nourishment at every stage of development, they are apt to neglect them.

However, there is a way to give your relationships the care they need and to make sure that you get the kind of relationships that will help you grow as a person and also enjoy life more fully. There is a way to make your relationships into partnerships. This is through the development of short-term alliances.

A short-term alliance can be defined as a "conscious contract" between two people to behave toward each other in a specific manner for a specific period of time or until one or the other asks for a renegotiation.

You need short-term alliances in order to make certain that you and your partner get the maximum benefits from your relationship and to make certain that neither takes advantage of the other. Actually there are unspoken contracts in all relationships— people agree to do things for one another. However, the relationship can be both stronger and more flexible when the terms are consciously selected by mutual agreement, made for a certain period of time and periodically reviewed.

In the past, it was not as necessary to work out individual agreements about how you'd behave toward people you were involved with. The rules of proper behavior were known and heeded by proper people. Everybody who was anybody knew what a woman or a man was supposed to do—at home, while traveling and when out in polite society.

People didn't spend time asking themselves what they wanted from friends, parents, mates and children. It was taken for granted how they should treat you and how you should treat them. Besides, people didn't make contact with very many others in the course of a lifetime and so didn't form very many relationships. And people didn't talk about relationships. That was too personal. Even today many people still assume it is cold-blooded, impolite or unnecessary to discuss and set a policy for a relationship. In fact, most of us fail to give our personal relationships the dignity and attention we give our business relationships.

When you go after a job and form a new relationship with an employer, you very carefully discuss the terms of that relationship —hours, salary, fringe benefits, job responsibilities. With your employer, you come to an agreement about how you'll work together, but the relationship does not become fixed with that first negotiation. Changes are frequently sought by you or your employer or required by circumstances. You may ask for a raise, a different schedule, a promotion. He or she may ask you to work overtime, to improve some aspect of your work or to take on additional tasks. Or your job may be outmoded by a computer and you may have to learn new skills or transfer to a different city. Both of you have the option to terminate your relationship if the other doesn't live up to the terms of the agreement. But you probably agreed to give a certain amount of notice when you first negotiated the conditions for employment. Usually in our business lives, though not in our personal lives, plans are carefully made for severing a relationship with as little discomfort as possible when it becomes necessary.

It is very different for two partners in a personal relationship. Often they just drift into that relationship without seriously talking or even thinking about its terms. Because of this, the relationship may take a form that is not entirely satisfactory to either,

and each may silently blame the other for not living up to the unstated wants and expectations brought to the relationship. Because the terms of the relationship are not clear, changes that
need to be made may not become apparent very soon. Thus they
may be delayed too long or not made at all for fear of ending the
relationship abruptly. Entering a new phase of a relationship, continuing to grow, becomes unnecessarily difficult. Ending it becomes
unnecessarily painful.

Just as an employer and employee have a ritual and a structure
that develop the policy for their interaction, so we need a ritual
and a structure to set the terms of our personal interactions. We
need not use the kind of a ritual usually used by management and
labor—negotiations that pit one side against the other. Although
this can result in the development of policy and a contract, it frequently leaves both parties with emotional bruises.

Luckily, we don't have to decide between no ritual at all or a
cold-blooded, impersonal one. The ritual used to develop the policy for an interpersonal relationship can be warm, friendly and
unhurried, and can help people on opposite sides of the fence understand one another better. It can lead to the kind of short-term
alliances that will keep relationships alive and growing or set them
aside with dignity and respect when it is time for that. The "We
Process" is such a ritual.

The "We Process" can be used when people want to clarify
their relationship—to make sure its "terms" are understood by
both partners; it can also be used when changes are desired in a
relationship. The only requirements are the recognition by both
parties that there *is* a relationship (i.e., that something is going on
between them) and a mutual interest in making whatever that is
more worthwhile. It is important to realize that a high degree of
emotional involvement is not necessary nor is the expectation that
the relationship will continue for a long time in the future. For instance, a man and a woman who are new lovers and planning a
trip could use the process to help them develop a short-term alliance for the time they will be traveling together. In this way, they
can avoid a great deal of conflict and misunderstanding and make
the trip more pleasurable and meaningful—even if they never plan
to see each other again after that.

However, the "We Process" is not just for forming sexual alliances. A divorced couple can use it to help each person under-

stand the other better and become supportive rather than vindictive. Family members, friends of the same or opposite sex and people who want to be friends will find many different uses for this ritual. Two women friends who have had a casual unstructured acquaintanceship for some time might enter a new phase in their relationship by forming a short-term alliance to lose weight. Using the "We Process," they may decide the terms of that alliance are to meet twice a week for exercise and low-calorie meal planning—for as long as it takes them both to reach their desired weight. They might encourage each other, for that period of time, to phone for help, anytime, day or night, if tempted to go off the diet. When their goal has been reached, their relationship may resume its more casual form or it may take on an entirely different structure. Again, if they wish, they can clarify the terms of that new phase and form a new alliance.

The "We Process" can be helpful for relationships in any stage. Those that are just forming can be gotten off to a good start if the partners use it to let each other know their feelings and what they want and don't want from each other. Or it can be helpful in examining ongoing relationships. Because so many people pass through our lives, we can be surrounded by people and yet lacking the kinds of relationships we want or need. "Spring cleaning" may be required. Most of us seldom, if ever, consciously think about which relationships are nourishing and which are draining, seldom take time to shine up, alter, eliminate and replace old ones and deliberately go out shopping for new ones. Doing this—deliberately choosing who and how many people you want in your life, getting your supply of relationships clean, neat and orderly—can give you greater control over your own life.

It is not practical nor is it appropriate for you to do the "We Process" with everyone you know. Nonetheless, just thinking about the process in connection with a relationship will help you better evaluate it—as you will discover once you have tried it.

Now, about trying it. The "We Process" is not difficult. The difficulty comes in making the commitment to try it—and more than once. No skill is perfected the first time around. However, we are certain that if you try it with three different people—if you will take the time to carefully do each and every step just as instructed—not only will you better understand the persons and the relationships you are trying to clarify and improve; you will begin to see new opportunities for clarification and improvement in many other relationships.

Following are the steps for the "We Process":

GETTING READY

1. Whom to ask

There is a part of all of us that wants to maintain the status quo at any price. This "stick-in-the-mud" part that is afraid of anything out of the ordinary can always find an excuse for not trying something new. Thus, even if you are able to think of relationships that you'd like to develop, clarify or improve, your "stick-in-the-mud" side may make you hesitate to ask your relationship partners to do the "We Process" with you. You may even keep yourself from having a relationship adventure by saying "logical" sentences like these:

> It would be too embarrassing to ask; I don't know him well enough yet. Or I know him so well he'd think I was crazy suddenly wanting to discuss our relationship.

> There is no use asking because she'd never do it anyway.

> I might hurt her feelings or she'd get mad or she'd laugh.

> I don't think she can ever change anyhow.

Or maybe the side of you that prefers the status quo will not even be able to think of anyone you'd like to do the "We Process" with. You may say to yourself that all of your relationships are already as good as they can be, or use the limp excuse that relationships go best if you just let them flow and don't discuss them too much. You may even convince yourself that it would be opening a Pandora's box to take a closer look at some of your relationships. No matter what "reasons" you come up with to avoid having to make changes in your life, the fact is that there is always room for some improvement in any relationship, and all people's lives can profit from relationship inspection and improvement.

The part of you that wants to stay in a rut can frequently be prodded into action by means of a guided fantasy. You'll probably be able to think of just the right person if you will close your eyes and let your mind drift through your relationships. Picture yourself as a baby or small child with your parents and then let your mind sift through your childhood chums and other people who have been in your past and gradually come up to the present. Pretty soon you'll focus in on one or two people who are in your life now and whom you care about and you'll recognize that things between you and them aren't as clear or as comfortable as you'd like. They are possible prospects.

Jot down the names of the people you are considering. Looking at your list, ask yourself if the relationship you have or think you might be able to have with each person is worth spending a couple of hours on. The "We Process" may take less time or it could take a lot more if you discover while doing it that it is working and decide to get all you can from it. However, you can postpone part of it until a later time (making sure you complete closure), so two hours is a safe amount of time to figure on. Once you have selected those you want to try the process with, you are ready for the next step.

2. How to ask

When it comes right down to it, many people find they are hesitant about asking a person to talk with them about their relationship. After all, the mere act of asking implies, "You are important to me, and I believe I am important to you." In a society as impersonal as ours, as afraid of feeling, conveying this message can be quite threatening. You may fear that someone you ask to do the "We Process" with you will turn you down in a way that will let you know you aren't important to him and have no business thinking you are. Or else you fear he'll misinterpret your request and think you are seeking more involvement and commitment than you really are. Don't let reticence hold you back. If you have feelings like this, it is an indication your relationship could profit from some clarification. Go ahead. Take a chance. Ask.

When you do ask, bear in mind that people can vary a great deal in their response. There may be some people who have a lot of trust in you, who are curious and who like to try new things.

With them you can just come right out and ask without weighing your words. However, with most people, when you ask them to talk about your relationship, they will become concerned. Many will assume you are mad at them and will bawl them out if they give you half a chance; others will assume you intend to pressure them into doing something they don't want to do.

You can frequently give a person reassurance if you are careful about the way you ask. Following are two suggestions for presenting the idea that can help prevent undue anxiety in those you ask:

> I really like our relationship and there are some ways I think it could be made even better. I'd like to talk with you about those ways. When could we talk about them?

> I read about this process for helping two people get more out of their relationship. Would you be willing to try it with me?

However you phrase your invitation, you'd better be prepared to convince a prospect that you don't intend to bawl him out or to demand anything. Be prepared with answers in case his stick-in-the-mud side comes out with some "logical" reasons for not doing it and staying in a relationship rut.

Caution: Don't use this process with people you don't really like or at a time when your feelings toward them are more negative than positive. THESE TECHNIQUES ARE NOT DESIGNED TO CURE A SICK RELATIONSHIP, BUT TO CREATE NEW RELATIONSHIPS THAT ARE SUPPORTIVE, AND TO MAKE RELATIONSHIPS THAT ARE ALREADY GOOD EVEN BETTER.

When you find a willing partner, get him to read this section if you can. If that isn't possible, take plenty of time and carefully explain the step-by-step procedure. Or better yet, write out the necessary instructions for him. While you're at it, make a few extra copies so you'll have them ready. (Once you've done this with one person, you'll probably want to do it again with another.)

BEFORE YOU GET TOGETHER

Following are several steps each partner should take before getting together to actually participate in the "We Process":

1. Fantasize

The purpose of fantasizing is to expand your mind in many directions—to free it of some of the "shoulds" and "shouldn'ts" that have limited you in past relationships and that may not be applicable to the present or to this relationship. Fantasizing can help you discover there are more options for behavior than you ever dreamed about and also give you the impetus to discuss what you *want* instead of limiting yourself to what you may believe you have to settle for.

How to do it: Sit or lie down in a comfortable quiet place where you won't be interrupted. Have a pencil and paper handy to record your fantasies. Close your eyes and relax. When you are relaxed, think of the person you plan to do the "We Process" with. Without forcing your thoughts in any direction, allow pictures of you and this person doing things together to appear in your mind.

When pictures do appear, observe them without judging them. For example, if a picture comes into your mind of you and your business partner holding hands and skipping along the wet sand on a deserted beach, don't turn off the picture by saying to yourself, "That's silly. You can't do that with a business partner." Just watch the picture as long as it lasts and see what the people do. If you should picture yourself and your partner engaged in sexual acts or overtures, don't say, "That's terrible. I'd never permit that." Just watch the picture until it disappears. Fantasizing is a way of letting your mind enjoy itself and explore what it wants to explore. Trust it. It knows its limits better than you do.

When you are tired of fantasizing or the pictures no longer appear, gradually sit up and jot down some notes to remind yourself of just how your fantasies went. Then examine them and try to figure out what they represent in terms of "wants" and "don't-wants" in regard to your relationship partner. Examine them from two different points of view—do you really want what you saw happening or is there a deeper symbolic meaning? For example, if you did see yourself skipping down the beach with your business partner, it could mean that you'd really like to take a vacation with him and do just that. Or it could mean you'd like more closeness and playfulness in your day-to-day relationship—that it has become too dull and ponderous, too "businesslike." Or that it has become too much play and not enough work and you are worried about that. Or there may be other interpretations.

If you have a sex fantasy about someone, think about it to see if it means you'd like to have sex, or a certain kind of sex, with him or her. Or it could mean you are afraid somebody wants sex, or sex of a certain kind, and you don't. A sex fantasy can also have a symbolic meaning—perhaps that you want more intimacy with this person than you now have. Only you can discern the real meaning of your fantasy. When the interpretation you come up with just seems to feel right, to fit, when you feel comfortable with it, it *is* right.

Don't worry if your fantasies seem immoral or impossible or ridiculous. You don't have to do what you fantasize, or even discuss your fantasies with your partner, unless you decide you want to. However, if what you fantasize or your interpretation of that fantasy intrigues you, you might want to discuss it with your partner and maybe the two of you together can figure out a way to make it happen. One woman had a fantasy of going on a long cruise with her boy friend. But she felt this was an impossible fantasy because he was working very hard and didn't have much time off. However, when they discussed it they realized that what she wanted was some quiet, intimate time with him to just talk and be close. They took a day-long cruise to a nearby island instead and made arrangements to include these "closeness cruises" in their relationship on a regular basis.

2. List your wants and don't-wants

Write down in a random fashion all of the wants and don't-wants in regard to your interaction with your partner that your fantasies have made you aware of, plus those that you have thought of in the past, or those that may occur to you as you are working on your list. Don't worry if they seem selfish or ridiculous or if you've asked for them before and couldn't get them. The purpose of listing any and all wants and don't-wants is to help you decide which ones are fair and reasonable, which you know you probably won't get and which you think are possibilities. This is not the list you are going to discuss, but the preliminary list you are going to examine. Since you can't examine your wants and don't-wants very well unless you look at them, don't leave any out, even if they seem preposterous.

There are many subjects to discuss that will occur to you as you contemplate your individual relationships, especially if you do the "We Process" again and again.

Following are some wants that it will usually profit partners to discuss:

TIME: How much time do you want to spend together and in what way?

MONEY: Whom would you like to pay for what, when, how, and why?

DECISION-MAKING: Whom would you like to make the decisions on what?

SEX: What do you want of your partner sexually now and in the future?

DURATION OF THE RELATIONSHIP: How long would you like this relationship to last and how long do you think it will last?

LIMITS: What kind of limits do you want on this relationship? How much or how little involvement do you want right now?

PRIVATE AND SOCIAL BEHAVIOR: How do you want your partner to behave toward you in private and in public? How do you want him/her to act toward others when you are out socially?

CONFLICT: How would you like to handle conflicts when they arise?

CONTACT: Who is going to initiate contact and how?

TRUST: How much are you going to share with each other verbally about other aspects of your lives when you are apart? *If* you have other sexual relationships, how will you handle that?

TERMINATION: How and when would you like your relationship to end?

3. Bring your wants into the realm of possibility and make a list of requests you intend to make and feelings you want to share

Look carefully at your wants and don't-wants and weigh them against what is fair and what is realistic. It doesn't seem fair for you to expect a person to be available whenever you call at the last minute yet not be similarly available when they want to make last-minute plans, or to expect to play the field while restricting your mate to monogamy. However, if you have a want that you feel isn't fair, you can bring it up for discussion. When you get together with your partner, you can tell him you don't think it is fair and yet you want it a lot and then see what he thinks. People's ideas about what is fair vary considerably and, besides, if you talk about something you really want and your partner helps you consider options, together you can frequently come up with an alternative acceptable to both of you.

As you peruse your list, take a look at what it is possible for you to get. If your closest friend is married, it may not be realistic to expect him or her to be available for prowling the singles bars with you. If your dating partner is unemployed, it may be unrealistic to expect him to take you out to more plays and dinners. If you have a sexual alliance with a married man who lives out of town, it may be unrealistic to expect more time with him.

When you have carefully considered your preliminary lists of wants and don't-wants in terms of fairness and practicality, start a new list—one you will share with your partner. Include your wants and don't-wants and feelings, for you will want to talk about all of those things. However, state your wants and don't-wants in such a way that you distinguish between a desire for a behavioral change and a desire for a feeling change. It can help a relationship to let a person know you'd like a behavioral change, but you can hurt someone when you ask for a feeling change. People can't change their feelings just because they want to. You can make them feel inadequate by implying they could if they would. Though it is very important to talk about feelings, prepare yourself so you can do it in a way that will make your partner feel good.

For example, don't write down, "I want you to love me more." That is a request for a change in feelings. Besides, you can't *know* how much he loves you. You can't get inside of him and measure his feelings. You just have a belief about how much he loves you and have made an arbitrary judgment about whether that amount is satisfactory or not. So when you have a want about your partner's feelings, translate it into a different form, one that lets him realize that you have a feeling that is making you uncomfortable. Make a statement about your own feelings without blaming him for it. Do not accuse him of having the wrong feelings or having done something terrible that caused yours. You might write down as a matter-of-fact statement, "I don't feel loved by you," or "I have trouble feeling enough love coming from you."

As soon as you make your feelings your problem, not his, it will be easy to take the next step—i.e., to make a request for a behavioral change. Whenever you write down a "feeling statement," if your feeling is an uncomfortable one, couple it with a request for behavior that you believe would help it go away. That gives your partner something concrete to work on and puts you in a vulnerable position. Though relationships are torn down by demands for compliance (especially demands that are beyond voluntary control), they are built by partners requesting help from one another from a position of vulnerability, by asking without whining.

Thus, follow your "feeling statement"—i.e., "I don't feel loved by you"—by a statement requesting a behavioral change similar to the following:

I want you to be more affectionate.

I want you to compliment me more.

I want you to buy me little surprise gifts now and then.

I want you to hold me in your arms and kiss me for a few minutes each night when we get into bed.

The more specific you can be about exactly what you want and when you want it, the better. However, don't worry if you find it difficult to be specific at this point. When you and your partner get together, you can work out the details. The main thing now is to stimulate and focus your thinking, to prepare yourself so that your subsequent interaction will be as supportive, enjoyable and productive as possible.

Here are portions of a list made by two close women friends, before getting together for a discussion. It contains behavioral wants considered fair and possible, some of which are coupled with "feeling statements."

Christine's List

> I want more contact with you—by phone and in person.
>
> I feel restricted by the rules you have against dropping by. I want to be able to drop by and see you without phoning first.
>
> I frequently feel judged by you in regard to my husband. I don't want you to criticize me when I stand up for him.
>
> When we are together, I frequently feel you withdrawing from me and I don't know why. When this happens, I'd like to be able to tell you about it and have us both work together to do something about it.
>
> I want you to tell me often that I am important to you and in what way.

Leona's List

> I don't feel as close to you as I'd like to be. I want you to share more of your feelings and needs with me, to call on me for help more often.
>
> I don't want you to act huffy or cold if I occasionally change my mind about coming over to your house for dinner if I get a chance to go out on a date—as long as you are cooking dinner for your husband anyway.
>
> I want for us to get together more often for an evening out alone—without your husband.

Here are portions of a list made by partners in a rather new sexual relationship:

> I want you to stop trying to get a closer relationship than I am comfortable with, stop pressuring me for more time and attention. I am cautious about relationships with men and need more space.

> I want you not to flirt with others when you are out with me.

> I want you to read some books on diet so you will understand what I am talking about and so that we can work together on developing a healthier life style.

> I worry about letting you know when I am upset. I want you to learn to put up with me when I get angry and not leave when we start getting into conflict with one another.

Here are portions of a behavioral want list considered fair and possible and made by a husband in using the "We Process" with his wife:

> I want some time at home by myself, preferably when you aren't there.

> I want to be able to develop some separate friendships on my own, with women as well as men.

> I feel bored.

> I don't want to spend so many Saturday nights with the same friends.

> I don't want to spend every Sunday with your mother.

> I want you to get a part-time job so I can work fewer hours—even if it means moving to a smaller house.

GETTING TOGETHER WITH YOUR PARTNER

While we strongly recommend going through the previous steps alone before getting together with your partner, sometimes it doesn't seem worthwhile—as in a brand-new relationship where you don't have a past history to think about. Or sometimes it doesn't seem practical—as with a friend from out of town whom you run into by chance, or with someone you mention the "We Process" to who is willing to do it *right now* and might change his mind if you put it off. Under these circumstances you can sit quietly together, each with paper and pencil, and take fifteen or twenty minutes to think and jot down some fantasies and wants. However, with a long-term relationship or one that is very important to you, there is a lot to think about. You'll do much better if you spend a while by yourself contemplating what you want. It pays to carefully prepare the phrasing of your wants and don't-wants and feelings so that they don't sound like accusations or demands.

While the time it takes to do the process varies according to how long you've known each other and how important the relationship is to each of you, arrange at least an hour together in a setting where you will not be interrupted. For long-term relationships in which there is a high degree of emotional involvement, two or more hours may be necessary. The setting is very important because doing this process can evoke some strong feelings. Therefore, don't try to do it in a crowded restaurant or bar where the presence of others might inhibit you. (And don't try to make it easier by taking an alcoholic drink. That might keep you from getting in touch with your feelings as well as communicating clearly.) Don't meet in a place where you are likely to be interrupted (your office, for example) or where one or the other might feel vulnerable (in your married lover's house while his wife is away). An isolated bench in a park makes a good setting, or your own house or patio (if you will keep from answering the phone or doorbell).

Sit where you can see each other's face clearly and where you can easily reach out and touch each other. Two overstuffed chairs drawn close together and facing each other is ideal; or sitting side by side on a sofa is O.K. Don't do this with a table or desk between you. It creates a psychological barrier and gives the whole thing a hostile ambience, like labor-management negotiations or a court of law, which is the last thing in the world you want.

Keep to the sequence in the following steps and follow the instructions and you will probably have a brief encounter in addition to ending up with a short-term alliance. (If you have a tape recorder and your partner is willing, use it to record this whole process. When you play it back you'll learn a lot!)

1. Start your mutual discussion by validating your relationship and each other

There is no sense going through this process unless you really like many aspects of each other and unless you believe that a relationship with this person will be valuable to you. Before you start, it is important to let each other know this. Do not assume it is known, or hint about it, but bring it right out into the open.

Sit without talking for at least ten minutes with pencil and paper in front of you. Think of all of your partner's good qualities, what you like about your present relationship, and what in particular it and he or she has meant to you in the past. Jot these things down. While thinking, look at your partner from time to time to stimulate your thoughts and to send a message of caring.

When you are both ready, take turns with one person at a time talking while the other person remains completely silent and just takes it all in. Read your list and augment it as additional things occur to you, remembering to look at your partner from time to time.

Give direct compliments preceded by the phrases "I like you because . . ." and "I like our relationship because . . ." For example:

I like you because:
> you are gentle
> you are handsome
> you are very bright
> you taught me to play
> you are sexy

I like our relationship because:
> it helped me grow up
> it produced two wonderful children
> it got me through a bad time in my life

Cautions:
Do not use disclaimers or say anything to take away from the compliment; don't use "buts." Be straight;

don't make jokes. Don't say, "I like you because you are lively and fun, but I wish you wouldn't talk so much."

Don't say, "I like you because you are gentle but I wish you could be a little firmer now and then."

Don't hurry. If you find yourself feeling deep emotion, just let yourself feel it and pay attention to what is happening in your body. Also pay attention to the expressions on your partner's face. If tender thoughts well up in you, articulate them. If you feel like crying, cry. Stop occasionally to take a few deep breaths. Here is an example of some thoughts expressed by two women friends as they came to the end of step No. 1, the validation procedure:

SANDY: I just realized that you still really fill a lot of needs for me. You are like a sister, a friend, a mother. I love you. I never really sat down and thought about how important you are to me until I started thinking about this "We Process." I have been so busy complaining that our relationship has changed that I haven't had time to look at how good it still is.

BARBARA: Outside of my husband, you are the person I am closest to in the entire world. I feel that if I have any needs or wants and tell them to you, you'll try to take care of them. I feel like I can always lean on you. You are the only person who knows what I am like inside because I have shared far more with you than with my husband because I feel he is limited in understanding the depth of my feeling. I guess I am really frightened of having you pull away from me because it would make me feel very lonely in the world.

2. Share relationship fantasies, feelings, wants and don't-wants

The purpose of this step is to get each of you to share important things about yourself that most people don't share nearly often enough—fantasies, feelings, wants, don't-wants. Since one person cannot share what another person will not accept, it is important that his partner be receptive, that he listen very carefully without getting upset if he hears what he doesn't want to hear.

Again, you take turns, one person talking while the other listens without comments or questions.

The speaker should use the notes and the list of wants and don't-wants he has made in preparation for this sharing, but he need not be limited by them. It is O.K. to augment or delete as you go along.

You may or may not want to share fantasies you've had about your partner or about your relationship with him or her. Telling a fantasy is a way of giving a very personal gift. However, as with other personal gifts, you must give some consideration as to how you think your partner will interpret it.

Whether discussing fantasies, feelings, wants, don't-wants or limits, the speaker must consider the effects of what he wants to say while at the same time trying to be as honest and open as possible. Do not allow yourself to be "brutally frank"; instead, endeavor to convey the "sweet truth." When expressing wants and don't-wants, it is of utmost importance that the speaker watch his tone of voice, to make certain he is not accusing or whining, and that he not hurry. This process should not be rushed.

In talking about feelings, express yourself with "I" messages: "I feel sad when you _____." "I get mad when you _____." "I am uncomfortable with _____." "I don't like it when you _____." Be sure to include some good feelings and don't just limit yourself to negative ones. "I like it when you _____." "It really delights me when you _____." Another word of caution. Take care to avoid the phrase "I feel *that you* _____." A thought preceded by such a phrase does not express a feeling even though the word "feel" is used. It expresses an interpretation of another person's behavior or motivation and will be detrimental to this procedure.

On the other hand, what can be most helpful is to share your hopes and fears about the relationship—where you think it is going, how long it will last, how it might end, what might happen if you make changes in it. When you share your hopes, don't be upset if your partner has different ones. Though hopes can influence a relationship, they don't determine or predict how it will go; they are just a way of expressing feelings about the future.

In sharing your fears, do not seek a guarantee that they won't happen. Instead, seek understanding and possibly help in dealing with some of them. If your fear is that your daughter will spend less time with you when she gets married, there is no way to keep that from happening. However, the very act of telling her about that fear may give you some precious moments of intimacy. And if the two of you put your heads together, you may figure out a way to share moments of such high quality that you will feel close even when you have fewer of them.

Many times people have fears of what might happen if they do get the relationship changes they want. If you have such fears, mention them. Perhaps you and your partner together can figure out what can be done to cope with them. You might want to broaden an existing friendship by adding non-exclusive sex to a friendly alliance but worry that your partner will become too heavily involved because of seeing sex as symbolizing a heavy commitment. You worry about slipping into a relationship that will either confine you or hurt your partner. If you talk about these fears, they are less apt to materialize, and sometimes they disappear as partners discover they each have the same fear about the other.

The listener, too, has an important role to play, even though he is to say nothing until his partner is through. He must try to be objective and hold back his emotional responses. He should try to put himself in his partner's shoes, to feel what he feels.

If, when you are listening, you hear things you don't want to hear, remind yourself that these are not demands for things you must do to be liked by your partner. He already likes you a lot or he wouldn't be sharing himself with you. It is natural to get shook when your partner asks for changes from you, but remember you do not have to do anything you don't want to do.

3. Discuss and pick relationship goals

When you have each had a turn stating your wants and listening to your partner's, it is time for a mutual free-flowing discussion in which you respond to what you have heard. Usually, both partners are experiencing some strong emotional reactions at this point. No matter how you are feeling—elated, depressed, spaced out, or furious—start your discussion on a positive note. Briefly list the requests he made that you *want to* comply with.

Here are some phrases you will find helpful:

I liked it when you said "you wanted to go out more" or "did not want a sexual relationship."

"Taking a class together" is something I can go along with.

I really want to learn to solve conflicts better. I hope we can figure out how to.

Seeing less of each other is something I thought about myself, but was afraid to bring up.

Avoid these phrases (or any other expressed in an accusing way):

That was a silly (or stupid, thoughtless, mean, unrealistic, etc.) thing to ask for.

You *always* ask for that.

You *never* think of what I want.

Avoid using the words *always* or *never* in all parts of this procedure. Remember, you are seeking a short-term alliance that can be renegotiated, not a lifetime guarantee.

After you've gone over your points of agreement, discuss your reactions to the fantasies, feelings and requests you heard expressed. Avoid interrupting each other or arguing. Don't try to talk your partner out of his feelings or opinions, even if they are very different from yours, and even if you wish he didn't have them. People can have quite different feelings, see things from a different perspective and have different reasons for doing what they want to do and still agree on what they are willing to do to, for and with each other. One of the factors that keeps people from understanding one another as well as they might and from making alliances both could profit from is that a discussion of feelings, wants and don't-wants often leads to arguments, insults, anger and resentment. This need not happen if people will follow the steps and conversational guidelines we have outlined and if they don't have unrealistic expectations.

Don't expect that you will want to do everything your partner wants or that he will want to do everything you want. The purpose of this step is to get a clearer understanding of the changes each of you wants as a basis for selecting some goals each will enjoy helping the other achieve. This can happen, but you must be a good listener, have patience and be willing to hang in there for a while.

As you talk, be sure to go over, at least briefly, all wants and don't-wants that have been mentioned. Don't skip those that have made you mad or hurt your feelings. However, in reacting to them, avoid all phrases that might tend to cut off dialogue or make your partner feel you are rigid or stubborn or don't give a damn about what he wants. Many times, when you find a request objectionable and know you can't or don't want to comply, if you can get your partner to go more into detail about it or to voice the thoughts and feelings that underlie it, that is enough to make him feel satisfied. If you cut him off, he is apt to feel that not only are you rejecting his request, you are rejecting him.

Thus, even if you feel strongly about something, even if you are certain that nobody in the world is going to talk you into cutting off your long hair, leaving your wife, going back to school or quitting your job, don't get in a huff and say, "I certainly will not consider _____."

Instead, try saying, "I don't believe I could go along with _____, but will you please tell me some more about it," or "Will you please give me some details about _____ and why it is important to you. Even if I can't go along with it, we might be able to figure out a mutually acceptable alternative, one that would make you happy and that I could go along with."

Continue your discussion, continue being open, honest and expressive, continue being patient and listening carefully and pretty soon some mutual goals and procedures will emerge. As those you both agree upon become apparent, jot them down, indicating whether each is a guideline—i.e., a simple behavioral agreement—or a goal or objective for which an action plan needs to be developed. Goals and guidelines should refer to behavior only—not to feelings.

Examples of guidelines:

> When we see each other or talk on the phone, we will start off our conversation by telling each other of good things that have happened since we last had contact instead of with complaints.

We will not flirt with other men or women when we are out together.

Sam will tell fewer jokes, particularly dirty ones, when he is with George. George will not make fun of Sam's bald head.

Examples of relationship goals:

We will go with each other to more plays, concerts and other forms of live entertainment.

We will work out a schedule for seeing one another that will not put stress on either of us and will make both feel as though we are important to the other.

We will find ways to bring more excitement into our sex life.

Guidelines that both parties fully agree upon require a minimum of discussion, but these questions should be answered: What shall we do when we notice the agreement is not being kept? When shall we get together again and talk about how these guidelines are working? Working out goals will take more time. Give each goal a number, ranking it in order of its importance. List only those goals that you both want to work toward now. When there is disagreement about the selection of a relationship goal, decide when you will bring it up for consideration again. People are more apt to graciously accept giving up a goal if they know that it will be considered in the future.

For example, if one member of a couple wants to change an "open" relationship to a monogamous one and the other doesn't, this is not the time to make this a relationship goal. However, a couple might be able to select a relationship goal that would achieve some of the benefits that usually go along with monogamy; i.e., they might agree to regard each other as a primary person when making plans for socializing activities and seeing others only when that did not require neglect of the primary relationship. Also, sometimes the wording of a goal can be changed so that both parties can get what they want. For example, if one wants more sexual excitement than the other, a non-monogamous relationship is not the only answer. If the goal decided upon is to provide that person with more sexual excitement, the couple can then work out the specifics as to what can be done (going to a sex workshop together, mutual sexual exploration, reading pornographic literature) that both can be happy about.

If you have many goals and if this has been a lengthy session, you may want to pick just one or two to work on in the next step and save the rest until a subsequent meeting. However, don't skip the next two steps. They are very important. You will probably be feeling quite excited at this stage, excited by the new things you've learned about yourself, your partner and the potential of your relationship. Whether what you've learned reinforces or contradicts what you believed about your partner and your relationship before you started this process, this much personal talk can sometimes make you want to be by yourself and think. Don't, however, stop this technique prematurely.

4. Make plans for achieving your goals and for subsequent evaluative discussion

Once a goal has been selected, deciding how to reach it is relatively easy. With an objective clearly in mind, brainstorming and planning can be great fun, for having a mutual goal brings out the creativity in people and makes them feel they are truly on the same team. If the goal is to spend more time together, one partner might think this can best be accomplished by setting definite times to get together while the other feels confined by a rigid schedule and wants to play it by ear. After a discussion with the purpose in mind of finding a plan that will help them accomplish their goal and that *both can feel comfortable with*, they might come up with a solution that gives each some of what he wants, such as to set aside one particular night every week to meet and to call each other on the spur of the moment the rest of the time. After all, there are many ways to achieve any goal and many paths that can be taken. If their goal is to help her spend less time in the kitchen, they might decide to (1) eat out more often, (2) hire a maid, (3) share the cooking, (4) buy frozen dinners, etc.

If one path doesn't get you there by the time you want to be there, you can try another path later on, or change your expected time of arrival.

Usually, by the time two people have gotten to this point in the "We Process," they have shared a lot of their feelings and wants, and much trust and good will have been built. They've gotten caught up in the fun of "orchestrating" their relationship, and they are more willing to give and take and to make compromises.

Deciding how to reach goals is not the end of the process. It is of utmost importance to set specific time limits for achieving each goal. People may say, with the best of intentions, "We just must get together more often," or "I really will see that the yard is kept in good condition," or "I promise to do more of the cooking." However, unless they settle on who is going to do what and when, they may never achieve their goals. Exactly when is the proposed action going to start? When is the expected completion date? When are they going to check with one another to evaluate progress? How will they know when they have reached their goal? (If the goal is to upgrade each other's wardrobe, when will they know this has been accomplished? When a certain closet has been cleaned out? When they have four complete outfits? Or two new ones? Or _____?)

In relationships as in work situations, such planning is a critical step that turns vague good intentions into a concrete alliance, a clear commitment. If not fulfilled, it can be examined in the future to see what has gone wrong. Such planning establishes policy which strengthens the relationship and gives the people in it guidelines that keep them on the track. It keeps them from resenting and blaming one another when they aren't satisfied.

And so, the purpose of this step is to look at each goal and to figure out exactly what each of you must do to accomplish it, to plan the sequence of steps, to agree on starting and completion times and TO WRITE DOWN THE STEPS AND THE TERMS OF YOUR AGREEMENT.

The most important part of this step is not what plan is chosen, but that both partners are convinced the one chosen is the best *mutually acceptable* one for their particular relationship at this particular time.

When you write down the steps and the terms of your agreement, be sure to include the following:

a. Be clear about the starting time of your agreement. Specify whether your agreement is to go into effect immediately or in a month or after you get back from vacation. When parts of the agreement have different starting times, specify them. If you have a goal of taking a class together, you may decide to start during the spring or fall semester. If your goal is to help one another get healthier, you must decide just when to start your diet and exercise plan. When the goals and guidelines are not related specifically to time, they can become just exercises in promise-making—the sort of "I'll diet tomorrow" resolutions we are all so familiar with.

b. Decide how long the various parts of the agreement will be in effect. If the agreement is a relatively simple one, the entire agreement can have a specified length of time. A couple may decide that their alliance will last for four months. On the other hand, some agreements are more complicated—containing many guidelines and goals. Some of these goals may take longer to achieve than others. So it is necessary to pick not only a starting time for each goal but also a completion time for each.

c. Set a time when the guidelines and goals will be brought up for discussion and review. You may want to set a certain date somewhere between the beginning of a particular plan and its completion; or you may decide on a certain time, such as in one month or four months, for a review.

5. Conclude the "We Process" and "seal" your alliance with some kind of physical contact that both of you are comfortable with

Spend a little time together during which you touch but do not talk. Bringing closure with physical contact is important for two reasons. In the first place, it is a ritual that both symbolizes and creates closeness and thus is a good way to indicate not only that you have agreed to but that you take pleasure in being on the same team. However, do not in any way pressure your partner into a kind of physical contact he is not comfortable with, and do not be in a hurry to stop any kind that is pleasant. Physical contact can take many different forms. For one pair, it may mean just holding hands and looking into one another's eyes for a few minutes. Friends might hug or kiss, stroke one another's hair or give a back rub. Lovers might want to stretch out somewhere and lie in each other's arms for fifteen or twenty minutes, or even longer.

It can take some time to "come down" after doing the "We Process." Much emotion can be generated, especially with partners who have a lot invested in each other—parents and children, close friends, mates and former mates. Here is how it affected one woman who did it with her lover. She says, "Afterwards, my stomach hurt and I felt like crying. My heart pounded like crazy as I realized I'd made a commitment and was really involved with a man for the first time in several years. It was almost too scary for me because I had been really super-cool in my relationships for some time. Now I had told a man my feelings and my wants and he had told me his—and rather than driving us apart, it had made us closer. Though both of us expressed the wish to go on together, just feeling I had made a promise made me anxious. Yet, at the same time, it was a different kind of anxiety than I had felt before when I had thought he might walk out on me. I think he felt the anxiety, too, because he got impatient and we almost got into an argument right there at the end. But then, suddenly, we just grabbed each other and hugged and hugged. I guess we both just really needed some reassurance."

It is important to remember that though the "We Process" is a system for making conscious contracts, it is not a rigid system. Though all steps and their sequence are important, how much time you spend with each step, how detailed and involved your discussions become, is up to you. How you feel about the person and the process during each step and at the end, when the terms of your alliance are clear, can vary greatly. Expect to have different experiences with different partners. Expect different experiences with the same partner if you do it more than once. Expect what you talk about, how you talk and what you experience to vary according to the type of contract you are forming; i.e., whether you are getting a new relationship off to a good start, deepening or broadening a friendship, forming or altering a sexual alliance or creating a new and different phase in a long-existing relationship. What is most important is that both partners end up with the feeling that they have taken a look at themselves, the other person and the relationship and learned something new. If that happens, the process has been successful.

Following is a brief summary of the essential steps in the proper sequence:

BEFORE YOU GET TOGETHER

1. Fantasize freely about your partner and your relationship.
2. List your wants and don't-wants about your partner and your relationship. Decide which are fair and realistic.
3. Bring your wants into the realm of possibility and make a list of requests you intend to make and feelings you want to share.

WHEN YOU GET TOGETHER

1. Validate your relationship and each other—one at a time.
2. Share fantasies, feelings, wants, don't-wants, hopes and fears regarding your partner, yourself and your relationship—one person at a time.
3. Discuss and pick relationship guidelines and goals.
4. Make plans for achieving your goals and for subsequent evaluative discussion.
   a. List relationship guidelines.
   b. List relationship goals.
   c. Pick a time for starting to operate according to agreed-upon policy and for starting the first step of each plan.
   d. Pick a time for attaining goals.
   e. Pick a time for evaluating policy and plans.
   f. Pick a time for terminating this alliance and each part of policy and plans.
5. Conclude with reassuring physical contact and some quiet time.

7

Elevating "Second-Class" Relationships to "First-Class" Relationships:
Betty's story

A great many men and women are reluctant to examine their relationships with members of the opposite sex. This became particularly noticeable when we tried to enlist as research subjects some friends and the participants in Emily's workshops, asking them to try out the "We Process" to clarify and improve their relationships (and record or tape the interaction for us). Usually they were quite willing—unless the relationship to be improved was with a member of the opposite sex.

It soon became apparent, from the excuses they used to avoid becoming "research subjects," that many were putting relationships with the opposite sex into two distinct categories—first-class ones (those in which a man and woman fall in love and commit themselves exclusively to one another forever) and second-class ones (those in which sex is not a factor or, if it is, where there is no "forever" commitment). And they did not want to use the "We Process" with opposite-sex partners in either category but for different reasons.

When it came to "second-class" relationships, most felt that these were not important enough to justify the time and emotional effort involved in establishing a short-term alliance. In fact, they seemed to think that second-class relationships could not even be improved upon. They were often seen as inferior "make-dos"—time fillers until the "real" thing came along.

The real thing, of course, was a "first-class" relationship but even when men and women were involved in this kind of a relationship, they were still hesitant to look at it too closely. This attitude is not surprising. In our society, there is a widely prevalent "mystique" about relationships between men and women, a belief that love is something that can happen to you when you look good and use the right toothpaste. It is a state you just fall into when you meet the "right person." It is nothing you do anything about, and it can strike when you least expect it. You can suddenly catch the eye of some attractive stranger across the room and just know that you are in love. You are then a helpless victim, so folklore has it, unless that love is reciprocated. If it is, if he or she whispers the magic words "I love you," the rest is automatic. "Naturally," if you really love each other, you'll want to get married—or at least live together. And "naturally," if your love is "real" and strong enough, you will be happy and will want to stay together for the rest of your lives no matter what crises and opportunities come your way. These beliefs are so powerful that even among the brightest and best-educated, there seems to be a lack of recognition that the building of a loving relationship is an act of continuous creation. Though very worthwhile, it is a difficult job, one that must be done consciously and deliberately, one that is never finished.

Unfortunately, what many people think is "love" is nothing more than a series of delightful romantic fantasies—wish dreams that would not survive the pinch test of reality. They imagine that this special person will automatically understand them, never be unhappy with them, won't give them the problems other people have given them and, in short, will give them what they want, when and how they want it—and without being told.

There is nothing wrong with romantic fantasies if you recognize them for what they are. It is great fun to have them. All love relationships start out with them. But they are just a bubbly phase and don't make a strong base to build on. Partners who try to keep the bubbly kind of love, who think love thrives on mystery, don't reveal themselves honestly to one another for fear that this could end the relationship; they hesitate to state explicitly what they want from their partner and what they are willing to give. Their relationship is based on illusion and when the illusion disappears, so does the love. And the cost of beginning a relationship with someone under the spell of an illusion is high; our divorce rate tells the story on a national basis, but it is the individual tragedies that are the most poignant.

Many people use up their lives sitting back and waiting for love to take care of everything. A particularly dramatic example is Ruth—bright, attractive, thirty-nine years old and suffering from terminal cancer. She recently remarked, "If I had known I was going to die so soon, I wouldn't have wasted all those years with my lover, Philip. When I thought I was going to live until I was eighty, I felt I had plenty of time to just sort of let little differences work themselves out. I see now our relationship never really was good—day-to-day solid good, I mean. Oh, it started out wildly romantic when we were each married to someone else and we took all sorts of risks just to be together. That made the whole thing an adventure, and the sex was great. But when we got our divorces and started living together, things just didn't work out. We were suspicious and possessive and kept each other from forming new relationships—even with members of the same sex. Even though we had more frustration than pleasure, I stayed because he said he loved me and would take care of me for life. I thought I had a sure thing. But now my lifetime is going to be a short one and Philip isn't around. He found somebody else and it's too late for me to do the same; who would want a lover who is dying of cancer?"

Ironically, lack of love wasn't the problem between Ruth and Philip; it was that their personalities and life styles, which fit so well when they were having an exciting affair, did not mesh so well when they attempted a full-time, committed, monogamous relationship. Because they saw no other alternative, their failure to successfully establish this sort of traditional relationship left them disappointed and bitter.

They believed, like so many people in our society, that if you love someone and he loves you, you *should want* and *should be able to establish* a sexually monogamous relationship for a lifetime. Though there is nothing wrong with wanting this kind of relationship, it simply isn't going to be possible or right for every man and woman—even for those who love each other.

The problem is that we have glorified one relationship pattern so much that men and women don't realize they have many other options. And when they do, they usually devalue these other options. How many times have you heard a man or woman refer to someone of the opposite sex as "just a friend"? In reality, this "friend" may be closer to them than a sexual partner, and may stay a friend for a lifetime as lovers come and go. Yet still the phrase "just a friend" is used as a disclaimer—an acknowledgment that this relationship couldn't possibly have the significance of a relationship with a sexual partner.

On the other hand, if a couple who enjoy one another's company get together over a period of time primarily for sex and without being "in love" or making plans for the future, both they and their friends tend to discount the relationship. To declare you are having an ongoing relationship based on sex rather than love is the same as confessing you are engaged in a second-class relationship. A "just sex" relationship has no more status than a "just friends" one. At best it is looked down on as "not going anywhere"; at worst, it is seen as shallow and meaningless in spite of the fact there may be much caring and it may be giving both parties exactly what they need or want at the time. Why should any sexual relationship—with a person married to someone else, or somebody who doesn't seem like long-time material because of religion, race, personality or age—why should any relationship that nourishes both partners be demeaned just because there isn't much hope that it will lead to marriage or go on for very long?

It is the attitude that deep caring and sex and durability are somehow tied together, or should be, that causes all of us sometimes to go after what we don't want and to deny ourselves simple pleasures available for the asking. Many times people will seek sex when what they really want is tenderness, affection, stroking and contact with the warm body of a member of the opposite sex. Other times they needlessly turn down the opportunity for sex that could be delightful and that would hurt nobody. But what is even worse, such an attitude causes many people, in order not to be thought shallow, immoral or stupid enough to get involved in "dead-end" relationships, to make disastrous, inappropriate and short-lived "lifetime commitments" when what they really want is some in-depth caring and emotional support and/or some glorious, passionate sex at a particular time.

Fortunately, it is possible to clear our minds of these old attitudes that make us compare one kind of relationship with another when it serves no purpose except to cause us to look down on some that are very good and avoid others that could be good if we'd work on them a bit. It is possible to learn to structure new kinds of relationships with the opposite sex—relationships with a commitment, not to marriage, not to staying in love forever, not to satisfying all needs, but a commitment to help one another get and/or keep something really wanted at the time. And if having sex is part of the agreement, that is fine, and if it isn't, that is fine, too.

Such relationships won't just happen, won't just develop "naturally." You'll have to deliberately expand your mind and you'll have to work against your cultural conditioning. You'll have to give up the notion that exploring and structuring a relationship will ruin it. You'll have to carefully consider people who seem at first glance to be poor prospects for any kind of relationship. And you'll have to consider doing things that you've never done before, some that your friends may call stupid and that you will sometimes suspect are stupid, too. And you'll have to prepare yourself to discover more truly worthwhile members of the opposite sex than you will have time for and to feel much, much loved by them—for that will certainly happen, too.

Although Betty had long agreed with these ideas intellectually, she came to terms with them emotionally during the writing of this book. She became one of her own "research subjects" and applied the "We Process" to two supposedly "second-class" relationships with men—one a "just friends" relationship and one a sexual relationship with a married man that might never "go anywhere."

BETTY'S STORY

When my twenty-four-year-long marriage ended in divorce, I decided never to make another long-term commitment. After all, that lifetime promise I had blithely made at eighteen to love and be faithful to one man forever proved to be impossible to keep in my forties. And, in breaking that promise, I had hurt my husband a lot, disrupted my children's lives and subjected myself to a lot of stress. I was terrified even of loving a man again because I thought love *had* to lead to that same sort of a lifetime commitment I had made—and broken—before. I knew I could never make a promise like that again in good faith.

And so, as a single woman, I tried to have love without commitment. The in-depth relationships I had were with men selected because, although I had deep feelings for them, it was clear they would not be around for very long. Though these liaisons were beautiful, they were also very painful. What happened was that, although I knew they could not go on for very long, my conditioning worked against me and I "fell in love" in spite of my resolution not to. Soon I found myself hoping for a lifetime commitment even when I knew this was impossible—as with a man many years my junior who had strong family and political ties in a foreign country where I would be socially unacceptable as his mate. When a love affair would end, although I had known from the beginning that it was going to, I felt as abandoned and betrayed as any wife whose husband has deserted her. The problem was that I had only outmoded attitudes and my past experiences to guide me; I had not developed a positive short-term viewpoint, the ability to make a supportive short-term alliance or the skill of bringing closure to a relationship. I really did not know how to take good care of a relationship while I had it, to use it well—and then to let it go.

Finally, deciding that loving someone was too painful, I tried to avoid it by carefully seeking an occasional temporary sexual relationship that had neither love nor commitment. This kind of relationship is the easiest to find. Today, a lot of men and women, disappointed and disillusioned by the failure of lifetime commitments, have decided not to make any sort of commitment at all. Linking love and commitment and believing that either will trap and hurt them, they have sworn off both.

Thus many of the men I met at this time had "rules" against getting emotionally involved just as rigid and confining as the old "love you forever" ones. As a result, the swearing off of traditional commitments wasn't quite the joyous and carefree experience I had expected.

It wasn't easy to just relax and enjoy the moment—not when we were both being so cautious and "cool" and trying to guard against any feeling except sexual passion. However, there were un-forgettable moments during this period—peak times of passion and fun and playfulness and caring, but these moments were only highlights in a long emotional desert of loneliness and desperation and sadness.

Sometimes I would get so frustrated with the man-woman struggle that I'd just withdraw from any contact with men. Frequently, these times were my happiest. I learned to get emotional support from family and friends and work—and to really enjoy celibacy. But I knew that until I came to terms with my feelings about men, I would not be leading a fulfilled life—at least my idea of a fulfilled life. I knew, though, that I had to learn to let men into my life in ways that would be pleasurable and nourishing and growth-promoting for all of us. I began to realize that I was going to have to learn how to develop relationships that were not only different from what I'd had in the past and different from what others thought I should have, but different from what I expected. I knew I was the only person who could create the type of relationships that would work for me, and yet I didn't know how to do it. I decided I'd start by taking a look at what I really needed and give up going after what I thought I should have.

After all, I no longer needed a man in my life for the same reasons I did at eighteen. Then, sexual relationships outside of marriage were frowned upon; the only way either my husband or I could get our sex needs met was to get married. At that time, with no education or skills at making a living, I needed a man to support me (or felt I did and society reinforced that belief). And I wanted to have children.

Today I want different things from men. I still want sex, of course, but society is now more "permissive." Not only can I have sex outside of marriage, I can even carry on sexual relationships with more than one man without encountering too much social disapproval. I still want the companionship of men, but I don't have to marry to get that. And I want the special feeling of being protected and cherished that I get from being held in a man's arms—but that feeling can sometimes be just as good when the man isn't my husband or lover, when we are "just friends." This doesn't mean I may never again want a monogamous sexual arrangement, but it does mean that I like to have a lot of different men in my life for a lot of different reasons.

With a changed viewpoint toward love and commitment and having the "We Process" to help me build first-class relationships, I was ready for Mark when I met him. When he and I spotted each other across the room at an early-morning meeting, it was "like" at first sight.

Mark, forty-one, was a medium-sized muscular man with a pirate-like black beard, a smile that invited me to smile back and a sadness in his blue eyes that made me want to hold him close and stroke his hair. I smiled at him; he walked over to me, and we started chatting as if we had known each other for ages. We spent the entire day together—going for a long walk at the beach and having dinner late in the day at a romantic little shoreline restaurant. We started seeing one another frequently. Soon I found it impossible not to entertain some romantic fantasies about having an exclusive, moonlight-and-roses type of relationship with him. While I was going out with a number of other men, none had the special qualities of gentleness and lovingness that he had. And I was getting tired of the "dating game" and thought it might be nice to have just one "romantic" partner for a while.

However, Mark told me that he was involved with another woman and that although they were having problems, he was hoping to work them out. So it looked as though the only relationship possible for us was to be "just friends"—something that at that point still seemed second-best to me. But I had a "hidden agenda." I figured that when his present relationship "blew up" he and I would establish a man-woman sexual relationship. Mark didn't have the same "hidden agenda" I had, but he had one. What he wanted was a close, but definitely nonsexual, relationship with a woman—something he had never had. He wanted to learn to understand women better, to have a confidante who was more sensitive than most men he knew and a friend he could be himself with, devoid of pretense. In his "traditional relationships"—first with his wife and then, after his divorce, with his present girl friend—he had always felt responsible for the interaction. He made all the plans, did all the paying and felt that he had to continually "please" his female partner. He wanted an equal relationship with an assertive woman. Since he'd never been able to have this with a sexual partner (and didn't believe he could), it was important to him that our relationship not be sexual. But I didn't find out all this until later.

Since, like many couples, we didn't talk about our sexual wants and expectations, the easiness we had felt with one another at first began to fade. About a month after we met, I even began to ask myself what was really in this relationship for me. After all, I was dating other men, I had more friends than I had time for and my writing was demanding a lot of my attention. Spending time with him seemed to be more bother than it was worth. I realized that it was necessary either to discard the relationship or to see clearly what was in it for me and how to get what I wanted. I decided to ask him to do the "We Process" with me.

It wasn't an easy thing to do. It is risky to say to someone, particularly someone you find sexually attractive, that you want to discuss your relationship with him. I thought he might say, "What relationship? You aren't my girl friend." So I played it safe and told him I wanted to test a technique Emily and I had designed for the book and would he cooperate. When he said he would, I felt a vast relief.

Doing the "We Process" with Mark brought out many tender feelings in both of us. When we shared what we liked about each other and our relationship, our voices frequently trembled with emotion, and at one point, I put my head on his shoulder and we both stopped talking for several minutes while we calmed down and got our bearings. I got so flustered from hearing only positive things instead of the usual advice and suggestions for improvement that I hurried through the process and even did part of it out of sequence. However, we managed to accomplish our goal —to clarify what we wanted and structure our relationship so we could get what would make both of us feel good.

As it turned out, Mark and I essentially wanted the same thing from each other: a bond with a person of the opposite sex we could trust, someone we could be open with, be ourselves with, ask for help from and give help to. In short, we wanted a partner, a pal. The only place where our "wants" varied considerably had to do with sex. Mark wanted a nonsexual relationship because in the past his relationships with women had been "one way." He always had to be strong, to be supportive. This time he wanted to be free to ask for help—to be "weak" now and then. I, on the other hand, wanted a lover, or thought that I did, for I believed a lover was the only person I could count on to be supportive of me. My husband had been a very supportive person—taking care

of me when I was sick, comforting me when I was emotionally upset—and I associated that kind of behavior with a sexual partner.
Believing that a relationship with a man had to be sexual in order
for me to be taken care of, I hadn't even asked myself if sex with
Mark was what I really wanted. I found him charming and attractive and thus just took it for granted that sex would be part of our
relationship.

It was quite a surprise to me to discover the relief I felt when I
found I could have a close, warm and supportive relationship
without sex. For years sex had loomed as all-important in my interactions with men—particularly at the start of relationships. In
fact, most times what happened sexually determined if there
would even be a relationship. Thus, every time I went out with a
new man who was attractive and who seemed to be relationship
material, I worried—would he want to go to bed with me, what
should I do and how would having or not having sex affect a potential relationship? Because of my assumptions about the importance of sex, dating became a nerve-wracking "test" instead of a
relaxed getting-to-know-you process.

Now I realize there can sometimes be advantages to a man and
woman giving themselves the luxury of time—time to find out
what is possible between them—before deciding sex will be part of
their relationship. And I can see one major disadvantage to the
sexual liberation movement. While it has "liberated" many of us
from a lot of sexual hang-ups, it has also led to a tendency for
many people to jump into bed immediately if there is any sexual
spark at all between them.

I see now that many times in the past when a man and I were
physically attracted to one another, sex quite soon became the
main focus of our relationship and other things we might do for
one another—i.e., provide intellectual stimulation, playfulness,
tenderness, moral support—were pushed to the background or
never even discovered. The platonic relationships I had were limited to men I didn't find very exciting and thus were *platonic by
default* and not by choice. I believe that often they didn't develop
into anything particularly special because they started from a negative base—being based on what wasn't there instead of what was
there.

After much discussion, Mark and I decided that what would
serve us best would be to have a nonsexual alliance and to become

one of each other's major support and comfort persons, one of the tender circle of dependable, intimate friends every person needs. Following is a bit of our actual dialogue as we decided on this important goal during the "We Process":

BETTY: Is it all right when I'm feeling really, really bad if I call you at three in the morning? I'm not sure I've ever done that with anyone but it is important to me to know I can.

MARK: Sure, but can we have a mutual thing? Sometimes I feel pretty bad too.

BETTY: I think we've just come across our first relationship goal —mutual comfort.

MARK: Mutual support.

BETTY: Mutual support and comfort. Support, including helping each other eat better and exercise more. And the comfort —feeling free to give each other our feelings. I want this to be our major relationship goal—to feel O.K. to call each other to talk and to do things together that are good for our bodies and souls. However, we need to make sure our relationship entails more than just getting together to cry on each other's shoulder about our other relationships. There has to be something of value going on between us.

MARK: There is. I care a lot for you. I'd like to see you get what you want out of life. If I can help you get what you want in any way, that is the way I'd like to help you.

One benefit of the "We Process" that Mark and I particularly enjoy is that now what we do with and for each other is no longer restricted by the fact that he is a man and I am a woman and that we must stay in set "roles." Instead, our relationship is governed by a contract of our own making. I feel free to ask Mark to help me with things that in the past I'd only have asked of a girl friend or sexual partner. When I needed some minor surgery, Mark took me to the doctor and waited anxiously until I was finished. He helped me to the car as carefully as a Boy Scout with an old lady and inquired solicitously how I felt. At home, he had me go to bed to rest while he fixed my dinner. He's also helped me get my house ready for a party, loaned me money, and gone shopping with me for new clothes—advising me from a man's point of view which styles and colors suited me best.

Mark's life, too, has been enriched in unexpected ways through our unusual alliance. With me, he's been able to express feelings he's held in all his life—feelings he's never been able to express to a sexual partner or male friend before, for fear they might consider him unmanly or self-pitying. I've held him in my arms as he sobbed out some of the sorrow he feels over his failing love relationship; I've been a sounding board for him to spill out the resentments he feels over his marriage—one in which he felt stuck and unappreciated in the traditional male role.

We take quite a bit of ribbing about our relationship from our friends. Some women think I'm stupid to "waste so much time" on a man who has a steady girl friend and who doesn't even take me to expensive places or buy me presents. Several men have suggested to me that "for my own good" I consider the possibility that Mark is "queer" since he doesn't want sex with me. On the other hand, some of his friends think he is being taken advantage of because he does so many things for me and isn't getting sex.

Looking at our relationship through the eyes of others, it is easy to see why people are so suspicious. Men and women just don't usually spend as much time together as we do unless they have a sexual relationship. And someone watching us together might wonder whether our relationship really is "innocent." We seem always to be making physical contact in some way or other—not to be sexy but to be affectionate or playful. We hug, we kiss, we rub each other's backs and sometimes we gently touch each other on the arm or shoulder for comfort or just to say, "I love you." And because we love and like and trust each other we also have a lot of fun—a no-holds-barred wrestling match on the beach, a fight with loaded "squirt guns" or simply taking a quiet walk in the park.

If I had to describe in one word my feeling about my relationship with Mark, the word would be "gratitude"—gratitude that I didn't discount or discard it because it didn't seem to fit into the traditional male-female pattern or because, at first, it didn't look as though I'd get what I wanted. But when I opened up my mind to the possibilities of our relationship, I ended up getting much more than I expected. Mark and I call each other "blood brothers" and our relationship has elements of all the positive relationships I've ever had with men—with my brothers, my father, my husband, my lovers—but it lacks the boundaries that have encompassed and limited these relationships. For the only boundaries we recognize are those of our own making.

We don't know how long our relationship will go on. It could be a month, six months, or years. Things could change drastically if he were to break up with his girl friend and find a new sexual companion who could give him the playfulness and understanding he gets from me. Or if I were to find a deep emotional involvement with a man and decide to live with him. But that's O.K.; we expect our relationship to change—maybe many times. We've already talked about that. When circumstances change we'll make a new alliance. Though we know now we'll always be something special to each other, we can't possibly know now what that will be and so it doesn't concern us.

Maybe, at this point, you are wondering if I am advocating nonsexual friendships with the opposite sex in lieu of sexual relationships. Not at all. As far as I'm concerned, sexual relationships are necessary to my well-being and emotional fulfillment and chances are, you feel the same way. I am simply suggesting that the world is full of a number of wonderful people of the opposite sex and that if we limit our relationships with them either to sexual ones—with touching—or to "platonic by default" ones—without touching—or if we insist that in sexual relationships we either have no commitment at all or the promise of a lifetime together, we simply won't be able to enjoy as many people as we will if we expand our ideas about what is possible between men and women and take advantage of what is really available.

Though it has been hard for me to give up the idea of finding a one-and-only to satisfy all of my needs forever, it seems to be even harder for many of my friends. My "short-term" attitude greatly disturbs some who are still hoping I'll run across "Mr. Right" and settle down safe and secure for the rest of my life. Every time I go out with a new man, they ask anxiously, "Did you like him? Will you see him again?" And I can feel the implied question, "Is he a potential husband?"

Being constantly measured against a traditional standard and found wanting (what's wrong with you that you can't find a husband?) makes it hard for me to feel the path I've chosen is O.K. and, undoubtedly, this sort of social pressure keeps a lot of other people from even seeing the possibilities of new kinds of relationship patterns. Thus, when I met a man named John recently and discovered, after a few weeks, there was something definitely going on between us (caring, a strong sexual attraction, mutual interests), I steeled myself for my friends' reactions when I announced I had a new relationship.

"Tell me about him," they said, and I began, "He is fifty, handsome, intelligent, has a good job, and he is interested in a relationship with me." They smiled approvingly until I added, "And he is married."

Immediately, they discounted him as a potential partner and, deciding that the relationship could not possibly be worthwhile, said things like:

"You can't trust a married man. They always stay with their wives."

"You'll get hurt. He'll just use you and leave you."

"You are wasting your time. There is no future in that kind of relationship."

And finally, "Why is it you always get involved with men who can't make a commitment?"

What they meant by that last remark, of course, was that if I was running my life right I'd be able to find a man willing and able to make a *lifetime* commitment. They couldn't understand that there could be value in any other kind of relationship, any other kind of commitment. Because he was married, a lot of other women had refused to go out with John. Their eyes on the future, they didn't even look to see what was possible in the here and now. What I saw was a man who, although legally married, was emotionally detached and "available"—a man who was lonely and loving and willing to get involved. I saw a man who was living at home (although in his own quarters) because he wanted to be near his children. I saw a man who didn't "sneak around"—who took me out openly, introduced me to his children and his friends and who was free to stay away from home as often as he wanted.

Therefore, I ignored my friends' advice. I knew there was something in the relationship for me even if I wasn't exactly sure what form our relationship would eventually take. What I wanted was for John and me to be able to spend enough time together to discover what was possible between us. I wanted to avoid what had happened to me a number of times in the past when either I or a man friend had gotten annoyed or bored and just drifted away before we had the opportunity to examine possibilities sufficiently. Because I thought we needed a framework that would provide enough emotional security for us to hang in there while we were exploring, I wanted us to do the "We Process."

Asking John to do the "We Process" was even harder than asking Mark. But a natural opportunity to bring up the subject occurred when John, about a month after we met, asked me to go on a trip with him. Since I could not take time off from my writing, he said it would be all right to spend part of the time on the trip working. I felt it would be worthwhile to clarify both our expectations for the trip and our relationship. My fear was that when I asked him to talk about our relationship, he'd think I was trying to tie him down to a commitment he wasn't ready to give. And that is exactly what he did think.

"I'm not sure our relationship is at that point yet" was his comment when I gave him a copy of the "We Process" and suggested we try it together. However, I soon convinced him you didn't have to know each other a long time or even be heavily involved to do it. Frankly, I think it was the idea of contributing something to the book that made him agree to do it. Maybe it also made it safer for him that way.

Validating our relationship and stating our wants and don't-wants taught us more about each other in an hour than most couples learn about each other in months. This is how we started out:

JOHN: I'm nervous because I don't know what it all entails. I worry I'll be exposed too much. I hope you'll be gentle with me. I'll try to be as interesting as I can but I'm not used to these things.

BETTY: The point is not to try to make this an interesting interview, but to try to be as honest with your feelings and wants as you can be. I'm nervous about doing it too because I only do it with people who are important to me. I'm nervous that maybe I pushed you into doing it and maybe you won't like me because you think I am too pushy or something. Anyway, let's start by telling each other what we like about each other and the relationship.

I found out that John thinks I am lively, dynamic, sexy, humorous, hard-working, entertaining and open-minded. He liked it that I had about the same energy level he did and wanted to spend about the same amount of time on things he did—such as pausing at a museum to view a particular painting, washing dishes, shopping, swimming, etc. He found out that I think he is intelligent, kind, an outstanding sexual partner and a man who truly believes in the equality of the sexes. I told him, "You are the kind of person I can appreciate more the longer I know you because there are a lot of things you don't show right away. There is a lot of tenderness that I didn't see at the beginning. One thing I really like is your cuddliness. You are like a great big cuddly teddy bear. I like the way at night you grab on to me and hold me really hard—so hard I can't move away. That feels good. I feel wanted and secure. I also like the fact that you give me space to be by myself to do things without you and that you do things without me."

Giving compliments was great, but the "We Process" also enabled us, right at the beginning of our relationship, to express some don't-wants—some things we didn't like about each other or the relationship—before they got to be a problem. For example, John was able to let me know in the kind way that the "We Process" provides for that he thought I talked too much about my work and that he'd prefer sometimes talking about other things. He was able to let me know that he pays a lot of attention to the way a woman looks and would like me also to pay more attention to my appearance and grooming. And he let me know that he didn't want me to ask questions about how he spent his time away from me since he didn't want a seven-day-a-week commitment.

What he wanted was an ongoing relationship—one in which we made a commitment to see each other once or twice a week and one in which we shared, not only a loving sexual relationship, but also many interests, including the taking of courses and classes together. But he wanted to be free to go out with others, as I did. When his marriage ended emotionally about four years ago, both he and his wife had started dating others by mutual consent. He had never dated much before he was married, and still wanted the freedom to explore other relationships. I wanted the same sort of relationship guidelines and goals, but I also wanted more. I wanted to be able to share my feelings with him without his getting defensive or making assumptions.

The day we set off on our trip, I mentioned to him I felt nervous. I hadn't spent so much time alone with a man for some time and I was not sure how I would handle the enforced intimacy. He assumed I was saying I didn't want to go and he got very upset—offering to return that night if I was unhappy.

Because we had done the "We Process," I was able to remind him how well it had worked when we just listened to the verbal expression of feelings without assuming we were being criticized and without taking it for granted that a change was wanted—unless it was specifically requested. He relaxed, and this helped set the tone; not just for our trip, but for our subsequent interaction. Now he can usually listen to my feelings without getting defensive or giving unwanted advice. If he forgets, I gently remind him. And he reminds me, sometimes, too.

It is much easier now for him to share his feelings with me. I'm certain that doing the "We Process" at the beginning of our relationship established a habit in both of us of giving each other feedback—of letting the other know our feelings, our wants and don't-wants, and when the other's behavior is causing pleasure or pain.

Settling on the terms of our alliance got our relationship off to a good start in many ways. We now know what is expected of us and how the other person can be expected to act under certain conditions. John and I know for sure that we will get together at least one or two days a week. We plan those days well in advance and are then free to make other plans—knowing we won't disappoint or upset each other. Nobody has to wait for a phone call. Either of us can call. Nobody has to feel unsure about whether or not to make plans, to worry about having a too full calendar or an empty one. Nobody has to get the feeling he or she isn't wanted because the other is too busy for a get-together. This structure, instead of confining us, frees us. Knowing I'll see him on a certain day enables me to concentrate on my work and think about other things. Because we have some structured meeting times, something to count on no matter what, we are able to be more spontaneous with the rest of our time, sometimes inviting one another to do something as a special little bonus. These times add a lot of fun and pleasure to our relationship, but we couldn't count on them alone to nourish and sustain us.

Along with increasing our behavioral freedom through guidelines of our own making, the fact that we have a firm, albeit short-term, alliance has freed us emotionally. Having a structure and continuity to our relationship gives us emotional security and we are thus able to relax and share more of our feelings, hopes and fears. In the past, when I had relationships with men that were not clarified, I was frequently afraid to "rock the boat"—to be myself—because I feared that might drive them away. Thus, I often acted very cool and controlled, and they never got to know the passionate, emotional, bright but sometimes irrational, tender-but-strong Betty.

John is very familiar with that Betty. Because I feel safe in the relationship—knowing we have continuity yet limits—I can let myself be emotionally vulnerable. At times, I am very romantic, writing him poetry and getting choked up over the lyrics of certain love songs. At times, I am childlike and vulnerable—curling up in his arms and wanting to be reassured that I am loved and cherished. And, at times, I am just plain jealous and possessive. At these times, I get upset when I think he is going out with someone else and I want to punish him—by making dates with many others, even when I don't feel like it, or by telling him I won't see him anymore.

However, I don't do these things, because underneath my insecurity, I have the security of our commitment. Instead, I have another way of coping with feelings I wish I didn't have: I share them with John. He realizes there are some things I just need to say. He has learned that if I can get them out into the open that is all I need and that I am not pressuring him to make promises he doesn't want to make and wouldn't keep if he made—i.e., never going out with anyone else. Because of being able to express our feelings, it seems that the uncomfortable ones and the desire for revenge just aren't as frequent as they used to be. In addition to learning new ways to structure relationships, I'm learning new ways to deal with my feelings.

It isn't easy to change the thought and behavior patterns of a lifetime, and to claim that I can always do with equanimity what I think should be done would be dishonest. But I am committed to learning new and more rewarding relationship patterns, committed to giving up behavior that implies a relationship either lasts a lifetime or is worthless, behavior that cost me so many good relationships in the past. I know that I'll have to work hard and long to rid myself of all of my old automatic emotional responses that don't pay off, but working on myself is fun when I have loving partners to help me.

Because John and I have a relationship "policy"—our short-term alliance—we are able to deal with his and my bouts of jealousy, insecurity and hurt feelings. Probably the area that causes the greatest amount of conflict and hurt feelings is the amount of time—above and beyond our set time—we should spend together.

Some weeks, when John is at loose ends or feeling especially devoted to me or maybe just lonely, he wants to get together almost every night. I start feeling "crowded"—unable to concentrate on my work or see my other friends as much as I'd like. On the other hand, particularly when I'm feeling depressed or my work isn't going well, I want to see him more than he seems to want to see me.

If we hadn't done the "We Process" our relationship might have exploded several different times in recriminations and blaming, with one or the other of us saying something like "If you really loved me, you'd want to spend more time with me." Or "If you really loved me, you wouldn't pester me." As it is, we discuss the fact that we do have a set policy about how much time we will spend together and we take a look at whether we want to renegotiate that policy or not. So far, we've decided to stick with it because it gives us both enough space to have other interests and other relationships as well as time to share a lot together.

However, we always keep in mind that our alliance is not a fixed, immutable contract that must be adhered to without reconsideration. We know our contract can be changed by mutual consent and that keeps us from feeling trapped. Therefore, we have the luxury of knowing we can take all the time we need before we make a change. We may make a change someday, but we won't make it under pressure or to conform to what others expect. We will make it when both of us are ready.

In the meantime, despite our own occasional self-doubts and despite some criticism from friends who want to see us move predictably to the next plateau of involvement—i.e., an exclusive commitment—we are trying to make the most of what we have right now instead of worrying about what we will have in the future. And what do we both have right now? A lot of immediate physical and emotional pleasure, someone to share our triumphs and failures with, someone we can cry and laugh with, and someone to be involved with in a dynamic relationship. We have the pleasure of learning about each other while knowing we are committed, but we are also aware we can and will change our commitment periodically. And, most important, we have the freedom to say "I love you" to each other without fearing it has to lead to something (i.e., marriage, living together). We both know we are getting all we can out of every moment. And, as for me, for the first time in my life I'm looking a lot more at what a man can give me than at what he isn't able to give me. And that feels great.

8

Defusing Money-Sex Power Lines in Man-Woman Relationships:
Sex

Today the sex act has quite a different place in a relationship for most people than it did in the past. Formerly, intercourse with a partner who was really cared about usually occurred at the end of a long courtship and signified the beginning of a lifetime relationship. Today, the sex act often occurs at the beginning of a relationship—as a means of getting to know one another.

What happens at that beginning—at that first sexual experience —can determine to a large extent if a couple will develop an ongoing relationship and, if so, what the relationship will be like. The way a couple gets over this sexual hurdle—and it is a hurdle— significantly affects their feelings about each other and about themselves as sexual beings.

When you have sex, you put yourself into another person's hands—symbolically as well as literally. You reveal parts of yourself ordinarily kept under wraps. Sometimes it is just your naked body but sometimes—and this is what can affect your relationship most profoundly—it is your naked soul. When you expose your vulnerability and your partner recognizes and respects it, a tender bond of trust develops between you. In addition, if your sex is a caring and pleasant experience, it creates what Masters and Johnson call a "pleasure bond"—a force that occurs between two people when they give each other pleasure. When people—whether friends, lovers or a parent and child—do things together for mutual enjoyment, they develop special close feelings for each other. Since sex with all of the affectionate touching that usually goes with it is one of the most fundamental and intense ways human beings have of sharing pleasure, it can be a powerful cohesive force. On the other hand, if things don't work out well—i.e., if you have put one another down instead of building one another up, because you have exposed yourself, it is easy to feel betrayed and resentful. Thus, having sex with someone will greatly affect how you perceive, treat and feel about him or her afterward, even when not having sex.

What makes a sexual relationship one that is worthwhile and memorable is the caring that two people show each other. To care for someone doesn't mean you have to be "in love" in the traditional sense—i.e., to want to live with or marry him. Instead, it implies a concern with and a liking that you express in your behavior. And in order to have such a caring relationship, a man and woman must feel and act like partners.

The best way to make a first-time sexual experience into a partnership is to act like gentle aggressors—i.e., for each person to be willing to take the initiative to get what he wants, as well as to take the responsibility for making it a satisfying experience for both. A partnership experience like that can leave both people feeling as though they have been given a gift by someone who values them highly. And this is possible whether this event is the beginning of a new relationship, a new phase in an ongoing one or a once-in-a-lifetime experience.

In this chapter we are going to tell you how to turn a first-time sexual experience into a partnership activity and thus to reduce some of the anxiety, make the experience a pleasurable one for both and bring about caring closure. With so many people having more first-time sexual experiences than ever before and having them earlier in a relationship—many times with people they have just met or barely know—we felt this new sort of sexual etiquette —one based on the principles of gentle aggression—was necessary. To find out what concerned people about first-time sex as well as to discover what their partners could do to put them at ease we interviewed many men and women—friends, people in Emily's workshops and strangers who heard about our project and volunteered their experiences. And of course, as with everything else in this book, much comes directly from our own struggles to have caring sexual relationships.

Chances are you have never thought much about what you might do to put your partner at ease or what he or she might do to put you at ease the first time you have sex. This is not surprising. Few people take the time to plan for gracious sexual activities the way they do for other at-home activities. In fact, most people still take a dim view of the sex act as an honorable and worthwhile way for human beings to relate and show affection. Evidence for this is that relationships that begin almost immediately with the sex act have much less social sanction than those that seem to be based on more "serious" values—like common interests. Many people believe that anyone who reaches out to them in a sexual way after knowing them but a short time is cheap and that they'll be thought cheap if they let their sexual wishes be known too soon. And relationships that are based primarily on sex are looked down on, too. But they shouldn't be.

James Ramey, sociologist and author of *Intimate Friendships*, points out that there are no valid reasons for automatically condemning a relationship because the attraction is purely physical, or a sexual encounter because it takes place soon or is a one-time-only occurrence. As he says,

> Would we condemn a couple for relating only on the social level, or the emotional level, or the intellectual level? I seriously doubt it. I suspect much of the negative labeling of relationships that involve only sexual intimacy are based on either the "Protestant Ethic" or on the theory that a one-night stand with a stranger involves the avoidance of intimacy. Yet even this most minimal of involvement may, and often does, lead to the development of a lifelong relationship. . . . It is easy to condemn people who are unsure of the degree to which they are willing to commit themselves when their limits are geared down to very minimal relating. Yet we all start somewhere, and any kind of a start is a beginning.

Rather than condemning sex that occurs very fast or occurs only once between two people, it is time we began appreciating the importance of sex in fostering better relationships between people. As a start, here is our Gentle Aggressor Etiquette to help men and women who have a sexual interest in each other feel and act like partners during three different periods in their first sexual encounter: before, during and after.

Before

What goes on during the before period—the time when men and women are deciding if they want to and intend to have sex—keeps many relationships from ever getting started. The most common complaint of women is that men make physical advances too soon and too strong. Women don't like "being pawed" and get turned off and angry when a man is pushy. Many a woman has told us that if a man had just been more patient, had given them more time, they probably could have gotten interested. However, when he tried to hurry them, his "demand" turned them off. A sense of urgency is insulting, for it seems as though he doesn't care how she feels but only if she will give in.

Only a few women ever complain that a man they'd like to have sex with won't make a pass. And that's the way it is put—as though it is *his* obligation to take the initiative. They don't say, "I've tried to get him to bed but he won't go." Very few women will ever admit to wanting sex when it isn't offered, and even fewer will take the initiative in making the first sexual overture.

As might be expected, the complaints of men are quite different. They grumble that women act insulted if a man openly lets them know he wants sex, but if he tries to be subtle about his wishes, he is left in doubt as to hers. As one man said, "I expect a woman to say 'no,' but I wish I knew how to find out what a particular woman's 'no' means. Does it mean 'no, not ever'? Or 'not tonight but maybe later'? Or does it mean 'yes, but I need coaxing'?"

Men complain about not being informed as to what a woman wants in regard to sex. The frustration of many men is expressed by one who griped, "I get irritated when I've spent a whole evening with a woman and we have had a lot of fun and talked about lots of things and I am driving her home and yet I don't have the faintest notion as to whether she is going to invite me in and, if she does, what she means by that."

However, problems involving "should we or shouldn't we?" largely disappear when a man and a woman act as if pleasurable sex is a prize that neither owns or has to have but instead is something they can obtain together if they choose to join forces. When this happens, they can talk openly about it. They can take time to ask themselves how they feel toward a particular member of the opposite sex at a particular time, what they'd like from that person in regard to sex and what they think would be realistic and desirable to do. And they can talk, talk, talk.

Suggesting that people talk with one another about sex to make certain they are making a decision both can be happy with, can bring screams of protest. "It takes away the romance," say some. "It's not necessary," say others. "It's cold and calculating." "It's too embarrassing." On and on and on go the excuses. However, they are excuses, not reasons. Excuses for not bringing the subject out into the open where it can be dealt with.

Robert Cromey, an Episcopalian minister and workshop leader, offers a plan that can be of great help in learning to talk more logically and in coming to a decision comfortable for both you and your partner. He suggests that couples ask each other and answer three questions early in their relationship, preferably on their first date. These questions are:

1. Do you find me sexually attractive?
2. Can you fantasize having sex with me?
3. Shall we have sex?

No matter what the answers are to these questions, people know where they stand with one another when they have answered them. Take the first question, for example. As you answer it, what you are becoming aware of and revealing is this: Do you feel a sexual charge when you are with this person or do you react more the way you would toward a sister or brother? That is certainly a straightforward question and neither person should feel insulted no matter how the other replies. We are not all sexually attracted to the same types of people; there is a certain kind of chemistry between people over which we have no control. Sexual attraction does not imply a judgment of worth. We can be highly attracted to people we don't even like or be sexually indifferent to people we admire, respect or even love. Nor does sexual attraction, when it exists, imply the necessity to act on what is felt. It merely denotes the presence of a particular kind of feeling.

The second question—"Can you fantasize having sex with me?" —has to do with how you react to the feeling of attraction. Another way of phrasing it would be to say: Does the thought of having sex with me appeal to you? Is it something pleasurable to think about? Again, a "no" answer should not be considered an insult nor a "yes" answer a request. Though a person might see you (or you him) as sexually attractive, the thought of having sex together may not be appealing for a variety of reasons. For example, you may remind him of a previous lover or a parent; you may be too tall or too short for his comfort, etc. He may not have any idea why the thought isn't appealing but it just isn't.

When you get down to the last question, even if both parties have answered the first two questions in the affirmative, there is still plenty to talk about here. The answer might be "yes," "no," or "I don't know." The last two answers don't necessarily indicate dislike of either the person or the idea of sex. They might indicate a desire not to get involved, not to get involved right now, the presence of other commitments, a lack of interest in sex or in a relationship, a lack of time, etc. Even a "yes" answer on the part of both partners doesn't determine what will happen next. There are still the questions of when and where and under what circumstances. However, when these three questions have been answered, the couple may then plan subsequent get-togethers knowing what to expect. The chances of feeling either insulted or taken advantage of if they don't or do go to bed have been greatly minimized. Being up-front and honest about sex, as about money, frees people to terminate their relationship without rancor or to start building the kind that both can be happy with.

Before foreplay

Let's assume that a couple has discussed these three questions and decided they want sex and they want it tonight. And they have arrived at either her or his home. What can be done to make this first experience a good one? What can each do to make the other feel comfortable and cared about? What should each have already done ahead of time in anticipation of this important occasion?

We shall confine our discussion to first-time sex that takes place in a home rather than a hotel, motel or the back seat of a car because the options in the latter instances are much more limited though the same principles apply but to a lesser degree. Even here each person should stop and think how he can behave to be a good host or guest.

The idea of trying to be a good host to someone you've invited into your home for sex is an idea that doesn't occur to many people or they'd probably be better prepared, and they'd undoubtedly be more gracious.

The host (or hostess) should begin acting like one as soon as the front door closes and the couple is alone in the living room. This is a time of nervousness and anxiety for both people though each person usually thinks he is the one who is in doubt as to what is supposed to happen next and the other knows just what to do.

For purposes of simplicity we shall assume the host is a she since first-time sex occurs more often in her residence than his. However, tips for making your sexual partner feel at home apply equally well to either sex.

What a host can do to make a guest more at ease

WELCOMING RITUALS

It takes a certain amount of time for a person to become comfortable after entering a new environment. It is the responsibility of the host to give the guest this time while doing things to set the mood for what is to follow. By her demeanor or words or both, she should say, "Welcome. Come in and make yourself comfortable."

WHAT TO DO

Take his coat, indicate where you'd like him to sit. (Perhaps the sofa, where you can sit alongside of him later.) Then offer him a drink, a cup of coffee or herb tea, etc. Put soft music on the stereo and then while he is sipping and listening, check on the basic essentials:

1. Make certain your bed linen is clean. If you wouldn't give a

dinner guest a napkin used by somebody else, then you shouldn't expect him or her to have sex on spotted sheets. Newly divorced men seem particularly prone to offend in this way. If you have invited someone to your home for sex and your sheets are soiled or your bedroom is in disarray, it only takes a few minutes to change the sheets and to quickly straighten things up. Extra care must be taken particularly for that first sexual experience so that it won't in any way seem sordid or dirty or cheap, so cleanliness is very, very important. (If you are a guest and are invited to go to bed in dirty sheets, it is O.K. to suggest that they be changed. With a warm and friendly expression on your face and a lilt in your voice, say, "Why don't you get some clean sheets while I pull these off and then we'll make the bed together.")

2. See that a clean towel is laid out for your guest in a conspicuous place in the bathroom. A person can feel very ill at ease if the only choices he has are to dry his hands on an already used towel or to open and close a number of cupboard doors trying to find a clean one. (If you are a guest, it is a good idea to ask where the bathroom is before you make love. You can wash your hands and freshen up and request a clean towel if none is laid out rather than waiting until afterwards and having to run the risk of either groping in the dark or getting the hostess out of bed to get you one.)

3. If you are in doubt about the availability of your lovemaking supplies, check on them. Make certain there is a soft, small clean towel within reach of the bed. Some people keep Kleenex on the nightstand, but a towel is both more efficient and more aesthetic. It is a gracious touch to keep a small stack of velour hand towels in a bedside stand, always ready and available, or perhaps some of the damask napkins your mother used to use at formal dinner parties. They are soft and pretty and just the right size and add a sense of dignity. Keep body lotion or delicately scented oil there, too.

To develop better relationships, as much attention should be paid to creating aesthetic lovemaking centers (and having supplies nearby) as to creating efficient cooking centers or friendly conversation centers. Time spent away from your potential sex partners will be kept to a minimum if, before they arrive, you take as much time to carefully prepare your home for "gracious loving" as you would spend preparing for a dinner party or drop-in guests. Give some thought to having extra niceties available, such as scented candles, peacock feathers, a vibrator, etc.

When your preparations have been completed, return to your guest, sit alongside him and turn down the lights as a signal that you are ready for the next phase. Remember that, as the host, you are responsible for the music and the lighting. Both should be soft and non-intrusive. Having candles around in both the living room and the bedroom is a nice touch, for all faces and bodies are more beautiful by candlelight, and the flickering little flames, reminiscent of a hearth, give a feeling of warmth and comfort.

If the first at-home stage consists of welcoming rituals and preparation, the next stage consists of touching rituals and intercourse. This stage is one in which the emphasis should be on slowing down because anxiety usually causes people to rush. Many times men hurry into intercourse because they are nervous and that gives them something to do when they don't know what else to do or because they think it is up to them to take the lead. Many women allow themselves to be hurried because they, too, are nervous and don't realize they don't have to follow a man's lead. They can take the initiative, and some of the things they initiate can slow things down without getting off course and, in this way, make it a more pleasant, longer-lasting experience for both partners. One of the greatest dangers of a man doing a hurry-up job in first-time sex is that it can give the impression he cares more about her genitals than about her. And a woman who thinks she will slow a man down if she just holds back and doesn't react is off on the wrong track. There is a better way: either partner can initiate activities to promote touching. Sex is a lot more fun if it includes many aspects of touching—not just breasts and genitals but hair, faces, feet, bellies and thighs. Touch here, there and everywhere in tender and playful ways.

Men as well as women like foreplay if they aren't the only ones doing it. And they seldom get enough because women expect to be made love to just as they expect their expenses to be paid for. If sex is going to be a partnership experience, then both men and women must share touching. Both must take the initiative to touch and also ask to be touched.

There are two before-the-sex-act body contact activities that can help a couple get to know one another quickly and keep them from feeling that they are either "being used" or are "using" someone else—feelings that are very unpleasant. These are massaging and bathing.

Either the guest or the host can bring out the body lotion and suggest a massage. Both men and women can be well-prepared guests by carrying with them a minimum of supplies when they go out on a date. It doesn't take much room in her purse for a small bottle of body lotion and a toothbrush. And he should keep in the car at all times a "ditty bag" that contains an extra set of shaving supplies as well as his toothbrush and some body lotion. (It is better to use lotion rather than oil for a massage before first-time sex as some hosts don't like oil on their sheets.)

There are all kinds of ways to massage. One can massage the other all over, but that takes a lot of time and energy. (There are many books on the art of massage, and it is well worth learning, but don't wait until you get good at it to try it.) Or you can take turns massaging certain parts of one another. A combination of shoulders and neck or else feet and ankles are especially good because most people carry a lot of tension in these areas which can be released through touch.

One woman adept at the art of gracious loving makes a practice of offering a new lover a foot-washing-and-massaging ritual she has perfected. Not all accept, but all appreciate the offer. Another suggests a bubble bath. She has found that taking a bath together takes the embarrassment from disrobing in front of someone for the first time. Also playing with the bubbles makes sex seem like good clean fun, and washing his back makes him feel super.

Bathing or showering together before sex is a great excuse for body contact as it is to be expected that you will wash one another all over. It also assures that both bodies will be squeaky clean and fresh so that lovemaking will not be impeded by unpleasant odors. The act of bathing together can be made part of a very lovely welcoming ritual. One popular bachelor we know has done just that.

When he brings a woman to his home for sex for the first time, he seats her on the sofa, gives her a glass of champagne, puts a stack of Mantovanni records on the stereo, sits on the floor at her feet, carefully removes her shoes and gives her a foot massage. When that is over, he takes her into the bathroom, where they shower together, and afterwards they slip into matching blue terry-cloth bathrobes in his and her sizes. He also has another very lovely custom, that of preparing a gourmet meal for her *after* they have had sex. If they have sex in the afternoon, he fixes a dinner of filet mignon with mushrooms and broccoli with hollandaise. If she stays overnight, he fixes her a breakfast of steak and eggs and toasted sourdough French bread. No matter whether their sex was good, bad or mediocre, the lady feels valued. And he makes sure he can show a woman he cares by keeping steak, broccoli and bread in the freezer.

There are many other ways you can prepare yourself to show your sexual partners that you care—both before you have sex and afterwards. Both times are very important. You can be very good at the sex act but ruin the whole experience by not being a thoughtful host. Here are some rules of etiquette that will raise your rating.

1. Keep extra toothbrushes around to offer unexpected overnight guests. Most people feel much more comfortable if they can brush their teeth before going to bed and when they get up in the morning and will appreciate your thoughtfulness.

There are some people—usually women—who wouldn't hesitate to offer a guest toothbrush to a relative or a same-sex friend who decided to spend the night and didn't have one, but wouldn't think of offering it to a sexual companion. Their fear is that if they seem to be prepared for casual sex they will be seen as promiscuous. However, it is the quality of the sex act that makes a person promiscuous—that is, if their sexual encounters are repeatedly self-destructive or thoughtless acts. Thus, when you are gracious and caring—of yourself and your companion—no matter how many sexual experiences you have or how soon in a relationship you have them, you are not promiscuous. So have that toothbrush ready.

2. Have an extra bathrobe—the kind that fits all sizes—available as a hospitable touch. One woman keeps in her closet a man's gold velour "happy coat" type short robe that has special meaning for her. Men love the sensual feel of the fabric and enjoy wearing it after showering or while having breakfast. But what really makes it special to her is that it was a "divorce present" to her from her twenty-five-year-old son, who helped educate and prepare his mom for single life.

3. Speak to your guest about your preferences in regard to his getting up to go home or staying all night—and inquire as to his.

Some men and women feel abandoned when the person they have just had sex with gets up to go home, while some feel imposed upon if he or she stays all night. Don't take it for granted that you know what your guest prefers, and don't assume that he knows what you prefer. Talk about it and decide what to do so that both of you can feel comfortable.

4. Treat your guest as you would a partner, not an opponent, slave or master when the unexpected happens—and it surely will. No matter how well you prepare yourself, you can be certain that everything will *not* go the way you expect it the first time you have sex with someone. It can be as minor as the fact that you both discover you prefer the same side of the bed and feel very uncomfortable and ill at ease on the other side. Or it can be as major as the fact that she suddenly starts to menstruate, gushing all over everything, or he doesn't get an erection. Or a child, supposedly away at college, unexpectedly comes home for the weekend, or— and the list could go on and on. It is what people do and how they treat one another when the unexpected happens that can really cement a relationship or can bring it to an abrupt halt.

In addition, be careful of your expectations. Don't expect first-time sex to be a fantastic experience. If you look upon it as an adventure in playing and caring, it may turn out to be fantastic sex, but if you set yourself up so that you are going to be disappointed *if you don't have fantastic sex*, you *are* going to be disappointed. Frequently women do not have an orgasm the first time they are with a new man. There are plenty of reasons for that but the reasons aren't what is most important. The frequency of the happening is. Also it is not uncommon for a man not to have an erection or to lose it—even young, very virile men. Don't worry about it. This is only the first time. Take it in your stride and there will be a second time.

When something happens that you don't want to happen, don't blame yourself or the other person. Instead share your distress or confusion with your partner so that the message comes over: "I'm sorry but I didn't expect this. What do you suppose we can do about it?" Remember that the purpose of the sex act is to share yourself in an intimate way with another person. It is not orgasm. When you share your feelings without being antagonistic toward yourself or your partner, you are sharing in an intimate way.

Here is how Evelyn shared her feelings with a first-time sexual partner in such a way that it not only made them partners but began a deeply satisfying ongoing relationship.

Evelyn, married for eighteen years, had been celibate for two years after her divorce. It wasn't that she lacked interest in sex but she was afraid that because she had only had sex with her husband, she was too inexperienced and wouldn't be any good in bed. She was convinced any man would be disappointed in her. One evening when her boss, whom she had been dating now and then for six months, brought her home from the theater, she invited him in for a cup of tea as she usually did. In pouring the hot tea, she spilled a good deal of it on her blouse and he jumped up to help her. After determining her burns were not serious, they found themselves kissing and hugging and ended up in bed. It was a lovely, tender experience, but as she came out of her euphoria, she suddenly became painfully aware that the bed they were in was the one she had slept in with her husband for many years. A feeling of somehow being disloyal to her husband overwhelmed her and she missed him and longed for him and started to cry. Though David, her boss, did not understand her tears, they didn't upset him. Though he could have interpreted them as her being disappointed in him, he didn't. Instead, he comforted her and she cried even more, letting out the pain of her loneliness in deep racking sobs. He took her on his lap like a baby, and stroked her hair and temples while she moaned, "I'm just a one-man woman. I'll never find anyone to care about me like my husband." As she cried and repeated the phrases over and over, she began to hear herself and to picture the scene she was involved in. She, naked, was being rocked by a gentle, naked man who had just made love to her and here she was, complaining that no man but her husband would ever care for her. As suddenly as she had begun to cry, she began to laugh, and though David didn't understand the reason for her laughter any more than her tears, he liked it better and soon joined her in it. And in no time at all, they were making love again and beginning a romance that was to last for several years.

What's wrong with one-night stands?

Although first-time sex sometimes signals the beginning of an ongoing relationship, as in the case of Evelyn and David, having sex does not necessarily signify a commitment to a special kind of relationship or even a desire to see each other again. In fact, increasingly often sex between men and women today is a one-time-only occurrence.

However, in our culture, there is a special term for this kind of an event, a derisive one: one-night stand. The thought of a one-night stand is one many people find disgusting, associating it, as they do, with "easy" sex and "cheap" people. Making this connection causes many women to appear unfriendly, to sometimes take offense at a non-pressuring invitation to sex from someone they don't know well or even at just a compliment that implies the giver finds them sexually attractive. It causes men to hesitate to offer invitations, even compliments, for fear they will be interpreted as insults.

In the past, the one-night stand was condemned because it was considered immoral—as were most sexual practices outside of marriage. Though our attitudes toward sex have changed considerably, this kind of sex, solely for the sake of pleasure, is still condemned. Since it is looked down on as shallow, as an avoidance of intimacy, the assumption is that if you were a decent person and if you cared about somebody, you wouldn't just have sex with them once.

It is strange because although a lot of other once-in-a-lifetime adventures shared with somebody (scaling a high mountain peak, dancing all night, watching the sunrise, etc.) are recounted glowingly to friends, it's not that way with a one-night stand. A once-in-a-lifetime sexual experience is seen as something rather tawdry. And the biggest sin seems to be enjoying it and valuing your companion. Though a man can brag about "conquest fucking," how he maneuvered this one or that one into bed, or even tell how he "scored with an old whore and hated himself in the morning," if he had a truly meaningful experience with a woman he respects but doesn't expect to see again, he doesn't mention it. And a woman doesn't dare say she enjoyed a "roll in the hay." Not if she values her reputation.

Old ideas about propriety and virtue die hard but we must put them to rest when they are interfering with basic human needs—the need for companionship, the need for sex and the need to express caring for and receive caring from other people. The censure of one-night stands does just that.

We're not saying that people can flourish on nothing but one-night stands or that everybody should have one or that all one-night stands are good. We're just saying that we had better get over the notion that they are bad because they are a necessary option in the world in which we live and lots of good people are having them.

In the "Brief Encounters" workshops given throughout the United States by the Man-Woman Institute, when the participants are asked how many have had a sexual encounter with a person they thought they'd never see again or, as it turned out, they never saw again, one quarter of the people disclose that they have. Though this ratio is probably not representative of the general population (those who attend these workshops tend to be largely unmarried persons who are considerably above average in intelligence, education and awareness), it is an indication of what is going on. One-time-only sexual experiences must be defended because in today's society we need them and because they have some unique possibilities for enhancing man-woman relationships.

We need to be able to speak of one-night stands with respect for several reasons. In the first place, we have more singles than ever before—approaching 50,000,000. And more and more people are choosing to remain single all of their lives. Though many are involved in committed relationships, many aren't. Though many become involved in ongoing sexual relationships, they aren't all of the time, and some never are. Even in committed relationships or marriage, there is an increasing tendency not to require absolute sexual fidelity, to realize that having a bit of sexual pleasure elsewhere doesn't necessarily hurt the primary relationship and under certain circumstances can even enhance it.

The mobility of people today also makes it necessary that one-night stands become a respectable option. Both men and women, single and married, travel more and move their base of operations more than ever before—for business and for pleasure. It seems foolish to allow being away from your home base to keep you from having sex and/or from enjoying the nourishing experience of sleeping close to a member of the opposite sex you like and who likes you. Travel and moving are draining emotionally and physically. Sometimes a good night's sleep is all that is needed to refresh you but sometimes there are other things that are better. People should be able to do what they need to do in order to feel tip-top as long as nobody is being hurt by their action. They will then be kinder to others and better able to do a good job.

And why should anyone, just because he doesn't have an ongoing sex partner, is on the outs with his partner, likes variety or is away from home, be deprived of the kind and amount of sex that will make him feel his best—and the tenderness, playfulness and ego-building that go with it. Because the sharing of sexual pleasure can make people feel close, more involved with one another, more trusting, more loving toward others, having a number of sexual relationships in a lifetime should be desirable. And so, what's wrong with a one-night stand?

What makes a sexual experience a poor one has nothing to do with the fact that you don't think you will have it with that person again—unless that thought really bothers you and makes you uneasy. In fact, the belief that the only time we shall ever have together is now, can sometimes enhance the experience, as it did for a young man we know.

Hank, twenty-six, tells of an experience he had when he was a crew member on a sailing ship. In port, the night before a race when he was the only one on board, he noticed an exceedingly attractive young woman on the pier, wearing an Indian sari that billowed in the breeze. They began talking and he invited her to share his evening meal. After dinner, carried away by the sea, the moon and each other, they had sex. She left in the morning and they never saw each other again. But he's never forgotten the experience. Says Hank:

> That experience with Claudia was the single best sexual experience I've ever had. She had a beautiful body and loved to make love. She touched me all over as if she really cared about me though she knew I was only passing through. And we tried all kinds of things I had never tried before and neither had she. We had oral sex—something most women I knew wouldn't even consider trying. I had been afraid to suggest it to my girl friend for fear she'd get upset, but after Claudia, I felt freed up and my girl friend and I added that to our sexual repertoire.

Let's take a look at some of the advantages of having sex with someone you don't know very well and don't know if you will ever see again.

1. The sex can be particularly good. When you don't have to think of the future, about impressing your partner so that he'll want another date, you can throw yourself with wild abandon into thoroughly enjoying the sensual and sexual pleasures of the moment. Under these circumstances, when you have nothing to lose, you can act out some of your sexual fantasies.

2. You can find a different kind of enjoyment in pleasuring your partner, giving to him because you like him the way he is right then. When your motives are "pure" like this, your partner can feel it and enjoy it and you can savor his enjoyment. You won't be paying him back for what he did for you in the past because you've had no past. And you aren't building up credit for the future because there will be none.

3. You can open up and talk about things you don't usually talk about; you can reveal yourself. When you have a pleasure bond with somebody you believe you aren't going to see again, when he shows you he cares, it is easy to get things off your chest. Many times you can say things and explore ideas you fear your friends would not approve of.

More one-night stands could be enriching experiences if we would get over our censure of them, study them carefully and see what are the factors that make them pleasant and unpleasant and learn to act in ways to stimulate more pleasant-producing factors.

One of Emily's fondest memories is of a lovemaking experience with a stranger—a one-night stand when she didn't even have sex. She had been divorced for but a few months after being married twenty-nine years and was feeling lonely and unsure of herself. Searching for self-improvement, she attended a program by a traveling lecturer who was giving a one-night-only speech in her home town. Impressed by what he said, she went up to the podium afterward to talk with him. They were immediately attracted to one another and he invited her out for a drink. Two hours flew by during which she heard among other things that he had never been in her city before and was tired of staying at hotels. Since she was trying to be more up-front and assertive in regard to men and sex, she decided to take action. Nervously, she invited him to stay all night at her large waterfront home, to drive him around town in the morning and get him to his plane at noon. She was careful to make it clear that he could either have his own bedroom or share hers, whichever he would prefer. He said that he would like to share hers but that he was married and was that O.K. with her? She hesitated for a moment because she had never gone out with a married man before, but after thinking about it decided "why not?" After all, his being married wasn't going to have any effect on their relationship since he lived two thousand miles away and they would probably never see one another again. Besides, being newly out of a marriage, she didn't want to get seriously involved with anybody just yet anyway and she couldn't see how their having sex would hurt his wife any more than their having a drink together.

At home and in bed another dilemma soon confronted her. After they had been hugging and kissing and stroking one another for a while, it became obvious that, for him at least, nothing was happening. This was a totally new experience for her, something that had never happened during all her years of marriage or in the very few sex experiences she had had since her separation. Disconcerted herself, but knowing that this is a very embarrassing situation for a man, she tried to think how to put him at ease. Uncertain as to how to go about it, she decided on a direct approach. Nervously, she blurted out, louder than she had intended, "It looks as if you aren't getting an erection."

Silence hung heavy in the room for what seemed like hours but was only seconds and then she hurried on, her voice much quieter, telling him that this was no problem for her, that she was enjoying just being with him doing what they were doing and didn't care if they never did anything else. Then, all of a sudden, as if her acceptance of what had seemed to him as his "failure" had released a pent-up torrent, he started talking from the depths of his soul—going back to his youth and telling her of his impotence the first time he had attempted sex and how the woman had ridiculed him and then going on to his present hopes, fears and problems. And she talked of hers, even crying on his shoulder about her "failure"—her failure to make her marriage last. All night long, they made love by listening to and comforting one another. Though they never did have intercourse, the quality of their time together—their caring—made it a memorable "one-night stand" for them both.

In examining Hank's and Emily's and other good experiences

and contrasting them with one-night stands we've heard about or had that left one or both participants angry, hurt, disenchanted or all three, there are several characteristics worth noting. In good experiences:

1. Both partners want sex. A good rule of thumb is: If you don't feel a strong physical attraction, if you don't feel lusty, don't. With a person you don't think you'll ever see again, don't just go along to be agreeable. You need the sexual charge to make it good.

2. Neither partner coerces the other. Since both partners need to feel sexy to make a one-night stand a good experience, it won't do you much good to try to pressure someone. Entice, but don't pressure. If you do and your partner "gives in," not only will he or she regret it but you will, too.

3. Both partners are honest with one another that their only commitment is for mutual enjoyment. That they will see one another again is not a prerequisite for their pleasure. They do not offer or require assurance they will. Though frequently people do get together after having spur-of-the-moment sex, enjoyment must not depend on that. If the belief that you will get together again is essential to your pleasure, avoid a one-night stand. And never lead anyone on to believe you want to or can see them when you can't or don't want to. If you do, you really will "hate yourself in the morning"—and you deserve to.

4. Each is interested both in his own pleasure and feelings of self-worth and in his partner's. They feel like partners on the same team. Don't sacrifice yourself for your partner, but, on the other hand, don't be so concerned with getting what you want that you forget him or her. Show your concern, not just for his physical pleasure but for his emotional comfort. If you sense your partner is uneasy, ask if he is and see what you can do to make him more comfortable. If this is your only chance to help make him feel good, take full advantage of it.

5. Both know what they are doing and don't get involved just because they aren't thinking clearly due to alcohol or drugs. One of the reasons one-night stands have a bad reputation is that people who are anxious use alcohol or drugs and then take on sexual partners without awareness and for the wrong reasons. Frequently, their anxieties re-emerge when they are in bed and they either can't function well or are insensitive to their partner or

both. Having a one-night stand is a sophisticated adult activity. You need all your faculties and so does your partner. Decline an invitation from someone who is high or loaded.

6. The partners do or say things that bring a sense of completion to the experience. In fact, in all first-time sexual experiences, whether it marks the end of the relationship or the beginning, there should be caring closure. Many times the type of closure or the lack of it is what determines whether a first-time sex experience will be a meaningless happening, a once-in-a-lifetime event or a part of something special that will go on further. Though caring closure is a critical phase, it is one that is usually ignored. It deserves much thought and planning.

Caring closure

Sooner or later a first-time sexual experience comes to an end—like all experiences. But sex is not like all experiences. Whatever else may have happened during your time together, you exposed yourself to a new human being for the purpose of mutual pleasuring. You risked. You are different from what you were before. Maybe you have renewed and strengthened your trust in yourself—or perhaps renewed your lack of trust. Or maybe your view of other people or your world has changed. You now have more trust than you had before—or less. Whatever has happened, it is important to discover what effect it has had on you. If the experience has been a significant one, it may take weeks, months or even years to fit it into its proper place in your memory bank of experiences. You can't do it all before you and your companion part, but it can be helpful to spend just a few minutes to quickly think through some important questions and to resolve to think more about them later.

The questions are these:

How do I feel about myself now, after this experience?

How do I feel about my partner? My world?

What did I do that I particularly liked?

What did my partner do that I particularly liked?

Did I get what I wanted?

Did my partner get what he/she wanted?

If I were going to do it all over, what would I do differently?

What would I like my partner to do differently?

What must I be sure to do to make my next first-time sex experience as good as possible?

We suggest a debriefing. Although debriefing a sexual experience is a procedure that few people ever think of doing or are too embarrassed to do, it needs to be done. However, it needs to be done in a soft, gentle way—not in a detailed businesslike way as you would debrief army maneuvers or a sales campaign.

The first suggestion for debriefing *is to talk about what your partner did that you particularly liked.* And to find out what you did that your partner particularly liked. When doing this it is important that you do not in any way pass judgment on your partner or ask him to judge you.

Though it can be both helpful and fun to discuss what you both liked, do not ask "How good was I?" or even "Was I good?" Even if you were good, if you ask it, it sounds as if you were asking to be compared with somebody else and put on a pedestal. People don't like to do that, and if they don't think you were good, they certainly won't want to tell you. On the other hand, asking to be told *what* your partner particularly liked that you did or that happened is an entirely different matter. In the latter case, you are showing an interest in your partner, in what he enjoyed. And people take it as a compliment that you are interested in what pleased them.

If you really had a good time, your partner deserves to hear you say it. And you deserve to hear him say what he liked, too. Sometimes when you both allow your enthusiasm to show, the critiquing can be almost as much fun as the original experience. It is dangerous, however, because people have been known to get so turned on by talking at breakfast time about what was so good the night before that they fall back into bed and are late for work.

In a case where you didn't really enjoy yourself, where perhaps you just didn't click sexually or else you've decided you don't like your companion after being with him like this, you will still be on safe ground if you stay away from judging behavior or personality traits or manners or anything else and just stick to what you liked. You can, if you look closely, discover something your companion said or did that you liked. Tell him about it with as much enthusiasm as you can muster. If the experience wasn't very good for him and especially if he flubbed it in some way and regrets it, he needs to be bolstered a bit. Be generous with your compliments.

That brings us to the second suggestion for caring closure: *say or do something that will show your partner you still value him as a person.*

There are many ways to let people know you care about them after your first sexual experience. Leslie and Reed did it by eating breakfast together. They met when both attended a rally for presidential candidate McCarthy in London, of all places. She was from California but was on a temporary teaching assignment there; he was from New York and on his way to Rome on business. After the rally, they went on to a late spot for a midnight supper and dancing and finally to bed at his hotel. It was one of those rare evenings when everything went right. They found they had mutual friends and much, much in common to talk about. The food was superb, the service unexcelled and they danced together as if they had been doing it all their lives. And it was the same way with sex.

The next morning and time to get up arrived all too soon, and it didn't seem very likely that their paths would ever cross again. Though she had to go to work and he had a plane to catch, he had suggested they get up early enough to have a nice leisurely breakfast at a nearby place he knew and liked. In spite of the fact that she didn't ordinarily eat breakfast and to do it would cost her an hour and a half of sleeping time—in addition to the calories—she agreed. At breakfast they talked about what the evening had meant to them, and he gave her his card and told her that if she ever came to New York she should plan to stay at his place. Two years later, she did go to New York and looked him up, and it was at that time she discovered that he never ate breakfast either but that he had been concerned that she would feel "cheap" if after having sex so quickly, they just got up the next morning and parted without talking about things. Inviting her to breakfast was the best way he could think of to find the time he thought they needed.

Asking someone to eat with you is an excellent aid to bringing caring closure to a sexual experience. Divorced men in particular appreciate having breakfast served to them without bickering, and a man who can and will cook breakfast for a woman is saying a lot. Whether the food is prepared at home or one invites the other out to eat, the sharing of food seems to say, "I care about what is good for you." But you must also remember to talk specifically about the night before and to say in words what needs to be said to convey that message or a similar message of caring.

Letting a sexual partner know you value him is relatively easy if you can spend the night and have breakfast together and if you have had a good experience, but what if you have to part in the middle of the night?

Even if you have to part hurriedly and you both are sleepy, if things are good between you, you can always squeeze your friend's hand, look him right in the eye and hold his gaze for a few seconds and say something simple, like "I really enjoyed being with you, and hope you enjoyed being with me," and then give him a big hug. Either one of you can then say, "I'd like to call you tomorrow and talk with you, what time shall I call?" And then the next day, you can phone and say all the things you didn't have time to say the night before. Or you can write a note or send a card. Or maybe flowers or an inexpensive gift of some kind. One very sensitive man always makes a point of sending a little something the next day if he has had a particularly pleasant experience or if for some reason he will not be able to see the woman again. In the first place, he wants her to have no doubt that the experience was a special one to him, and in the second place, he wants her to know that he respects her and the intimacies they shared.

Sending a note, flowers or a gift the next day is usually thought of as the gesture of a gentleman, and so it was in Grandma's day. But times have changed and now that has become the gesture of a caring person of either sex. At present, for women this gesture is not yet common, so that one who does it gets double her money's worth. Very few men in this world have been thanked for sharing themselves sexually with a woman, and she can make herself feel very powerful and him feel very good by doing this.

To protect tender feeling, both partners should express their thanks for the sharing even if they don't want to share again. It doesn't hurt to say just that—"Thanks for the sharing. And good night." Be sure to look him in the eye. And make some kind of friendly physical contact. If you don't feel in the mood for a hug, squeeze his hand or give him a pat on the shoulder. Letting him know you still want to touch him if only in a very limited way is also important.

There is a third step to remember in bringing a first-time sexual incident to a close. It is talking about seeing each other again. Caring closure should be honest closure and in addition each of you should let the other know your wishes regarding further contact. Many men, insensitive to a woman's tendency to feel soiled somehow by sharing herself sexually, will just depart saying something vague like "I'll call you." A woman has no idea what this kind of remark means. Is he just saying something polite to get off the hook even if he has no intention of ever seeing her again? Or is he saying he likes her a great deal and is enthusiastic about seeing her again? If he is enthusiastic, she deserves to know it and to have his enthusiasm demonstrated by the setting of a definite time to get together again.

But all the responsibility should not rest on the man. Women, trained to be passive, will usually say nothing at all about a subsequent get-together. Not only will a woman not bring the subject up, if he says something vague like "I'd like to see you again," she won't even say, "I'd like to see you again, too." This is a good place for a woman to take the initiative. If he says he'd like to see her again, she should say something that will stimulate the making of concrete plans, like "That would be nice. When shall we get together?" Or she can speak up first before he has said anything at all and invite him to come over for dinner on a particular night at a particular time. If she makes it sound like an invitation and not like a demand that because he has had sex with her, he now owes her his time, he will be delighted. If she is worried that he may not want to accept, she should remind herself that he is worried about the same thing every time he asks a woman to do something.

Sometimes a man and a woman may enjoy each other a great deal but know they don't intend to see each other again. Perhaps they met on vacation and live too far apart to want to even try to maintain an ongoing relationship. Or maybe one or both are heavily involved with someone else or even married and don't want their sexual interaction to be anything more than just that. Whatever the reason, when this is true, it is best to talk about what you would like to happen in the future—i.e., "I'd like you to drop me a line to let me know how you are doing but I'd rather not get together again," or "This has been very enjoyable but I'd prefer it if you didn't write or call in the future."

And you should also talk about how you'll handle it if you do run into each other socially. For example, you might say, "I'd like it if we should meet for you to smile and give me a special warm kind of handshake and then just kind of ignore me. I'll do the same, but I'll know you are there and that will be nice."

Caring closure does not mean that everybody will like to hear what you have to say when you part. It is possible to be kind even when you are telling someone that you do not care to see him again, or that you realize you do not want to have an ongoing sexual relationship with him. If you do not want to, or don't have time to talk about this when you part, you can just mention it and set up a time that is good for both of you when you can get together for a little while to discuss it or even talk on the phone. Though it is not necessary to go into a lot of details if your mind is made up already, it is an act of kindness to let him know if your decision is the result of a personal preference or if he did something in particular that was offensive.

The ability to tell someone something he doesn't want to hear and to do it in a kind way is not a talent people are born with; it is a skill that can be developed. Following is a technique that Joel Springer, instructor of "dating" techniques at the University of Minnesota, and marriage counselor, has devised. It is called "I Want to Tell You." Here are the instructions for doing it:

Look into his/her eyes and take his/her hands in yours. Then say, "I want to tell you something, but I am afraid to because it might . . . (hurt you, make you angry, etc.). It is negative yet if I tell you I think it will strengthen our relationship. May I tell you?"

As you say this and whatever you say afterward, it is important to be gentle and caring. Your attitude is what makes the difference. Though you are giving a person some negative feedback, the idea is to do it in a way that will make it feel like a hug rather than a slap.

Asking a person's permission to tell him something negative gives him a chance to decline if he doesn't want to hear it; you aren't forcing it upon him. He is also reassured, from the way you are going about it, that you will be kind, that you value him and the relationship.

One woman said to a man, "I want to tell you . . ." and what she told him was that he never seemed to initiate a conversation. She felt if she didn't keep talking they'd lapse into an uncomfortable silence. That gave him a chance to reveal that he was shy and found it hard to talk to people until he knew them well. Just saying that relaxed him and made her understand him better and they started a lively conversation about how hard it is to get to know someone of the opposite sex in an honest way.

In the above case the man and woman never were lovers again but they did develop a warm and loving friendship. And this is the way with caring closure. It is frequently a new beginning as well as an ending.

9

Defusing Money-Sex Power Lines in Man-Woman Relationships:
Money

Money is as important a force as sex in a man-woman relationship. In fact, men and women all too often tend to turn their relationships into power struggles centering on sex and money. This power struggle gets its start in the traditional "dating game" —a game that is more manipulative and destructive than playful and nourishing. Here is how the "game" goes:

Usually the man begins the "game" by asking a woman for a date. He picks her up at the agreed time and provides the transportation. He hopes to impress her and win, if not her love, at least her sexual favors. So he pulls out his secret weapon—his wallet—buys her drinks, dinner, perhaps a present or two, takes her to expensive places and frequently spends more than he intended to or can afford.

Sometimes, however, a man will deliberately play it cool—see if his "date" will like him or perhaps even have sex with him if he spends little or nothing on her. (This is what many men do in the belief they are getting out of traditional roles, but such behavior is just the flip side of the same old record. It is a test devised by someone who is suspicious and wants to entrap. It is not the act of a trusting partner.) Usually she will pick up on his suspicious nature. Even if she does agree to see him again or even if she agrees to sex, she will certainly not reveal very much of herself whether she is aware of what she is doing or not. Human beings just don't open up when they sense somebody is testing them to see if they are worthy.

Her ploy, with sex as her bait, is usually more subtle. In response to his overtures and expenditures, she behaves demurely and dependently, is nice and agreeable, attempts to be a good companion, and though most women will deny this, holds out the promise of sex. When he lets her know he wants sex, she usually feels somewhat "obligated" because he has spent money on her (and because she has been taught spending money means he values her).

She responds in one of three ways: (1) declines to go out again, (2) "gives in" or promises to on the next date, or (3) says she doesn't intend to have sex until she is married or going steady. (This is the ultimate test.)

Sometimes a woman will respond to a man's spending money and then asking for sex by scurrying away—not because she doesn't like him but because she doesn't want to take advantage and either doesn't want sex or isn't sure yet. Sometimes, especially if she wants the security of an ongoing relationship or simply another date, she will "give in" or promise to soon.

For some reason, the third date seems to be the magic number for both men and women. Many women believe they are not promiscuous if they wait that long before having sex and that they will not be asked out again if they wait any longer. Men feel that they have surely "earned the right" to sex by the third date, and if she doesn't come across by that time, she probably never will.

If she doesn't agree to sex, the man usually concludes that she doesn't care for him very much. He then feels that he has been "used" as a "money object." Even if she does agree to sex, her heart isn't usually in it since her behavior is motivated more by the desire to impress or win him than by her sexual feelings. And besides, he may still feel like a loser. How can he be sure that it is him she likes and not the things he buys her? She frequently feels uneasy, too, for she can't really be sure about the extent to which he cares about her or is buying her sexual favors. She feels especially bad if, after having sex, he stops seeing her. Then she feels "used" as a sex object.

Perhaps, at this point, you are reacting like some of our friends who read our manuscript before publication. "Wait a minute," our men friends would protest, "maybe a lot of men do expect sex if they spend money on a woman but not me. I'm not like that." And it is a rare, rare woman who will admit that her sexual behavior might be even a tiny bit influenced by the fact a man has spent money on her.

However, while people may not consciously be aware they are making a connection between money and sex, their behavior is influenced by unconscious attitudes. To find out what your attitudes are, think about the following questions. One is directed to men and one to women, but you'll learn a lot by thinking about both questions.

To men: Suppose you had a relationship in which a woman paid all of the expenses. Would you feel you were somehow cheating her if she made sexual overtures and you turned her down? If so, can you say that you don't think the person who always pays is entitled to sexual favors?

To women: If another woman gives you a gift, takes you to dinner or goes out of her way to drive you someplace in her car, do you feel some sense of obligation? Afterward, if she wants something from you, do you feel obligated to put yourself out for her, to do something she wants even if you may not really want to? If so, can you say you don't feel a sense of obligation when a man spends a goodly amount of money on you?

We have some suggestions to help men and women act like gentle aggressors in regard to the way money is spent when they are together. And the basic gentle aggression principle behind all the suggestions in this chapter is that men and women *both* must take responsibility for the time they spend together. They can do this by (1) sharing expenses, (2) talking openly about money and (3) taking turns initiating get-togethers.

SHARING EXPENSES

Saying that couples should share expenses isn't the same as saying couples should always go 50-50—the famous "dutch treat." That may be one way of sharing and perhaps one couples prefer much of the time, but to make it a rigid rule would be just as unfair and as limiting as the present rigid rule that a man should, automatically and always, pay. Sharing has a slightly different connotation. We are using it to mean that a man and a woman should apportion or divide their joint expenses between the two of them.

There are many ways to apportion expenses. Sometimes one or the other can treat, such as for a special occasion or when one is feeling flush. Sometimes you can split the tab right down the middle, as when your expenses are about equal and it isn't worth the trouble to figure it all out. Sometimes each can pay just for what he orders, as when one person is drinking a lot and orders lobster and the other isn't drinking and orders a hamburger. Sometimes one can pay for dinner, the other for theater tickets or for after-dinner drinks and the tip.

Sometimes it will be best for each to be fully responsible for all of his own financial obligations; other times just a token gesture of paying for some little thing or perhaps just offering is all that is needed. However, a woman must not think she is doing her part if she always makes the token gesture and never takes full responsibility.

When trying to decide what is "right" and "fair" in regard to money and the opposite sex, use as a guide your behavior with a member of the same sex. For example, if you were in a bar and began talking with someone of your own sex, chances are you'd feel O.K. continuing to talk for quite a while without money being spent at all. Neither of you would feel you had to buy the other a drink for the privilege of just talking together, nor would you feel the other should buy you one. After you talked for quite a while, if you liked each other and if your glasses were empty, *one or the other* might offer to buy a round. If you stayed together longer and decided to have another round, the person who had accepted the first drink would probably pay, but the relationship would not be burdened by a sense of obligation even if there was no second round. All things being equal, the less obligation a person feels when treating, the less obligation will be felt by the person accepting the treat.

Thus, it is not so much how expenses are divided that makes the difference in man-woman relationships as the context in which it is viewed. Money must not be looked upon as something the man alone has and accepts the responsibility for allocating. He must not spend it in an attempt to control her behavior. She must not consider the amount spent or even the act of spending it as a measure of her worth. Instead, money, like time, must be seen as a mutual resource—to experience and enjoy together. It must be apparent that with money as with time, men and women each have some. But quantities are limited, and how much each will want to spend varies with the circumstances and the partner.

Let's face it, it does cost money to have many of the experiences that make a relationship enjoyable. Though sex creates a "pleasure bond" between a couple that is one of the strongest bonds that can occur, there are experiences other than sex that a couple can share which can add to their "pleasure bond"—such things as attending a play, listening to a concert, sharing a delicious meal in a nice restaurant, roller skating, bowling, etc. If couples see money for what it is, a medium of exchange to buy some of these pleasurable experiences that enhance the quality of the time they spend together, and thus of their relationship, money can lose much of its awesome weight as a symbol of other things like love and caring.

Here are some things to take into consideration when deciding how to share expenses, whether for one evening or as the basis of an ongoing money policy.

The financial resources of each

We don't mean that a couple should compare income-tax returns or their bank balances to work out a fair money policy. But we think they should be sensitive to how much income their partner has, his responsibilities, etc. And it isn't fair to make this decision on the basis of sexual generalization. For example, many women say they are not willing to pay their own way because men make more money than women. While it is true statistics show the average yearly income of men is higher than the average yearly income of women, that doesn't take the individual man you may be dating into account. He may be unemployed, may have a low-paying job, may be a student and only earning enough to get himself through school, or he may make a good salary but have a lot of obligations to his divorced wife and children. And even if a man makes more than a woman, why should he be expected to subsidize her? If she went out with a woman friend who made more, would she automatically expect that woman to pay? And what about going out with men who make less than she does? Will she pay for them or will she decline to go out with them because they can't pay for what she wants to do?

A man must be equally sensitive to what is going on in the life of the particular woman he is dating. Some men, confused at the changes happening in male-female relationships and unsure about how to cope with them, make hostile statements to women like "Well, if you are so liberated, pay your own way. And if you really believe in equality, pay for me, too, like men have been doing all along." However, a man should not expect the women he meets now to make up for all the times he and other men have been used as "money objects." Besides, some women can't always pay their own way if they go to the places some men can afford and want to go to. If she is older and divorced or widowed, she may have just re-entered the job market; she may be supporting children; or she may be struggling along on a small salary while trying to develop a career that will someday bring in more money.

The latter was true of Carol, a secretary, when she began going out with Ken, a salesman. Although Carol believed, in theory, in sharing expenses equally, she couldn't afford to do that if her date wanted to go out in style—dinner at the "best" restaurants, plays and concerts, skiing weekends. Ken, it turned out, did like this style of dating and since he knew Carol's income was limited and since he made more money than she did, he picked up the tab.

However, after they had been going out together for about six months, Carol was promoted to an executive position in her company at a much higher salary. In fact, she now made almost as much money as Ken. To her surprise she found that even though she now had the money to pay her own way when they went out and even though she was intellectually committed to the concept of sharing expenses equally, she found it difficult emotionally to put this concept into practice.

Despite her emotional misgivings, she suggested to Ken that they now go "dutch" when they went out. When he thought it was a great idea, Carol felt chagrined—she even fantasized that he simply didn't care about her as much any more. In addition, she found the reality of "dutch treat" dating too cold-blooded. For her one of the main pleasures of dating was being taken out now and then and treated to something—whether a movie, a hamburger or an art exhibit—and she missed that. It occurred to her that maybe Ken would enjoy being treated now and then too and she suggested they take turns "treating" as their way of sharing expenses rather than splitting the tab down the middle each and every time.

At first, they tried alternating evenings—she paying one night and he the next. However, that didn't come out fairly since one evening they might go to an expensive restaurant and the next take a walk and have a light snack.

After much trial and error (something all couples must go through to work out a system that fits them) they came to their present "sharing" policy. But they also realize they must be flexible enough to change it if their circumstances or feelings change. On weekends they each pay their own expenses whether they go out of town for the weekend, to a movie, play or dinner. On Saturdays and Sundays they spend the most money and it seemed the most fair and beneficial to the relationship to have each pay his own way at those times. However, during the week they take turns treating. If one wants to go out, he or she calls the other and invites but with the understanding the one doing the inviting will pay. This way, they share responsibility for initiating get-togethers and each gets a chance to treat.

The total amount of expenses incurred on a date

Many times women just automatically assume that men will pay for little incidental expenses when they are together—parking, tipping the parking attendant, checking hats or coats, toll fees. Today these expenses can add up to quite a bit of money and should be considered as part of the total expenses to be shared by both.

Another expense that should be considered is one that women ordinarily don't even think about: transportation. Traditionally, the man picks up the woman and so, traditionally, he has been responsible for the transportation. Whether he drives his own car, rents one, takes the subway, hires a cab, etc., she should be aware of this expense and share it. If she provides the transportation, he should be equally sensitive to the cost.

Baby-sitting is another costly item that should be discussed and shared. While it is usually thought of as a woman's problem, it isn't. It is a single parent's problem. Today, more and more men are rearing their children and have to get baby-sitters in order to go out, too. The ordinary way of handling this expense is for the parent of the children to pay for it, although there are some women who take it for granted that, after a date, a man will just naturally take the baby-sitter home and pay her. Men complain about this, and they should. A person should not have the decision as to what he will pay for imposed upon him. How expenses will be shared should be discussed in advance so that no one will get an unpleasant surprise by being expected to pay for more than he is prepared for. If two partners who have gone out several times want to be together and one or both has to pay baby-sitters to accomplish this, that money should be considered one of the evening's expenses and examined when decisions are being made. It may be that on some evenings they will want to pay for the sitter jointly and then do something inexpensive, while other times the cost of that item will loom so high they will prefer staying in. Or together they might think of another single parent they can exchange baby-sitting services with.

When the resources of two heads and two pocketbooks are used, many different actions are possible. And this applies when guests are asked to bring food or drink or both to a get-together. The custom of sharing costs between guests and host has become increasingly common, but what usually happens among singles is that women are expected to bring casseroles, desserts, dips or some kind of food while men bring liquor. Or else if one half of a couple was invited, he or she will prepare or pay for whatever is taken. When partners go together to a gathering, no matter which was the "invited" guest, both should share in paying for what they bring. And items should not be allocated merely on the basis of sex. Women shouldn't automatically be expected to bring food and men liquor.

The degree of interest

In addition to the total amount of expenses, there is another consideration when it comes to deciding each partner's "fair share" of expenses. This is the *degree of interest* in an activity. People just don't ordinarily like the same things to the same degree. And this is ever so true of men and women in sexual relationships. He may love football and hate ballet; she may hate football and love ballet. If they expect the other to occasionally share their favorite activity, they may have to compromise some on the concept of sharing. If he wants to go to the Superbowl and get the best seats, she may not be willing to go "dutch treat" even if this is how they share most of the time. He may have to pay more or even all of the price of the tickets if he wants her to go with him. But she can pay for the hot dogs, the parking, the incidentals or even nothing at all and this can still fall within the framework of sharing—providing it doesn't always happen this way. It is of utmost importance that a man and a woman frequently remind themselves they are *sharing* both their money resources and their right to pick an activity. Without a reminder, it is all too easy to backslide into the old ways where he picks the activity and pays and she doesn't pick but anything she pays for is a "bonus" to be praised and exclaimed over.

Partners sometimes like an activity equally well, but one wants to do it more often or do it in a more lavish style than the other. Herman and Joanne both loved to ski, but Herman, a schoolteacher, could only afford to go about twice a season. On the other hand, Joanne, who had inherited considerable money, wanted to go every weekend when the snowpack was good. But skiing wasn't all that was important to her, she wanted to go firstclass. And with Herman. Therefore, she subsidized the difference between what he ordinarily paid to go skiing his way (the dorms, the charter bus, etc.) and what it cost to go skiing her way (the rented chalet, lessons with the pro, après-ski cocktails with the "in" crowd, etc.).

At first, this caused them to have some rather uncomfortable feelings, which they talked about. He felt like a gigolo, and she felt like an over-the-hill woman who had to pay to have male companionship, but they got over that feeling by doing a little playacting. When they asked themselves what would be so bad about the situation if he was her gigolo, it became apparent that it would mean they were both undesirable. Thus, one weekend, he decided to pretend that he was a gigolo but a very handsome, expensive and much-wanted one. And she pretended she was a very beautiful, young, rich woman who could have her pick of men but wanted to be with this particular one. Through changing their thinking and imagining themselves desirable, both were able to really get into their new roles and enjoy them, even to act them out with a flair now and then just for the hell of it.

Having the well-heeled partner pay is not the only way of coping with a great financial disparity. A couple might sometimes decide to do only what the "poorer" partner can afford. And this need not be a case of sacrifice for the one who has more money and is used to more luxurious habits. In fact, deliberately seeking ways to spend less money or even none at all is a way couples can enrich the time they spend together.

In our money-oriented society, it frequently happens that partners will get into the habit of always relying on money for amusement, of thinking that to have a good time, they must go someplace to be entertained and spend considerable money. Doing this can cause them to overlook each other and their personal resources. Thus, in addition to learning to use money in ways that will enhance their relationship, partners need to learn to not spend money sometimes.

A good way to do this is to keep a "Cheapie File." A Cheapie File consists of things available in your own or nearby areas that either cost very little or are free. You store in it clippings of free concerts, picnics, lectures, hobby displays, art shows, etc., that are going on in your town. There are always many, many cultural events available that are free of charge or that cost a mere pittance, especially if you live near a college. Or you can get some tourist brochures and find out what people visiting your area find interesting and what free attractions are available. (Many times your town's main tourist attractions are the very thing you have taken for granted and ignored.)

A convenient way to file your clippings is to toss them all into a glass fishbowl and then when you want to do something that doesn't cost much money, draw one out and go to it. This way you can have two kinds of fun—that of being surprised and that of seeing how little money you can spend.

One couple had an unusual and memorable date one rainy Sunday when they had planned to go on a picnic. In their Cheapie File, they discovered a lot of coupons they had accumulated for discounts on take-out food. They drove around town collecting a free Coke at one place, a pizza that was half price at another, two hamburgers for the price of one at another and so on. They came home bearing their "junk food" assortment and had a picnic on their living-room rug. And without any ants. They entertained themselves reading the Sunday funnies aloud, acting out some of them and making up comic strips of their own using their favorite characters. It was one of their most creative dates and yet cost a total of $3.77—plus, of course, the gas they used.

Another important consideration in the sharing of expenses is the *amount of time each person wants to spend with the other.* Men and women, especially those who have just begun a relationship, rarely have the same amount of interest in each other or agree totally on how much time they should spend together. In fact, Joel Springer, instructor of a course on dating at the University of Minnesota and a marriage counselor, found when he took a survey of 1,000 college students that conflicts over time and commitment differential (i.e., interest in and commitment to the relationship) caused more relationship problems than conflicts over sex.

When Raymond and Pam started going out together Pam wanted to spend more time with Raymond than he with her. It wasn't that he didn't care about her. It was just that he was going to school full time, worked part time and had a lot of men friends he liked to hang around with. At that point, he wasn't ready to sacrifice his other activities in order to find time for Pam.

When they went out on their once-a-week date, they shared expenses 50-50. Even then they stuck to movies and drive-in hamburger joints because Raymond didn't have much money. Pam, on the other hand, while not wealthy, had a steady job and could afford a few luxuries. Pam soon realized if she wanted to see more of Raymond it was up to her to take action. She had to "get his attention"—to make him want to spend more time with her. Thus, once a week or so, she started getting tickets to something she knew he would like—a football game, a play, a concert—and inviting him to go with her. Since Raymond enjoyed Pam's company as well as the entertainment she was offering, he frequently found it worthwhile to rearrange his schedule and spend this extra time with her.

Sharing expenses *will* change your relationship—usually for the better, but not always. A change in money policy may even mean the demise of a relationship. However, if a relationship folds because you are trying to make money matters more equitable, you can be certain it was on a very shaky base to begin with. And as you try to work things out, though it is bound to be uncomfortable at times, you will learn much that will pay off for you in your next relationship.

Women and sharing

Some women have learned to like the idea of sharing expenses. They say that when they pay for their own dinner, they can order just exactly what they want instead of limiting themselves to what they think he can afford. In addition, they feel freer to express their opinions as to what they should do and where they'll go. After all, when it is their money, too, they are less likely to just be "good sports" and go along with things they don't really enjoy. One woman found when she started sharing that she didn't really like going to bars or out to dinner all the time—activities many men just rely on because they don't know what else to suggest. All the eating and drinking had been hard on her waistline, but when it became hard on her pocketbook, too, she took action. Now, no matter who pays for what, she frequently suggests to a companion that they take a walk, or ride on a sight-seeing bus, or go swimming, or horseback riding, or shop and cook a simple low-calorie meal together, or do something that is inexpensive and that doesn't make her fatter.

When a woman takes more responsibility, it makes the date itself more enjoyable for both. Felice is fussy about where she sits in a restaurant. To begin with, she prefers a booth where she can sit next to her date and have physical contact. Also, she doesn't like to look into the kitchen and she doesn't like to be in the line of traffic. She enjoys the illusion of being isolated and private. When she was being a man's guest, she never mentioned she didn't like a particular table for fear of sounding fussy. Now she feels free to ask the waiter to move them to a better table. If her date objects to her speaking directly to the waiter, on the basis that she is "taking over" the man's prerogative, she gently assures him that she is trying to relieve him of the total responsibility for their time together—not trying to "take over" the relationship.

Many women who have learned to share say the very best part is not feeling obligated because a man has spent a lot of money on them—obligated to be nice even when he is boring or offensive, obligated to act as if they like everything even if the meal is mediocre, the waitress curt and the play a flop, or obligated to go to bed. Some have admitted that it wasn't until after they started paying their own way that they realized the number of times they had gone to bed without much enthusiasm but just because they sort of liked the guy and he had spent a lot of money on them and they didn't want to make him feel bad. When they shared expenses, not only did they begin to feel entitled to refuse sex, they began feeling enthusiastic about initiating it and some even got up enough nerve to make the first overture, an act usually considered a male prerogative.

And this sharing of responsibility can improve relationships by helping each sex understand the other better. One never-married woman, Louise, found, in her years of dating, that she was inclined to get upset when a man did not want to use the valet parking—sometimes parking quite a distance away to avoid doing this. Not only would she resent having to walk half a block or so all dressed up but she resented what she thought of as the man's "tightwad" attitude. To her, valet parking was a symbol of being taken care of—of being deposited at the door and of having someone take over the chore of parking the car. With most men she suffered in silence, but with Dave, a man who had become important to her, it all came to a head on a New Year's Eve. He didn't want to use the valet parking but she insisted—adding in a sarcastic way, "Don't worry. I'll pay the dollar for the tip." The conflict over that incident ruined their evening and almost their relationship. To Louise, Dave seemed like a man who was so intent on saving a dollar and so insensitive to her needs that there was no use trying to save the relationship. To Dave, Louise seemed like a spoiled woman who wanted luxury and attention. Later when they talked it over more rationally, Louise found that Dave didn't like valet parking because he hated turning his expensive foreign car over to anyone else. He feared the transmission would be ruined by someone who didn't know how to shift gears and he didn't like the idea of someone he didn't know having the keys. He also worried about leaving it unlocked in a parking lot. Once Louise understood how important his car was to him—and that valet parking symbolized the possible destruction or loss of it and had nothing to do with either money or her—she didn't mind the inconvenience to her of his parking his own car.

When women share responsibility and expenses, they get to understand men's feelings better, especially the resentment many have built up by being expected to do all the paying. Women have the opportunity to discover how incredibly expensive it is to go out for an evening. Some don't want to face this painful fact and really would like not to think about money at all and just let the man take care of everything. However, more and more are becoming convinced it is good to be forced to face reality. Many say they have learned to appreciate men more than ever before and that now, when a man does take them out or pays for anything, they make certain to thank him. This new system helps to keep them from taking a man for granted.

But some women still can't quite accept the concept of sharing. They say things like "Well, if he values me, he'll be willing to pay for my company." But a woman who really loves herself doesn't sell very much of her time to the highest bidder. Instead she seeks out the company of men who are so worthwhile that it is a joy to be with them even if they aren't paying.

Other women say they don't want to take a man to dinner or pay for their own dinner when with a man, but that they are willing to invite him to dinner at their home. We say that isn't good enough. To begin with, the expense of eating at home doesn't equal the expense of dining out. But the cost isn't the main issue. The point is that she is not willing to accept her share of responsibility for whatever they decide to do together. She wants to stay in the stereotyped role that associates woman with home and man with the outside world.

That some women will find excuses for not paying their own way and want to keep the status quo is to be expected. Everybody likes to get something for nothing. But liking isn't the issue. Establishing new customs that will foster better relationships between the sexes is. Besides, when a woman always lets a man pay, she isn't getting something for nothing. She is paying a high price because what she may be settling for is a series of inferior relationships.

Men and sharing

Men, too, have different reactions to the concept of sharing. Although a lot of men say they would really like to have women share expenses, other men would prefer to keep on being a "money object." After all, when a man pays, he can call the shots. He can phone a woman when he wants to go out, take her where he wants to go and come home when he wants to come home. And she is expected to be grateful for the fact he has spent money on her.

Not only will the sharing of expenses help women grow up and face reality; it will help men do the same thing. After all, if a man's popularity with women depends upon how much money he spends on them—i.e., if he is vulgar, pushy, dull, unkempt or for some other reason unpleasant to be with—he'd better find it out. On the other hand, if a man's popularity doesn't depend upon how much money he is willing to spend—i.e., if he is gracious, exciting, kind, well groomed or for other reasons a delightful companion—he's entitled to find that out, too.

And men may experience a lot of discomfort when women pay their own way or even pay for them. One man who was taken to dinner by a woman said it was excruciating to have to sit there passively while she ordered, discussed with the waiter the vintage of the wine, the ingredients of the house specialties, then tasted the wine, and later paid the check. He felt like crawling under the table—as if his manhood were being diminished And he was sure the waiters were snickering at him.

It is good for men to experience that "bought and paid for, being at someone else's disposal" feeling, for it gives them an idea of how women have felt for centuries. However, when expenses are shared, that uncomfortable feeling goes away, and rather quickly. It is replaced by a new feeling, unfamiliar to most men—the feeling of being valued for the kind of person you are, the feeling that your presence is so important to a woman you care about that she is willing to spend money to have it. When a man can really revel in this new feeling, it is possible to give up the compulsion to conquer and control, possible to give up playing the role of the "great white hunter" and become more of a human being and a partner to women in the best sense of the word.

TALKING ABOUT MONEY

Even for men and women who think the sharing of expenses is a good idea, there is the problem of who brings it up—and when—and how you can work things out so that everything is fair. Usually each sex thinks it would be just fine if the other would bring up the subject. Although both sexes are going to have to learn to talk about money honestly and openly, men have to take a special responsibility in this area. They are more likely to be conscious of a need for a change than women for they are the ones who are being unfairly burdened now by the cultural expectation that they pay.

Here are some tips on how and when to bring up the embarrassing subject of money.

The first and most important thing to do is to *talk about money in personal, direct terms as it relates to you and a member of the opposite sex in a particular situation.* People tend to want to use generalizations and assumptions when it comes to discussing money; it helps them avoid the real issues and not deal with this emotionally laden "symbol." As was said earlier, making generalizations like "A man should pay because men make more money," or "If women want equality, let them pay for a man," does no good at all and just fans the flames of resentment between the sexes. This is not the kind of talking we are suggesting. A man and a woman have to look at what is happening between them in regard to money—who pays for what, how it is decided and how each feels about it—and then discuss it. They must realize it will make them uncomfortable, maybe even angry sometimes, but they must also realize that, in the long run, it will improve their relationship.

Talking with members of the opposite sex about money is important, not only because it can improve an existing relationship or get a new one off to a better start but because if people don't talk about money, some may go without any relationships at all. Joe was such a man. Returning to school in his mid-forties to learn a new career, he had a limited income and an old, shabby car. He had convinced himself no woman would want to go out with him because she would think it unseemly for him to be so poor at his age. So rather than risk explaining his situation to anyone, Joe had chosen to wait until he had more money to ask a woman out.

What a waste! How different it could have been if, when he met a woman he liked, he would explain his present money situation openly and honestly and if she were still interested, take it from there. We suggested this to Joe but he said he just couldn't bring himself to do it even though he believed that money isn't all that women are interested in and that it is only fair for them to put out some money, too.

Later, he tried it but had a couple of miserable experiences. In discussing them with him in detail and having him act them out, it became apparent he had two difficulties. One was that in his gut—not his head—he still believed there was something wrong with him as a man if he couldn't pay. Though this made him angry at himself, he came across as being angry at women for not liking a man unless he had money. His second difficulty was that he didn't know just what to say or how to say it. He would try to convince a woman that his philosophical viewpoint on men, women and money was the right one instead of getting to the point and saying specifically what needed to be said, namely (a) that he liked her and (b) that he would like to see her again.

We gave him some sample statements that didn't sound abstract or self-pitying or hostile and had him say them over and over until he could do it naturally. And don't think it was easy for him. Even with us, his friends, he stammered and stuttered at first and literally could not get the words out. The sentences we had him practice were: "There is a great play on at the college that I've been wanting to see before it closes. I really like being with you and would like you to go with me, but I don't have the money to pay for us both. How would you feel about going with me and paying your own way?"

After Joe practiced for a while, the statements came out sounding matter-of-fact and honest, and we sent him on his way with instructions to try it out and let us know what happened. We haven't seen him since, but he did call to say he was dating, even using one woman's sports car now and then, and that learning to talk about money was the best thing that had ever happened to his relationships with women.

The second thing to consider in talking about money is timing. *Talk about it when it is appropriate.* You may never, in some short-term relationships, need to discuss money. You may have a brief affair on a cruise ship where it isn't necessary to spend any; and you can meet people at a party and have a great rapport but never see them again. It isn't necessary to lay out your philosophy on money as soon as you meet. In fact, it might be, and usually is, totally inappropriate to do so. Though it can make for an interest-ing discussion, the topic, like politics, sex and religion, carries a heavy emotional load and you'd better ease into it.

The best time to talk about money is when you need to. You do need to talk about it when you are inviting someone to do something with you. Do not take it for granted that the other per-son will know what your intentions are. Not even if you have had a long discussion about money the night before and she said she was willing to pay her own way on a date. What people say in ab-stract discussions doesn't always reflect what they want to do or will do in real life. And don't think you can wait until later to say what your intentions are. It may be too late.

One woman, curtly turned down when she suggested to a man that they go to dinner together, discovered later he thought she was trying to cadge a free meal and hadn't realized she was offer-ing to pay. Some women do ask men to take them out and ex-pect them to pay and some men resent this, and they should.

On the other hand, Ted, a young man in college, complained that women always got mad when he asked them to go dutch and so we asked him to tell us step by step exactly what happened and we discovered why. It seems that he asked a woman he had gone out with before to go to a movie with him and when they got to the box office he went ahead of her and bought one ticket. Then with the ticket seller watching, he stepped to one side, saying, "I've bought my ticket. Now you can buy yours. I want us to start going dutch." In the first case, had the woman made her inten-tions clear when she invited the man, he probably would not have refused. In the second case, had Ted informed his date he wanted to start a dutch-treat policy, she could have decided how she felt about that—and Ted—and not suffered the humiliation and em-barrassment she felt when he made his intentions clear in public.

If you are a man, you may hesitate to talk about money. After all, if you ask a woman to share expenses she may think you a cheapskate. But if you go about asking in the right way and are careful with your timing, you will be able to avoid this initial reac-tion or at least get her over it quickly. It is probably not a good idea to suggest sharing until you have treated her to a little some-thing. Thus, unless you have met her under circumstances where you have bought her something—if only a drink or two—your best bet, before you bring up the subject of sharing, is to invite her on a traditional date—i.e., one where you pick her up and pay. It need not be an expensive one, however, or lengthy, but she needs time and the right circumstances to build up some trust in you before you broach this ticklish subject. This is a very sensitive area for women, not because they consciously want to take advantage of anyone but because, as we have said before, they associate the payment of money by a male with his wanting to protect them, take care of them, even to care about them. If a man they don't know very well doesn't want to pay, they are apt to think he doesn't care about them. And if he doesn't care about them and still wants to go out with them, so their unconscious logic goes, he must be interested only in sex or else have some other ulterior motive.

Probably the best time to talk about sharing is at the end of the first date, when you know you like this woman and are pretty certain she would like to see you again. Start off by telling her that you are interested in doing whatever you can do to develop really good friendships between yourself and women and have done a lot of reading about this subject. Tell her that studies show that man-woman relationships get off to a better start when both parties work out a way of sharing the costs of dating in a way that is comfortable for them and that because you'd like to spend more time with her in the future you'd like to talk about that. Be careful not to make it sound like a threat or an ultimatum but like a request for a discussion of an important subject. Don't hesitate to cite this book as evidence of the need for men and women to learn new money etiquette. Then suggest a trial period. Tell her you'd like to try out one "sharing date"—and soon—because you'd really like to see her again, and that you can evaluate the system after the trial.

Undoubtedly, if she likes you a lot, she won't mind sharing at least for your next date. The idea may even intrigue her and make her feel less obligated. If she goes for it, suggest that she pick the activity and the time for trying this new system. This will let her know you'd like her to be more involved in your dating activities, and so you will be off to a good start. Decide between you, in advance, what form this initial sharing will take—whether it will be 50-50 or whether one will pay for entertainment, the other for food, or however it is agreeable to both of you.

Now, if she doesn't take to the idea right away, you have a decision to make. Maybe she really isn't a person you'd like to see more of after all, or maybe you like her well enough to give up the idea of sharing expenses at this time—you might take her out and pay a few times until she builds up more trust and you can talk about it again.

Talking about money and deciding how to deal with it in a way that makes both of you feel comfortable is something that must be done again and again in a relationship. Not only do people change their ideas about what is "fair" and "right" and "proper"; circumstances change so that what was fair at one time is no longer fair. The important thing is that expenses are shared; there is no one and only right way to share them. As we have said, each person's financial status, obligations and preferences must be taken into account, and a couple must figure out a system that makes them feel good about themselves and each other, and change it when it no longer does the job.

TAKING TURNS INITIATING GET-TOGETHERS

Expenses aren't all that should be shared if two people are to feel like partners—to feel that they are equally involved in their relationship. Women should take turns with men in initiating get-togethers. This doesn't mean keeping score; it does mean that she will invite him to do things on a regular, reciprocal basis. That may sound threatening to many of you women, but think about it. If a female friend invites you to something, you like to reciprocate. On the other hand, if you keep inviting a friend to do something and she never invites you, sooner or later you decide she isn't very interested in your relationship. You feel used, exploited, unappreciated, the same way men feel when they repeatedly ask a woman out and she never invites them to do anything. When a woman invites a man to do something, it indicates she is interested in him, in his company and in maintaining a relationship.

An excuse many women give for not inviting is that the man may expect them to do all the inviting (and paying) from then on. But it might be good for women to experience that fear of being automatically expected to keep on paying forever. Men have known that expectation very well. But if a woman invites a man and he never invites her back, she can take it as a sign he isn't very interested—the same way she would with a woman she had just met and wanted to start a friendship with. And on the first date, she can talk with him (just as we advised men to talk with women) about her philosophy of sharing if it appears they'll want to see each other again. She doesn't want to get stuck in the giving role any more than he does.

Another reason a woman will balk at inviting a man is that she has to be willing to phone him. Some women say they have never phoned a man and just don't know how to go about it. Others say they are afraid of being too aggressive. Some claim men don't like women to call them. And all are afraid of being refused.

The idea of women phoning men may seem like a big hurdle but it really is nothing at all once you make up your mind and start doing it. When you think about it, it is senseless and archaic for a woman always to have to plan her time so she can be around home, waiting by the phone, in hopes he'll call.

Naturally, men and women need to talk with one another about this and work out some plan that is acceptable to both of them. Shortly after they meet and decide they like one another, she should ask for his phone number and ask if it is O.K. to phone. Or at the time that he asks for her phone number, she can ask for his and also inquire as to the most convenient time to phone, just assuming that what is sauce for the goose is sauce for the gander. Or he can offer his phone number and invite her to call. However they go about it, each should let the other know what times are best to phone and what hours are bad. It is also helpful if they will work out an agreement that will allow either to terminate the phone call quickly without hurting the other's feelings in case the call comes at an inconvenient time. Men and women who are sexually involved seem particularly sensitive when the person they call seems brusque or quickly terminates a call, and yet it will happen sometimes. The person being phoned may be deeply engrossed in something or be feeling crabby or sad or some other way that has nothing to do with the caller or the fact of being called.

Some men really like the idea of women phoning them. Others don't like it at first but when they think about it and talk about it, it becomes O.K. One young man said, "I thought it was a terrible idea when I heard about it. My immediate thought was what if she phones me when I have another woman at my place? That would be terrible. We could even be in bed and she would be interrupting us. And then a thought struck me like a bolt of lightning, and I said to myself, 'I wonder how many times I have phoned a woman when another man has been there. I wonder if I have ever interrupted her when she was in bed with somebody else.' "

Just the thought of the opposite sex doing things you expect to do or vice versa can bring many insights as to what life is like for them and thus it can improve understanding and cooperation. A woman can get in touch with how a man responds to being invited by looking at her own reactions. Most of the time she is delighted to be invited to something even when she doesn't particularly like the man. Although she may refuse, she can carry around a glow that someone sought her out because he wanted to be with her.

The truth is that men aren't different from women at all in this respect. The majority of men love to be invited out by women. They usually feel flattered and appreciative, even when the woman is one they don't particularly care for. They like to feel wanted and popular every bit as much as women do. However, just like women, they don't want to be made to feel that they have to accept, that something is wrong with them or with the person who asks if they refuse. And, of course, they don't like to be hounded. Occasionally, there will be an old-fashioned man whose masculinity is threatened by having a woman ask to take him somewhere, but this particular breed, ill equipped to function in today's world, is rapidly becoming as extinct as the dinosaur. More often than not, if a man reacts negatively, it is because he is so surprised at this unexpected bit of good fortune that he doesn't quite know what to do or say.

So, if you are a woman, don't be held back by the thought that a man might not like you if you invite him out. There are a lot more men who appreciate the kind of woman who will take the initiative in regard to paying and inviting than are put off by it. The odds are in your favor. In fact, you can probably increase your popularity if you let it be known you are the kind of woman who will share expenses and sometimes even treat.

If you are a woman who is newly divorced, back in circulation after a broken romance, new in town, or who for any reason wants to let a number of men know you are now "available" for dating and if you are willing to try out our concepts of sharing expenses, here is a suggestion:

1. Buy some tickets to the midweek performance of a play or some other event going on in town.

2. Make a list of all the men you like and are interested in seeing.

3. Begin calling these men, one by one, and inviting them to the event you have tickets for, making it clear they will be your guest. However, first call the men you think will be least likely to accept because of their work, because they take night classes, belong to a bowling league, etc. The idea is to get as many refusals as you can before you get an acceptance. This way you'll get more mileage out of your tickets. By phoning and inviting a man to go out you are letting him know that you like him, are available for dating, are an assertive woman willing to take the initiative and pay and that you enjoy plays or whatever other event you selected.

4. Use the phone calls as an opportunity to talk and get better acquainted. The chances are every man you call will be delighted to have been asked and probably several who turn you down will call you later and ask you out.

In phoning a man and inviting him out, it is imperative to make it clear that you are paying. As we showed in an earlier example, men aren't always sure what a woman means when she calls him and invites him out. It is a new situation and it is a courtesy for her to make it clear she'll handle the financial arrangements. But we think that she should do more. If it is possible, she should also take care of the transportation.

For years, men have been burdened by having to do all the driving or the arranging of transportation. It is a pleasant surprise to many men to be picked up and driven around all evening. They find out how delightful it can be to settle back and be taken care of for a change.

Couples who start sharing will soon get in the habit of discussing who is going to pay for what, how much should be spent, who will drive and so on without embarrassment or rancor. These items become details to be worked out—not symbols of caring or worth. In fact, one couple—Peter and Mary—always negotiate before every date as to who will provide transportation and how they will share expenses. On a recent occasion Mary had invited him to a party held in a beach city halfway between their homes (they live about twenty miles apart). They didn't want to meet at the party because that wouldn't give them time to visit and it seemed rather cold to arrive separately. On the other hand, each had a busy schedule the next day and they had already decided they couldn't stay all night with each other. Therefore, they decided to meet halfway at a restaurant and have dinner. In this case, Peter paid for dinner because Mary brought a bottle of liquor to the party as her contribution. They left Mary's car at the restaurant and went on to the party. When they left, Peter drove Mary to her car and they went home separately. Had they not viewed the situation as partners, Peter would have been expected to pick her up (a twenty-mile drive), go to the party, take her home and return home—approximately eighty miles of driving. Probably, had she not been willing to share the driving, Peter would have said "no" to her invitation.

We hope the suggestions in this chapter have heightened your awareness about the connection between money and sex in man-woman relationships and also shown you the importance of becoming sharing partners. To further heighten your consciousness and to help you change some of your social customs regarding money, we suggest you go on a Gentle Aggressor Mini-Date.

The Gentle Aggressor Mini-Date

This involvement-promoting format can be followed with members of the same sex or the opposite sex you have known a long time and have no sexual interest in; frequently it will stimulate a brief encounter. However, it is particularly effective with a person you are sexually attracted to and it is a great structure to follow for a first date. It provides a safe and reassuring structure for getting below the superficial level quickly and either a man or a woman can take the initiative. It neutralizes the power lines of money and sex.

In the first place, it allows a person to invite another to do something for a short period of time. The present custom of a man inviting a woman he'd like to get to know better out for a whole evening, frequently to dinner, not only entails that he spend considerable money but is a big commitment of time for both of them. This date requires very little time. In the second place, very little, if any, money needs to be spent. It is O.K. to invite someone for a walk along the beach, for a visit to a museum, for a hamburger, a cup of coffee or a glass of wine. In fact, it would not be appropriate to invite someone to an event where you would both be observers, such as the theater or a ball game, as the purpose is to get to know, not to entertain or impress. In addition, because the person who initiates the date also takes care of the money, it helps couples get out of the traditional expectation that the man will always pay.

Another feature is that specifying "no sex" permits both partners to be more personal in their conversation and to touch in friendly ways without worrying about the possibility of sexual overtures. It encourages both men and women to be gentle aggressors, to initiate interaction and take responsibility for the quality of the time they spend together and also to be sensitive to and listen to the other person's feelings. The structure of talking freely about personal matters and then critiquing, debriefing, giving one another feedback, not only helps establish a relationship fast and on a healthy basis; it serves as a model for future get-togethers that will help keep the relationship going.

INSTRUCTIONS FOR A GENTLE-AGGRESSOR MINI-DATE

Invite someone you'd like to know better to be with you for *at least* an hour. Specify the activity you'd like to engage in. Give him/her permission to accept, decline or negotiate on time or activity, but let him/her know that the following "rules" must be agreed upon:

1. If there is any *cost* for anything during the time you are together, the inviter (whether male or female) will pay it.
2. There is to be *no sex* or erotic touching on this date.
3. Both parties will be *more personal* in their conversation than they ordinarily are. They will talk about subjects to help them get to know each other's background, hobbies, interests, values, goals, opinions, feelings, hopes, fears, etc.—and what they have in common.
4. Both parties will *touch* each other more than they ordinarily would—but with much sensitivity to the other's reactions. They

will tell each other their feelings when being touched and request changes when uncomfortable.

5. At the end of the time together, *at least* fifteen minutes will be spent critiquing the time spent together through discussing the following questions:

    a. What were your *concerns* about this get-together beforehand?

    b. What did you particularly *like* about this experience? About what each other did, said, wore?

    c. What did you *not* like about the time together, about what the other did, said, wore? Be specific. Be honest. Be kind.

    d. What could your partner have done or said that would have made the time even more pleasurable? Be supportive but direct in making suggestions.

6. Before parting, each will make a point of telling the other if another get-together is wanted and the circumstances under which it is wanted—if it is.

10

Enriching Your Life Through Supportive Circles of Friends

Caring kinds of sexual relationships can be very important in a person's life. But they aren't available to everyone all the time. Even when we have them, they don't always last very long. Even one that lasts and lasts isn't enough to fill all of our "people-needs." What we really need are friendships. Lots of them. Good ones. Close ones. A variety of different kinds. We need to have them with members of both sexes. And we need to realize most aren't apt to go on forever. Thus, a part of daily living is creating from bits and pieces—from relationships that may be short or lasting, sexual or nonsexual, intimate or arm's-length—a patchwork quilt that will be our security blanket.

That one relationship, no matter how good, isn't enough, should be obvious. We've been warned since we were kids about what happens when we put all our eggs in one basket. But it is only recently that behavioral scientists have shown us that when we act as though happiness and emotional satisfaction depends entirely upon finding and keeping a mate, we are headed 180 degrees in the wrong direction.

Their recent observation, one that hasn't made headlines but should, is this: The best-functioning people—those who are happiest and most productive, who like themselves and get along well with others—may or may not have a mate, but they *do* have a supportive network of friends. This is a network with a particular kind of structure, a network of three circles of friends, one in which most relationships are by necessity short-term. Though a mate might be a member of the network it is the fact that there is a network—a lot of supportive people available—that makes life easier. And it is how that network is structured—how many people are in it, how accessible they are and what they can and will do for, with and to you—that makes life more fulfilling.

It took being widowed and groping for several years in the wrong direction to teach Sandra, thirty-eight, what friends could do for her. But what she learned turned her life around. Says Sandra:

"I think my whole life until recently has been one long search for love. I always thought that love was in short supply, that except for certain blood relatives, the only way you could get love was from a person of the opposite sex. When I became a widow, I thought I was condemned to hunger for love until I found another mate. And so I went on a frantic search for this mate and my life was, for quite a while, a series of shattered dreams. I would think I had found my perfect partner and then discover I hadn't. It took a while to discover my friends and how they could help me find pleasure in so many ways: in building a nest for myself, finding a new career, tuning in to nature, learning what I needed to learn to readjust, and much, much more."

Sandra said her first insights occurred when she discovered that the periods "between" relationships were often the times she felt most satisfied and secure. Besides being motivated to revive friendships she had neglected when totally engrossed with a "one-and-only," she also made new friends. And she took time to develop new interests and to share them with friends rather than zeroing in on making a relationship with a man "work" in the anxious hope that it would guarantee her lifetime security.

Gradually she came to an important conclusion: "When I realized that a lot of the love and security I was seeking was coming from my friends, I was able to stop searching so desperately for a mate—not that I don't want a sexual partner or maybe even a lifetime one someday—but from now on my lover must become a part of my support group, supplementing it instead of supplanting it."

Unfortunately, because of the emphasis on coupling in our society, most people never learn what Sandra learned—that supportive friends are what make one's life rich and full and satisfying. Seeing salvation as lying in a mate leads to four chronic approaches to everyday living that keep a person in a rut and limit his enjoyment: (1) deprivation, (2) disillusionment, (3) desperation and (4) resignation. The beliefs that go with any of these attitudes limit what must be an ever-continuing task: the building and nourishing of a network of constantly changing friendships.

Deprivation is what can happen to a person who has found a mate, who really likes him or her a lot and who would like to be partners forever. If he thinks he has found the magic key to happiness, not only will he not deliberately seek out the other relationships he needs, he will often avoid them, engulfing himself and his mate in a smothering cocoon of "togetherness."

On the other hand, when men or women who have found their mates aren't satisfied, they are apt to feel that they've been lied to or that something is wrong with them because they have what should make them happy but they aren't. *Disillusioned*, they tell themselves that this is just one of the sacrifices that living together or being married makes necessary. Or else they decide that they must have picked the wrong mate and discard him.

Those without a mate who think they must have one, have their problems, too. Many, in *desperation*, make it their life's work to seek the perfect person who, if found, will make them happy forever. In their search for perfection, they overlook the many people who could add to their happiness as they go along. And then there are those who *resign* themselves to unhappiness because they either don't want, or believe they can't find, a mate. This group includes those who don't have a wide selection of partners to choose from because they are older or not very attractive physically, those who don't choose to pair up because they have a commitment to a career, a cause, a religion, etc., or simply because they have a low sex drive. These people often feel the price they must pay for not coupling is doing without love and caring—which just isn't so.

Furthermore, the idea that it is mandatory to have a mate of the opposite sex to be fulfilled forces people to compete with each other to obtain one. If people believe the only way they can be happy is to be part of a couple, some people are going to be left out. The numbers of men and women aren't equal—especially as people get older; people aren't all equally attractive or desirable to the opposite sex and some people attract more than their fair "share" of partners. Sometimes men and women believe the only way they can get a partner is to compete for one or to take one away from someone else. But it is not necessary to compete for members of one's supportive network. A person can be a member of your network and of other people's, too. And you have so many to choose from. Anyone of either sex who has something to offer you and who wants what you are willing to give can qualify. You don't have to limit yourself to emotional involvement only with people who don't have partners or to people you would consider as a mate. Because so many people are possibilities, there is no scarcity of members for your group or anybody else's. Nobody needs to be without a group.

Before we go on further, let's make it clear, we aren't saying people shouldn't couple—only that they shouldn't couple out of a belief that this is the only way they can feel loved and function well. And neither should they think that a romantic, stable coupling with one person will, in and of itself, eliminate the need for other supportive friendships.

It is not just the emphasis on coupling that keeps many people from getting as much out of life as is possible. It is also the lack of a clear picture of the kind of support system needed in today's mobile, highly specialized, transitory world, and the lack of guidelines for developing this system. It is the purpose of this chapter to show you the reasons a network will work well for you whether you are married or single, old or young, male or female, and to provide the conceptual framework necessary to develop such a supportive group. Once you get started, you will find that you will rapidly develop a "kinship of spirit" with many people and contribute much to each other's growth and feelings of well-being.

The first thing you must do in order to develop your supportive friendship group is to change some of the pictures in your mind about relationships. We all direct our lives according to mental images and to the extent that these images limit and confine our thinking our lives are limited and confined.

Now the ideal relationship "picture" or "model" most people carry around in their minds is of a couple—a male and female, a momma and daddy, an inseparable pair. The bonds between the male and female are seen as strong and mutual with the people functioning not as two separate individuals, but as a "we."

In contrast, the kind of relationship model we envision, the supportive network, consists of three friendship circles that surround and enclose the individual at the very center. Though you might at times have a sexual alliance with a primary partner, the strength of that bond does not cause you to always act as a "couple-unit." As an individual, you make the separate connections with members of your three circles that will give your network the beauty, strength and flexibility you want it to have, sometimes choosing to act in unison with various others as a couple, a triad or a larger group.

Here is a brief description of the circles, which will be expanded in greater detail later. The first circle, the one closest to the center, is the "tender circle." It is composed of four to seven people who have very strong ties to the person being "supported." Though there might be legal, financial or blood connections, these are not the basis of the support. The ties come from emotional rapport and depth of involvement.

The second circle—larger than the tender circle and further away from the center—is the "congenial comrades" circle. It is composed of fifteen to twenty people, each of whom is involved with the person in the center. The involvement is not as strong as that between the "supportee" and his tender circle, but these people are important to his life and he sees them fairly regularly.

The third circle is called the "outer rim" and is composed of from thirty to fifty people. The ties with these are the weakest because of infrequency of contact, but there is still some sort of stated or unstated alliance regarding what it is they expect from each other.

Maybe, at this point, you are thinking that this all sounds a bit complicated and, besides, who needs it? If you have a mate and feel that most of your needs for interpersonal interaction are being met, you might tell yourself it could cause conflict in your marriage to develop these circles. However, the truth is that you will be doing a favor for the one you love most by developing a supportive network. Your relationship will be enhanced, not harmed.

If you are single, you can also live more happily whether you have a number of friends already or not. Deliberately and sensitively structuring friendship circles for yourself will make it easier for friends to satisfy more of your interpersonal wants. (We prefer to use the term "wants" rather than "needs" to refer to the things that people can give and get from each other in order not to confuse them with physiological needs. You can live without getting any of your interpersonal wants met, but the quality of your life is higher when more are satisfied.)

Here are the reasons everyone should develop his own circles of friendship:

1. *A supportive network provides a "safe" structure within which people can form a number of opposite-sex friendships that are non-possessive and non-threatening to other relationships.*

A young wife remarked plaintively that the thing she disliked most about marriage was that she longed to have friends of the opposite sex but that there was no existing social structure within which she could do this and still appear to be a faithful wife. It is true that close, nonsexual male-female friendships are not customary in this country and, in fact, there is a myth to the effect that such friendships are impossible to maintain because of the possibility of a sexual attraction turning them into sexual relationships.

However, Paula Menkin, Program Specialist at the University of Southern California and creator of a course called "Friending: The Art of Making, Nurturing and Ending Friendships," says such friendships are not only possible but healthy. Says Ms. Menkin, "I spend time with several married men friends who are not unhappy with their wives, are not about to leave their wives, but who like having a close woman friend. I think the kinds of things they have talked about with me and the kinds of experiences we have shared have made a number of my married men friends feel more understanding of their wives."

Emily, as a married woman, began seeing the ridiculousness of the myth that men and women can't be friends when she realized that that myth cut off half of the world's population as possibilities for meaningful relationships. She talked this over with some of her married women friends and they agreed to experiment with taking each other's husbands out to lunch with the object of getting to know them as individuals. In her book *Making Friends with the Opposite Sex*, Emily elaborated on this idea with her "Take Your Friend's Husband to Lunch" plan. The rules include the following: There is to be no sex, the woman who invites is to pay the check and the husband is told the objective and rules and given an opportunity to refuse gracefully if he wishes.

What Emily and her friends did was set up a social structure that made it acceptable for them to get to know each other's husbands without having to worry about jealousy, sexual "complications," etc. As you form your supportive circles, you will build in safety because as you place people in your circles, you will make agreements to act as guidelines—keeping confusion, misunderstandings and stress to a minimum.

A structure that makes it safe to get together with many members of the opposite sex—if only for a few hours and for the mere purpose of talking honestly—will encourage you to include more of them in your life. As you do, you will get out of traditional roles because you'll find you react quite differently to members of the opposite sex when the wish for or the possibility of sex is not uppermost in your mind. You will find yourself paying more attention to the individuality of those opposite-sex others, realizing how many other factors there are that are far more important (for most purposes) than whether a person has a vagina or a penis, one X chromosome or two. This will keep you from "stereotyping" the opposite sex as much as usual, a practice that creates misunderstandings and resentment. Being limited to a knowledge of one man or woman encourages people to make generalizations about the opposite sex based on their particular partner—i.e., "All women are jealous," or "All men like football."

2. A *support network provides a structure that recognizes the importance of in-depth same-sex friendships.*

Besides having myths that prevent men and women from forming meaningful friendships, we also have some that make it difficult for members of the same sex to maintain more than superficial "bridge table" or "golf course" contacts. The most common myths are the beliefs that:

> You are different from others of your same sex and that they couldn't possibly understand you.

> Physical and emotional closeness with a member of your own sex implies homosexuality.

> The members of your own sex are competitors and can't be trusted.

The women's movement has done a lot to break down these myths as they apply to women. Women have been encouraged to be less competitive with each other and more supportive; in fact, to become "sisters." In consciousness-raising sessions all over the country, women are getting together to discuss their problems and their feelings, and in a variety of body workshops they've learned that it is possible to give each other physical tenderness and affection without these leading to homosexual activity.

And women, on their own, can make alliances to try to get beyond the superficial "gossip" relationships they may find themselves in. For instance, in one group of married couples who have known each other for over twenty years, the wives often got together for afternoon coffee and chitchat. Their talk was usually superficial and they never really shared their concerns and feelings —that is, not until the afternoon one of them suddenly began to cry and blurted out she was getting a divorce. That seemed to open the door for them to level with each other—about the status of their marriages, about their concerns in the present and fears for the future, and about how much they valued each other as individuals and as a group. Since that first opening up, the women's get-togethers have taken on a very different tone—the result of a conscious decision not to waste time on idle gossip and superficial discussion, but to serve as a support group for each other. Group members now show more concern with what the others think, feel and do than in trying to keep up a façade of being a "good wife" as they used to do. In fact, the one who is no longer married is still a member of the group and her status has not diminished.

Unfortunately, there has been no widespread men's movement as yet, and most men find it difficult to get beyond the usual kind of male camaraderie—talking of sports, bragging about sex and jobs—to the sharing of feelings. Interestingly and contrary to the myth that men and women can't be friends, many men are able to talk with women friends on a level of intensity they can't with a man. If you ask around, you'll find that more men have close women friends than have close men friends and many have no other man with whom they can talk on other than a superficial level. The need to be aggressive and competitive makes it hard for a man to let another man see his weaknesses and fears, to let his hair down, as it were, since even the idea of letting one's hair down just isn't masculine. It is very important for men to develop deeper, more honest and more expressive friendships with each other if they wish to develop their total personalities. As friending expert Menkin says, "Though there are things a man can be with a woman that he cannot be with a man, there are also things a man can be with a man he cannot be with a woman—if he will."

3. *A supportive network provides a security blanket, in the form of a number of people that can be depended upon when there are unsettling changes in one's life.*

Change is the norm today—in jobs, homes, relationships. And changes often take place at such bewildering speed that they interfere with physical and psychological well-being. As Alvin Toffler points out in *Future Shock*—a book which deals with the impact of change on our society—there are limits on human adaptability. Says Toffler:

> When we alter our life style, when we make and break relationships with things, places or people, when we move restlessly through the organizational geography of society, when we learn new information and ideas, we adapt; we live. Yet there are finite boundaries; we are not infinitely resilient. Each orientation response, each adaptive reaction exacts a price, wearing down the body's machinery bit by minute bit, until perceptible tissue damage results.

However, while everyone is subjected to the physical and psychological stresses brought about by rapid change, some people seem to be able to withstand the stress of change better than others. These are people who develop "stability zones" in their lives that give them a sense of security. A man might, by driving the same car for years and keeping the same job practically all of his life, be able to absorb many new ideas and develop numerous relationships. A woman traveling a lot in her job, staying in different places, meeting different people, might, to maintain some stability zones, make a practice of always getting up at the same time, following the same exercise and rest routine during the day, and eating the same breakfast—no matter where she is.

In the past, most people didn't need to seek out interpersonal relationship patterns that would give them "stability zones" because these were built into their lives. Their families—those aunts and cousins and grandparents who had known them since birth— and their marriage partners—whom they could count on being with until they died—gave their lives stability and continuity. And they needed this continuity and stability, for even in the past people suffered the stress of change brought about by a war, a depression or a new invention such as the railroad. The difference is that this change did not come about as fast as it does today. The television series "The Waltons" is a good example of how a supportive family served, in the past, as a bulwark against the stresses of changing events—in this case, the Depression.

But today, the family can no longer serve as the exclusive bulwark against change. There is too much change. Few people have enough relatives living nearby to be able to count on them alone in time of crisis, much less on a day-to-day basis. And just being related doesn't equip a relative with the ability to give the kind of emotional support people want. In addition, more knowledge and encouragement from trustworthy people are needed now than ever before.

This isn't to say that a person shouldn't look to his mate as an important source of stability. However, to rely on your partner for all of the stability you need or even the major portion can leave you stranded if you should break up or if—for a variety of reasons, including illness or prolonged separations (military, business, etc.) —your partner is unavailable. Besides, even one person who is always there when you need him just isn't enough stability in these times of accelerated changes. Building friendship circles, making alliances with many people, is the only way to assure yourself of enough people to fall back on.

4. A *supportive network helps people grow in every way possible* —*intellectually, spiritually, physically, emotionally.*

It takes the stimulation of many people for us to achieve our potential as human beings. Unused potential, like unused muscle, atrophies. If you neglect your own growth by restricting yourself to just the few long-term relationships that come your way, even though they may be very nourishing and very fulfilling, you will never find out what you are capable of becoming. Growth requires that you reach out and stretch yourself.

Sometimes couples—married or unmarried—believe they don't need other people because they are so content. And it is true, they may not *need* friends for many of the reasons single people do. For example, they may not *need* someone to bring them chicken soup when they are ill because they take care of each other; they may not *need* someone to go to the movies or theater with because they go with each other or they may not *need* someone to travel with because they have each other. But having someone to do things with is not the dimension of friendship we are talking about here—the kind that helps you grow.

It is through involvement with a variety of different personalities that we grow. Because we connect with different people in different ways and at different places, different facets of our personality come into play. You may take the lead when you are with one person, follow when with another; you may be creative with this one, and analytical with that. One person can bring out "masculine" qualities and another "feminine." Even when you do the same things with different people, you do them in different ways, thus providing the opportunity to discover whole new parts of yourself. And the talents, abilities and strengths you develop with one person will enrich your relationships with all others. No matter how old we get, personal growth need never stop if we have frequent contact with many people who can and will interact with us in meaningful ways.

CHARACTERISTICS OF SUPPORTIVE FRIENDSHIP CIRCLES

Now that you've seen the reasons everyone, *including you*, needs to develop a supportive network of friends, let's take a closer look at the characteristics of each circle. Let's see how they differ from one another and what attributes to look for in selecting members for each. If you deliberately seek out people with the qualities we recommend (or help those you know develop these qualities), we guarantee that you will develop an interpersonal support system with a good combination of basic emotional security and many opportunities for personal and social growth.

Bear in mind, however, as you read our recommendations that we are describing an ideal, much as we might describe what to look for in an ideal husband or wife. But, just as if you wait until somebody comes along who has all the qualities of an ideal mate, you will never get married, so you can't wait for "perfect people" before including them in your friendship circles. You and the people you know will never exactly fit all of each other's requirements, but adjustments can be made, and in fact, the process of making these adjustments (such as by the use of the "We Process") is part of deepening a relationship. Besides, when you have many supportive people around you, and you picture your relationships as being in concentric circles, you can in your mind move a person from one circle to another with little or no bother until you find the place where he fits best.

We shall describe the characteristics of each circle as if they were indeed separate entities, but you will find considerable overlap when you try to see where your friends fit best. Don't let this bother you. The main thing to remember is that a person's position in your different circles depends upon two factors: your depth of involvement—i.e., the time and energy you want to commit—and the purpose of your relationship—i.e., what you do for, to and with each other. Remember also that both of these factors change—and sometimes rather quickly. *It is the existence of a network that provides you with stability although the network itself is a dynamic entity.*

Depth of involvement, as we are using the phrase, refers not to how much you care about a person but rather to what you want to do about the caring. You may care for a person very deeply without wanting to or being able to *take care* of him or even to spend much time with him. The involvement that is the basis of our supportive circles is a behavioral one. It refers to the amount of time, energy (emotional, psychic, physical) and resources you want to and are able to share with someone you care about. By deciding how much involvement you want with a person, you are not "rating" him as inferior or superior, important or unimportant. What you are acknowledging is that different people have different things to give and get from each other at different times in their lives and that is O.K. When you use that knowledge as the basis for a greater appreciation of what each individual has to give, you are on the way to higher-quality friendships.

First we will discuss the characteristics of each circle and what to expect of the people in them. After that, in the next chapter, we will offer some suggestions as to types of alliances that can be made with people in your support system.

THE TENDER CIRCLE

The tender circle is that group of people who form the basis of your emotional support system. They are your core group, those you are most intimately involved with. They don't have to know each other, but each knows most of what is going on with you. They know the external happenings and your internal gropings. They keep in touch with what you are doing in regard to your work, in your relationships, financially and in terms of your health. They are the people you really level with, the people who know your story, who know you. If you have a mate, he or she is usually a member of your tender circle. However, sexual partners, per se, may be members of any of your circles. Just because you have sex with someone doesn't mean you are intimate and it doesn't mean he is easily accessible or that you see him frequently —prerequisites for tender circle members.

To function optimally, you need to have at least four people in your tender circle, to make it fairly certain that somebody will be available when you need them, but also so that you'll have enough diversity of emotional expressiveness and opinion to keep you from falling apart or from getting lopsided. The people who are closest to you become part of you and mold you.

Following are the requirements to bear in mind when selecting people for your tender circle:

1. *A tender circle member is readily available.*

Each member of your tender circle must give you a high priority in terms of his time and emotional energy. Each must make a commitment to be emotionally and physically available to you whenever possible. This does not mean that every member of your core group will be available whenever you want, but it does give you the assurance that whatever happens to you—day or night, midweek, weekends or holidays—one or more will probably be available. And in a crisis, the resources of these people who are closest to you can sustain you.

A number of our friends and Emily's students who have followed our suggestions in building their relationships frequently tell us the many ways members of their tender circle help them.

Art, forty-eight, is one of them. After his twenty-year-old son was killed in an accident, Art, who is usually well organized and efficient, was too numb to do anything. His tender circle members took over—each one handling what he had the time and ability to do, and contrary to what frequently happens when relatives try to help, there was no bickering and quarreling because there was no rivalry, no competition. Mary, who had a lot of time because she was unemployed, stayed at Art's home for a while, helped him handle his grief by letting him talk and cry and swear, and also made the funeral arrangements. Phil made his home available to some out-of-town relatives who came in for the funeral, and Evelyn took upon herself the task of keeping track of who had sent flowers, etc., and writing thank-you notes later. Art, who had always taken pride in being able to "stand on my own two feet and handle anything and everything without anybody," was convinced the time he spent developing his tender circle was more than worth it—just for this situation alone—not to mention the numerous other benefits he has gotten.

Tender circle members can also be available in more routine, day-by-day ways. June and Phyllis live together and are very good friends. In structuring their relationship, they made an alliance to be a support person for each other in time of need—in a crisis or just when one or the other gets out of bed in the morning feeling like she can't face the day and doesn't know what is bothering her. They carefully spelled out how they would live out their alliance. Since both women work at home and each has her own office there, they made an agreement that if the door of either office is closed the person working would rather not be disturbed. However, if the other needs some emotional support, it is O.K. to knock on the door and explain the situation. At that time, the person being asked for support has the right to say, after listening to the problem, whether or not she will take time out from her work to help. Sometimes one or the other will put her work aside for a while, but sometimes the job at hand has a higher priority, and each has agreed not to take offense if refused, but to find other ways of coping.

It is imperative in committing yourself to those in your tender circle that while you make it clear you will certainly make every effort to live up to all aspects of your commitment, you do reserve the right to be unavailable sometimes and want them to do the same. Unless you know you can occasionally say "no" to some-body without his getting all shook, you won't be comfortable agreeing to be available. It is difficult to make a request unless you can trust a person to refuse if what you ask is just too incon-venient or out of line. Nobody likes to intrude or take advantage. Those who are in each other's tender circle must make an extra effort to be straight with one another.

2. *Tender circle members understand you and like you as you are.*

Select as members of your tender circle those you believe under-stand you pretty well now—your limitations as well as your assets —and who want to understand you even better. Then, with them, you can really be yourself, without pretense, without façade. How-ever, make certain they do not try to keep you the same so that it will be easier to "deal" with you, that they do not view new ideas you may have or a change in belief or behavior with alarm. In-stead, they should help you in exploring your feelings, your belief systems and your world.

And remember, people feel closest to you when they can share your triumphs as well as your sorrows. Sometimes we hesitate to tell our friends when we are particularly happy for fear of sound-ing as if we were bragging. Besides, it has become the custom to gripe and complain and it seems easier for people to feel sorry for us when we have problems than to rejoice for us when good things happen. Our success brings envy—the feelings of "Why couldn't it have been me?"—and sometimes a fear of no longer being needed. But because the members in your tender circle un-derstand what makes you tick, they should also understand what a particular triumph means to you. Although they may have a few momentary pangs at your success, they must be able to take wholehearted joy in the good things that happen to you and be willing to help you celebrate. And they should know how to offer comfort—physical and emotional—in times of crisis without hav-ing also to offer advice (unless you ask for it). When they do offer advice, they should show they are clearly on "your side" while also trying to be objective. You don't want "putdowns," but neither do you want blind adoration.

Don't expect the kind of treatment you want to happen auto-matically. You'll have to guide your close friends. Gently let them know how you want to be treated and also take heed when they guide you. All of this is part of the process that promotes and re-sults from understanding. It is well worth working on, for there are many payoffs, as George, forty-four, a married man with two children discovered. George had taught school for almost twenty years—had tenure, medical insurance and a retirement plan—but he was fed up. Suddenly, he announced he was quitting to go into real estate. Many of the people he knew—including his co-workers —viewed his idea with alarm and warned him that he probably wouldn't make enough money to live on and that he was making a big mistake. Other friends applauded his courage, said "right on" and assured him he was doing the right thing to get out of a dead-end job in favor of one that had more potential.

However, those in his tender circle did neither. Two, in fact, ar-ranged to sit down with George and help him look at the entire picture—his objectives, his options, the problems and payoffs, the probable effect of various alternatives on himself and his family. They helped him come to a decision that was right for him be-cause they understood him. As a result of their thorough but sen-sitive probing and suggestions based on understanding, George de-cided to teach half time and work in real estate half time—a compromise that enabled him to earn enough for his family's basic needs and still have enough time to pursue his new career.

And his core group stood behind him. They did more than just "understand" him and offer advice. They sent friends to him who were interested in buying homes; they offered to loan him money if his part-time income proved inadequate. They supported his dream with both words and action, which brings us to the third requirement for those closest to you.

3. *Tender circle members must be dependable.*

Pick as members of your tender circle those you can count on. Those people who not only say they care about you but show it. You need people who do what they say they will do, or if, for some reason, that becomes impossible, let you know they cannot and are honest as to why. Today, it has become commonplace for friends and acquaintances to make lip-service social remarks like "Let's get together soon," "I'll call you this weekend," or "I'll drop by someday next week," and then take no action. It is even common to cancel social engagements at the last minute with relatively little explanation or even just to fail to show up. Many people have come to expect this social undependability and think there is nothing they can do about it. Though it is not malicious but the result of the fast pace of life that keeps everybody on the run, it is perpetuated by people not realizing the effect of their behavior on themselves and on others. Though we can't change society totally overnight, we can change certain parts of it. We can and must let those close to us know we have to be able to depend upon them, to know—to use an old-fashioned phrase—that their word is their bond. For if we find that we cannot count on the word of someone close to us, even in such seemingly small matters as keeping social engagements, it will soon shatter our sense of trust, make us feel they don't care about us and sooner or later ruin our relationship.

Take Pete and Harry. They call themselves close friends and have been buddies since army days, but because they've never thought much about what being "close" really means, they sometimes let each other down.

This happened not long ago when Pete promised Harry he would take him to a big-league sports event for his birthday. A very excited Harry told all his friends how he was going to spend his birthday and even turned down several other invitations. But when he called Pete to find out what time to meet on the day of his birthday, Pete exclaimed, "Oh my gosh. It simply slipped my mind. I forgot to get the tickets. Things have been so hectic at work I'm sure you'll understand, old pal. Let's do it some other time, and, by the way, happy birthday."

"Oh, it's no big deal," said Harry, but he was hurt. Disappointed, he spent his birthday all by himself drinking morosely in a bar. Because he and Pete had never consciously spelled out the terms of their friendship, Harry didn't know whether he was within his rights to expect more dependability of Pete. Though both felt uncomfortable about the incident, neither ever brought it up. Eventually because they didn't know how to discuss their relationship openly in terms of their expectations and feelings, they began seeing less and less of each other until their friendship just withered away.

4. *You must be able to see members of your tender circle frequently.*

It is essential to live close enough to be able to keep up the frequent contact tender circle alliances require. While it is possible to maintain emotional rapport and caring over space and time, it is not possible to maintain day-to-day understanding and get the kind of emotional support we all need from people who live far away or whom we don't see often.

Strangely, people rarely consider how important proximity is in relationships. Many times people, when asked to list their closest friends, will list people who live long distances from them and whom they have not seen for years. The kind of closeness that helps us function the best can come only from people we can reach by walking, by a few-minute trip in the car or by phone when there is no toll charge. Though you may think you'll never find another friend like the one who moved away—and you may not—you had better not delay for too long looking for a satisfactory substitute that you can see frequently—one in your apartment-house complex or neighborhood. The new friendship you deliberately develop may even be better than your former ones if you start developing it right from the beginning and nourish it with frequent contact.

A change of circumstances as well as a physical move can interfere with frequency of contact and must be taken into consideration. Jean and Lois discovered this when they began to feel upset and disappointed with one another. Jean, twenty-eight, and Lois, twenty-nine, had been best friends and college roommates and had lived together for several years after that. But two years ago, Jean got married and is now the mother of a baby girl. Lois, who lives alone and has no particularly significant involvement with a man, felt keenly the loss of Jean as her primary person— one who always had time to listen to her, advise her, comfort her and do fun things on the spur of the moment. However, she felt self-conscious about going to visit Jean for fear she would intrude on her relationship with her husband. And then when the baby arrived, she felt even more like an outsider. Jean, on the other hand, felt that Lois didn't come over because she was finding her dull now that she was "just" a wife and mother.

All of this came out into the open when we encouraged them to do the "We Process." As a result, they decided they wanted to re-establish their "tender circle" level of involvement. Since they still lived near to one another, it was no problem and they set up the following guidelines to make it happen:

Both agreed to:

1. Drop by each other's place frequently and also permit the other to drop by with short or even no notice.

2. Make contact by telephone at least twice a week.

3. Get together at least twice a month for a planned evening out—without the husband.

All factors that interfere with close friends getting together often should be of concern and should be talked about. Take moving, for instance. People take a lot of things into consideration when they move—how close they'll be to their job, how much rent they'll have to pay, what stores are nearby—but they rarely consider how a move will affect their relationships and to what extent they will be cutting themselves off from important people who are supportive of them. It is even more important to locate where you have a friend you can be open with or where there are people who are likely to be willing to take the time to develop close relationships than to have that extra bathroom or lots of closet space. Since the quality of our lives and our personal fulfillment depend upon our emotional support circles, we should carefully explore the "people-resources" of an area before deciding we want to live there.

CONGENIAL COMRADES CIRCLE

The second ring of people in your supportive network should contain from fifteen to twenty people, those whom you can count on seeing on a fairly regular basis, but with whom your depth of involvement is not as total as with your tender circle members. These are your "congenial comrades," and while the main function of those in your first circle is to give you emotional support, the main purpose of those in this category is enrichment. The people in this circle can help you expand your life in many directions—especially if you choose comrades with a wide variety of personalities, interests and viewpoints—or they can simply be pleasant companions for certain day-to-day activities.

The characteristics of this supportive circle are as follows:

1. *Congenial comrades see each other regularly (although not necessarily frequently) on some kind of conscious basis.*

Since we need many people in our lives in order to grow—physically, mentally, emotionally, intellectually, socially—we have to figure out ways to make time for them. And we have to face the fact that we simply cannot make the same amount of time for everyone. The congenial comrade circle contains people you like very much but whom you cannot (because of distance, time or other emotional commitments) or do not choose to give as high a friendship priority as those in your inner circle. Your relationships with them are not automatically inferior because you spend less time and energy with them than with your tender circle; the terms are just different. However, the terms include the idea that congenial comrades are enough a part of each other's lives that they manage to get together on a regular basis. They do not meet just by whim or chance. Sometimes these meetings might be planned in advance on a sort of schedule. At least, congenial comrades Susan and Sandra always meet once a month for lunch on a regular basis to catch up on what is going on in each other's lives, offer each other advice and comfort and just have fun. However, the rest of their meetings are spontaneous—they may ask each other out to dinner, to a party or just get together to talk, but sometimes they may go months without getting together except for their luncheons. On the other hand, they sometimes go into social flurries and see each other several times in one month. It all depends what is going on between them and in their individual lives.

Barbara and Jim have a sort of internal time clock that tells them when it is time to get together. They are congenial comrades (and sometimes lovers) who have a limited involvement centering on some similar intellectual interests. They don't really keep up on what is going on in each other's lives but about every three weeks one or the other will feel the need for the enrichment the other provides and call him or her. They understand each other in a special way no one else does and they've found they start missing each other or even feeling uneasy wondering if the other is O.K. if they don't make contact every few weeks.

2. *Congenial comrades provide companionship for enrichment.* Dr. Abraham Maslow, founder of the human potential move-

ment, said that men and women must fulfill certain psychological needs before they could achieve their full potential—which he called self-actualization. According to Dr. Maslow, those needs that must be fulfilled first (after physiological needs and physical security) are love and self-esteem. And one of the purposes of the tender circle is to provide that love and self-esteem so that a person is able to go on and develop other aspects of his personality— to explore new interests, to learn new skills or perfect old ones or pursue some specialized interests. Congenial comrades help us explore and learn.

Having a tender circle serves as an emotional foundation that frees us to reach out to many others in more limited ways, to enrich ourselves with congenial comrades who don't appear to be "our kind." For example, Philip is a very intellectual man. He is a college instructor and so spends a lot of time reading, grading papers and discussing abstract ideas. Since most of his friends are also college professors, his life tends to become unbalanced. As a result, his head gets more "exercise" than his body. But Philip has always wanted to explore the terrain of his own body; it's just that, since his natural inclination is to be "bookish," he needs a little guidance and encouragement in his exploration.

Therefore, he values his special friendship with Steve—an engineer who is also a "rugged" outdoorsman. Now and then Steve suggests that they go backpacking into a wilderness area or that they take a mountaineering course or go skiing. Since Steve has a lot of expertise in these things, it becomes a learning experience for Philip as well as a pleasant outing and a chance to use his muscles after sitting all week. With the help of his congenial comrade, Philip is, literally, getting out of his head and into his body. His personality and his life have expanded.

It isn't important that Steve and Philip don't share a lot of feelings or intellectual interests—Philip has his tender circle for the former and his colleagues for the latter. However, without Steve it isn't likely that Philip would have ever really discovered the world of nature and his own physical self as he has.

While the enrichment that congenial comrades can help provide in your life can take you into some dramatic and exciting areas, it can also make your daily life more interesting and fulfilling. Alice and Sophie could be like the many bored housewives they know, women who have let housework and child care become monotonous and unrewarding tasks. However, they have chosen to serve as congenial comrades for each other for the purpose of enriching their lives as housewives and mothers. Together they take their children on some interesting and educational excursions—to parks, museums, theaters—and in the process they find they too are being educated and stimulated. They baby-sit for each other so that each can take a class or pursue some outside interest or simply enjoy shopping without the hubbub of little children. And in their daily "coffee klatches" they attempt to avoid gossip or small talk and discuss ideas—as they jokingly say, "We have ideas the same age as well as children."

Alice and Sophie share a lot of each other's daily lives but they do not share many of their feelings with each other. They do not have that understanding of each other that makes for close emotional rapport. However, they are two congenial people who play an important enrichment role in each other's lives.

THE OUTER RIM

The third supportive circle is called the outer rim. It contains from thirty to fifty people. These are the people you are least involved with in the sense of the time and energy you devote to them and the activities you share. Again, the word "involvement" does not refer to the amount of caring you may have for these people. You may have an old childhood friend that you keep in touch with. Maybe you exchange letters at Christmas and see each other every few years. You are committed to staying in touch but you are not really involved in the daily activities of each other's lives. Yet, when you are together, the closeness you've always felt is there—real and tangible.

On the other hand, you may have some friends and relatives in the outer rim with whom you are not very close—people who are sort of "have-tos." You may "have to" see them occasionally at holidays or family occasions because you are related or have been friends a long time, but you may not have much in common except blood ties or memories. Still you want to keep them in your life in some way because of loyalty or because they give your life some continuity since they knew you "when."

The two important functions of your outer rim are that its members provide stimulation—cultural, intellectual, physical, sexual, spiritual—and that they serve as "resource" people—people you can call on for help in getting a job, in getting tickets to a concert, in learning how to play chess.

These are the characteristics of the outer rim:

1. *The contact with outer rim people is infrequent and generally not on a regular basis.*

You will not be able to see all of those in your outer rim group on either a frequent or a regular basis. There are simply too many of them and you don't have enough time or energy for very many of them very often. But these people are in the background of your life and you know you can reach out and contact them when it seems like a good idea. Maybe you'd like to reminisce about old times with a childhood friend, to laugh and be carefree with a playful pal, to find out more about a specialized subject that this particular "outer-rimmer" knows a lot about.

There may be a few outer-rimmers that you see infrequently but on a regular basis—certain relatives or friends, for example, with whom you have established some special "rituals." Larry and Tim meet once a year. They call on the phone now and then and drop each other a line occasionally, but that is generally their only other contact. But the one day that they meet is very special—it is New Year's Day and they always go to the Rose Bowl game together—a tradition that started when they were in college together. This day is a special one for them—a "bonus" day—and they wouldn't give it up for anything. Yet they don't feel the need to be involved in other aspects of each other's lives.

And sometimes you can maintain outer rim contact by phone. This may include those you simply don't have time to see, don't care to spend time or energy on or those who live far away. It may also include some very dear friends, those you have put on "hold" until circumstances change and you can have closer and more frequent contact. Whatever the reason, it may be worthwhile to call them now and then because they inspire you or stimulate your thinking or make you laugh or because they are ill or have a birthday or just because you've been thinking about them. But, no matter how your contact comes about—by planned meetings, by phone, in response to a specific need or by sheer joyous chance—the time you spend with them can be like a "bonus" to your life.

2. *Some of the people in the outer rim add stimulation to your life.*

Although you may not see these people very often, they usually have a unique sort of stimulation to offer. Perhaps they spark your intellectuality; their heads enrich your head, as Paula Menkin puts it. Ms. Menkin believes that we should be careful not to overemphasize the "feeling" level of friendship at the expense of the intellectual level. According to this friendship expert, "Some of the most beautiful friendships and the ones we don't develop and value enough are friendships with people whose minds spark our minds."

One woman got this sort of intellectual stimulation from a woman she met in the elevator who works on a different floor of her office building and with whom she has had two very intense, very exciting lunches. Though they seldom see one another, they enjoy and stimulate each other because there are some things they can talk about more clearly with each other than with anyone else.

For another man, going to the opera with a friend who used to be an opera singer is a form of cultural stimulation. He says it "nourishes his soul" even though he only sees his friend once a year during the opera season.

And some outer-rimmers provide a very special sort of sexual stimulation—the kind of excitement that comes with a partner one knows and expects to see again, yet who always seems new because of the infrequency of contact. For five years in a row, Janet spent part of her annual vacation in a rustic lodge in Vermont where the attractions included wonderful meals, a great view and a handsome night clerk. Each year they resumed the sexual affair that had started on her first trip. The sex was great and stimulating, but they did not have enough in common to build a full-time relationship; therefore, they made the most of the time they had and parted without regret.

3. *Some of the people in the outer rim serve as "resources."*

If you really sit down and think about it, you probably already know a lot of "resource people." It could be the tennis player in your apartment complex who can help you with your backhand; it could be the teacher you met at the psychology conference who can help you get your class in order; it could be the wine taster you met at a recent party who could help make your cheese-and-wine-tasting party a smash. Today, with so many things to learn about and such constant change, it is impossible to learn everything you need to know for yourself. You can use other people to help you find the best buys, make better decisions, locate services you need and so on.

When Sally wanted to change jobs she found out just how many resource people she knew. She was a secretary for an insurance firm who wanted to become an insurance agent—a field hard for a woman to break into. However, she had an outer-rimmer who was active in the women's movement who advised her on how to make sure her civil rights weren't being abridged when she did apply. Another outer-rimmer, an insurance man, gave her some tips on how to construct her résumé and yet another introduced her to the manager of a large insurance firm—where she got her job.

All of your circles are important to your well-being, and each level of relationship deserves to be nourished. But even with the best of care, your network will never be a static thing. It is a living security blanket and nothing that is living stays the same for very long. You will find people moving from one circle to another—because of a change in circumstances, because you decide to move them or because of a decision they make. People will weave their way in and out of your life. Many will be in your supportive network one year but won't be there the next. In fact, probably most who are in your inner circle won't be there five years later, not necessarily because you don't want them to be or because they don't want to be, but because life today is like that.

This movement of people is nothing to worry about. It has advantages and disadvantages, but it is something to recognize and prepare ourselves for. The only way we can prepare ourselves is by learning to reach out easily, to build good relationships quickly, to bring closure comfortably and, most important, to savor short-term relationships, for they are the very fabric of our existence.

11

How to Form Your
Supportive Network

After reading about supportive networks, you may be saying, "I'd sure like to have one, but I don't know how to get it," or "It all sounds like too much work," or "I already have a bunch of people who care about me, so there's nothing for me to do," or "I have a more than full-time job—how will I have time?" Whatever your reaction, if you suspect you might benefit from learning how to get more emotional security, enrichment and stimulation from your friends, *it is time to take action.*

FRIENDSHIP EXAMINATION

The first step toward organizing your supportive network is a friendship examination. This is a process that involves deciding what you want from people at this particular time in your life, identifying the significant people in your life and the circle into which each fits and evaluating what you are getting from those relationships. Such an examination will require thought and energy, but the time spent will be exciting because you will be learning about you. And building a solid foundation for yourself takes a lot less effort than trying to function without it.

Though we will focus on your wants because this is your supportive network, remember that in friendship alliances both parties must benefit. You must be willing to give to those in your network—sometimes more, sometimes less than they give you, sometimes the same as what they give you, sometimes something entirely different. But there is always an obligation. To want people as friends, they must satisfy some of your wants; to keep them as friends, you must supply some of theirs.

So set aside at least two hours when you won't be interrupted, and get started. Be prepared to experience some insights and ideas that can turn your life around.

Part A

This will help you discover just what it is you want from the other people in your life and how important those wants are to you. It is your own collection of wants that helps give you individuality as a human being. Thus, you must deliberately develop the relationships that will fulfill many different wants.

Some of your people-related wants are vital to you; unless they are satisfied you cannot function at your best or enjoy life fully. Other wants are sort of "bonuses"—pleasant surprises if they do get satisfied but not necessary to your well-being. Not only do your wants vary in intensity but they change from time to time as you change. This is exactly why you must look at your list of "wants" every now and then.

Following is a list of "Interpersonal Wants" coupled with a scale of numbers of 1 to 7. After each item on the list, circle the number that shows how strongly you desire that item. Number 1 means that your desire is only slight, while number 7 means that it is very strong. The items presented here will probably not be all-inclusive of your wants, and are intended only to guide your thinking. Change their wording as appropriate and add other items at the end of the list to represent your wants as specifically and precisely as you can.

INTERPERSONAL WANTS

	VERY LITTLE					VERY MUCH	
I WANT SOMEONE TO:							
1. Talk to for companionship	1	2	3	4	5	6	7
2. Eat with	1	2	3	4	5	6	7
3. Sleep with (without having sex)	1	2	3	4	5	6	7
4. Have sex with	1	2	3	4	5	6	7
5. Have fun with	1	2	3	4	5	6	7
6. Share intimate feelings with	1	2	3	4	5	6	7
7. Give love and affection to	1	2	3	4	5	6	7
8. Receive love and affection from	1	2	3	4	5	6	7
9. Work with	1	2	3	4	5	6	7
10. Learn from	1	2	3	4	5	6	7
11. Cuddle me and give me physical strokes	1	2	3	4	5	6	7
12. Give me ego strokes	1	2	3	4	5	6	7
13. Go out with	1	2	3	4	5	6	7
14. Help me be creative	1	2	3	4	5	6	7
15. Play sports with	1	2	3	4	5	6	7
16. Go shopping with	1	2	3	4	5	6	7
17. Help me with tasks that are too big for me	1	2	3	4	5	6	7
18. Be spiritual with	1	2	3	4	5	6	7
19. Give me intellectual stimulation	1	2	3	4	5	6	7
20. Enjoy nature with	1	2	3	4	5	6	7
21. Encourage me in what I do	1	2	3	4	5	6	7
22. Commiserate with when I'm sad	1	2	3	4	5	6	7
23. Help me in my personal growth	1	2	3	4	5	6	7
24. Travel with	1	2	3	4	5	6	7
25. Care for me when I'm sick	1	2	3	4	5	6	7
26. Help me make important decisions	1	2	3	4	5	6	7
27. Share living space	1	2	3	4	5	6	7
28. Help me with my children	1	2	3	4	5	6	7
Others (Write in additional wants)	1	2	3	4	5	6	7
	1	2	3	4	5	6	7
	1	2	3	4	5	6	7
	1	2	3	4	5	6	7

(Man-Woman Institute, October 1978)

Part B

Take three sheets of paper (8½ × 11 size or larger) and label one at the top "Tender Circle," another "Congenial Comrades" and the third "Outer Rim" to represent the three circles of your supportive network. (You may actually require more than one sheet for the second and third circles.) Think about your friends and acquaintances and how they are functioning in your life at the present time. Based on the descriptions of the circles in the previous chapter, list the names of these people down the left-hand side of the appropriate sheet. Write in pencil so you can erase and move names around until they are all on the sheets where they seem to fit best.

Next, divide the remaining space on each sheet into two equal columns. Label the first column *"Wants Being Satisfied"* and the second column *"Wants Not Being Satisfied."* Now, starting with your Tender Circle sheet, think through your relationships with each person one at a time, deciding which of the wants on your Interpersonal Wants list are being satisfied by that person and which are not. Write the numbers of the wants that are being satisfied in the first column of the sheet, and in the second column write the number of additional wants that you *would like* to have satisfied by that particular person. Do this for each of the three sheets. You will probably have a number of duplications, but don't worry. It is common for one person to satisfy several wants and for the same want to be satisfied by several different people.

Part C

The information you have on your Interpersonal Wants list and the three sheets representing your support circles will clearly show you the organization of your supportive network. You will be able to tell a lot about the numbers and kinds of relationships you have, what you are getting out of these relationships and what is lacking. You can now begin to draw conclusions that will indicate what changes should be made to give you the complete support you need. Answering the following questions will help:

Which of your circles have the recommended number of members? Which do not?

Are you under- or over-peopled? Do you need to weed out or add people to your circles?

Do you have too many close involvements that might be sapping your time and energy? Or are most of your involvements limited ones that cannot give you the kind of support you need?

Which of your wants are being met adequately? Are these your strong wants?

Which of your wants are not being met adequately? How strong are they?

Do you have too many people for some wants, not enough for others?

Are your various wants being met by people in the proper circles? For example, are people in the Tender Circle meeting the wants appropriate to that circle?

Which people in your network have the potential for satisfying certain wants they are not now meeting? Which wants will require bringing new people into your life?

Even if you find that you have a number of good relationships in your present supportive network that are meeting your strongest wants satisfactorily, all may not be as good as it can be. While it can be helpful to have several people available for your most important wants, it may be that you are automatically seeking out people for the same reasons time after time when you don't really need them. To lead a better balanced, more well-rounded life, it could profit you to pay attention to your lesser wants and to seek out people to satisfy them. For example, some people continually find friends for sharing sexual pleasure or for intellectual stimulation, but entirely ignore those who might bring out the spiritual side of their nature. On the other hand, some surround themselves with spiritual friends, meditators and do-gooders, and neglect their creative or devilish sides. All sides of us need stimulation through interpersonal relationships.

REMODELING YOUR SUPPORTIVE NETWORK

Your Friendship Examination may indicate that your network is not giving you all the support or exactly the kind of support you need. This section contains several suggestions on how you can remodel it.

1. *Weed people out*

If there are too many people in your network meeting the same wants or some who do not have the capability of meeting the wants you'd like them to, you should consider removing them from your network to make room for other people. You'll probably find that as you become more conscious of your wants, their relative importance and how well they are being satisfied, you will also become more selective about the people that occupy space in your network. We will not go into detail here on how to take people out of your network, but in later chapters will discuss ways to "unpeople" and to end relationships with minimum difficulty and pain.

2. *Change the nature of certain relationships*

Arrange to have different wants fulfilled or to have the same wants met in different ways. This may result in people being moved from one circle to another.

Contact those people in your network who are not meeting your wants as well as you would like but who have the potential for giving you greater satisfaction. Let each know that you have an unfilled interpersonal want and that you believe they can help fill it. Ask them to do the "We Process" in order to clarify the nature of your relationship and exactly what you can give to each other. If they do not want to do the "We Process" but are still willing to help you, together you can work out a plan for a one-time-only trial action.

Make explicit what you want done for you and what you are willing to do in return; devise a plan for trying it out; and then be sure to talk about it afterward, to find out what you and your partner liked and didn't like and what you would do differently if you were to do it again.

It is especially recommended that you ask the people you want to have in your Tender Circle to do the "We Process" with you. These are the people from whom you will get your major support, and it is important that your relationships with them be clear and maximally effective. You will not have the time nor is it necessary to use the procedure with everyone in your network, but your tender circle people are critical.

Pick out certain individuals in your network that you think have special qualities and entice them into doing something with you that you have never done before, something that will expand or deepen your relationship. This might be the "We Process," a mini-date, a one-time-only action plan that will fill an interpersonal need or help you act out a fantasy, or maybe an alliance for a particular purpose for a particular amount of time.

3. *Bring new people into your network*

Deliberately seek out new people who seem interesting to you and might have potential for satisfying your wants. Follow the suggestions in Chapters 3 and 4 for getting acquainted and striking up friendships.

Go to places where there are apt to be people interested in developing supportive relationships that may not last a lifetime but that will be good for now: growth centers, nontraditional churches, and adult education classes at progressive universities and community colleges. Visit them while carrying a copy of this book under your arm and use it as a wedge in opening a conversation regarding the acquisition of supportive relationships. Use it much as Diogenes used his lantern when seeking an honest man.

Bring up the subject of building supportive circles of

friends at a get-together of people you already know. For instance, the gang at the nineteenth hole, the coffee klatch, relatives at a holiday dinner, your friends at PTA, or church, or at the après-ski gathering. Stand up and make the announcement that you want to give more emotional support, enrichment and stimulation to the people around you and to get more from them, too, and that you have some ideas as to how to do that and you want their ideas and help. Explain the idea of a network to them and also the idea of making interpersonal temporary alliances or contracts. Or ask them to read this book and set up another meeting later to discuss these matters. Become a missionary for better relationships. You'll find a lot of new friends, and your old friends will become better friends.

4. *Arrange a "Group Date"*

Another way of building new friendships or deepening old ones, while at the same time fulfilling wants for companionship in recreation, is through a "group date." Gather together a small bunch of people, some from your network and others that you don't know as well, to go out as a group and have fun. Make it an odd number of people, with members of both sexes, none of whom are married or "going with" each other. Whatever activity you decide on for the date, make it clear that the main objectives are:

a. To get to know one another as quickly and as well as possible.

b. For each person to look at himself and how he handles social situations in regard to things like money, transportation, seating, the purchase of drinks, etc., when he is on his own and functioning as an individual and not as half of a couple.

c. To have fun while also seeing that others have fun, too. (You will if you picture yourselves as members of a team with each person's purpose being to see that he *and* his teammates all have a good time. This attitude creates a synergistic effect—i.e., what comes out of the group is greater than the sum of its individual components. So expect some surprising things to happen on your group date.)

The idea behind the group date is that each person has much to gain by getting used to going out socially as an individual who is a member of a temporary social "team." He needs practice in learning to interact freely with members of both sexes, in being able to both initiate action and follow it and in looking after his own comfort and that of the group. Because of the expectation that people should go every place in couples, married people seldom attend social events as individuals (except for same-sex functions). And single people are usually busy looking for a partner if they don't have one. Or, if they do have one, they are concerned with being sure to say and do only what their partner will approve of.

This makes them ignore many opportunities for spontaneity and rewarding social interaction—with both their own and the opposite sex. In addition, few of us ever learn much about functioning as a member of a group in social situations. Our tradition of "rugged individualism" translated into action means that if people can't be part of the traditional social unit (a couple), they'll do it alone or not at all. We have not had a tradition of group dating in this country as there is in some other countries, though it is now beginning to catch on in some youth groups.

You will have to initiate the group date by inviting the other people to participate. The activity for the date can be decided either by you in advance or by the group when it first gets together. Once you have organized the group date and given everyone the "rules," however, you are not responsible for the interaction that follows. Do not act as the sole host or hostess. It will be puzzling to some people to be in a group with no assigned "leader," but the idea of the date is partly to encourage different people to take leadership at different times rather than to have a permanent assignment as either a leader or a follower.

Rules for a Group Date

In order for a group date to be most effective, these rules should be followed:

1. Everyone is to go as an individual. Whether a person is mar-

ried, in a committed relationship or dating, he/she is not to take a sexual partner on this date.

2. There is to be no hustling—no sexual passes—on the group date. Because we associate "dating" with sex, men on a date tend to be concerned with if or when to make a sexual overture while women worry "Will he or won't he?" This makes people nervous and causes them to pay less attention to the people around them and to the social activity they are supposed to be enjoying. The object of this date is not sex, but the enjoyment of several people at one time.

3. There should be both men and women on the group date. It is not a group date—at least, our idea of a group date—when couples or people of the same sex all go out together. The interaction in those kinds of groups tends to be along traditional role-playing lines, and we are trying to avoid that by our structure.

4. To help prevent "coupling" there should be an uneven number. This will force you to deal with some social situations that you might not know how to handle—i.e., if you go dancing and there is an extra, what do you do? Is it O.K. to leave him or her sitting alone at the table? Is it O.K. to ask strangers to dance to even out the numbers? etc.

5. Everyone should pay his or her own way. How the group handles the money will have to be decided at some point (does each person pay his own bill, do they pool their money, do they take turns?) but each person will be responsible for his own expenses.

6. The transportation should be decided on the basis of convenience, not sex. The men should not automatically have to serve as chauffeurs on this date. Whether cars are taken, the subway, taxis, etc., the group should decide upon it mutually as a group responsibility.

7. Whatever activity the group picks for its date, it should be one that allows people to have a lot of interaction and to move around. Sitting in a row at a play might not be the best activity unless the group also plans to meet later for a discussion. Some good group date activities are dancing, field trips to unusual places (factories, breweries, museums), physical activities such as roller skating, or even a camping trip (as long as it is made clear there will be no coupling or sexual interaction). The date can give everyone a chance to try activities his mate (if he has one) may not like, to explore unusual places with the safety of a group or to try a new physical activity with friends who won't criticize him for

not doing better or feel embarrassed if he is clumsy (as a sexual partner might).

8. The group date should be followed by a short meeting to discuss what went on among the participants and their feelings about the date. This is an excellent opportunity to gently point out to one another ways in which your interaction was good and ways in which it might be improved. It also can take care of any left-over feelings that people might have (someone felt left out, someone felt he got "taken" financially, someone resented the obvious coupling of someone else). And chances are at this critique session you will want to set up another group date.

TEMPORARY ALLIANCES

There are some things people need or want from one another that are particularly difficult to get in our society. Tender physical stroking is one, ready companionship when one doesn't have a mate is another. Forming temporary alliances is an excellent way of meeting such wants. The group date described in the previous section is really a temporary alliance made for a specific purpose.

We strongly encourage you to develop the practice of forming temporary alliances to get more of your wants fulfilled—from people both inside and outside your supportive network. You don't have to know people very long or very well in order for them to give you exactly what you need at a given time. People will do unbelievably lovely things for you—and enjoy doing them—if you will just follow these simple steps:

1. Be sure you have a feeling of caring about the person or persons you intend to ask something of.
2. Let them know exactly what you want.
3. Find out exactly what they want.
4. Decide what you are both willing to do.
5. Take action to do it.

We have described below some types of alliances that might help you get your wants fulfilled. You undoubtedly will be able to think of many more.

Tenderness alliances

There is a song that encourages men, when life is not going right for their wives, to "Try a Little Tenderness." But the truth is that all people need tenderness, no matter what sex they are, and they need it every day of their lives. However, tenderness, which should be one of the most available commodities around—because of the pleasure that comes with dispensing as well as receiving it—seems to be awfully hard to give and get enough of. What makes it so difficult is that we tend to associate a desire for tenderness with weakness of character, and the display of physical affection among adults, with sex. Nobody wants to admit he sometimes feels weak and needy and longs to be cared for and stroked like a baby, but we all do. And we act as if we think that hugs and pats and kisses must be reserved for lovers or children. As a result, most adults are starved for physical affection. Though some people turn to bed-hopping as a means of getting the tenderness they need, there are much better ways.

Ways of giving tenderness (of allowing our softer feelings of caring, compassion and kindness to show—through words, sounds and touch) and a willingness to let others express their tenderness toward us, are limited only by our imagination. And by our ability to let others know what we want. Emily discovered—when she was newly divorced and without a loving sexual partner for the first time in twenty-nine years—that, to her surprise, she didn't have to do without tenderness. She recalls one experience in particular when she found that tenderness could come packed in an unlikely form.

Emily had been living with a divorced friend who had a nine-year-old daughter. One Sunday morning, Emily woke up in a very bad place emotionally. She knew what was bothering her and had no desire for advice, but needed someone to stroke her and reassure her and let her cry. But her friend, whom she knew would understand and help her out, was sleeping late. The only one around was the slip of a daughter unconcernedly munching corn flakes and reading the funnies. Emily looked at her appraisingly—the germ of an idea brewing in her head—could the little girl help her get past this emotional crisis? Would she dare ask?

She decided to take a chance. And so she—without realizing

that was what she was doing—proposed a sort-of tenderness alliance with the little girl. Very gently she explained that she needed to cry and get her feelings out but that she needed some help in doing it. She assured the child that there was nothing seriously wrong and no cause for alarm, just something that happens to grown-ups sometimes. When she asked the little girl if she would be willing to help her with her feelings, the child said she would. Then, following instructions, she sat on the couch, took Emily's head in her lap, and patted and stroked her and made soothing sounds while Emily sobbed. Soon Emily felt much better and showed it. And then for a while they talked about what had happened like equals. They both had gotten a lot out of their temporary tenderness "alliance." The little girl had an opportunity to give comfort—to take the adult role for a change. This made her feel strong and realize she was more than just a helpless child. And Emily learned that comfort is available from almost anyone —even when that "anyone" is a little girl.

You, too, can make a variety of alliances to give and get tenderness. Following are a number of examples we hope will stimulate you to think of ways in which you might get more for yourself and give more to others. Always keep in mind that alliances can last for but a few weeks, days or even hours and yet be of immense benefit.

A short-lived but useful tenderness alliance was one formed by a man and woman who lived in the same large apartment complex. Shortly after becoming acquainted, they realized they had something important in common; because of some stressful situations in their lives both needed someone to just listen to them—non-judgmentally—without giving advice or criticism and to hug, stroke and pat them. So, for several weeks they met every morning at seven-thirty, before they began their daily activities, their meetings lasting about an hour. Each took a turn talking without interruption for fifteen minutes, and then they spent some time in dialogue, giving feedback, reassurance and physical affection. Although they never "dated" or developed a romantic involvement and the meetings ended when their period of stress was over, the time they had spent was treasured by both, for it helped them get through a difficult time more easily.

A group of single friends (three men and five women), in order to get the tender touching and nonsexual physical contact they wanted, formed a massage workshop. They met every other Saturday afternoon, each time in a different person's home. They arranged for a professional masseur to come in for a few times and instruct them so that they could develop a matter-of-fact, nonsexual attitude toward massage as well as the skills necessary for giving the type of massages that are satisfying physically and emotionally rather than just excuses to "paw" one another. Not only did this workshop make them better able to touch each other with affection and without anxiety; it has carried over in their relationships with others, and they have become more tenderly affectionate and less nervous with other friends, too.

An unusual tenderness alliance was made by two men, George, forty, and Paul, thirty-one. George was basically a lonely man. Divorced, he had "girl friends" and male acquaintances but no men he could share his softer feelings with. As a result of his need for tender talking and affectionate touching, he became a minor-league "Don Juan." Often he found himself having sex with women he wasn't really interested in just because he was starved for soft contact and didn't know how to get it any other way.

However, when George went to Europe for six months on a long-term work project, he discovered that in some other cultures men are able to touch—physically and emotionally—without homosexual implications. He became involved in a beautiful friendship with a European man that had both masculine camaraderie and caring. When George came back to this country, he decided he wanted the same kind of friendship here, but he just wasn't able to find it until he met Paul at a workshop on divorce. The two men found themselves part of a "dyad" during an exercise that involved the sharing of experiences and feelings about divorce. Afterward, they felt so good about themselves and each other they wanted to keep their relationship going. After the workshop, they formed an alliance to meet once a week to talk, to listen, to hug without embarrassment and, if it seemed appropriate, to cry. Their alliance has helped them both see that they need not be dependent on women for tenderness and, as a result, their relationships with women are better.

Tenderness exercise. Emily and her partner in the Man-Woman Institute, Dr. Keith Tombrink, often use tenderness-promoting exercises in their workshops for singles because the lack of it is a big problem for most of them. Following is one of the exercises they sometimes use. It is called Temporary Tenderness and is patterned after one of the techniques originated by Dr. Herbert Otto, psychologist, director of the National Institute for the Development of Human Potential. You can form a short-term tenderness alliance by getting two other people to try this exercise with you. Remember, you don't have to be single to do it. Everyone can use all the tenderness he can get.

Form a triad which includes a member of both sexes. The object is to take turns rocking and stroking one another in ways reminiscent of parents and children.

There are three roles. Each person is to have a turn in each role. The entire exercise is to be done without talking.

Start out with one person, who plays the "mother" role, sitting either on a sofa or on the floor with some support for her back. Her legs should be spread apart so that the person playing the "baby" role can put his bottom between them and curl up and cuddle like a baby, allowing his head to be supported by the "mother's" arm. The "mother" should support and rock back and forth a bit now and then while the third person, the "father," strokes the "baby's" forehead, hair, face and body—slowly and gently. The reclining person is to let himself go, not to worry about being too heavy, but to allow himself to be supported, stroked and cared for with his eyes closed—as if he were a helpless infant.

After five to ten minutes, slowly and quietly, without talking, they should change places, repeating the whole process. After each person has had a turn in each position, they should look into one another's eyes for a few minutes, still without talking, trying to sense how their partners are feeling and becoming aware of how they are feeling. Then, when they are ready, they should talk softly with one another, focusing their discussion around the following questions:

What were your feelings during different parts of this exercise?

What did you particularly enjoy?

What bothered you?

In what ways are your feelings toward your partners different now from what they were before this exercise?

How do you feel after this experience?

Did sexual feelings bother you? How did you deal with them?
Did homosexual feelings bother you? How did you deal with them?

Doing-good alliances

All human beings are capable of doing far more than they think they can, and have more sides to their personality than they develop. But they often need someone else to help them discover just how much they are capable of and to bring out some of their hidden inclinations. One of the benefits of having short-term alliances with many people is that we get to do things we could never do alone and we discover facets of ourselves we didn't even know existed.

A part of everyone's personality is the urge to "do good"—an urge to change the world for the better in some way, to make it matter that one has spent some time on this planet. Many people are unaware of the "do good" urge in themselves; they don't recognize it as a side that, if developed, will benefit them personally, as well as others. Or they don't find enough opportunities to express this particular facet.

Betty discovered the power in the "do good" facet of her own and others' natures when she was teaching in high school. Her students appeared on the surface to be very "cool"—to be uninterested in anything beyond their own little world. They acted self-centered and selfish. But Betty soon learned that if she pointed out people who needed help, or problems that needed solving, and if she gave them encouragement to let their strength be felt—and the resources for doing it well—they jumped at the chance to "do good." And she found that the classes always learned more, were better behaved and accomplished more when they banded together in a common "do good" cause. It didn't matter whether this alliance was to save the fish in a nearby golf-course lake when the lake was drained (as one ecology class did), to adopt a needy family and give them a marvelous Christmas (as five social science classes did) or to get petitions signed for a state-wide initiative (as a politics class did). What mattered was that the students accomplished something they felt was worthwhile, learned to feel better about themselves and learned to work in temporary teams to reach a common goal.

Adults enjoy the camaraderie of "doing good" together, too, and sometimes a group of people spontaneously develops a "do good" alliance when they see a need. When Adele, fifty, became seriously ill, her friends rallied round, giving her all the support she needed and giving themselves a chance to "do good." Adele, who had the responsibility for two children and a house, had a well-paying job that provided sufficient money for meeting day-to-day living expenses, but not for the massive expenditures entailed by a catastrophic illness.

One by one her friends came over to help—cleaning her house, baby-sitting, doing the shopping, mowing the lawn. But some days there might be two or three people there and other days no one at all. So the friends decided to "get organized" and they held a meeting for all people interested in being part of Adele's support group. They drew up a list of chores to be done and assigned people specific times to do them. They also made sure there was always someone in charge every day—someone who either came over to be with Adele or who checked with her on whether she needed anything beyond the chores already being taken care of. Adele's supporters even put on a fund-raising party that raised over $3,000 toward her medical expenses.

What they had done—although they didn't know it—was to form a short-term alliance to see her through her crisis. As Adele improved, the larger "do good" alliance dissolved, but a smaller group of close friends formed a sort of tender circle alliance to be supportive to—not just Adele—but everyone in the group.

But "do good" alliances needn't be group efforts and the "do-gooding" cause needn't be a crisis. Two friends, Thelma and Sue, formed an alliance to visit some elderly relatives together. Thelma's aunt was in a convalescent home and Sue's grandmother lived alone in an apartment. They felt an "obligation" to see their relatives at least once every several weeks, but it always seemed like a terrible chore because of the difficulty of finding something interesting to talk about. But when they started doing their visits together—first to the aunt and then to the grandmother—they found it no longer seemed like a chore. Sue was able to bring out facets of Thelma's aunt that Thelma hadn't been able to; Thelma found she and Sue's grandmother had a common interest in weaving rugs. The visits became livelier, the rapport of the women with their elderly relatives closer, and the aunt and grandmother thrived on this new and warmer sort of attention.

Doing-bad alliances

"Doing good" isn't the only urge we have that others can help us develop. We also have a need sometimes to "do bad"—to let out the devilishness in us. And companions can help. Strange as it may seem, this kind of activity can benefit us and others.

It is a custom in our society for people to tell each other in many ways, some subtle and some not so subtle: "Be good," "Be nice," "Be polite," "Play it safe," "Don't rock the boat." When we try too hard to do these things (and all of us do sometimes) we lose our zest and energy, become tired—and tiring. A saint is a bore. It takes a dollop of naughtiness not only to rev up our corpuscles but to make us seem human and alive. For their own and others' well-being, people need to be encouraged to "do bad" now and then—to be a bit naughty and self-indulgent when no one is being hurt by it. To be daring and adventurous. To do some things that seem foolish or that go against conventional mores, but that are fun.

Most people have a hard time doing bad because they've been conditioned for so long that everything they do must be worthwhile (including their play time) that they feel guilty if they do something just for the "hell" of it—something that may not be meaningful or have a deeper purpose than enjoyment. Many people often devote their leisure time only to "worthwhile" activities—to learning to play tennis, for example, even though they don't enjoy it very much but because it is the "in" sport. Or they subject themselves to monotonous forms of exercise like jogging or weight lifting because that is good for them rather than skipping to work or doing the hula or belly dancing for the sheer pleasure of it—which would also be good exercise.

People are afraid to try things that seem unconventional for fear others will disapprove. To break through these fears and "do bad" now and then, it is important to have just the right teammate. This is no time to take along the sort of person who will keep saying things like "You can't do that," or "Stop, people are staring." You need someone willing to enter into the spirit of devilment with you and then you'll think of ways to "do bad" that will astonish and delight both of you.

But there is another reason to have just the right "do bad" companion. All of us have areas in which we are shy or fearful, and many times when we try to overcome these fears by ourselves by trying something new and devilish, we go about it the wrong way or at the wrong time. With a companion to offer another viewpoint you are more likely to do things in ways that will not get you rebuffed or in difficulties. And if you do have some problems that result from your attempts to "do bad," it helps to have someone to comfort you or help you form a plan to get out of trouble. By forming a "do bad" team you can set up a safety and comfort system.

Joyce, forty-two, and Doris, forty-five, found they were exactly the right "do bad" companions for each other after their long-term marriages broke up. Both had been "proper" wives and mothers and now wanted to experience life in new ways. Though they were like two babes in the woods, somehow, between the two of them, they always came out O.K. from their adventures. An example was the night they decided to go out and defy all the rules they had ever been taught about how to meet men. First, they went out to dinner and flirted with all the men in the place—but in such a charming way that even the women companions of their male "targets" found it amusing. Then they went to a bar alone since they had been told this is definitely something nice women don't do. Their third—and by far the greatest "do bad" achievement of the evening—was to take the aggressive role in making contact with men at the bar. They wrote a note on a napkin that said, "Dear handsome man. We are two ladies who would like to talk to you for a while. Do not be alarmed. We mean no harm." They selected a likely candidate and sent the note, via the bartender, to the man. Their first response was a note on a business card that went like this: "Dear ladies, I would love to talk with you but I am having a business meeting with my boss. Too bad because I *do* mean harm." Signed, "Handsome man." You can imagine what fun they had the rest of the evening sending their "pickup" note out several times.

Here are some suggested "do bad" activities that you and your friends can make short-term alliances for:

1. Deliberately flirting and trying to get acquainted with

members of the opposite sex you ordinarily would be afraid to reach out to.

2. Playing hooky—taking a day off from work, school or housekeeping—to goof off with a friend.

3. Trying out some new activity that you are a little apprehensive about—getting a massage at a massage parlor, going to a gay bar or a pornographic movie, going to a nude beach or a nude camp.

4. Having an affair with someone who is married or who is much older or younger and discussing it as it develops.

5. Buying and wearing clothes of a very different style—clothes that bring out a different facet of personality or that seem outlandish.

6. Playing a role—acting as if you were someone else. The purpose is not to take advantage of anyone or to fool him, but to see what being someone else feels like, to give you a sense of being very important and to find out what happens when you act as if you are. For example, before going out for an evening you fear will be dull or nerve-racking, make a pact with a friend who is also going that each of you will assume a new identity and act it out as much as possible. Each will keep track of the other—complimenting when the role is being played well, reminding when it seems to have been forgotten. In this little game, you don't lie to anyone about your identity, but just act the part. You'd be surprised what fun a dull gathering can become when you carry yourself and talk and treat others as if you were the Queen of England or Albert Schweitzer or the author of a best-selling novel or the chairman of the board of a billion-dollar corporation or a South American playboy or Madame Du Barry.

An adventurous married couple tried this when they found themselves vacationing at a hotel where there was a convention of the American Psychological Association—a very serious and prestigious organization. They had made friends with two psychologists attending the convention and when they showed interest in attending one particular session, their friends offered to lend them their badges for the evening. With that, she became Dr. E. Pratt, editor of a psychology journal, and he became Dr. S. Leonard, a psychology professor at a big university. They had fun reaching out to people at the session in their new role, and then when they went to dinner, they really got into the spirit of the game. Whenever the waiter came around or was within earshot, they talked with one another as though she (Dr. Pratt) was interviewing him (Dr. Leonard) for an article in her journal, and to top it off they had themselves paged at the restaurant so they could feel even more important. They laughed more than they had laughed in years, and that night back in their hotel room their lovemaking was different, as might be expected. Two experts in psychology make love in ways an ordinary married couple would never ever think of.

While this type of "doing bad" can do you a lot of good, it isn't bad for anyone else. You don't do things that can hurt others physically or emotionally or that can get you in legal trouble. Usually the worst that can happen is that you might raise a few eyebrows or get some disapproving stares.

Working alliances

Because most of us were brought up to play male-female roles, we also only learned to do certain types of jobs—those that were considered fitting and proper for our sex. That upbringing made most people very dependent in many ways. Sometimes marriage—at least traditional marriage—doesn't give us a chance to grow out of these dependencies. So the married woman never learns to change a tire, or the married man to cook. And sometimes when relationships do break up, the man and woman both discover they are crippled in some respects—that they cannot live autonomously.

Dr. Stephen Johnson, the author of *First Person Singular: a guide for single living*, makes the statement: "I am convinced that one of the primary reasons people have such difficulty in living single is that they are simply unaware of what they need to do in order to live a reasonably fulfilling life alone." And one of the major things they have to do, adds Johnson, is "perform all self-care functions that have been previously shared or delegated. The more unfamiliar these tasks are, the more difficult you will find learning how to perform them. The more division of labor and mutual dependency in the previous relationship, the more difficulty there will be in getting along alone."

We believe that all adults need to be autonomous; after all, most adults live alone or with a same-sex roommate at some point in their lives—before marriage or when they are "between relationships." And married people may have to take care of themselves at times—the wife may get ill, the husband may go away for extended periods on business. And to learn what it is they need to know in order to be autonomous, people can form alliances.

When Bill became a widower he was not only grief-stricken but virtually helpless—at least around the house. Although he could run a machine shop, he couldn't do his own laundry, shopping or cooking. Bill found himself wooing and about to marry a woman he had known during his marriage simply because she was able to take care of him. But his daughter—sensing the relationship was based more on convenience than love—made an alliance with her dad. She agreed to teach him to take care of himself if he would help subsidize her in a new apartment so she could try autonomous living herself. Before long, Bill was taking care of himself and seeing the lady less. A lot of marriages are based primarily on mutual dependency—two people shoring up each other's needs—which breeds possessiveness caused by a fear of desertion. Helping each other learn to be self-sufficient can ensure non-clinging relationships.

Of course, no matter how autonomous we are, life is far too complex for any of us to do everything for ourselves. There are some things we can't ever be very skilled at; there are some things we don't want to do. This is O.K. It is only when you think you can't do some things because of your sex, or that only a mate of the opposite sex can do them, that you are trapped. It doesn't take a penis to do the plumbing.

A group of people can form an alliance to help each other do the pesky time-consuming jobs around the house that no one wants to do. One such group, made up of three women and two men, all single, all living alone, calls itself the Labor Patrol. Three members own their own houses and two have apartments. They got together because they were tired of spending so much time and money fixing up things around the house—cleaning, etc. Here is how the Labor Patrol works:

Once every two weeks the group spends four hours (usually on Saturday mornings) at the home of one of the members. They rotate until everyone has had a chance to enjoy the fruits of the group's labor and then they begin again. The "laboree" prepares a list of tasks to be done and is responsible for providing all the materials. The tasks are divided according to who wants to do what and who has the skills—not by sex. However, they make an effort to see that everyone tries to learn how to do some of the messiest and most difficult jobs so no one gets stuck. So they all participate in painting jobs and heavy cleaning. Strangely enough, when encouraged to work at what they really enjoy, one of the women discovered she really likes to mow the lawn, another that she has a knack for electrical repairs, while one of the men selects vacuuming and dusting whenever he can because it gives him time to daydream.

And people in jobs can also form alliances to help each other at work. Two women became friends by virtue of the fact they were the only women in the social science department of a large high school. They soon discovered that unless they took action, their chauvinistic male colleagues were going to see they got all the bad assignments and had little voice in department policy. They formed an alliance to look out for each other's interests—and they even worked out an effective strategy to achieve this aim.

One of them, Patty, was very aggressive verbally and had a way of turning the men off by attacking them—the other, Lisa, was the opposite. She would never speak up, even in discussions that affected her personally. The women made an alliance to give each other feedback on how they came across at department meetings. Thus, every time Patty toned down and said something in a way that gained support for their cause and didn't alienate, Lisa would point it out in their post-meeting sessions. When Lisa spoke up, Patty would do the same. Not only did they help each other come across more effectively, but they also became a respected force in the department because of standing together.

Eating alliances

Nobody seems to eat together anymore—not even families. A survey of meal habits of American families showed that the family dinner is almost a thing of the past. It seldom takes place more than three nights a week in any family and when it does, the television set is likely to be on.

Families and married couples, at least, do have the option to eat together—even if they don't always take advantage of it. But single people often say the one thing they hate most about single life is eating alone. In our society we associate food with love—

with being cared for. Thus, to eat alone seems to tell us or anyone else watching that we are not loved—which is one reason people hate to eat alone in a restaurant.

In the following section we'll describe some eating alliances suitable for either married or single people—alliances that can help people fill the social needs that were once filled by the custom of the family dinner, alliances that can serve as an "enhancer of communications" between people, alliances that guarantee that no one person gets stuck in the role of "chief cook and bottle washer" and alliances that may keep single people from getting remarried primarily to have someone to eat with.

1. One man frequently forms a one-evening alliance with certain friends, a time to get together at his house to cook and eat a meal together. It is his custom to invite a different person each time—sometimes a man and sometimes a woman, sometimes a married person, sometimes a single one—and they discuss the menu in advance. Then, since he is interested in being involved with the person as much as possible and in having them not stay in the "host" and "guest" roles, he and his guest make out a shopping list together, go to the store together, do the cooking and cleanup together. This way his men friends have a chance to learn some cooking skills and his women friends don't get stuck in the role of cook. No one has to feel like a servant doing a boring job alone, for even unpleasant chores like washing dishes can be fun with two doing them. Everyone benefits from learning about different kinds of menus, different ways of doing things, and, of course, he benefits from sharing such a learning and fun experience with so many people—and it is much cheaper than taking a friend out to dinner.

2. Two women friends have an alliance to seek out unusual restaurants. They each live alone and get tired of the struggle of trying to fix nutritious and interesting meals for themselves. So once a week—in the middle of the week—they select a restaurant (after careful study of the restaurant section in the paper, the phone book, recommendations of friends) and eat out. They are particularly interested in inexpensive "ethnic" places since neither has a very big salary. The alliance has livened up their palates and their lives in some interesting ways. First, they've met a lot of new people during their dining-out adventures and second, they've started asking their men friends out to dinner at some of their favorite

colorful places. The men are delighted to be taken out and many times, in return, cook a meal for the women.

3. A group of friends have formed an alliance to meet at a local restaurant one night a week to eat together and have some lively discussions. After having them as steady customers for almost six months, the owner invested in a good-sized round table for their weekly dinner meetings. Subsequently, the group requested that any people who came alone—either sex, any age—be invited to eat at their special "round table." This way, they also get to meet some new people and the group doesn't get so "ingrown." The restaurant owner, seeing the potential of his round table, has started a policy the rest of the week of seating people without partners at it and giving them a chance to form their own temporary eating alliances.

4. And it isn't only unmarried people who should consider forming eating alliances. One young couple we know has a certain bachelor friend to dinner twice a week. It is an alliance because the friend contributes the main course in return for the company and for having it cooked. He helps their food budget and they provide him with company and a home-cooked meal. He usually departs shortly after dinner—leaving them free to enjoy the evening together and guaranteeing their alliance doesn't become the kind of tedious social occasion where everyone is expected to make conversation when they would really rather be doing something else.

While reading these many ideas, you surely must have thought of something you'd like a friend or two to do for you or with you. You may like the suggestion of forming temporary alliances yet hesitate to get started. A good way to get going is to set a definite goal. Here is what to do: Write a reminder to yourself in big letters on a piece of paper and tape it on your bathroom mirror. It should read like this: "I will take the initiative for making *at least* one temporary alliance each week." If you live up to this plan for two months, you can then throw the note away. You'll not need it anymore. You will have so many exciting and rewarding experiences you will be hooked. You will keep on making temporary alliances and enjoying them all the rest of your life.

12

Short-Term Relationships:
What are they doing to you and others?

Though the terms "supportive network" and "temporary alliances" may seem rather strange to some people, they won't be that way for long. Like the once strange "telephone," "television" and "computer," they will become part of daily life, for they are new "inventions." Such inventions are important because though they are dynamic, they offer stability in a world of change.

And whether we like it or not, one such new invention, the short-term relationship, is here to stay. Already long-term relationships are the exception in most of our lives. As Alvin Toffler says in *Future Shock*, long-term relationships

> are like long-stemmed flowers towering above a field of grass in which each blade represents a short-term relationship, a transient contact. It is the very durability of these ties that makes them noticeable. Such exceptions do not invalidate the rule. They do not change the key fact that, across the board, the *average* interpersonal relationship in our life is shorter and shorter in duration.

The fact that most of our relationships even now are short—and frequently not very satisfactory—and that we are going to have even more and shorter ones in the future is a source of concern to many people. Although we've demonstrated that short-term relationships can be nourishing, they can also be harmful if people don't develop certain skills and attitudes.

People who get involved in many short-term relationships sometimes use and then cold-bloodedly discard each other. Sometimes they fail to make meaningful commitments and they feel helpless and rootless as a result. Sometimes they become so "overpeopled" that the quality of their lives diminishes as the number of people in them increases. But it is just as foolish to blame short-term relationships for this kind of behavior as it is to blame telephones, television and computers when they annoy or upset us. People do have choices as to whether they focus on the drawbacks of new inventions or see them as possible aids.

And they can change. Though you may be willing to change when you look at the world and your life and see the inevitability of short-term relationships, you may still have plenty of worries about them. There are three questions that people most frequently ask about what short-term relationships can do to them and others:

Question 1: Doesn't having a lot of short-term relationships cause people to use each other?

Answer: Yes, and that is good because people need to use each other if they are to grow, to be fulfilled, to feel worthwhile.

It is O.K. to use others to satisfy your needs and to facilitate your growth if you also have sufficient regard for what you may be doing to their lives, particularly to their emotions and to the connections they have with other people.

Ginny is a good example of a person who was able to get exactly what she wanted from somebody else and yet hurt nobody. Ginny thought a lot about what she needed people for. She realized one of the things she wanted was a sexual alliance that would give her pleasure and affection but which would not make too many demands on her time and energy while she was involved in a time-consuming and demanding project at work. She wanted a man who was sensual, attractive and caring and who was not seeking a permanent or primary relationship, and then she met Ron. He was all those things and was infatuated with her besides. He might have been the perfect candidate except for one rather important drawback: he was her girl friend's husband. Because she didn't want to cause pain to either her friend or Ron, and because she didn't want to jeopardize a friendship, Ginny passed over this eager candidate for a short-term alliance. She opted for Bob. Though not as sensual, attractive or caring, he wanted the same sort of limited alliance she wanted but he had no other entangling commitments. So Ginny "used" Bob—and both she and he flourished.

Although people don't have to worry about "using" each other in loving and caring ways, what they do have to watch out for in any relationship—short or long—is abusing each other.

Here are three common ways people abuse each other in short-term relationships: (1) by promising something you can't or don't intend to deliver; (2) by abruptly dropping a person without a caring termination process when he no longer meets your needs; and (3) by not letting a person know just what it is you want or expect from him or from your relationship. The following story is an example of a false promise and thoughtless termination—the kind of abuse that can take place when a person doesn't sufficiently value a relationship because he doesn't think it will last very long.

Tom needed a place to stay for just two months. He had been evicted from one apartment and didn't want to rent another because he was waiting for a condominium he bought to go through escrow. Gary, his new friend at work, owned a house and was looking for a permanent roommate to help share rent and household chores. Tom asked Gary if he could move in, not telling him about the condominium and implying he would become a permanent tenant if he and Gary were compatible. In his mind, he justified his critical omission by telling himself he had only known Gary a short time and so it wouldn't make any difference if it was him or somebody else as long as the rent was paid and that he'd find Gary another good tenant when he left. Gary, who really enjoyed Tom's companionship, was delighted to have him as a housemate, but when two months later he was informed Tom was moving into his own home, Gary felt abused—and rightfully so. Tom couldn't understand Gary's upset, and thought him unappreciative for the replacement he had found. But having somebody to pay the rent wasn't the issue, the issue was making a false promise.

Many times people like Tom who are adept at initiating short-term relationships but inept at ending them can make others feel "discarded." In this chapter we'll discuss how to temporarily "un-people" in kind but firm ways and in a subsequent chapter we'll tell you how to bring relationships to a close in ways that will permit you and others to feel good and not abused.

Probably the most common way we abuse others is by not letting them know what we want and expect from them. Though it has become rather popular lately to say of a relationship, "I have no expectations. I just go along with whatever is happening and make the best of it," that just isn't true. Whether we admit it or not, we have expectations of our friends and lovers. There is something we want from them or we wouldn't bother to get involved. When it comes to lovers, we usually know at least some of our expectations. We want sex or marriage or to live together or frequently all three. And, of course, we want to be reminded that a person cares about us—by words and deeds. However, even when we know what we want from mates, lovers and potential lovers, we frequently don't let them know, and this can cause plenty of difficulties.

On the other hand when it comes to our friends, we haven't usually thought much about what they have to offer or what we want. In fact, we aren't used to thinking about people in terms of what we want from them, particularly in regard to the expression of feelings. You probably seldom, if ever, stop to ponder what a friend could do to show you he or she cares. A person is apt to call himself cold-blooded or calculating if he even thinks about such things. There is a prevalent belief that if you have to let your friends know what you want, if you have to ask them to do something nice for you in order to get them to do it, it doesn't count. They don't really care. As a result, we develop some vague general expectations of what our friends might do to show us they care, but we don't tell them. Instead, we expect them to read our minds.

Carl feels very strongly that a "real friend" is one who remembers his birthday with a present. To him, a birthday present is the most important symbol of affection and caring. But because he never tells his friends of his expectation, those he has not known long or seen much of usually fail to acknowledge his birthday. When this happens, he acts pouty, spiteful or aloof without telling them why. As a result, he is constantly feeling let down by friends, and many drift away because of his behavior.

A lot of people are like Carl, always disappointed in their relationships, and they often blame their relationship failures on our mobile, transitory times. But the truth is that this insensitivity and unintentional mistreatment of our friends isn't a recent development.

The problem is that in America friendships have never been structured and ritualized as sexual relationships have been. Our culture doesn't make it clear what a good friend is supposed to do. Though we have expectations as to what a friend should and shouldn't do, these vary considerably from person to person. Thus friendships lack the cement of both well-defined obligations and mutual expectations.

Though lack of structure and ritual gives us freedom to create many different kinds of relationships, according to Myron Brenton, in his book *Friendship*, this freedom is a "double-edged blade." Says Brenton,

> it slices us free of restrictions but it also cuts us off from the comfort and security of knowing exactly what is expected of us and how we should behave with our friends. Unlike members of primitive societies, we make up our friendship rules as we go along. We make decisions relating to our friendships—and there are a lot of decisions to make—as we go along. Decisions such as these: how open we can be with this person, how far to commit ourselves in that relationship, whether to encourage a potential new friendship, how much time to give this friend or that.

The problem is that we don't usually know how to make these decisions. We haven't had "friendship" training; we don't have criteria and guidelines to help us. Ignorance frequently causes even those who are bright and well-intentioned to fail to follow through on some promising new friendship or to let some developing relationships die for lack of proper nourishment. We even will allow a relationship with a long-standing and cherished friend to just drift off into oblivion when we form a relationship we believe must be all-important—i.e., marriage or a "living together" arrangement. We do all of this without realizing how badly we are abusing each other; we take it for granted this is the way things are supposed to be. As a result, not only do we abuse our friends without meaning to, we don't get the closeness, fun and support that we could get.

Anthropologist Robert Brain, author of *Friends and Lovers*

and expert on friendship patterns in different societies, is convinced that our culture's lack of concern with friendship plays a big part in making Americans feel all alone, helpless and depressed. Though many of us suffer from feelings of loneliness much of the time, the custom is to hold those feelings in and try to deal with them all by ourselves, or to go to a physician for tranquilizers or "pep pills" or to a minister or psychotherapist for comfort and guidance—rather than to a friend. We aren't taught to make good use of our friends, and even "best friends" frequently don't know how to be good friends.

Brain points out in a *Psychology Today* article (October 1977) that in contrast, the tradition of friendship in many other cultures is rich and varied, though expectations and obligations may vary considerably from one culture to another. These may entail being godparents to each other's children, shouting playful insults when the friends meet in public, being pallbearers when a member of the other's family dies, spending a lot of time in each other's company, etc. But the point is that people know when they become friends, they take on these obligations; they know the terms of their friendship alliance. The obligations are similar to those of marriage. In fact, in some Latin societies men have deep friendships with other men, called *camaradería*, which are so ritualized that if they have a quarrel and decide not to be friends any longer, there are certain procedures they go through to officially separate them. Friendship bonds are severed with the same seriousness as marriage bonds and legal contracts in this country.

We are not suggesting that Americans should develop the same sort of unchanging friendship patterns we have just described. But what we *are* advising is that friends realize that they do have expectations of each other and find out what these expectations are so that they won't abuse each other by expecting something the other is unaware of or may not want to give. The only way people can do this is to develop friendship rituals of their own. As Brain inquires, "Why should marriage and not friendship be celebrated?"

We believe people can use the trend to short-term relationships to build even better types of relationships than have been customary in this country. They can learn to "celebrate" their friendships by developing friendship rituals that allow them to use but not abuse one another. The "We Process" we describe in Chapter 6 is one sort of friendship ritual. But you, using some of our suggestions and a lot of your own imagination, can devise many other friendship rituals of your own. As you do, the length of time your relationships last will become less important than the quality of them as you go along.

Question 2: Will having a lot of short-term relationships keep men and women from making in-depth romantic commitments to each other?

Answer: On the contrary, it should encourage people to make commitments they can enjoy and live up to both within and outside of marriage.

However, people will have to learn to think of commitment in a new way. Usually when people think of commitment between a man and a woman, they think of marriage. And they don't think of the many kinds of commitments that are possible within marriage but think of the "traditional commitment." It is traditional commitment and not marriage that is causing problems for so many people today.

In a traditional commitment, a man and a woman, without a discussion of abilities or preferences, slip into the traditional male-female roles and stay there. The man becomes the major breadwinner and decision-maker and the woman the homemaker and support person—even if she works. They do not pick their roles and change them when it becomes feasible. In addition, they take literally the pledge to "forsake all others" which is part of many marriage ceremonies. They give up other close relationships with friends of the same and opposite sex and sometimes even those with members of their family, taking it for granted their mate will satisfy all their emotional needs. Furthermore, they make "forever" promises—to love each other forever or to live together forever—*and expect to keep them.* They fail to recognize these promises for what they are, not an inviolate, irrevocable, lifetime pledge, but the expression of a hope for the future.

It is these aspects of traditional commitment that make it unrealistic in today's world. It just isn't sensible to expect yourself or your mate to stay in a rigid sex role or to function well without a goodly number of other meaningful relationships. Nor is it possible to love each other in the same way forever just because you would like to. And nowadays when a relationship is not working, people are less inclined to stay together than they were in the past.

In the past there were three strong forces that pushed men and women into staying together for a lifetime: sex, money and children. She would commit herself to him in exchange for economic security; he would commit himself to her in exchange for exclusive sexual availability and acts of service on a full-time basis. And then they would settle down and raise babies.

There were lots of reasons for maintaining this union even when it became more frustration than fun. Divorce was difficult to obtain and carried a severe social stigma. Most women couldn't support themselves and besides were not able to mingle freely in society or the world without the protection of a man. Most men didn't know how to cook or keep house and it was considered unmanly to do either. Sex was a problem because unmarried women were not supposed to have sex, and while unmarried men with money could find "professional" sexual partners, the average man needed a wife to make certain of his sexual pleasure. For couples with children—and most had them—rearing them without a mate was almost impossibly difficult.

Today the forces bringing and holding men and women together are not as great. Sex and money are no longer the powerful "committing agents" they once were. Since the sexual revolution has made sex without marriage more respectable even for "nice girls," men find it much easier to find available sexual partners. They do not need to promise to support a woman for life in order to have a satisfying sexual relationship. And many women, since the women's liberation movement, have found it easier to establish a career or find a well-paying job and thus aren't willing to form a relationship with a man just for economic security. Not that sex and money don't play an important part in male-female relationships; they do. It is just that more and more people are hesitating to make old-style lifetime commitments primarily to get them.

Not only that, but divorce is easier to get and much more socially acceptable. Children, too, are no longer the bonding agent they once were. Many people have discovered that the rearing of children is not the unalloyed joy they have been led to believe. It is but one of the many ways you can choose to spend your time, money and energy. And like all choices, it may bring certain pleasures but it will certainly bring problems too.

As a result, many couples are choosing not to have children so they can be freer to do what they want as a couple and as individuals. Many individuals who want children have them without having a spouse at all now that single persons are permitted to adopt children. Both men and women have discovered it is possible to rear children to adulthood with no more than the usual number of traumas whether or not they ever have a spouse or whether they have several different ones.

Becoming aware of our options is a mixed blessing. Because today's men and women have so many options in their relationships with the opposite sex, many find themselves reluctant to make a significant commitment of any kind. As Dr. William Glasser, author of *The Identity Society*, says of the men and women he sees in his own psychiatric practice, "For some people, particularly those in certain positions in life, who are attractive, who have money, or who have power, life becomes like a cafeteria line. There is such a wide selection that if you take one thing you may not have room for another." Adds Dr. Glasser, "These men and women ask themselves, what good is all this money or being so attractive if I get stuck with someone who isn't right for me? When you make a commitment, you narrow your options and people who feel they have a wide range of options hesitate to make a commitment."

However, a person can make romantic commitments, can even marry, without tying himself down to the impossible-to-keep "traditional commitment." A person doesn't have to choose between making no commitment or else marrying and making the traditional one. The right kinds of commitments can give a person the security, affection and companionship he desires within the framework of marriage or without it. Specific, practical and realistic commitments can enrich marriage by providing room for growth and change. They can also give those who are not married much of the security that is supposed to come automatically with marriage—but doesn't. Commitments can be more freeing than confining if, after much open and honest discussion, they are custom-made in bits and pieces, subject to revision and change. New-style commitments differ from traditional ones in these ways:

1. Men and women in making them pick the roles they want to

play in their relationship with one another and change them by mutual consent when they are no longer suitable. The way decisions are made and who does what chores are not the result of a person's sex but are tied to ability and preference.

2. The need for more than one meaningful relationship in a person's life is recognized. Whether or not a committed couple decides to marry or to be monogamous, they allow themselves to have significant relationships with a number of others. Also people without a primary partner can make new-style commitments to a number of others.

3. Two people don't have to live together or love one another forever in order for a new-style commitment to be considered worthwhile. In a new form of marriage ceremony, the bride and groom promise to stay together as long as they both shall love. New-style commitments include terms that give a person a feeling of security while they last and keep him from feeling he has failed when they end.

If new-style commitment sounds a lot like making temporary alliances, it is because the making of alliances is an integral part of new-style commitments. Today it is necessary for the terms of romantic commitments to be consciously made and flexible in order to give the people in them what they want and to let them grow and exercise many of the options now available. That means making a variety of specific kinds of alliances with each other for varying amounts of time. A vague "love, honor, and obey till death do us part" just won't work any more. Those who make the new-style commitments must know specifically what they are promising and take responsibility for the pledges they make. The more they do this, the more comfortable they will feel, the more loving they can be.

Question 3: Won't I get "overpeopled" by having a lot of brief encounters and short-term alliances?

Answer: Sure you will sometimes. However, you can stop that "overpeopled" feeling and sometimes even avoid it by learning how to "unpeople" yourself.

"Overpeopling" results not just from having too many people in your life, but also from having people around that you are not "in tune" with or that treat you badly or drain you. However, when most people become overpeopled, they usually think they have but two choices: to let things go on as they are until something changes or to drop some people entirely.

There are times when neither of these options is desirable and yet your life is too busy or stressful or you'd just like to have more time to yourself. At these times you need to practice the art of "unpeopling"; you need to pull back from people, but with sensitivity and caring, and put other relationships on "hold." It is possible to drastically cut back the amount of time spent with some people, arrange to not see certain ones at all for a while and just keep up with others now and then by phone.

The skill of unpeopling, in fact, may be a necessary "survival skill" once you have developed the skill of making quick but intimate contact and growth-promoting alliances and have discovered how fascinating each person can be and how much each has to give you. Then it is all too easy to find yourself overwhelmed with people. Not just ordinary, run-of-the-mill people but those you really care about, those it would profit you to spend more time with. And you'll find you have to make choices, not so much between interesting people or dull ones, bright or dumb, kind or thoughtless, but between people all of whom are interesting, stimulating, creative and fun.

What a problem! If you complain about it, you'll probably get as much sympathy as if you complained about having too much money. "I sure wish I had your problem," your friends will say. But it can be a problem, and a serious one.

Important as interpersonal relationships are, you don't want to get so "hooked" on them that you don't have time to be alone, to get inside yourself in solitude. A person must find time to work in a concentrated way toward goals, some of which will not be accomplished in his lifetime; he must learn to put people out of his mind sometimes while he concentrates all his effort on what he and he alone can accomplish. He must pare down or eliminate some relationships in order to concentrate on others. He must make his short-term alliance with the forces on this planet pay off and not exhaust his potential by spreading himself around like mayonnaise.

The point at which you sense you have gone beyond your "people limit" is strictly an individual one and it depends on what is going on in your life at the moment. Sometimes being surrounded by people can be a blessing, as during a prolonged illness or an emotional or financial crisis. At times when you are unable to work or concentrate on mental activities, you may welcome the attention of all of your friends and have plenty of time for everyone who wants to be with you. But these times are usually few and far between. And we all go through periods when requests for the pleasure of our company from friends we truly cherish seem like a demand, when other things in our lives take higher priority.

Since friends can sometimes feel abandoned, angry or rejected when you suddenly don't have time for them, you need to learn how to "unpeople" gracefully when it is necessary. *The most important step in learning to unpeople is to decide on your own priorities and let your friends know where they stand on your priority list.* Dale, who is normally a very busy and involved person, found herself with a lot of time on her hands last summer. During this period she made friends with a young relative of hers—a cousin that she had never spent much time with or gotten to know well. He needed her because he had just broken up with his girl friend of four years and was burdened with a combination of grief, guilt and resentment. As a good listener, she helped him understand what was happening to himself as he flip-flopped between anger, despair and relief. And as a good talker, she helped him understand what probably had happened to his girl friend. He bolstered her self-confidence by letting her know how much she was helping him and by telling her how much she had changed in the past few years for the better. He remembered her as a rather "up-tight" middle-aged lady who was removed from him by the "generation gap" and by the fact she was married. Divorced now, on her own for the first time in many years, worried about being attractive to men and unsure of her ability to take care of herself and to find others who would find her interesting, she needed to sense the pleasure he so obviously took in being with her.

However, their little idyl ended when the summer ended, for she had to go back to her teaching job. Suddenly she didn't have much time for him, but he still had lots of time and the need to spend it with someone who would comfort him. Things came to a head when, after she had finally set aside a weekend for them to be together, she canceled because of some unexpected work obligations. He got very angry and blurted out, "Well, it's obvious I just don't have a high priority in your life any more."

Because his words sounded like an accusation, Dale started to deny this. But suddenly she realized he was absolutely right. He didn't have a high priority in her life any more. Her work plus a new romantic relationship were taking more of her time and she wanted to give them top priority. This didn't mean she thought less of him in any way. It simply meant that, while she still valued their relationship and hoped they'd have other periods of intense rapport and closeness, at this particular time, her main interests were elsewhere.

When someone says to you, directly or indirectly, that you don't seem to have time for him, he very often makes it sound as if that is a bad thing. It is difficult not to get defensive and deny what sounds like an accusation. But it is a good idea to stop and think about what he is saying. Maybe he is right; maybe you do have other priorities; maybe you would like your relationship with him to take a back seat for a while.

Don't blame yourself if this is true. It is only natural that priorities change sometimes. When this happens, the important thing is to help the person you have been involved with not take your unwillingness or inability to give him what he wants as a rejection of him as a person. A change in your priorities doesn't mean there is anything wrong with him.

When this happens, you will do your friend, yourself and your relationship with each other a favor if you face the fact and say, in effect, "Yes, I do have priorities elsewhere with other people and other things." To protect people from the fact that you simply don't have or want to make time for them at the moment is to protect them from growing up. Growing up is painful and you can't keep from hurting people if they are going to get hurt by your not doing what they want. You should present the truth in as kind a way as possible but not attempt to protect them from it.

In an earlier chapter, we suggested that every once in a while you do some relationship "spring cleaning." This means consciously sorting out your priorities—evaluating what you are giving to and getting from people—and then deliberately altering some relationships and letting go of others. When you have systematically examined your relationships you'll find a number of people you wouldn't miss very much if you didn't see them as often as you do. Or maybe you know who they are right now. At any rate, the men and women you might choose to "unpeople" from probably fall into three categories: (1) those you really don't want to spend any private time at all with; (2) those you find uninspiring or uncomfortable to be with yet feel obligated to see now and then; and (3) those you genuinely like but don't want to spend much, if any, time with at the moment because you are either too busy with other things or else you don't seem to have as much in common with them as you used to.

Though it is difficult to let go of or change relationships, you'll feel so much better after you've done it, for having too many or the wrong kind of relationships can drain your energy and poison your system every bit as much as too much or the wrong kind of food. And just as spring cleaning tasks are easier when you select the kind of tools that are right for each job, relationship cleaning is easier when you select the way that will best suit your relationship with a particular individual and his personality.

There are probably a number of people in your life that are pleasant enough to chat with at parties, in the grocery store, while hanging around the water cooler or on a coffee break but that you really wouldn't want to spend time with privately—i.e., invite to your home, go out to lunch with, etc. Though there is nothing particularly wrong with them, your personalities just don't click and you don't feel enough rapport to make you want to pursue the relationships further. These people may be members of the same club, neighbors, business acquaintances or just someone who travels in the same social circle.

Sometimes one of the people in this category wants to spend more time with you than you want with him, and you find yourself the object of his telephone calls, drop-in visits and invitations. It is awkward to continually make excuses, impossible to avoid seeing him or speaking to him on the phone and embarrassing to you and hurtful to him to try to discourage him by "cutting" him in public or being rude. And actually, all of these things are unnecessary.

To unpeople from those in category 1—people you don't want to spend any of your "private" time with—the tools you need are directness and firmness. You will have to be quite direct and let them know exactly where you stand. You will have to tell them that you are unable and unwilling to give them as much of yourself as they want. You can do it and live through it. And they'll live through it, too.

Take Janet, for example. She had a neighbor who was constantly dropping in on her—for a cup of coffee, to borrow something, etc. Any excuse seemed to do. Then she would sit down and talk and talk and talk for hours. Janet did not relish her company much in the first place, and in the second place, she didn't have the time for these extended coffee klatches. She tried saying she was very busy, moving around impatiently, leaving the kitchen where her neighbor was sitting and going into the bedroom to make the bed. But her neighbor wouldn't leave. She would just follow her about and help her make the bed, and all the time chatter continuously. Janet didn't want to insult her neighbor by telling her never to come over and so finally she asked us for advice.

It will be difficult, we said, but this is what we suggest. Invite your neighbor over for a cup of coffee, telling her you have something important you'd like to talk with her about. (This lets her know you value her.) Then when she is there and you are sipping your coffee say something like this to her. "I have a problem and it's hard to talk about it. I frequently get the feeling you want to spend more time with me than I care to spend with you. Now, it's O.K. for you to want my time and I'm glad you like me. However, it is also O.K. for me to not want to spend so much time with you, to want to do other things instead. It's no reflection on you. What I'd like is for you not to drop in on me without phoning first and then when you do come over, I'd like it if you didn't stay very long. However, I would like to be friendly to say 'Hello' when we meet and that sort of thing. I just don't want you to expect a lot of my time and then be disappointed when I don't give it or when I seem impatient."

We had Janet compose her own variation of this message and say it out loud to us a couple of times so that we could help her adjust the tone of her voice and a word here and there. We wanted her delivery to be both kind and firm—not apologetic or punitive.

When you have a message you want to get across to someone and are concerned about it, you will find it helpful to ask a friend to listen as you say it and to coach you on your presentation. (Tender circle members are especially good for something like this.)

Janet followed through with the plan and although the neighbor got a little huffy, she also got the message, and stopped dropping in. Though for a while, things were strained when they met, and the neighbor would visibly stiffen and clamp her jaws, Janet would smile pleasantly, remaining calm and friendly. And now they both smile and wave when they see each other on the street and even give each other's children rides to school and do other neighborly favors without their turning into lengthy visits.

It would have been awkward and unnecessary for Janet to tell the neighbor to get lost; she couldn't very well terminate the relationship entirely because she has to see her almost every day. But it would have been equally uncomfortable for Janet to continue spending so much time with a person who was draining her energy.

Another category of people that you can profit from seeing less of is those you don't care much for but feel obligated to spend time with now and then. But you don't want it to be very much time. These are not "chosen" friends but "have to" relationships —perhaps a business associate or an aunt. In the case of relatives, there can be some special problems because relatives rarely clarify their relationships with one another and as a result there are usually hidden expectations and resentments.

Dorothy, for example, has a sister that she just doesn't get along with. There has always been competition between them and even now, though they are in their fifties, much of it is still there. Dorothy has outgrown a great deal of her resentment, but her sister hasn't. Every holiday the sister, who is married and has four children living at home, invites Dorothy, who is divorced and lives alone, to dinner. Then she proceeds to drink too much and get hostile—always to Dorothy and many times to her own husband and children. This year, at Christmas, she again invited Dorothy and in the same manner that she always does—as if she were martyring herself by making this big family dinner for the sole purpose of helping poor single Dorothy who has no one. Dorothy, who has many friends and is never at a loss for someone to spend the holidays with, had already made up her mind not ever to spend another holiday at her sister's home because of the "bad vibes." She had managed to be out of town at Thanksgiving but decided she couldn't keep inventing excuses and that it was time she told her sister the reason she didn't want to join her. What she said was this: "I find I am quite uncomfortable with all of the tension in your home. I know you didn't mean to, but the last time I was there you had a few drinks and then hit out at everyone, especially me. I really appreciate the kindness of your invitations, but I know we'll both feel more comfortable if I spend Christmas elsewhere."

Sometimes we simply have to tell people they make us uncomfortable. Though it is difficult to do, if properly done, it is an act of kindness. Frequently people have no idea how their behavior is affecting others and need to be told in a way that is both firm and direct but which doesn't make them out a "bad guy." It takes skill to be able to describe to people what it is about them and their behavior that bothers you and/or others without at the same time seeming to judge them as no good because of it. However, it is a skill that can only be perfected through practice, practice, practice, and you will get better at it the more you try to do it.

Unwanted invitations from people you want to see occasionally, but not that often or not under the circumstances offered, are a problem to most of us now and then. In one case, a woman had a ritual of having a family dinner every other Saturday night for the few relatives she had living nearby. It was her way of keeping the family together. Her nephew, Everett, went reluctantly, for he was single and Saturday was date night. When he complained, she insisted he bring his women friends so they could meet the family. When he started going steady, his new woman friend went twice, was totally bored and refused to go again. Because Saturday night was the only night he could spend with her, he was stimulated to think of an alternative. He suggested to his aunt that she go out to lunch with him instead—just the two of them. She was delighted not to have to cook and this turned out to be just the right way for them to get the contact they wanted from each other. In the course of their luncheon they found they really enjoyed being together, exchanging ideas, feelings, family gossip. For years, they had only gotten together when other people were around and had never had a chance to really get below the surface level with one another. Now they look forward to meeting occasionally for a drink or a lunch and their get-togethers have been removed from the "have to" to the "want to" category.

In cases like the above, it is sometimes necessary to make it clear that you cannot schedule the time of your girl or boy friend. Many times people that we want to see will automatically invite our spouse or lover because of the "couple assumption" idea that we discussed in an earlier chapter. However, such an invitation can be an imposition on a person who does not know them and may not even care to. In such cases, it is best to let them know as tactfully as possible that your mate or lover has other things he would prefer doing. Or you might let them know that you prefer coming alone so that you can really visit with them instead of dividing yourself by feeling responsible for a partner. If you will be honest but kind and especially if you will do as Everett did and offer a suggestion as to a different way of getting together, you can often ease yourself out of an uncomfortable situation and into a better one.

The people who are usually the most difficult to "unpeople" from are those you really care about but, at the moment, don't have time for or else don't feel a close rapport with. These are the ones you may want to put on "hold," to carefully set aside so that you can pick them up again at some later date. Just how to do that in a way so that you can both feel comfortable is a challenge.

To begin with, it is hard to admit to yourself that you can't somehow find enough time to be with those you really care about. It is easy to keep thinking that maybe next week or after vacation time or the holidays, or when I finish a certain project, then I'll surely find more time and we'll get together. It is easy to put off facing the issue as it really is and admitting to yourself, "There are just too many interesting, lovable people in my life and only twenty-four hours in each day, seven days in each week." Frequently, by the time you get around to recognizing that you are just not going to be able to put eight days in a week, you have already hurt some of your friends by promising to get together with them and not doing it, canceling dates, not returning phone calls or showing other signs of lessening interest. When people suspect a lowered interest in seeing them, they are apt to misinterpret and think the amount of your regard for them is also lowered and then to feel hurt. If at this time you suggest not seeing them at all for a while or even just cutting back on the amount of time you have been in the habit of spending with them, they are apt to feel even more hurt. And because you care so much for them, their hurt can be very painful for you. However, the situation can be dealt with and in a way that will usually be pleasant for both of you.

With those who are most important and who you believe understand you well, the best way to handle the situation is to talk over your dilemma with them. Tell them first of all about your admiration, regard and love for them. (Don't be afraid to use the word "love" when you have strong feelings for a friend. Don't just save the word "love" for a mate. Friends and relatives need to be told that you love them, too—and frequently.)

Tell them what they and their friendship have meant to you. Give a specific example if possible. For example, I'll never forget "the way you took care of me when I had that awful case of poison oak" or "how competent you were that night in Rome when our luggage was lost, they didn't have a reservation for us at the hotel and we couldn't speak the language," or "how much fun you were the night you passed your bar exam and we got drunk together."

Then tell of your mixed feelings—that you want to spend time with them and yet you can't seem to find the time or that you don't have enough in common right now because of the different paths your lives are taking or whatever the reason. Level with them as to what the reasons really are. Then explain that you have to find a way to create more time and space for yourself, to temporarily put some distance between you and them, and yet you worry that they will think you don't care as much about them as you do.

If you know how you'd like to handle the situation, let them know, but also be sure to ask for their ideas. This is one of those times when two heads are better than one. Even if they have no thoughts on the subject, or if what they propose isn't feasible, you have let them know you value them by asking, and that is very important.

Though each relationship is different and thus a plan suitable for one seldom fits another perfectly, here are some suggestions that many others have found helpful in temporarily unpeopling from good friends. You can undoubtedly adapt some for your own use.

1. Agree to have a moratorium on your relationship with the idea that you will get together at the end of a certain period and reevaluate by looking at the options and opportunities open to you at that time. Decide not to see each other or have any contact at all for a fairly long period. Make it long enough for some

significant things to happen in both of your lives—say three months or even six months.

If you decide to do this, pick a definite date at the end of this time period for a reunion. Mark it on both of your calendars and do not break that date. Make contact by phone a week or so before that date and set up the time and place for your reunion, making certain to pick a place where it will be quiet enough for you to talk and where you won't be interrupted. Do not have others join you at this reunion. This should be just for the two of you.

2. Arrange to have "phone dates" on a semi-regular basis—for instance, once a month or every two months. Plan a time when you can talk uninterruptedly for at least a half an hour, better yet an hour. The phone is a great substitute to offer in place of a get-together for a lunch, dinner or party. It takes a lot less time because you don't have to dress up to go out nor do you have to drive any distance at all to get to the place of your rendezvous. And even if you talk with somebody who is not in your area code, chances are the cost will be less than you'd spend for food and transportation. Besides, for people who want to catch up quickly on what's been happening in each other's lives, telephone conversations can sometimes be even better than in-person contact. There are apt to be fewer distractions. You aren't looking around at things as you might be in a restaurant and there is no waiter to butt in and ask if you are ready for dessert or if you'd like your coffee cup refilled. You can really concentrate on listening to every word and on talking.

Use the phone between "dates" for quick contact—to call and say something like, "I don't have time to talk right now but you are in my thoughts and I just wanted you to know it. I love you."

3. Agree to not see each other for a while and to have contact primarily by letter with an occasional short "touch-base" phone call. Make a pact that you will write a letter every so many months—one or two or three or whatever seems comfortable to both of you. When you write your letter, be sure to make it very personal. Reveal yourself. Be sure to talk of your feelings. Tell what is going on in your inner world as well as what is happening in your external world. And make a point in each letter of telling the person something specific about him or her that you particu-

larly value—e.g., a quality you admire or something he once did or said. Let him know the ways in which he has affected your life.

Most people don't want to write letters, especially to people who live nearby. They say it takes too much time or that they are no good at it. But what letter writing can do is pinpoint and clarify your thinking, so it can be a very profitable activity. In addition, when it comes to nourishing a relationship, an hour or so spent in letter writing can be worth three or four hours drinking coffee or cocktails with someone. You can say nice things in a letter that you'd probably be too embarrassed to say in person. And a letter can be and frequently is read and reread, so a person can feel your presence many times.

The practice of writing personal letters prevalent before the invention of the telephone and the automobile needs to be revived. After all, a letter is the most unobtrusive way of making contact, and unobtrusive ways need to be encouraged in a world where overpeopling is a daily hazard of living.

Probably not all of your friends will understand and find it acceptable when you want to put your relationships with them on "hold"—when you want to cut back your time with them or stop seeing them at all for a while. Some are bound to see it as a rejection. Paula Menkin, "peopling" expert, told us of an experience she had recently in this regard. Said Paula, "I have one friend who I enjoy doing certain things with but in the present tenor of my life I don't have much time for her. I like her and would not want to lose her completely, but she makes it difficult for me. She believes because we were so close at one point in our lives and spent so much time together that now, when my life is so full, I've deliberately cut her out of it. There is no way I can possibly fill up the void in her life by saying 'Hey, I really do value you but my life now calls for a smaller portion of you than it did before, but that smaller portion is still valuable to me.' I do know the one thing I cannot do that I would like to do and that is to just call now and then and touch base. I've tried it and she gets very accusing—asking why I don't spend more time with her, etc. I sincerely hope she will be available to me sometime when I come back and say 'Let's pick it up again,' but she may not be. I just may not be able to save this friendship because she has such great needs."

With people who act like this, who get accusing or angry when we try to be nice, it is a big temptation to just write them off completely, to tell them something like, "I guess we just weren't meant to be friends and I never want to see you again." Though it might feel good at the time to tell someone off, it isn't worth the risk. Just as it is unwise to count on a relationship lasting forever or even for a very long time—because the odds are against it—it is also unwise to count on someone being out of your life forever. It's amazing how many times you cross paths with the same people in your sojourn through life. Things change and people pop up in the strangest places. Sometime in the future that person you tell off may turn out to be your boss or a neighbor or even the person who has to O.K. your application for a loan.

And people change, too. You'll cool down and so will he. And then maybe, if you leave the way open and are patient, that relationship you once enjoyed may be revived.

The many changes that take place in long relationships and the increasing frequency of short-term ones do present problems. There is no way to guarantee we will never feel hurt, deserted or overwhelmed by others. But the problems are not insurmountable. In fact, they are but challenges that can get us to try new behavior —behavior that can create better interpersonal relationships than have ever before been possible.

13

Enriching Long-Term Relationships Through Short-Term Principles

There is no way to assure a long-term relationship. A pledge of eternal friendship is not a guarantee, merely the expression of a hope; a vow to love forever at a marriage ceremony can be broken the following day; and even a so-called "airtight" business contract can be severed in court.

Nor is a relationship necessarily a good one just because it has gone on a long time. Mates who live in the same house for twenty years may believe they know each other perfectly yet know but very little of the important things that go on down deep inside. Most couples, even the most well-meaning, because they don't know one another as well as they could and are unskilled at using creativity in their relationships, fail to get more than a fraction of the tremendous joy available from a relationship that goes on and on. They could get more if they didn't see a long-term relationship as something completely different from a short-term one, and would take advantage of short-term principles and practices.

The best long- and short-term relationships have the same base. Both require the same attitudes and skills. In fact, a long-term relationship is nothing but a series of many brief encounters and short-term alliances with the same person.

Remember that special afternoon or evening when something clicked and you and your spouse made slow tender love. Or that night you clung to one another in mutual grief at the death of a close relative. Those were brief encounters.

And in the course of your long-term relationship, you've made many alliances with one another, had many mutual goals, some of which you reached, others you gave up on. When your children were babies, the emphasis in your alliance was probably on keeping them healthy; your home environment and life style reflected that. As your children grew, the terms of that alliance changed and you focused on helping them learn as much as possible and deal with the struggles of growing up. Had you and your mate known you were making an alliance (and been fully aware of its purpose), you might have been more cooperative, had more fun and helped your children even more. As part of your alliance, you probably had a goal to make money and get ahead in your work, a goal that required you to develop new skills at certain times and to drastically change your habits at others. And when your children grew up and left home, you had to develop yet another new alliance with one another, perhaps to change some of your money goals and habits, to rediscover each other, to concentrate more on growing yourself, to live in a smaller home or maybe even to separate and live alone. You've had many mutual goals, made many contracts.

The skill of making contracts and developing short-term alliances is certainly one that can be used in enriching and expanding long-term relationships. And so can the other short-term principles and practices already presented in this book (i.e., developing the skill of gentle aggression, creating your own social rituals, using the "We Process," etc.). However, relationships that continue over a long period offer special challenges just because they persist. On the one hand, when you have a history of shared experiences, you have the opportunity to try new things, to be adventurous. You already have a base of knowledge and trust to build on; you can take bigger risks. On the other hand, this same history makes it easy to keep expecting what you have always expected from one another, to do what you have always done, to give of yourself what you have always given—in short, to get stuck in a rut.

Thus in this chapter we shall offer some special suggestions based on short-term principles and practices that are designed to bring new joy into sexual relationships that have gone on quite a while and look as if they are going on even longer. However, most are also applicable to long-term relationships with a friend or relative.

These suggestions include: (1) enrichment exercises to help long-term partners see and hear each other in new ways; (2) special kinds of short-term alliances partners can make to enrich and expand an already good relationship; (3) ways to create an environment in which "brief encounters" can happen; and (4) new ceremonies and rituals to mark the existence of a deeply committed relationship that doesn't take the form of marriage and to help long-term partners express their appreciation to each other.

Because these suggestions are pleasure- and not problem-oriented, they are for partners who already have a good relationship and want to make it even better. However, though not geared to treat relationships that are in serious trouble, they will make some problems disappear and prevent others from happening.

Preparations for your adventures

Enriching a long-term relationship requires an important short-term attitude: the willingness to risk. It requires daring. All adventures do.

First, you must be willing to risk your feeling of being worthwhile. You must be willing to try some behavior that you worry might make you appear awkward, stupid, thoughtless, calculating, impolite, unfeminine or unmasculine or something else you don't want to be. This may be difficult because people are most anxious to appear at their best in front of those with whom they are sexually involved. There is a way around this, however, and that is by reminding yourself that there are just two ways to go through life. You can stand on firm ground and look up at the apples in the tree but never taste them, or you can scramble up the tree after them. If you take the latter course, you may appear awkward, may tear your clothes, skin your knee or even fall and break your arm, but you won't get any apples unless you take the risk. And the same is true when you risk trying behavior that may make you appear unattractive to a long-time lover. But there is a reward. For if your spouse or lover sometimes finds you awkward, stupid, thoughtless, calculating, impolite, unfeminine or unmascu-

line or something else you don't want to be and still finds you
sexually attractive, you know he really cares.

A way around this risk is for two partners to agree ahead of
time that they will not make fun of, bawl out or put one another
down when trying new behavior. Or if they do, the other will
catch them up on it and they will stop immediately and apologize. (Incidentally, this is a good agreement to keep in force for
all times during your relationship.)

The second risk that must be taken is that of setting a precedent. Strange as it may seem, a major worry that long-term partners have of trying new behavior is that their partner *will* like it.
Their concern is that if they do something once and their partner
likes it, he will then expect them to keep on doing that same
thing forever—whether it is playing bridge, skydiving or doing the
dishes. For example, Harold and Mary have been married for
fifteen years and their relationship has been quite traditional.
Harold has not been involved in helping around the house and
Mary has never worked. However, Mary recently started doing
some painting at home as a hobby. Her work was so well received
by her friends that she got the courage to enter her art work in a
local competition. The weeks before the competition were hectic
and she wasn't able to do everything she used to do around the
house. One morning Harold, moved by her franticness to try to
get the housework done as well as prepare for the show, went out
into the kitchen and cleaned it from top to bottom. "But," he
muttered to Mary as she stood at the door in wonder, "I'm just
doing this because you are busy. Don't expect me to do it all the
time." Harold had tried some new behavior—and in fact had enjoyed the challenge of cleaning the kitchen in record time—but he
feared that by so doing he was creating, in effect, a new alliance—
one in which he, too, would be expected to do housework.

Partners need to be able to try some new behavior just once—
for ten minutes, or half an hour or half a day or two weeks—
without being committed to acting that way "forever." If they
can't experiment with new behavior, how can they know what
new kinds of short-term alliances they might be able to develop?
Therefore, a woman should be free to try backpacking—just once
—to see how she likes it without her husband automatically expecting that now they will include backpacking as a regular part
of their recreational life. A man should be able to send his wife

flowers or write a tender poem—to see how that behavior feels—without being pressured thereafter to produce poems or flowers regularly.

The way to keep the fear of setting a precedent from interfering with your trying new things is to remind yourself that it is O.K. to do something just once—or twice or three times—and never do it again. Also, make an agreement with your partner that neither of you will use pressure to make the other feel guilty for not repeating what he has done before. (Again this is a good agreement to keep in force for all times during your relationship.)

The third risk you must be willing to take is the risk of losing the relationship itself. It is true that when you expand and enrich a relationship, you change it. Most of the time these changes will be for the better. However, there are no guarantees. Shaking up the balance you've maintained in an ongoing relationship for years can make it obvious that you've outgrown each other or have nothing in common or simply don't want to be together anymore.

But on the other hand, if a relationship never changes, if the people in it do not frequently form new kinds of short-term alliances, then they are stuck in roles. They are in a rut. They are not growing and neither is the relationship.

A static relationship is not necessarily a "safe" one. We've all heard stories of the husband or wife who suddenly walked out of a "perfect" marriage—i.e., one in which there was no conflict, no change, and each partner was a perfect lady or gentleman at all times. When a couple sees change not as a threat but as an opportunity to try something new, when they jump at the chance to try what might prove stimulating and helpful, they will create a relationship that is vibrantly alive and healthy. Thus there is nothing to do but risk losing a relationship to keep it.

ENRICHMENT EXERCISES

When two people who have known each other a long time get together, many times they don't really make contact—i.e., tune in on each other. Though they may shake hands, pat or even kiss and hug, these are perfunctory gestures. Seldom do they deliberately make the effort required to establish contact in more than a superficial way. One or both will fail to look the other in the eye to get a sense of what he is feeling. If they touch, they won't even feel what they are touching. And when they talk, neither listens but just waits for the other to take a breath and then babbles on as though what he has to say was prerecorded. As a result, they stay two separate entities locked into their separate thoughts and feelings rather than connecting and getting in a "together" space where they can share.

It is this failing to connect that makes people feel lonely even when they are with another person. Though it is easy for mates and lovers to fall into this kind of habit pattern because mechanical ways of treating one another are so much a part of our cultural customs, it is also easy to get out of—and fun besides. Here is an alternative way to greet your spouse or lover at the end of the day after work or any other time after you've been apart for several hours or more:

Looking, touching and talking

As soon as you see your partner, look into his eyes and hold his gaze as long as you can *without talking*. As you do this, allow yourself to become aware of these things in the following order: (1) your own breathing—all of the places in your body that you can feel it (take a few deep breaths); (2) the thoughts and feelings you believe your partner is having at this very moment; (3) the sentences that are going on in your mind and the kinds of emotions you are feeling.

Take hold of your partner's hands and *still without talking* lead him or her to a place where you can sit down, look into one another's eyes and hold both hands. Maintain this position for at least three minutes (five is even better) while allowing your consciousness to shift from being aware of what is going on in various parts of your body (e.g., my armpits are sweaty; my jaws are clenched; my neck hurts), to what you believe your partner is thinking and feeling (e.g., he looks sad; he's thinking he doesn't like my hair fixed this way; he's tired), to the sentences that are going on in your mind and what you are feeling (e.g., he's going to be mad at me for suggesting this. I'm tired. This is a silly thing to do. Why do I feel like crying?).

When the three to five minutes are up, relax and then talk with one another for five minutes or more about what you each experienced. Tell what was going on in your body, what you thought the other was thinking and feeling and what you were thinking and feeling. Make certain you both have a chance to talk and to listen, and then carry on and do whatever feels good to you to do.

Don't just spring this on your partner or it won't work. It takes the cooperation of both of you, so talk it over with him first. If he is reluctant, try to get him to do it with you just once and agree when that will be. Talk about what you got out of it afterward and if you both got anything at all, agree to try it three or four times in a row. You can't be expected to do this exercise every time you come together after being apart for any length of time, but if you do it several times, you will begin to establish a new habit, one of tuning in on your thoughts and feelings, sharing them with your partner and inquiring about his. Use this ritual now and then to reinforce this new habit and on special occasions, for this is a nice little "welcoming" treat for the one you love.

Looking at your partner with new eyes

When you've known people for quite a while and they become important to you, it is difficult to see them as they really are—for a number of reasons. In the first place, the way we see a person—in regard to his appearance, his moods and his behavior—is greatly influenced by how we feel about him. Certainly, at some time in your life, you've met a person you thought at first glance was rather unattractive. And then he became your friend. Later when you took another look, he was quite handsome. Or else you have experienced the reverse. You met someone you thought a real beauty, but when you got to know her, she became unattractive.

In the second place, many of the qualities we attribute to a person are largely the result of our wishes or fears. For example, we call a person gentle or passive, competent or pushy according to whether or not he is doing what we'd like him to do.

And there is another occurrence that keeps us from seeing a person as he is, one that keeps our perception of a person from being up-to-date. Though people change little by little, our perceptions of them don't change that way. What happens is that at various points in a relationship we form a certain mental image of a person and keep it until something dramatic happens that causes us to see with new eyes. A mental "set" frequently blinds us to what is really there. As a result of a perception lag, we can fail to notice that a child has become an adult, a formidable parent has become weak or a usually cheerful spouse has become depressed.

Thus, sometimes we fail to take action when we should. Because you may not even notice that your husband's clothes are way out-of-date, you will not prod him to get new ones. Or on the other hand, when he buys new clothes and would enjoy your comments, you may not even see them and thus fail to compliment him. Perhaps your wife may have lost the color in her cheeks, be dragging around low in energy, and could profit from your gently pointing out these things and suggesting that she get a physical checkup. Or perhaps, she who used to be shy and inept socially has become more self-confident and outgoing and deserves your praise but you don't give it because you still see her as she used to be.

Compliments from those we've known a long time are frequently lacking because they don't see us as we are. Besides, there is a cultural tendency to emphasize the negative and neglect the positive. And when we stress the negative over long periods, as is customary in many long-term relationships, we can come to believe that our mate or lover has more negative than positive qualities.

The inability to see a person as he is and the failure to reinforce his positive qualities can be circumvented by occasionally indulging in a special kind of people-watching called "partner-watching."

People-watching is a popular pastime. Most of us enjoy going someplace where we can do it. We can sit and watch strangers for hours. And yet how many of us ever sit silently and watch our mates? Unless, of course, we are upset and are out to gather "evidence" that they are not behaving the way they are "supposed" to or unless we are suspicious and want to see if they are flirting or ignoring our mother or doing something else they had better not do.

There is another form of "partner-watching" that you probably haven't tried. Not only will you enjoy it but you and your mate will both profit from it. The idea is to watch carefully—to pay close attention to every detail of your mate's appearance and behavior—but with a positive purpose in mind instead of an ulterior motive. The purpose is to see him as he is right now, to get to know him better, to become acutely aware of his positive qualities and then to tell him about them. Here is how to go about it:

"Partner-watching"

Pick a time when you can observe your partner without it bothering him. It might be some evening at home when you are sitting in the same room reading. Or perhaps a time when he is helping the children with their homework and you are doing the dishes. Or it might be when you are at a party or out to dinner with friends. The time doesn't matter except that you will learn different things when you are in a social situation from what you learn when you are alone with him. And so you will want to do this exercise several times and to vary the circumstances.

You can plan ahead of time when you are going to do it or you can just get somewhere and suddenly decide, "Tonight's the night." However, before you do it, talk it over with your partner so that he will know what is going on. This way, if he notices he is being watched, while he will probably feel self-conscious, he won't be upset thinking he has done something wrong but will interpret it as a compliment and know that you are looking at him with love.

Instructions:

1. Before you start looking, prepare your consciousness: Close your eyes for just a few seconds and repeat silently several times: "This is someone I care about and who cares about me. I want to see him as he is so I can show him more caring." With this preparation, your gaze will be softly exploratory and not invasive. You will appear to be stroking your partner with your eyes, not examining him with a magnifying glass.

2. Start at the top of your partner's head and go slowly all the way down to his feet, examining carefully as you go each part of his anatomy and attire. As you observe, evaluate from a personal perspective whatever you see. Pay particular attention to what *you like*, but if you notice something that bothers you, don't just skip it. Become aware of exactly what it is about it that bothers you

and why. But then see if you can find the positive side to a negative discovery before moving on. For example:

> His hair is brown and curly and it is not as full as it used to be. (Observation) He may be getting bald and I won't like that at all. But I'll still love him. (Evaluation)

> Her lips are full and her mouth turns up at the corners. (Observation) I really like to kiss those soft lips and I like her chronic bubbliness. (Evaluation)

> His hands are small. (Observation) He is a gentle, sensitive man. (Evaluation)

> Her shoulders are very broad. (Observation) They are too broad for a woman. But she is strong. I like her strength; she is somebody I can lean on. (Evaluation)

> He is wearing the blue sweater his mother knit for him. (Observation) I'd like to talk him out of wearing it. It never did fit very well. (Evaluation)

3. In the same systematic way, observe your partner's movement, manners and behavior and evaluate them. Again, focus on positive aspects, but if something bothers you, become aware of what there is about it that causes you concern. For example:

> She speaks up a lot more when she is with women than when men are around. (Observation) I wish she would hold her ground more with men. (Evaluation) I'm afraid she will be taken advantage of. (Cause of concern)

4. Make a mental list of what you liked about your partner's physical appearance, personal qualities and behavior. Write these things down under a heading of "I like you because . . ." Make another list of what you didn't like and why it bothered you. If the list of what you liked is at least twice as long as the list of what you didn't like, you are ready to share your "I like you because . . ." list with your partner. If it is not twice as long, repeat this process, focusing just on what you like until you can get a long list of positive qualities and strengths to share. When you get together with your partner, share only the positive. *Do not*, at this time, bring up the negative. Save those for another time—perhaps

when you do the "We Process." You need to take time to sort them out so that you can present your negative feedback in a positive way.

SPECIAL SHORT-TERM ALLIANCES FOR LONG-TERM RELATIONSHIPS

Long-term relationships require short-term alliances for three reasons: (1) to get out of ruts; (2) to prevent dependencies; and (3) for personal development.

When a relationship is ongoing, partners make numerous behavioral agreements, many of them unknowingly. They fall into habit patterns. It can't be helped. Each "stakes out" certain areas in which he is comfortable. Each then can feel he alone owns, not just the right to have the yard or kitchen the way he wants it, but the exclusive right to issue social invitations, initiate sex or even to cry or get mad.

To have your roles and status in a relationship well established can be very helpful. It is reassuring to know how you and your partner are expected to act. And it certainly is convenient to take control in some areas and give up responsibility for others. However, when you continually do the same old things in the same old way, daily life can become a monotonous bore. Even a very good life with a very good mate. In addition, partners can lose the knack of expressing themselves in various ways and the ability to handle certain situations. They can become, in a very real way, partially crippled.

The way to avoid this situation is by getting involved in a variety of role-expanding short-term alliances. There are three kinds of role-expanding alliances most couples can profit from, those that have to do with new experiences, and with being autonomous—in day-to-day living and in social functioning. We will discuss and give suggestions for all of these alliances, but first of all, here are some tips to help you get started:

1. Talk the whole idea of "role expansion" over with your partner. Tell him what you want to do and why. Try to create a pact between you to develop more interesting and elaborate "selves." And then when you have a particular kind of an activity to sug-

gest, make certain to bring the subject up in a way that doesn't sound like a complaint. Don't say, "I want you to take more responsibility for fixing meals" or "I'm tired of always being the one to initiate sex." Instead, say in a more positive way: "I sure would like to see you plan and cook a whole dinner sometime. You could tell me what to do and I could help you." Or "Why don't we take turns being master and slave in sex play? We can flip a coin to see who is which tonight." Remember alliances are for increasing pleasure, so approach your partner in a way that makes it clear you are interested in enriching an already satisfactory relationship—not in "saving" your marriage or "improving" an inadequate partner.

2. If you meet resistance, don't give up. Back off and try a different tack. Remember that to those who have not experienced the benefits of "role expansion," the thought can be quite frightening. In most cases we suspect that women will be the ones who are trying to initiate a change in their relationships with men. This is because women are generally more interested in personal relationships than men and since in today's world women's roles are changing drastically, they tend to be more flexible in trying out new things. Even very mild changes can be threatening to men who confuse a request for role-expanding activities with the desire for role reversal and suspect that any significant changes will put them in a subordinate, menial position. Assure your mate that even though what you suggest may sound like role reversal, it isn't. You don't intend for him to give up any roles, just to add additional ones to his repertoire. And you don't want to take over, you just want to share more responsibility, become more flexible and become a more interesting person. It's hard to argue with those objectives.

However, if he or she is adamant, suggest a trade-off. Offer to do something he wants if he will try something you want. One wife agreed to learn to skin-dive—something her athletic husband had been urging her to do for years—if he would work on developing his gentler, more passive side by letting her take leadership in some new situations.

3. Don't wait to get your partner's compliance before starting your own role-expanding activities. There are many things you can do on your own without your partner's help or approval that will benefit your relationship and you. There have been numerous

ideas for new ways to act thus far in this book, and when you read about autonomous-living and social-functioning alliances, you'll find some more. But don't just read about them. Let them stimulate ideas in you and then act on them. Don't wait. Get started as soon as possible.

New-experience alliances

After a relationship has gone on a long time, it would be impossible to discover all the areas in which one partner automatically takes over without even thinking about it or questioning, "Why me?" And besides, it isn't necessary. Rather than constantly trying to discover and renegotiate all these "staked-out" areas, get involved in something that is brand-new to both of you. Try out a new religion, take up sailing or racquet ball, investigate spiritualism, camping or swinging—any activity that intrigues you and requires the participation of both of you will do. The object is to pick a new situation and then to make it as different as possible. It isn't enough to just decide on something new to do and do it. You must discuss in advance what each of you can do in this new situation that is different for you, that will help you add new roles to your wardrobe of behaviors. It takes prior planning to take full advantage of the opportunity to create more elaborate selves.

When you find a new mutually agreeable activity and decide to explore it by behaving in new ways, you have no precedents to deal with, no ruts to overcome. It becomes easy and fun to behave differently with one another. For example, one couple decided to travel to a foreign country—something they had never done. Since neither of them knew the language and it was a relatively undeveloped country with fewer conveniences than they were used to, they knew they would have to adapt to new customs and make friends with strangers.

He wanted to get over his tendency to be taciturn and gruff and to learn to meet people easily. Thus, when they made plans, his "role expansion" assignment became to talk with as many people as possible as a means of learning as much as he could about the country, the customs and each individual. Since she was by nature a "plan everything ahead and live by the clock" type, her role assignment was to be a spur-of-the-moment, adventurous person. On the trip, they found themselves eating in out-of-the-way restaurants on an impulse—merely because she liked the decor—rather than spending time seeking one that had four stars and had been recommended as "safe." And they "talked" with people everywhere—in the next booth, on the street corner, in the hotel lobby, on the beach—even though their "talking" was done with few words, much, much sign language, and many interruptions because of references to a pocket dictionary. Naturally, such behavior caused a number of complications that could have been avoided by more conventional behavior. But it also caused much laughter. Besides, it was through coping with the complications in a strange environment that they discovered new creativity in themselves and each other.

Another couple picked canoeing as a new experience they could share. They wanted a physical activity but one that would not be too strenuous for the wife. Their object was to try out a relationship that was entirely equal in every way. Their agreement was to share every activity—carrying the canoe, paddling, pitching the tent for overnight stays, cooking, etc.—as if they were two men or two women, each expected to carry his own weight and not be waited on. She found that sometimes she got aggravated when, toward the end of a hard day, she was very tired and yet he made her keep paddling or pitch the tent because it was her turn. He found that something in him expected her to cook and serve the evening meal and he felt neglected when she didn't or when she declined to fetch things for him during his turn to break camp. Though making these discoveries was uncomfortable, because of them, they were less inclined to take one another for granted when they got back home and resumed their regular routines.

Getting-along-without-you alliances

What usually happens when a man and woman love and live together, whether married or not, is that they develop inhibiting dependencies, both social and personal, and their personal growth slows down. It is the nature of a man-woman exclusive coupling in our society that causes this. Though this relationship is a remarkable combination of sex, domesticity and comradeship which can be very satisfying, it is also very limiting. Because of the custom to live only for each other, after a couple lives together for a while, they can come to believe they can't get along without one another, and sometimes they really can't. When this happens, whether it is a fact or just a belief, a relationship will go downhill. People will either cling and the relationship will stagnate or they will seriously inhibit one another's growth—or both. But crippling dependencies don't have to occur if couples will make alliances with each other that will help them learn how to get along alone.

Some people would not like their spouses or lovers to discover they could get along without them. They fear it would ruin their relationship, for their partner might want to leave them. Actually, what usually happens is the reverse. When two people know they are staying together from joyous choice and not from neurotic or actual need, they feel closer. It is working together for each other's benefit because of caring, and in spite of the risk of personal loss, that brings them closer.

Partners who choose to cooperate in a getting-along-without-you alliance are in effect making two quietly affectionate statements to one another: (1) Your personal and social growth is of utmost importance to me, and (2) I am willing to do a lot to see that, if something happens to me—or us—you'll get along just fine. You'll have the skills and friends you need. There are two kinds of alliances that partners can make to help each other function well as independent adults: autonomous-living alliances and social-functioning alliances. The first involves teaching each other skills.

Autonomous-living alliances

If there is one activity that a couple can share that, at times, can give even more pleasure than sex, it is learning. Particularly when one is the teacher, the other the student. Because of all of the things that take place during a teacher-student relationship, this can bring many moments of intimacy and exhilaration *if* they take turns being teacher, *if* one is really interested in learning what the other wants to teach and *if* both are convinced they will gain from their efforts. However, if the same one is always the teacher (and thus in the one-up position), and if the viewpoint is that the student is rather stupid because he doesn't know what he should know already, or that the learning is bound to be an unpleasant process from which only the one will benefit, it just won't work.

It can be great fun to teach your partner tennis or art appreciation or to play the piano, and this is well worth doing, but there is a certain kind of teacher-student experience that will enrich a relationship in many more ways. When two partners will help each other learn their jobs and sometimes trade jobs temporarily, both will reap a variety of benefits.

Now, we are not suggesting that a couple totally change jobs, such as has been the theme of movies and books in which a housewife becomes an executive overnight and an executive takes over in the home with the kiddies. That is fantasy material and good for a lot of laughs but that is all. Nor are we suggesting that each try to become proficient at everything the other does. That is not practical, possible or even desirable. There are bound to be some tasks each hates and has no intention of ever trying to learn, and there will be others they couldn't learn if they tried. But there are many tasks that one has taken over that the other can and should learn in order to assure his ability to function as an autonomous person and to improve his knowledge in an area where it is lacking so that he can contribute more to decision-making.

For example, whoever keeps track of household expenses, insurance payments, income-tax records and all of the bookkeeping and check-writing matters might carefully instruct the other as to what he has been doing—and why and how—and then turn over those tasks to the other for six months, talking about the process frequently and acting as a consultant. At the end of this or some other mutually agreed-upon period of time, they would carefully re-evaluate and see whether they want to continue the same system for a longer period, go back to the old way or reassign various tasks according to a different plan. Or the one who does the grocery shopping and cooking or the yard or car maintenance could teach the other those skills.

The husband who learns to bake a pie from scratch, do the laundry and fold it so that it not only smells good but looks good, who tries to arrange the living room so that it is easy to keep clean, aesthetic and comfortable for all family members, will appreciate his wife all the more for being able to do those things. The wife who learns how to take care of a car, accurately describe symptoms of malfunctioning to a mechanic, change a tire or the oil, who takes over the responsibility for the yard, will certainly appreciate her husband more.

Learning the other's tasks can lead to suggestions for new ways of handling jobs and also for life-style changes. There was an older couple who both worked and who tried to maintain—mainly on weekends—a large home and an even larger yard with a pool. When the woman took over the care of the grounds and the man the housekeeping and cooking, even before the trial period they had agreed upon was over, both had made important discoveries. The woman found that the time required for upkeep left her no time to enjoy the garden and pool. Though with modern equipment she was strong enough to do the work, because of having to rake leaves, mow the lawn, clean the pool, prune, plant and fertilize, most of her free time disappeared. She suggested they hire someone to help with these chores—something she had claimed they couldn't afford, until she had to do it. The man discovered that he really enjoyed spending more time indoors and that he especially liked to cook and to cook what he liked. However, he found out that cleaning three bathrooms, dusting, vacuuming, etc., was dull work and took too much time. He suggested they move to a condominium, something she had been wanting to do ever since their children moved out.

The idea of two partners teaching each other their particular skills is really a very practical one. In fact, Dr. Adele and Sam Scheele, who are partners in their social engineering consulting firm in Los Angeles as well as long-term marital partners, say that in some organizations, the members of a work team all teach each other their skills so that if someone is missing the work group doesn't have to slow down or stop. And, they add, there is an extra benefit from learning another person's job. Say the Scheeles, "You get an appreciation of how well certain people do certain things which you can't know until you've tried it yourself. If you've never tried to type error-free for an hour, you don't know what an accomplishment it is and when you have tried, you can appreciate someone who can do it."

Thus this kind of "on-the-job" training that we've been talking about can not only help each partner become autonomous but can also be useful in time of emergency. It benefits a man-woman team if bills get paid on time even if the person who usually pays them is in the hospital or away on vacation. It makes a home a more comfortable place to be in if the drains can be unclogged even when the person who usually unclogs them isn't available.

And when one partner learns to do the other's job, he appreciates more the amount of effort and creativity it takes to do even seemingly small tasks well, tasks such as taking care of house guests, talking with the children's teacher or a stockbroker, accountant or insurance agent, or ordering lumber to build a bookcase.

Smooth functioning and greater appreciation are direct results of on-the-job partner training you can count on, but there is another surprise benefit that occurs now and then: the discovery of a previously unrecognized talent. This happened to Zack. It happened in a very roundabout way. Mildred, Zack's wife, had taken a part-time job, and the usual routines for running the home had become disrupted. Though Zack was trying to help her with some of the household tasks, it wasn't working out very well. We suggested that they give up the idea of his *helping her* with *her* tasks. Instead we proposed that they look at all the jobs necessary for the optimum functioning of them as a team under the present circumstances and see what each could do to help them function better. We had them look at their resources and how they could best use those resources. It became apparent that housecleaning, cooking, laundry and sewing were the jobs that weren't getting done very well, that she was an important resource because of her specialized knowledge in these fields and that he had more time than she had. He was spending considerable time on his hobby of woodworking while she had no free time at all. We suggested a teacher-student alliance, and that he should pick out the job that interested him most and she could teach him. He picked out sewing because the idea of making something from a pattern appealed to him. (And when you stop to think of it, it is not too far from his hobby of woodworking.) This opened up a whole new world for him. Actually, Mildred is a mediocre seamstress and only made very simple things. She sewed just because it was cheaper to make the children's clothes than to buy them. But Zack was good at sewing and loved it and soon was making up his own designs. He started sewing for her and for himself, making garments that were minor works of art. Though we had thought of his learning to sew as but a first step to his learning more of the household tasks, he still hasn't gotten around to the cooking, cleaning and laundry. However, their relationship has perked up and they have worked out some new ways to get these things done that are comfortable for both of them.

Relationships do flourish and a couple will find ways to work things out when they learn to look upon all jobs necessary for the optimum functioning of them as a unit as *our jobs,* and the performance of any task as *temporary.* Even the most onerous task is bearable if you know it doesn't have to go on forever and you can usually find ways to make it interesting when your teammate understands your difficulties and will help you learn what you have to learn and do what you have to do.

Social-functioning alliances

It is easy for men and women in long-term relationships to let their social skills get rusty. Because of common social customs and the belief that if you have a mate, you don't need a close rapport with anyone else, many people lose the knack of forming close friendships with members of their own sex and never fully develop the skill of forming close friendships with members of the opposite sex. Most think that once they have found a mate they are out of the male-female "game" and thus don't bother learning how to be warm, open and cooperative and still set their own limits as to what they will and won't do. They lack the relating skills necessary to relax and thoroughly enjoy themselves when alone with someone who is sexually attractive to them—when conquest is not uppermost in their minds. Very few know how to let a member of the opposite sex know they are attracted but are not sexually available. Nor do they know how to handle the cost of food, drinks and transportation in a way that is both gracious and yet fair. Or even how to have a conversation that gets beyond the barriers of sexual innuendo into something more meaningful.

Married and living-together couples tend to become a "we" socially—going everywhere together, rarely separating at parties except to have "man talk" or "woman talk," and falling into routine social habits. It is not uncommon to play bridge every Saturday night with the same couples, eat dinner out every other Friday and have family dinner on Sunday. A member of a couple seldom if ever reaches out to others as an individual.

A way a couple can enrich a long-term relationship is to help one another learn to function well as autonomous social beings, particularly in regard to members of the opposite sex.

This does not mean that we are suggesting that sexual partners

teach their mates how to "make out" with others. The art of se-
duction takes a different set of skills and that is not at all what we
are talking about. What we are talking about is learning to cope
with your sexual feelings other than through acting in accordance
with or ignoring them. And even the most happily monogamous
couple can benefit from learning these skills.

The truth is that men and women don't cease to be sexual
beings just because they are half of a pair. Unless you stay home
all the time and don't answer the doorbell, it is impossible to iso-
late yourself from people who are sexually attracted to you or vice
versa. Learning to handle such people in a gracious way is not
going to turn you into a "swinger," or someone who is constantly
on the prowl. The fact is that sometimes married people get involved in sexual situations they don't really want because they
don't know how to be open, warm, gracious and complimentary—
to have a meaningful relationship—without having sex. Being able
to recognize but get beyond your sexual feelings in social situations will make you more confident as a person. And two
confident people who know they can handle the "singles scene" if
necessary are better marriage partners than two who are staying
together mainly because they can't stand the thought of the hassle
of having to deal with members of the opposite sex if they were to
part.

There are two ways partners can help one another function
more effectively as autonomous social beings: (1) They can coach
one another in gentle aggression techniques to be used with
members of the opposite sex. (2) They can encourage one another
to "uncouple" occasionally, sometimes by going to social functions separately, other times by separating when they attend a social gathering together.

This behavior, although essential for couples who want to learn
to function well socially in today's world, violates two old-
fashioned "thou-shalt-nots": (1) Thou shalt not show any interest
in attractive members of the opposite sex. (2) Thou shalt not go
to social events where there are members of the opposite sex unless accompanied by thy mate. Thus there is the risk of censure,
but the possible rewards are well worth it.

Let's take a look at the usual behavior of committed couples in
social situations. If the only way they know how to deal with
members of the opposite sex is in the old traditional sexual roles,

they are very limited and frequently create problems for themselves. Take James, for instance, a married man who is happily monogamous. But if you watch his behavior in public you will think he is definitely "on the make" most of the time. This is because James knows only two ways to behave with women—ways that he learned during his dating days some fifteen years ago and has never outgrown. If a woman is considerably older than he or doesn't appeal to him physically, he tends to ignore her or is exceedingly deferential. He has never learned to talk to a woman as a person and doesn't know how to start and maintain a conversation that isn't business or sexually based. On the other hand, if a woman appeals to him, he eyes her body, makes suggestive remarks and touches her in a way that implies a sexual invitation. He is unable to get past sexually based innuendos into any kind of meaningful discussion.

When it comes to money dealings with women, James is just as limited and rigid in his behavior. Frequently, he'll sit at a table in the company dining room and if there are women in the group, he finds himself offering to pay for their meals. Sometimes everyone from the office goes out after work for a drink and if he happens to sit at the bar next to one of his female colleagues or at a table full of women, James always picks up the tab.

Married women also usually fail to make meaningful contact with individual men as persons because they immediately put them into two categories—those who are sexually attractive and those who aren't—and then treat them accordingly. Some will ignore those who aren't and flirt with those who are, since acting seductive is the only way they know of letting a man know they like him. They believe they are "safe," that any "nice" man will know they are also "nice"—meaning not sexually available. And if he doesn't, and becomes sexually aggressive, they rely on their husbands to get them out of an embarrassing situation. Others, unaware of what they are doing, get in the habit of acting hostile or mothering around those who are attractive, dumb or helpless around those who aren't. Or vice versa, but always acting in some way that puts up barriers.

Not only does this tendency to place members of the opposite sex into two categories confuse and demean other people; it isolates the person who is doing it because it keeps him from making person-to-person contact and getting the kind of personal attention all human beings need. This contributes greatly to the loneliness many married people suffer from—loneliness that sometimes becomes so intense it causes marriages to break up.

It is normal and natural for people—even those in nourishing committed relationships—to want attention from many members of the opposite sex. All of us do. And one of the advantages of being half of a long-term couple is that you can form an alliance to help each other get attention from others and, at the same time, enrich and expand your own relationship.

Tia and Harris got into an alliance like this for an odd reason—because he was losing his hair. Baldness ran in Harris' family but he thought he had been spared. All of his life he had had a handsome crop of hair which was his pride and joy. And then, all of a sudden, when he was forty, it started falling out.

He became very depressed, and when his depression continued, he and Tia talked to see what was at the bottom of it. It turned out that he had a great fear that he was not going to be attractive to women with a bald pate. He had no doubt that Tia would still love him, but what if she died, then what would he do? And besides, though it was difficult to admit to Tia, he was concerned that young women no longer found him attractive the way they used to. The thought of being old and shunned by women was just too much for him.

Tia tried to reassure him by telling him all of her women friends really liked him. His answer was "Sure, they treat me like a big brother, but who wants that all the time?" Then Tia said, "You treat them all like little sisters, too, except for the young or real pretty ones. You barely talk with them and then walk away. Some think that you don't like them." And then she laid it on the line, saying, "If you want some other kind of behavior from women, I think you are going to have to change yours."

And so they made a pact. He agreed that at social gatherings he would deliberately seek out women he thought attractive. He would consciously make eye contact and small talk and then try to get into something more meaningful. (In essence, to follow the suggestions for making contact we discussed in Chapters 3 and 4.) She agreed that whenever possible, if he was around women, she would try to listen to what he said and watch his behavior and then to tell him later her reactions and suggestions. She agreed to coach him as to how to look at women, how to talk with and touch them so that they would see him as an attractive man and not as a brother or as somebody else's husband on the make.

A number of things happened because of their new behavior. To begin with, they had such fun that he started coaching her on how to be more effective with men. What they were doing was teaching each other the role-expanding techniques of gentle aggression—i.e., how to get involved with other people while being sensitive to their needs and letting them know what you want from them.

At home, Tia and Harris also talked a lot about what they could do to break up the cliques and improve the atmosphere at mixed social gatherings. They noticed that so often men would gather in one group and discuss business or sports and women would gather in another and discuss housekeeping and hairdressers. If a woman attempted to join the men's group, the men would immediately start cracking jokes or making remarks with sexual overtones, while if a man joined the women's group, they played up to him by acting coy. They pointed this pattern out to some of their friends and requested their cooperation in trying to change it.

While everybody didn't want to change, many did, for they, too, felt bored and isolated by the old routines and wanted more contact and more opportunity to be expressive without censure. Though it took a long time and there were problems along the way, they did change, not only their own way of interacting with members of the opposite sex, but their interactions with the same sex, too. They began seeing them more as individuals instead of as competitors for attention, and the mood of many of the social gatherings they attended changed as a result.

Harris' hair did not stop falling out, and young women did not ever swoon over him, but many found him interesting to talk with when he made the effort to reach out to them. But what was most important, women in his own age bracket discovered that he was an exciting man, one who took action and made things happen. And they let him know it. He, in turn, found women of all ages much more stimulating and understanding than ever before. Harris and Tia did, however, have to give up some of their old stick-in-the-mud friends, especially those who criticized them when they started going to some social functions without each other and even sometimes with another person's mate. For that was the next step they took in trying to improve their social life, their feelings of self-worth and their relationship with one another. And that is a step we recommend to you. Here's why:

Chances are, that if you were to poll all the couples that attend cocktail parties, football games, plays and concerts, who go together to dances, fashion shows, bowling alleys and restaurants, and if you were to inquire if both parties really wanted to be there or not, you'd be in for a surprise. More than likely, in over half the cases you'd discover that one really didn't want to be there but had given in, either because he would have felt guilty or because the other would have made it unpleasant for him if he didn't.

Rather than both going or both sitting at home, why shouldn't couples sometimes consider the option of going to things separately? Bring this up to your partner the next time one wants and the other doesn't want. And then talk about what you fear might happen if you were to do this daring thing. Yes, people might talk. They might think your behavior is a bit odd or even that you must be on the verge of breaking up, but so what? Are you going to let what people might think keep you both from doing what you'd like to do? Or what if the person who went alone were to feel lonely or uncomfortable? Good, that will present him with the opportunity of learning to handle those feelings instead of expecting a mate to do it for him. On the other hand, he might not be lonely or uncomfortable at all but might feel very free and have a wonderful time. That is another worry people have. If their mate goes out alone, he might discover he has a good time when she isn't around. But is there anything wrong with that? It is possible, even desirable for a person to have as good a time without you as with you. That doesn't mean he doesn't love you or that you aren't important to him. It just means his happiness does not depend entirely upon you *and that is good*. However, if he frequently has a *better* time when you aren't around, you'd better talk about what makes the difference and then together do something about it.

And then there is one more worry, the real clincher, that keeps many couples tied to each other's apron strings: What if, while out without me, he meets somebody he likes better than me? Well, if your relationship is good solid stuff, the chances of that happening are highly unlikely. And if your relationship is a flimsy thing, you aren't going to be able to keep him by following him around like a puppy dog. If losing your mate to another is what you are worried about, you'd better both stay home and talk about it and then take some positive action to build up trust before you try to enrich it.

For those of you who do trust one another, try going alone to places where you usually go as a couple but with these two guidelines in mind: (1) Talk with your mate beforehand—to plan how you will handle any difficulties you believe you might encounter— and afterward—to share your experiences and to deal with uncomfortable feelings either of you might have. (2) Prepare other people for this change in your behavior. For instance, don't just show up at a home where you both were invited for dinner and say, "I came alone because Jane didn't want to come and I did." Instead, call ahead of time and explain that Jane has other things she needs to do. (Don't lie and make up a sick grandmother or something. Lying won't help people get used to your new behavior. The idea is to be truthful but with concern for your hostess's feelings.) Then say that you are really looking forward to her dinner party, and is it O.K. if you come alone or will it upset her seating arrangement?

If you are a man, you'll probably be graciously welcomed. An extra man is usually considered an asset to any gathering. It is assumed he will take care of others, like deaf old Aunt Sadie.

If you are a woman, you'll also probably be accepted. But not so graciously. Or you might even get turned down. This is because in most social circles, a woman without a man is still seen as a person who has to be taken care of, a burden. A hostess is apt to believe it will fall on her shoulders to supply the lone woman with someone to talk with or even to see that she gets home safely. Thus if the hostess doesn't seem enthusiastic about having you, don't take it personally and back away. Go anyway. And if by chance you do get turned down, be bold and inquire as to why. Then give reasons to combat the objections. You deserve the right to go places without a big daddy to take care of you. See that you get it.

When you get to wherever you decide to go alone, whether you are a man or a woman, keep in mind your objectives: to practice functioning socially without a mate to lean on, and to enrich and expand your relationship with your mate. To accomplish these objectives requires that you make your time enjoyable and that you have some exciting experiences to share with your mate when you get home. So don't hover in a corner alone. And don't, whatever you do, let yourself get stuck with deaf old Aunt Sadie. Or a lecherous bore with halitosis. Instead make this an adventure. Seek out people who seem interesting and try to get to know them. Try things you never dared try before. And all the time be aware of what you are thinking and feeling and doing, so that you'll have an exciting story to tell.

When you go alone to social events usually attended only by couples, you are being a real pioneer. You are breaking precedent and making social history. You deserve congratulations, but don't just sit back and rest on your laurels. There is one more step before you can brag that you are not trapped by outdated and nonsensical social taboos. This step consists in going somewhere that couples usually go—*without* your mate but *with* another member of the opposite sex.

While this might seem too risky and purposeless, it isn't. If you want a companion, your reasoning might go, why not take your mate? The truth is sometimes your mate doesn't really want to go where you want to go and sometimes it is just nice to have someone else to be with for a change—and not always a member of the same sex. And it won't hurt your relationship, if you go about it in the right way. It will give you ideas on how to treat members of the opposite sex and will add enjoyment to both of your lives.

Take Neil and Ardyce, for instance. For the twelve years of their relationship, Ardyce had been going to football games almost every Saturday afternoon to keep Neil company. He loved football, and she hated it. Then early in the football season one year, right after taking assertiveness training, she told him she didn't want to go anymore. Because he had season tickets on the 50-yard line, it was easy to find a male crony to go with him. But then one Saturday morning, just before the USC–Notre Dame game, the friend who was to go with him came down with the flu. His friend asked Neil if he would mind taking his wife, a rabid Notre Dame fan, instead. Neil took her and learned a lot in the process. Not only did she know a lot more about football than he did; she had a totally different type of personality than his wife. While his wife was rather self-effacing and subservient, this woman was totally confident and self-sufficient. He did not find her attractive to look at but he enjoyed her enthusiasm and the way she took care of herself. It was quite an enlightening experience, and he went home with much more appreciation of what his wife was trying to accomplish through some of the self-development courses she was taking.

If you would like to try going someplace with a member of the opposite sex other than your mate, here is how to make it a memorable event:

1. Talk over the idea with your mate first. Make certain that he or she understands your motivation, that you want to learn to function better socially without being dependent upon a mate and that you want to learn things about yourself and members of the opposite sex that can enhance your all-important love relationship. (This is the time to give a mate a great deal of reassurance. They usually need it. Some compliments can help here.) Decide together whom you will invite. While you don't want to let your mate pick out the person for you to invite, neither do you want to invite someone he or she is terribly jealous of.

2. Explain your motivation to the person you are inviting and assure him or her that your intentions are not sexual. If this person has a mate, explain it to him or her also.

3. All of the time you are with the person you have invited, try to get to know as much as you can about him or her and share yourself also. A good format to follow is that of the Gentle-Aggressor mini-date.

4. During the time you are with this other person make mental notes of what is happening, particularly in regard to your thoughts and feelings.

5. When you get home, tell your mate all about your experience. Be sure to clarify and share what you learned and what you would have liked to have done differently. And then start making plans together for subsequent similar outings—for yourself and for your mate.

MAKING BRIEF ENCOUNTERS HAPPEN IN LONG-TERM RELATIONSHIPS

One night, Ken and Lucy, who had been married for twenty-three years, were putting their groceries away after their weekly Friday-night shopping trip. The radio was on and suddenly it began playing "Deep Purple," their song, which had been popular when they were going together. Ken closed the refrigerator door, put his arms around Lucy and they began to dance slowly around the kitchen. Then, the rest of their groceries forgotten, they began to reminisce about their courtship and the early years of their marriage.

Among the things they recalled was how they loved to dance to the music of the big bands at the old Palladium in Los Angeles. So Lucy put an old album of swing music on the stereo and for the next hour they jitterbugged around their large kitchen—dipping and twisting the way they used to. After a while, they brought out a bottle of wine and toasted their relationship—the many good years they had had together. And then a little later, slightly tipsy and ever so playful, they made love on the floor of the living room—in a more sensuous and appreciative way than they had for a long, long time.

Ken and Lucy had a brief encounter. They have them every so often because they have a relationship that they work to keep alive and growing.

You've probably had some experiences like this with your long-term partner, and if you are like Ken and Lucy, you can't predict when they are going to happen. It doesn't seem to hinge on how much money you spend; going to a posh restaurant where the lights are low and violins play romantic music is no guarantee. It doesn't seem to happen on the nights you'd like it to—like New Year's Eve or your anniversary, and, in fact, it seems as if these are often the times you end up having a terrible time or even a quarrel. You just can't seem to plan for it to happen. That weekend you sent the kids away and expected to be so great was a disaster.

While you can't, it is true, make brief encounters happen when you want them to, they do happen to some couples more than others. And it is no accident. There are things you can do to set up the kind of environment in which they can happen. And you can prepare yourself to let them happen. It is important that long-term partners do these things, for brief encounters are the punctuation marks in a relationship. They determine its form, meaning, and value, much more than a series of anniversaries.

In the following section are some suggestions as to what you can do to make brief encounters happen more often to you and your beloved. Many of these suggestions come from Dr. Adele and Sam Scheele, whose own exciting and successful relationship is proof of the validity of their advice.

One of the first things most couples need to do is to allow themselves to "hang out and hang loose" more often. Sam Scheele calls it "doing nothing creatively." Instead of crowding your calendar with highly structured social events—dinner parties, dances, card parties, conventions—and filling in all the blank spaces with spectator activities—particularly TV—time must be made available when things can "just happen."

Here's one idea. Why don't you set out some weekend with the object of being available for "happenings"? Start out to go someplace but don't make a reservation. And don't have your heart set on getting there at any particular time—or even on getting there at all. Then dilly-dally along the way. Avoid freeways and busy thoroughfares in favor of less traveled routes. Explore those little side roads you never explore when you are trying to make a certain destination before dark. Open yourself to people along the way. Stop and talk to the woman who is arranging goodies in the bakery-shop window, or the man selling fruit from the back of his truck, or the farmer plowing his field. If you do this with an open mind—i.e., not having any expectations that something terribly exciting or offbeat will happen—you just might have a brief encounter. With each other or with somebody you meet. And in any case, you'll have a lot of fun.

This is what happened to Don and Marguerite last spring. It had been a long, cold winter. In fact, for them, it had been a series of long, cold winters. Don, always a heavy drinker, had slipped over the border into alcoholism. His work had suffered and his relationship with Marguerite—sexual and emotional—had deteriorated greatly. And he had had two drunk-driving arrests. It was these arrests that finally stopped his drinking. He was given the choice of enrolling in Alcoholics Anonymous or losing his driver's license. Once he stopped drinking, his work and his relationship with Marguerite began improving, but though both were really trying, the spark between them was missing.

One weekend, Marguerite suggested they just get in the car and drive and then find someplace along the way to stay all night—just as a change of pace. Ordinarily Don not only insisted on making reservations but planned almost every moment of a trip well in advance. He liked the security of knowing just where they were going and what they were going to do and hated the thought of being stranded with no room or having to stay in a poorly run motel or eat tasteless food in a dirty coffee shop. But this time she somehow convinced him to give it a try. In talking about it, they agreed to set reason aside for two days, to give in to their impulses and make whatever happened a lark.

They started off, meandering along the coast, stopping now and then to take a picture or have a bite to eat and then in the early afternoon, on one of their stops, they spotted a small hotel over-looking the ocean. They looked at each other and without a word drove up to the hotel and signed in.

That evening, according to Marguerite, "It all came together for us." They took a long walk among the fragrant pine trees which stood all over the hotel grounds, shyly holding hands; they talked softly but nonstop during dinner, a talk not clouded by alcohol; and they laughed a lot at their bumbling waiter, at the garish decor of the dining room and at themselves—what they had thought and done in the past. And while they talked and laughed, they seemed to rediscover those things in each other that had caused them to marry in the first place. And that night, in a cozy old-fashioned down bed, they talked more and made love. And afterwards he cried and told her how afraid he was of her leaving him. And she cried, too, because she had found him again.

Now we don't want to imply that all of Don and Marguerite's problems were solved and that they lived happily ever after. It's just that this particular brief encounter was a turning point for them. It let them know the spark was still there. And afterwards they began to do more things to help them have more brief en-counters and to build the kinds of alliances they needed to help them feel close and secure.

There is another way in which to provide a context in which brief encounters are likely to occur. This is by taking on an unfa-miliar but rewarding task that must be completed within a rela-tively short period of time, something like canning a lug of fruit or assembling a bicycle for a child's birthday party. The idea is to create for yourself a sort of "crisis" situation in which you have to help one another do something important neither of you has ever done before. This way you are likely to develop the same sort of cooperation and creative solving of problems that complete strangers often achieve during emergencies such as earthquakes, floods or other disasters.

During the first power blackout in New York, many people reported having a memorable brief encounter with another person —a stranger, someone they had known well or even a long-term partner. This is not surprising. While keeping up each other's morale in a stalled elevator, or simply trying to find something to do to occupy their time during hours of darkness without television or lights to read by, people dropped their usual roles and related to each other in new ways. What happens is that in "crisis" situations, there are no set rules of behavior. People have to rely on their own creativity and their ability to work with others to solve their problems. In addition, the feeling of urgency engendered by sharing common dangers or discomfort can enable them to work together more cooperatively.

In creating your own "crisis context" at home here are some things to keep in mind. (1) Make sure your task is complex enough so that you have to work out a process for doing it. It must be such that you just can't assign parts of it to each other and do it. For example, scrubbing and waxing a kitchen floor is a task but it does not involve a very complicated process. (2) Make sure you are both unfamiliar with the task. Otherwise, it is easy to fall into boss-employee roles. If it is something the husband is good at, the wife will become the employee and vice versa. This task should be approached by two partners of equal knowledge and ability (or rather, inability!). (3) Make sure that the task can be completed in a relatively short period of time—i.e., at one sitting. You'll lose your sense of urgency—and some of your opportunity for brief encounters—if this task is the kind you can easily stop in the middle of and finish later. (4) Pick a job that results in a specific product. To be motivated enough to continue, you need to have something to show for your efforts. Twenty-four cans of homemade pickles is a product. So is a batch of homemade noodles. So is an assembled bicycle. Or a bookcase.

Martin and Angie had a brief encounter because they decided that they just couldn't let a crop of ripe apricots go to waste. In a new home but a few months, they found themselves overwhelmed with the huge amount of apricots produced by one tree in their backyard.

One Saturday morning, dismayed at the number of rotting apricots on the ground—and sick of eating fresh apricots—they impulsively decided to make apricot jam, and neither of them had ever made jam before. Although they thought they were just being thrifty, they were really creating a crisis context for a brief encounter. And they had one.

They didn't realize the complexity of their task until they had launched into the process and by then it was too late to stop without having a batch of rotten fruit on their hands. First they had to devise a plan to pick all the ripe fruit—even that at the top of the tree. Then they had to wash it, remove the pits, cook it and watch and stir it until it turned into jam. But that wasn't all. In addition, they had to go out and buy canning equipment, locate a recipe for apricot jam, buy sugar and pectin and sterilize the jars before they could fill them with the jam. And they had to finish the process by sealing each jar with paraffin.

This is what Martin has to say about the whole thing: "Now I understand why people were a lot closer in the old days when they had quilting bees and the like. Angie and I stayed together until every last apricot had been turned into jam and was in a clean jar topped with paraffin. It took until three in the morning, and once she threatened to quit and once I did. But for the most part we were caught up in the excitement of it all. It was like creating our own little factory, and devising a new form of technology. We really got into the process—discovering the best way to pit the apricots, ladle out hot jam without getting burned, coordinate cooking the jam with sterilizing the jars and pouring the paraffin so it didn't make bubbles. Before long, we began to talk on a different level than we ever had before. It became a total flow. We gloried in the challenge and took pride in every single jar of jam—which we labeled and gave for Christmas presents. It reminded us of the early days of our marriage when we had to struggle more. We realized we had achieved many of our goals and had stopped struggling, but we had also stopped challenging ourselves. Now we are aware that that needs to be part of our relationship, too."

Here are some more suggestions as to how long-term partners can create a context within which brief encounters will sometimes happen:

1. Use your environment in different ways. Try camping out in your living room overnight—or in the backyard. With or without the kids. On a rainy day, have a picnic in the living room. Spread a

beach towel on the floor to sit and eat lunch on. Schedule a whole day in bed together. Don't get dressed all day or answer the phone. Bring your meals into bed and eat them propped up on pillows. Do purposeless things. Read a "dirty" novel; take lots of catnaps; watch things on TV you usually don't watch; write a poem; talk about what you would do if you won the Irish Sweepstakes or were eighteen and a real knockout and knew what you know now.

2. Trade residences with some friends for a day or a weekend. You will get a different sense of yourself and each other as you try to cook in someone else's kitchen, find out where they keep their Kleenex and throw their trash, as you read their books and play their records.

3. Try some different forms of socializing. Give a painting party —either one where you invite friends over for the express purpose of painting some room in your home, or your pool deck or a fence, or else to experiment with painting pictures. In the former case, you supply all the materials and the food, and in the latter case, either you can supply food and materials or each person can bring food for a potluck dinner and art supplies for potluck picture painting.

Or give a housecleaning party or a cleaning-out-the-garage party, thus having fun and forming a short-term working alliance as was discussed in Chapter 11.

4. Set aside a half day or an evening to devote to doing a series of unusual personal things for each other, such as washing each other's hair, giving each other a shower or mending clothes and polishing shoes. Or help one another clean out a closet and decide what clothes need to be thrown away. Or devote some time to helping one another clean and organize desk or bureau drawers or a filing cabinet.

5. Dress each other for the evening—either when you are going out or when you are staying home but are planning to do something special. Pick out all of the items you would like your partner to wear and as you help him into them, tell him why you'd like him to wear each one.

6. Use reading material in creative ways. Each of you can read a section of the paper you don't usually read and then tell each other about it. If you don't usually read the sports page or the entertainment or travel sections or the items on fashion and social

events, digest them thoroughly and give your partner an accurate and detailed account of what you learned. It is bound to stimulate discussion. Or take turns reading aloud to one another, stopping now and then to talk about what you have read. Reading aloud is particularly helpful in staving off boredom and keeping in touch with one another when you are on long drives. You can give the driver a reward by allowing him to pick what he wants to hear.

7. Make it a frequent practice to invite your partner out for a just-the-two-of-you prearranged date for which you make all of the plans as if you were inviting out a new boy or girl friend. Treat him or her as you might if you were on a first date. Dress to please him; pay close attention to everything he says and does; compliment him frequently; draw him out in conversation. You might even want to make a pass or two.

Joel Springer, marriage enrichment counselor and teacher, always recommends "dating" your own partner as a good short-term treatment for long-term doldrums. He suggested it to one pair who had come to him because the fun had gone out of their relationship. The man was a student tied up in his books and she a housewife tied up with the kids, and so he gave them the assignment of going out on a date on which they would talk about neither. And he told them to flirt with one another.

At first, they objected, saying they had been married for years and that married people didn't do that sort of thing, and besides, it was silly. He agreed it sounded silly but explained that one of the things that went wrong in marriage was that people forgot how much fun it was to be silly.

And so she invited him to a movie one night—a Western. She didn't like Westerns, but he did. And afterwards, she bought him a double-decker ice-cream cone. A week or so later, he got her mother to take the kids and invited her to a candlelight dinner which he cooked. And they playacted like they were lovers meeting in his bachelor pad. And then on their next "date" she invited him to a rendezvous at an "adult" motel where they tried out a water bed and watched a "porno flick" on closed-circuit TV. Together they rediscovered fun.

8. Playact with your partner. Playing make-believe is a way children try out new roles and prepare themselves to become grownups. Grown-ups who want to keep growing can profit from

playacting, too. And it is good for rejuvenating and enriching relationships because it brings out new facets in people.

A favorite form of make-believe used by many couples is "Pickup." The idea is for one or the other to sit at a bar and play it sort of cool and nonchalant while the other approaches him and tries to pick him up.

Another variation of make-believe is "You be and I'll be." You do it like this: When you are about to go out for the evening or do a task that you don't like to do—like wash the car, clean up the yard or entertain some relatives you don't care for—one partner says to the other: "You be _____ and I'll be _____." You can fill in the blanks with characters from history that are easy to impersonate—Abraham Lincoln, Mata Hari or Napoleon; or movie stars—Marilyn Monroe, Gary Cooper, Katharine Hepburn; or character types—a successful businessman, a drunken bum, a rock star; or anything else you can think of. And then each of you assumes the selected role for the duration of the evening or the task, staying in character and interacting with each other and with other people as if you were that person. It is great fun to watch Elvis Presley vacuum the rug or to make a pass at Whistler's mother. This is one of our favorites and if you try it once and if you pick a character who is quite different from you and really get into the role, it will become one of your favorites, too.

NEW CEREMONIES AND RITUALS FOR NEW KINDS OF RELATIONSHIPS

Many people today discount the importance of ceremonies—those occasions when we gather with family and friends to mark the important rites of passage—birth, puberty, marriage, death. They tend to discount them because they have been to far too many weddings or bar mitzvahs or christenings or funerals where the cost of the flowers or the lavishness of the food and liquor or the number of guests seemed to be more important than the occasion for which people had been brought together. A solution for many is to eliminate ceremony from their lives. Unfortunately, by so doing they also eliminate some other pretty important things—a sense of drama and meaning. Ceremonies are important. As people prepare for and share with friends a ceremony to mark their movement from one common life stage to another, they can get a strong sense of their connections to others and of the flow of life.

What we do need to do is to make our ceremonies more meaningful—to make them reflect a short-term philosophy—i.e., a belief that every moment, every stage is meant to be enjoyed and that life is meant to be lived as a celebration and not a chore. And many couples who are getting married today are doing just that by writing their own wedding ceremonies and their own vows. But in addition, we need to devise new kinds of ceremonies to mark new kinds of life styles. For example, many couples today who are living together in a committed and serious sexual alliance feel a need for some sort of ceremony that would help honor and give social sanction to their relationship even though it is not legally recorded, even though they don't know how long it will last. In this section we are going to describe such a ceremony—one devised by some friends of ours. But first let's talk a little about what living together means these days.

It used to be that men and women not related by close blood ties or marriage did not live together. Nor was a sexual involvement without marriage considered worthwhile, serious or socially acceptable. If you had one, your mother didn't want her friends to know about it. It's a different story today. It is true that in some geographical areas and to certain people, living together is spoken of in derogatory terms as "shacking up." It is considered, if not a sin, then at least a sign of a lack of commitment. However, to enlightened people, it is not that way. A sex life is seen as the right of all human beings, and marriage as but one way of getting it. In a number of respectable families, a divorced mother and father and their grown children may all be "living with" someone and even Grandma can talk about it without blushing.

However, there are problems of status, dignity and respect even where the practice is morally acceptable. It's hard to know what a couple who are living together mean to one another. Sometimes they are simply sharing living space and sexual pleasure in a very casual and temporary way; sometimes they are going through a sort of trial period to help them decide whether or not they want to get married. And sometimes they are in a very intense, loving and supportive relationship but don't intend to get married. Although in the latter case their involvement with each other may be at least that of the average married couple and many times even deeper, their relationship is not given the respect automatically accorded a married couple. It might be if there was a ceremony that would announce and clarify such a relationship for their friends and relatives. And besides, such a union deserves a celebration.

Since there are no traditional ceremonies to honor unmarried but committed couples, people have to devise their own. That is exactly what some friends of ours—Suzanne Taylor and Olaf Egeberg (their real names)—did. They called their creative and unusual ceremony a "waylinking."

A "waylinking" ceremony

When Suzanne and Olaf started planning for their ceremony, they were not seeking anyone's approval of what they were doing. What happened was that, after living together for two years as romantic and business partners, they wanted to celebrate. They wanted friends around but not to witness an exchange of promises to behave a certain way in the future as is done at weddings. Instead they wanted friends to help them rejoice that their relationship existed in its present form at that moment in time. And so they decided to have a party specially designed to celebrate the coming together of two people in a New Age manner, linking their lives for as long as seemed right.

In selecting the form for their waylinking they had several requirements. First of all, they wanted to create a sense of aliveness and playfulness in the ritual itself and in the before and after activities. To them, too many marriage ceremonies were like too many marriages: deadly serious and lacking in laughter. In addition, they wanted all of their guests to feel important and honored. They wanted to avoid the idea conveyed in most wedding ceremonies that there are but two important people there—the bride and groom. And they wanted their guests to meet one another and share themselves in meaningful ways. For them, it wasn't enough that each of them should meet the other's friends, a tradition at such events. They knew their friends would like each other and wanted to make it easy for new friendships to start.

It was with the idea in mind of combining pomp, ceremony

and humor that Suzanne and Olaf had decided to do a sort of parody on weddings as a means of investing with new meaning certain rituals that are popular and understood. They included a reception line, a wedding "cake," a wedding "march," a ceremony at which they both spoke, presided over by a person of status, and an official ending at which everyone joined in wishing the couple well. But these were different from what anyone who attended had ever seen before. You couldn't help but laugh; you couldn't help but feel important; you couldn't help but participate; and you couldn't help but meet and get to know a lot of fascinating people.

To create a mood of fun, guests were requested to come in costume, to wear clothing that would bring out an undeveloped side of themselves, a side they seldom got to show off. The waylinking partners realized what fun it can be for grown-ups to dress up and to express themselves, and since they were going to do it themselves, they wanted to encourage their friends to do it, too. The result was that you could learn a lot about the guests from just a glance at what they wore, and you were encouraged to look. As each guest arrived, he was met by a team of greeters dressed in funny costumes, his name was announced to the other guests grouped on the patio and then as he walked down a short winding path lined with rainbow-colored balloons and crepe-paper streamers, they repeated a singsong little ditty over and over: "Jerry, Jerry (or whatever his or her name was), you sure look good, just the way that we knew you would. La-de-da, la-de-da, la-de-da." In this way, everybody got to know everyone else's name and the group singing energized the crowd.

When all of the guests had arrived, they were ushered into the living room for a group meditation followed by a series of "ice-breaker" games that required looking carefully at other individuals, touching them and sometimes talking with them. After a while, each guest was given a piece of paper with one of the following written on it: *dum-dum, de,* or *dum.* They were then asked to line themselves up so that a person who had a *dum* was after a person with a *de,* and that person was behind the person with a *dum-dum.* With guidance from a leader, each person in turn sang his syllable. As the whole line repeated the syllables, what resulted was a rendition of the wedding march—very much out of key. As people realized what they were doing and tried to make it better, repeating over and over, *dum-dum, de, dum,* Suzanne and Olaf made their appearance. They walked slowly down the stairs to stand in front of the fireplace, their backs to the guests. A person dressed as Harpo Marx was waiting there. Harpo, in pantomime with much eye-rolling and toots on his horn, performed a wordless ritual, a takeoff on the marriage ritual. After the laughter had subsided, Suzanne and Olaf turned to face their guests seated on cushions scattered all over the living-room rug. Then one at a time, with a voice full of pride and tenderness, each talked about the other and their relationship. They told how they met; they told of the qualities they most admired, describing incidents to demonstrate those qualities. They told why they were with one another, what they were getting from the relationship and the ways in which their lives had been changed because of it. And as they talked, the mood changed to one of deep reverence and love.

When they finished, they kissed and hugged one another and then formed their version of a reception line. First they had all of the guests join hands to make a large circle and quietly look at one another with the idea of seeing something they liked in each person. Then, with Suzanne and Olaf leading the way, the circle was broken and a serpentine line formed which doubled back on itself so that eventually every person stood in front of every other person there—and gave him or her a ritualistic hug.

This was followed by a cutting of the "cake," which was not a cake at all but a huge heart-shaped, fancy-looking but sugarless multi-layered sandwich concoction. It was created from health breads and a variety of fresh vegetables, fish and cheeses, and topped with a "frosting" of pink cream cheese. This was New Age food for a New Age ceremony but the champagne served with it was quite old-fashioned. After some more games designed to help the guests meet one another and express feelings of playfulness and tenderness, each was given a helium-filled balloon and three small pieces of paper. They were asked to write on the slips of paper a wish for Suzanne and Olaf, a wish for themselves and a wish for the universe and tie them onto the balloon string. Then all gathered around the edge of the swimming pool, sang a joyful song and at its conclusion released their balloons—and their good wishes—to float skyward.

You can be certain there were no bored people at this New Age ritual. And we wager to say all went home feeling good about themselves, Suzanne and Olaf and people in general. If you are living with someone now or think you might be in the future or if you are planning a wedding, we'd like to suggest that you create your own rituals to honor the existence of your relationship the way it is. Though you may not want to create an event as elaborate as the one we just described, it should give you some good ideas.

Have your friends in your supportive network help you plan a ceremony to honor your relationship. Use your creativity to make it both meaningful and fun. In this way, you can be a pioneer in creating the rituals our society needs to bring more affection and liveliness into daily life.

Affirmation rituals

If there is one thing all of us could use a lot more of, it is affirmation. Partners who want a long-term relationship especially need to develop rituals for frequently telling one another of their strengths—i.e., talents, skills and personality assets. If they fall into the prevailing relating patterns, they will do just the opposite —i.e., frequently remind one another of their faults and shortcomings but seldom mention good points. Such behavior will sooner or later erode their relationship.

It says a lot about the emphasis in our society that we have many common ways of showing someone we disapprove of him— the shaking fist, the scowl, the upraised finger. And we find it easy to give advice, to imply through words, gestures or sometimes just tone of voice, "You aren't trying hard enough," or "You aren't doing it the right way." Also, giving faint praise is common, saying such things as "You were pretty good at the party last night— didn't drink nearly as much as usual." But we have very few universal signs of approval, nonverbal ways to indicate, "You did well, friend." And most of us find it difficult to give praise without feeling foolish, or to accept it without suspecting the motives of the person giving it. In fact, there seems to be some sort of "taboo" against praise, that makes us put it down as unnecessary, or to label it flattery and discount it as insincere and phony.

When we have something nice to say about a person, we usually say it behind his back rather than to his face. Notice next time you are with a group of people how often, *after a person has left the room,* one person will turn to another and say about the person who has left, "Isn't John handsome?" or "Doesn't Mary have a wonderful sense of humor?" It is quite common for a person to brag to family and friends about his mate ad nauseum, relating in detail what she has done and said and yet never let his mate know of his pride. If this behavior is pointed out, the rejoinder frequently is: "Gee, I don't have to tell Mabel she is pretty"—or a good cook or well organized or a logical thinker—"she knows it already." The truth is that she may not know it already, or even if she does, she'd like to hear it from you.

As a result of the common practice of emphasizing the negative and ignoring the positive, we are all, to some extent, starved for praise. And when we don't get it, we don't give it. When you feel impoverished, it is hard to give away what you need yourself.

There is a way out of this downward spiral that can drain the liveliness out of even the best of relationships. Invent rituals to reaffirm your partner's value. Not only will you keep your relationship alive and lively, you will bring out the creativity and caring in one another. People who have their good qualities recognized, develop more of them. People who are frequently told they are lovable become more loving.

Here are two suggestions:

1. Occasionally, have an end-of-the-day Stroking Ceremony. Set aside about fifteen to twenty minutes to spend with your partner in a quiet place where you will not be interrupted by the children, your neighbors or sounds from the radio or TV set. Position yourself where you can look into one another's eyes. Be silent for a minute or so, holding one another's gaze and hands. Take a few deep breaths. Then take turns and one at a time, while continuing to look into your partner's eyes, say to him or her, "I love you because _____," enumerating all the reasons you can think of. One partner should keep this up for *three minutes* without interruptions. The other says nothing except "Thank you." The partner who is giving the compliments may repeat one thing several times if one is especially important or if he runs out of things to say. It is not necessary to repeat the introductory phrase, "I love you because," with every compliment but do repeat it a number of times. Your partner will enjoy hearing it.

2. Give your mate an Affirmation Party. This kind of a party is particularly nice as a birthday party or it can be given for other oc-

casions when a person particularly deserves or could use some compliments. It is based on the idea that the best present you can give a person is a compliment. When he receives a series of them given by a number of people in a ritualized way, he will not be able to discount them as is so frequently done when a person hears good things about himself. Instead, he will feel his value as a human being on a deep level and will also recognize his importance to other people.

If giving a birthday party, plan it and invite guests as usual but ask that they don't bring presents. Instead ask them to think about the guest of honor in advance and to be prepared to tell him three things: (1) what they have noticed about him that they particularly like, (2) why they love him, and (3) a memory they have of an incident involving him that was significant to them. Then at the time during the party when presents would ordinarily be unwrapped, have the birthday person sit in the center of a circle with his friends around him and have them one at a time tell him the three things.

This compliment ritual is bound to have a profound effect on the person being honored. Even the most blasé person will be touched by hearing things he would not ordinarily be told, and tears of ecstasy sometimes flow as a person feels his cup runneth over. Have the Kleenex handy.

It is a good idea to tape-record the compliment ritual. First of all, people are usually so overwhelmed at hearing good things about themselves that they can't absorb it all; they shut out a lot of what they are hearing. If they have a recording, they can really hear what was said later, when they are alone. In addition, the recording (or a transcription of it) serves as a wonderful memento. No one can be oversaturated with love and compliments and positive things, and a person being honored at an affirmation ritual will probably treasure a permanent record of that moment more than any other "material" gift he might receive.

But don't wait for your mate's birthday to give him an Affirmation Party. The variations on this theme are endless. Right now, if you really tried, you could think of a way to set it up for your mate to get complimented, honored and/or thanked by you and some other people. If you find yourself thinking that you can't do it or that he or she wouldn't like it if you did or that the whole idea is rather silly, set those excuses aside for a while. Probably the

truth is that you are out of the habit of affirming and complimenting one another and so this seems rather odd to you. But
come on, take a chance. Remember, this is a short-term ritual.
You don't have to repeat it. It is just designed to make you and
your mate feel good right now. Following are some examples that
can give you ideas.

One woman gave her mate a "This Is Your Life" party when,
he, at the age of forty-five, finally got his Ph.D. degree. It had
required his doing graduate work for ten years part time while
working to support her and their children. She invited forty people who had been significant in his life—from his parents, a
woman who had cared for him as a child when his parents
couldn't and buddies from childhood, to his present friends, his
business partner and the chairman of his Ph.D. committee.
As she told the story of his life, she introduced each person, telling of his relationship to her husband, and they, in turn told, very
briefly, of the qualities in him they admired and his importance to
them.

Another man, whose wife was in the hospital in traction for
quite a while, helped her have a party to raise her spirits even
though her friends could not be with her. He asked a number of
them and also her children and grandchildren each to write a letter telling her of her special qualities and what she meant to
them. And to mail it so that she'd receive all the letters on one
particular day. On that day, he brought a big bouquet of flowers
and some special goodies to eat. Not only did the letters make the
day a special one; they made the discomfort of subsequent days
more tolerable, for she, of course, saved and reread all of them
many times.

The writing of letters of affirmation to your mate is another
practice to be encouraged, for letters can be saved and used as a
spirit booster over and over again. Unfortunately, because of the
invention of the telephone and the greeting card, many people
gave up the practice of writing personal letters or never bothered
to learn how. It used to be that a collection of love letters written
before marriage was an important part of a person's possessions
to be savored in private in old age, but even in the past they were
seldom written to your mate. But they should be.

Letter writing is another affirmation ritual to be tried. And it
doesn't take very long—certainly not as long as it takes to look

through all the cards in the rack at the drugstore or stationery store. Here is a quick and easy form to follow as a starter. If it goes over well, you can write something longer and more complex later.

Take any piece of paper that is handy—some memo paper, the back of a laundry list, a piece of brown paper bag, a sheet of folder paper or some fine stationery. Write at the top of it with pen, pencil, crayon or even lipstick:

To _____: a person who is (or has) _____, _____, _____. (Fill in these blanks with three good points, ideally a physical attribute, a personality asset and a talent or skill, but any three complimentary words or phrases will do.)

This is just a quick note to tell you I'm thinking of you right now at this moment—Monday, June 2nd, at 10:45 A.M.—and that I care a great deal about you.

Much love,

_____

(your name)

If you feel like it, you can draw some funny little flowers or hearts around the edges, sort of silly and childlike, and maybe add some XXXXXXs and OOOOOOs at the bottom. It will add to the fun. Then put it in an envelope and mail it and wait for results. Try this today, and if you get a good reaction, see if you can talk your mate into the end-of-the-day Stroking Ceremony or maybe you will then think of a good idea for an Affirmation Party. Try a praising ritual. You'll like it and so will he or she.

It could even be the beginning of a whole new phase in your long-term relationship. Long-term relationships are special. We put a lot of time and energy into them. Why not put just a little bit more to make them even better by following some of our short-term suggestions?

PART III

14

Successful Endings and Caring Closure

•

Have you ever had a romantic relationship end before you were ready to break up? How many times have you suffered pain or embarrassment in bringing a relationship to a close? Are you in a relationship now that you'd like to terminate but don't know how? This chapter is about ending relationships in a friendly, caring way, with minimum pain. It will make you more comfortable with relationships that have already ended, help you terminate with minimum discomfort those that need to end and show you how to prepare yourself for those that might end in the future.

Although our suggestions pertain to all kinds of relationships, they are designed specifically for people who have been sexual partners and who have had an emotionally significant involvement. It doesn't matter whether the involvement has been marriage, living together or exclusive dating, or if they have been close for twenty-six years, six years or six months. What matters is that they have been important to each other and that parting hurts.

While most people think of parting with dread, the process of bringing closure to a relationship is one that few think about at all. And one that even fewer do anything about. The kind of closure we are talking about is emotional closure—separating yourself from another person emotionally. Closure is the transition process that starts as a relationship begins to end and is complete when the relationship has been put to rest in your mind. The way you know you have had closure is when the thought of what he or she did or didn't do just doesn't bother you very much anymore. The process of caring closure involves people doing things, sometimes as individuals and sometimes with others, to make the transition period easier for all concerned.

Most endings to intimate relationships result in anger, resentment and bitterness. But it is possible to part and continue to be friends, or to become friends, even very special people to each other later. There will still be pain, if you meant anything to each other at all, because separating from someone you loved is like losing a part of yourself. You may also feel offended, disappointed, sorrowful, remorseful or guilty afterward, but what you do as you actually end your relationship and what you do afterward to achieve emotional closure can minimize the pain and help you cope better with your other feelings, hasten your recovery and even make you a better person for it all.

But to end a relationship with grace, consideration and style you need to understand two things: (1) how to achieve a successful ending (physical parting) and (2) how to bring about caring closure. To help you achieve these two goals, we have devised a new etiquette for terminating relationships. The etiquette of the past included no such procedures at all, for a broken relationship was seen as a failure. Even today, man-woman relationships that are deeply intimate are supposed to last forever. If they don't, so goes common belief, either you didn't do a very good job of picking a partner or you are an inadequate person who can't make a go of it in the relationship.

Since ending a relationship is considered a failure, few people are interested in developing any "goodbye" skills. After all, they reason, unless you expect failure, you don't prepare for it. The result is that when people realize their relationship is in fact ending, they feel helpless, guilty, desperate and panicky. They lack the appropriate skills, are fearful of being a failure and dread facing the future without their partner. Other people aren't much help either. If your relationship is in trouble, everyone from the laundry woman to your banker will advise you to "save" your relationship, no matter what you have to do. Your family and friends will put enormous pressure on you to hold it together—so you won't upset your sick mother, for the sake of the kids, for financial reasons, so you won't be lonely in your old age. You will be bombarded with hundreds of reasons for staying together, along with advice on how to do it, and vivid descriptions of the terrible things that will happen if you don't. But nobody tells you the terrible things that might happen if you *do* stay together. Nobody suggests that it might be time to part, or offers to help you look at what both of you might gain from separating.

As a result of this lopsidedness, people frequently stay too long in relationships that are not mutually gratifying. Not only do they subject themselves to unnecessary pain, but so many bad feelings are built up that bringing closure with caring becomes extremely difficult. Often the relationship is severed brutally with words or deeds that sour the memory of the good things that were shared. Or if one partner doesn't want the separation, he or she may cling so hard the other will find it almost impossible to say goodbye in a kind way. And sometimes one or the other, because he doesn't know how else to do it, will just "cut out" without any discussion at all, leaving his partner feeling abandoned and confused. Men and women in general do not end romantic relationships in a caring way.

Despite this fact, few people will encourage you to get out of a relationship that is no longer satisfying, and fewer still will show you how to turn an ending into a base for a new beginning. However, some professional counselors are now beginning to work with clients to bring about successful endings and caring closure. One, Dr. James L. Framo, calls himself a divorce therapist as different from a marriage therapist. His specialty is couples who have decided on divorce, for he believes that most counselors stop working with couples right at the point they are needed most—i.e., when their clients decide to separate. Then the couple is usually turned over to a lawyer, because their "problem has been resolved." The assumption is that all that remains is to decide on the disposal of property, custody of children and spouse support. But that just isn't true. Dr. Framo's purpose, which he states in a February 1978 *Psychology Today* article, is to help couples "disengage from a marriage with a minimum of destructiveness to themselves and their children, and with the personal freedom to form new relationships." The sad thing is that, according to Dr. Framo, the couple themselves often believe this is impossible. Even couples who aren't married have the same attitude.

Friendly endings are not only possible; they will someday be the norm. But it will require new attitudes about relationships, and new skills. Fortunately, more and more people are now accepting that it is O.K. for an intimate relationship to have an ending, that it doesn't mean the relationship or the people in it were failures. However, the manner in which an ending is brought about is indeed crucial to the well-being of the people in the relationship and to their readiness to get involved in new relationships. An ending can take place without needless hurt and in a way that shows that two people still respect and care for each other although not in a way that would enable them to continue the relationship.

Successful partings

When a relationship ends, most people, both the partners and their friends, need to blame somebody. To make themselves comfortable, they must point a finger and say he or she did it. He drank too much. She was a sloppy housekeeper. He ran around with other women. She let herself go. He was uncommunicative. She was cold. In fact, as long as a person loves his mate, and thinks she is a very nice person, it is very difficult to bring about a separation. You don't feel justified in parting just because you are no longer comfortable living with a person. Or because you want to move on to a new life style or to have some new experiences, to explore, to grow. And friends make it hard by asking, "Why? Why?" and telling you that with love and patience, you can make anything work.

As a result of having to justify their wants through blame, most partners wait until one or both have come to hate the other, or until they are suffering from severe emotional stress, before they part. This is unnecessarily destructive because the truth is that no one person is ever to blame. To begin with, what people usually see as causes of a separation are really descriptions of what they don't want, and therefore should not be held as reasons for blame. The real causes are far more difficult to pin down, even when they may seem obvious, with everyone agreeing on them.

Take, for instance, if a man is a drunk. Surely then, he is to blame if his wife divorces him. Or is he? Maybe he drinks because she is crabby. And she is crabby because he drinks. Then who is to blame? After all, not everybody gets crabby when married to a drunk, so there must be a contributing cause within her. Maybe she gets crabby because her health isn't good. And the reason her health isn't good is that her family was poor and she was malnourished as a child. Then who is to blame? Him or her? Or is it her parents' fault? Or is it society that should be held accountable?

And what about him? Not everybody becomes a drunk when married to a crabby woman. Maybe he drinks to excess because his genes make him oversusceptible to alcohol. Then who is to blame? His parents? His grandparents? How far back should a person go to find the culprit or culprits?

The truth is that there is no culprit. There is never just one cause of a relationship becoming unsatisfactory, and the many factors involved can never all be known. So it's erroneous and a waste of good energy to blame someone.

The end of a relationship often comes simply with the passage of time. What happens is that gradually the bonds that hold a couple together wither and die. Or the spark between them goes out. Or the goals that brought them together are accomplished or set aside as unrealistic. Or interests change. Or nowadays, with increasing frequency, expectations change and one or both want more out of life and their relationships than they used to and need to try a different path. Why can't a parting, like a car accident, be labeled "no fault"?

Saying that no one is to blame does not mean that a person is not responsible for what he does or that what he does has no effect on a relationship. A person is responsible for his behavior, and how he behaves certainly does affect a relationship. But blaming, like bawling out, doesn't improve the situation. Rather than blaming, it is necessary for each individual to accept responsibility for his own happiness. And sometimes taking care of your own happiness may mean leaving your partner.

Separating from a partner when a relationship is no longer gratifying is an action that people need to be encouraged to take sooner, and more often, and with more finesse. Parting is an art that needs to be developed.

Blake and Shelly Wilson made an art of their parting. Married fifteen years and the parents of three children, they made their decision to part mutually. The fact that their decision was mutual does not mean that each didn't see different reasons for the demise of the relationship. Or that they didn't vacillate for a long time over whether or not to part. But it does mean that they were able to agree upon how to part and to help one another through the parting process.

The Wilsons chose a lengthy, gradual process for backing out of the love and intimacy they had once shared and for detaching themselves from each other. During this time, they worked hard to resolve their negative feelings and to preserve their positive feelings of respect, caring and even affection. Realizing their problems were mutual, they continued to help and support each other even when they wanted to give up and run. The result, according to Blake, was that "slowly but steadily, instead of falling into love, we raised ourselves back out of love. But we'll always be special people to each other."

Here is how they went about their gradual process of "backing out of love."

It took the Wilsons two years to decide to divorce. The question of whether or not to separate would come up after a quarrel, and then with a variety of emotions—anger, sadness, fear, helplessness, anticipation, love—they would discuss their relationship and the issues of conflict between them. But one night there was an incident that made them realize that they should and would separate. As Blake tells it:

> It happened one night as a result of an argument. We were angry, and my wife stormed out of the bedroom into the den, where she slept on a sofa bed. She stayed there several nights, and I was unable to persuade her to come back. It was then that we both knew that we would never sleep together again and that our relationship was truly coming to an end. Fortunately our house was large enough so thereafter we could each have a room to ourselves.

However, although they both knew their decision to separate was final, they decided to stay in the same house together for a while—partly for financial reasons but more because it was important to them to bring closure to their relationship with good feelings. And for them, this process of a gradual instead of abrupt separation seemed to work well. They still quarreled, but because they had always been good friends as well as lovers, they were able to give each other support and companionship during this painful time their relationship was ending. They tried to avoid blaming each other for the breakup, rather accepting it as a sad but mutual process of growing apart. They made a point of including in their conversations the highlights of their years together and what their relationship had meant to them. They became allies, helping each other through a difficult common experience.

Blake explains how their growing-apart alliance worked:

> We continued to fulfill our traditional married roles—I as the provider and the weekend gardener, she as the mother, homemaker, and cook—so that the home would run smoothly and not be a source of further upset to us or the children. We still made plans and decisions about the home jointly, worked together there, and took the children on outings together. We went places as a couple, and served as escorts for each other when needed, for example at social functions given by my employer.
>
> We supported each other in testing our skills at being single and dating other people again. We talked about our dating experiences and shared ideas on where to go and how to relate to the opposite sex. I remember that several women I met were reluctant to go out with me, because I was still living at home and they couldn't believe I was free to date. I asked one in particular that I was very interested in to call my wife and check it out. She did, and my wife not only assured her that it was right and proper for me to date, but extolled my virtues and told her how fortunate she was to meet a man of my caliber. On another occasion, I took my wife to her first singles dance and introduced her to some of the men there. As it turned out, she did not meet anyone particularly interesting to her, so we wound up going home together. Again we shared our experiences of the evening.
>
> We agreed not to bring anyone into our home for an overnight stay. However, we felt that it was important for the children to begin seeing us date other people and to realize that this was O.K. with us, so occasionally one of us would invite someone in for a few minutes to meet the children. (We had long since discussed our separation with them and the fact that I would someday move

out of the house.) Also we checked with each other and coordinated our dating schedules so that one of us would always be home with the children.

Seeing each other date and knowing that we were now giving to others the love and affection that was once exclusively ours was a source of considerable pain. However, our dating came about gradually also and thus contributed to the steady process of detaching ourselves from one another and starting our new separate lives. While it was painful, there was also comfort, because after a date, particularly one that did not go well, we still had each other as friends to come home to.

Blake continued to live at home for about a year after he and Shelly had decided to separate but then he accepted a job in another city. But even as he moved out of the house—feeling like a "young bird leaving his comfortable nest to begin a new life in a strange world"—they continued to give each other help and support. Shelly helped him pick out things from their kitchen that he would need to start housekeeping on his own—pots, pans, utensils and a cookbook. And she wrote many of his favorite recipes on index cards for him. In the same spirit of cooperation and caring, they decided on the sharing of their furniture on the basis of who needed what the most rather than being concerned about whether everything was "equal."

After he moved out, Blake continued to be caring to Shelly by giving her both financial and emotional support to get an academic degree so she could pursue a career and eventually become self-supporting and by making repairs to the house whenever he came to visit the children. She made sure the children maintained contacts with him by mail and phone and treated him like an "honored" guest when he came to town to see them. Although their divorce was not entirely without rancor once it reached the stage of the final property and financial settlement, the good feelings they built up in their three-year de-escalation of love have paid off in a "friendly" divorce—one which has done a minimum of emotional damage to the entire family.

When the decision to part is not a mutual one, the difficulties of separating are increased for both. To begin with, the person who is left is automatically seen as the victim, the one who has been wronged. He himself feels this way, and others also take it for granted he is the "good guy" who was "done wrong." In addition to suffering a loss, a person can become vindictive.

When people place blame, they feel justified in acting in destructive ways, and often acts of revenge are encouraged by family and friends. One woman whose lover moved out painted his car windshield black, and her friends applauded, saying, "The bastard really deserved that."

Actually a double loss is suffered—the loss of a loved one as well as the loss of self-esteem. The loss of self-esteem is the hardest to bear. It is exemplified by the thought "If he could leave me after all I've done for all those years, then I must really be an unworthy, unlovable person." It is not uncommon for someone whose mate has left to do irrational things, hurtful to himself, to his partner or to both. Some begin dating madly, with anybody and everybody, trying to prove to themselves they are still desirable. Some mope around the house, never going anywhere because they believe no one else will ever love them. Others may do something spiteful to a partner or even attempt suicide.

Friends can also worsen the situation by giving advice on how to get a partner back through trickery and manipulation, totally ignoring the real issues. "Lose weight and buy some sexy underwear," women are told. "Take her on a trip or buy her a diamond," men are told. Perhaps the worst advice of all is "Make him/her jealous." This is an old familiar standby and one that is usually successful only in the movies.

Feeling like a victim can make it doubly hard to let go of a relationship and take the inevitable in stride. Although each person in the relationship should do everything he can to make it work, there is a point at which he also has an obligation to give it up. When the issues between a couple cannot be resolved, and it becomes clear that one partner wants out, letting go gracefully—even when one doesn't want to—is an act of caring closure.

Here is how one couple handled their parting when only one wanted to end it. Tammy had started a sexual relationship with Cal (who was married) soon after her divorce. After a year, she wasn't happy with it. The fact that Cal was married didn't bother her, nor was he doing anything that displeased her. To the contrary, she was very fond of him and told him so. She said, "It isn't you. I'm sure of that. I can't quite explain it except that I feel confined. Perhaps our relationship just isn't meant to be right now. Maybe it started too soon after my divorce."

Cal was devastated. He didn't want to lose Tammy. As an alternative to breaking up—a way of buying time—he suggested that they take a temporary leave of absence. They decided that for six months they would not date or even talk on the phone. At the end of that time, they would meet and re-evaluate whether they would pick up the relationship again or end it for good. Before they parted, Tammy suggested Cal use his time to work on his relationship with his wife. Cal had been trying to improve his marriage during the time he was having an affair with Tammy, but he had concentrated more on Tammy than on his failing marriage. And Tammy decided to use her time for personal growth, to focus on learning more about what was going on inside her rather than in relationships.

Shortly before their six months was up, they met accidentally at a conference they were attending as part of their work. After spending some time together, both realized the intense phase of their relationship had passed and all they wanted now was to be friends. Cal and his wife seemed on the way to establishing a firm and dynamic basis for their marriage, and Tammy was more certain than ever that she was not yet ready for a close involvement. They kissed goodbye tenderly and without regret.

While being left is painful, sometimes the pain of being the one to leave is even greater. Nobody wants to break up a relationship if it can be avoided. It takes courage to say, "It's over. I want out." To do it, that is, not in a moment of pique but after carefully considering the issues, the alternatives and your own and your partner's feelings. It is so much easier to drift, hoping things will work out, waiting for someone else to make a move. What makes it even worse is that a person who wants to leave seldom gets encouragement. Nor does he usually get support for the uncomfortable feelings he is bound to have afterward. If there seems to be no "good reason" for a person to leave (i.e., he has not been obviously abused or neglected), he will get no sympathy at all. In fact, he may even be called selfish. Because he appears to be in command, to be decisive, it is assumed he is perfectly capable of taking care of himself. If there seems to be a "good reason," if a mate is unreliable or abusive, he is supposed to be happy that they are apart, to have no regrets, to feel no loss. And, of course, if he leaves because of another involvement, he is branded as unfaithful and seen as a "bad guy" who deserves any uncomfortable feelings he might have.

Little consideration is given to the fact that there are mixed feelings at the ending of important relationships and feelings of grief because there is loss. Just because you choose to give up something doesn't mean you can't miss it. And the decision to leave is sometimes made only after a tremendous amount of thought and the greatest pain. Here is what one woman said about leaving her seven-year marriage: "If I hadn't left, I would probably have died. I felt like I was at the bottom of a pit and couldn't climb out. Yet nobody seemed to know that—not even my husband. Despite the arguments and problems, he seemed to think everything was great. Finally, one night I couldn't stand it any longer and blurted out, 'I want you to move out.' He was stunned. For weeks we talked about it but every time we talked I said the same thing. And he finally moved out. But he was able to go to all our friends and say I kicked him out. I was barely holding myself together but I couldn't seem to convince anyone of my pain. In fact, one night my husband stopped by and I was crying. I tried to express some of my feelings to him but he looked at me coldly and said, 'You wanted this didn't you? Well, live with it.' I didn't want to go back together but I wanted some acknowledgment that it was hard for me, too. But everyone acted as though I were some kind of monster and many of the men I later dated would say, when they found out I was the one who wanted the divorce, 'Your poor husband—to be kicked out like that when he loved you so.' I even began to feel I must be an unloving person to have done such a thing."

But later, this woman's husband came to see her and thanked her for having the courage to end it. "I can see now," he admitted, "that it was for the best. But I don't think I'd have ever done it."

Sometimes, a person just has to leave—no matter how much his partner cries, screams or threatens—for the sake of both of them. And sometimes this leaving can't be done gradually in the sort of weaning-away-from-intimacy process we described earlier. Instead, it has to be done "cold turkey"—abruptly and finally. But even leaving a person cold turkey can be done with caring although it probably won't appear that way to the person being left and to many outsiders. It was that way with Charlie and Pat.

After a sixteen-year marriage to a very dependent wife, Charlie knew he had had it. Though over the years he had encouraged Pat to develop herself, she had built her whole life around him and the kids. She had no other friends, no other interests, no other resources. But each time Charlie tried to discuss leaving, she went into hysterics, and Charlie, cowed, gave up the subject. But one day he felt desperate enough to persist. He got Pat to listen and made a deal with her.

"I'll stay just two years more," he said, "until Lisa [the youngest] is out of high school, but on the day she graduates, I am leaving. I will be as supportive as I can be to you and the kids, but I will also be planning for the time I go out on my own. If you want to go back to school or go to work to prepare for that day, I'll help with money and household chores or whatever else I can. This is all I know how to do because I just can't promise to stay with you forever."

Although Charlie reminded Pat of their deal now and then, she made no effort to prepare herself for his leaving—other than three sessions of a Fascinating Womanhood course during which she tried to seduce him at the door wearing only an apron. But she soon lost interest in trying to hold him by sex appeal much less in learning to take care of herself. And a few weeks after their daughter graduated, Charlie kept his word. He packed his bags and said goodbye. He told his wife he would not be talking with her for a while but that he would keep in touch so they could work out a fair property settlement. He said to her as he left, "I'm not leaving out of hate or anger. I don't hate you. But the kindest thing I can do for myself is to break away and get free of you. And the kindest thing I can do for you is let you know it is final so you can try to make a life for yourself. I hope that later on, when we have had time to adjust, we can have contact and be friends."

Unfortunately, that never happened, for Pat never forgave him, but he was able to live with that because he knew he had done the best he could do in a difficult situation.

Sometimes two people part not because either of them wants to but because of circumstances beyond their control. They may be enjoying their relationship, and have no idea of parting, but then something comes up that makes it necessary for them to say goodbye. Perhaps he has a job offer in another city and she must stay where she is because she has a sick mother. Perhaps she has a chance to study on a scholarship in Europe and he can't leave his job here. Or maybe the fact that they are of different religions—a fact that didn't make much difference when they were going out on a casual basis—has raised insurmountable problems now that they are talking marriage. It really doesn't matter what the circumstances are—moves brought about by a career, family obligations, religion or age differences. The point is that two people who don't really want to part find they have to. Or at least, the price of not parting is heavier than they are willing to pay.

The remarks of family and friends, all hoping for a happy ending, can make a decision to separate even more difficult. They may say things like "If you really cared about him, you'd give up school (or put your mother in a rest home) and go with him," or "If he really loved you, he'd give up his religion (or his chance to study at the Sorbonne or to do field work in New Guinea) and stay with you."

When you hear remarks like this, you don't have to let them go on and on. A good way to turn them off is to say, firmly and clearly, "I know you want me to be happy, but you are hurting, not helping. Please stop saying those things. I do not want to hear them."

It is important that you do not let others pile guilt on you or make you feel that your partner did not care about you. It is also important that you accept the fact that you will have some feelings of guilt and also some suspicions about your partner's feelings for you. This just happens when important relationships end, no matter what the cause. It is normal for a person to beat himself with "if-onlys" for a while, to have thoughts repeatedly go through his mind like: *If only* he hadn't gotten that job offer. *If only* I had gone with him. *If only* we had tried harder to work it out despite the problems. *If only* he or she or I had or hadn't done this or that, things might have been different.

Thinking things like this is just part of the process of closure and is nothing to worry about, but the discomfort will move away quicker if you will frequently repeat to yourself: "We both did the best we could do. Not even a deep love can overcome all circumstances. I am a richer person for having loved. I can never completely lose a person I have loved; he is a part of me forever and will help me carry on."

Sometimes, with a couple who are parting because of circumstances beyond their control, there is a moment of parting, one day or evening when they get together to say goodbye. Often at this meeting—which can be very dramatic—the word "goodbye" is never spoken. Or even if it is, it is accompanied by "maybes"— either at the time or later, in phone calls or letters. *Maybe* we can see each other at Christmas. *Maybe* I'll get transferred back in a few years. *Maybe* we'll be together someday, someplace. I hope. I hope. I hope.

Though some of the "maybes" may be realistic, most usually aren't. They are a way of hanging on to hope until a person has had time to get accustomed to the fact that it is over.

Knowing in advance a relationship is going to end can, in some ways, be an advantage, for you can plan to end it with finesse. Johanna, a German girl, did this after she started a relationship with Cliff, a U.S. Army sergeant stationed in her country temporarily. During the year and a half of their involvement, she planned for a future that didn't include him. She worked on developing her career, enlarging the small dress shop she owned and expanding her staff. In addition, she led a full and active social life, part of which did not include Cliff but did include warm, though not sexual, relationships with other men. But because he meant a greal deal to her and because she wanted him to have something to remember her by, she planned a little ceremony for their last night together. On that night, she presented him with a letter of recommendation to a future lover. Written in businesslike style and addressed "To Whom It May Concern," it enumerated his virtues in exquisite and sometimes humorous detail. Needless to say, he loved it.

Not only was this a beautiful testimonial to all that Cliff had meant to her; the giving of it was tangible evidence that this was really goodbye and added to the process of caring closure. However, preparing for an ending in advance should not be the prerogative only of those who know for sure their relationship will end. Anyone in a relationship is more likely to be able to end it successfully, as well as go through the process of caring closure, if he does certain things in advance.

THINGS TO DO IN ADVANCE TO PREPARE FOR SUCCESSFUL ENDINGS AND CARING CLOSURE

(1) Anticipate that your relationship may end and (2) prepare yourself for getting along without your partner in case it does.

Anticipating the ending means that you accept the fact that everything ends—a brief encounter, a short-term alliance, a long-term relationship, a meal, a day, a life. We have learned, as a society, to accept and prepare for some kinds of endings better than others. Thus, we all know how to end a meal or a day with ease. And we adjust—maybe with a few pangs but more often with hope for the future—to the ending of our high school or college days or our time in the service.

Endings are beginnings, too

As long as we see the ending of relationships as "unnatural" events—as tragedies or failures—instead of as part of the natural ebb and flow of life, we'll never be able to see them as the positive steps they can be. Many times we have to end one relationship to make room for another—one that might be even more meaningful and gratifying. Many times an ending gives us space in our lives to discover new things—things we would never have discovered without that ending. As a matter of fact, Betty met Emily because of the ending of a relationship.

What happened was that the man she had been seeing a lot phoned and canceled their plans for the weekend and at the same time told her he didn't want to see her again. Although they hadn't been getting along very well, this was pretty abrupt, and she dreaded the thought of a lonely Saturday night without a date. However, the day after he called she got a letter from one of the directors at Elysium Field, a growth center in Topanga, California, inviting her to attend an Emily Coleman workshop for singles. She had sent the director a manuscript she had written about other workshops she had attended, and he believed an Emily Coleman workshop would be a different sort of experience than she had had before and that it would provide her with interesting material to write about. It was and it did. It led to a four-year collaboration that has produced two books and a warm friendship. But had Betty not been at the ending of one relationship she wouldn't have had the time or inclination to explore new areas—and she would never have discovered the new and more positive relationship awaiting her. If we can just see endings as an inevitable part of life and learn to say goodbye with finality, with caring, with dignity and with the support of family and friends, it can lead to personal growth and to all sorts of unexpected new horizons.

Dr. Keith Tombrink, Emily's partner in the Man-Woman Institute, learned this lesson when he was in the Navy during World War II. Dr. Tombrink served aboard an aircraft carrier with 2,500 other men. He refers to this time "as a valuable education" in terms of his relationships with other people. Says Dr. Tombrink:

> Men were constantly arriving, leaving, being discharged, or being killed or wounded. Since we all knew and accepted the fact that we couldn't count on knowing someone very long, a sort of short-term attitude developed on the ship—the attitude that our friendships would be of limited duration and that this was an O.K. way of life. And from this experience I learned that a relationship can give me great fulfillment and happiness even when I know at the outset that it isn't going to last very long. I learned, however, that I must be willing to plunge into the relationship, get involved quickly on a deep level and then when it is time, let the relationship go without trying to hold on to it. What usually happened was that when I met someone I liked, the two of us would spend a little time with each other on the ship, and then go on liberty and have a few drinks and talk and laugh together. Sometimes this relationship would quickly develop into a very close one. Ordinarily we talked very little about our past lives; rather our friendship seemed to develop out of sharing who we were at the present time. We lived only for the present, the past was irrelevant and who knew (or cared) what lay ahead in the future. We might not even live to find out. When either of us left the ship or the friendship broke up for other

reasons, we let it go—knowing we had derived as much pleasure and satisfaction from our relationship as we could while it lasted and knowing there would be other friendships to look forward to.

While it is easier to anticipate endings in wartime—when people are aware that their relationships might well end, and soon—you can, with a little effort, develop this short-term attitude yourself. And it is helpful to anticipate the ending of your relationship with your partner by talking with him or her about it.

Planning for possible partings

This does not mean that you just go up to a partner and suddenly say, "I want to talk about ending our relationship." Naturally, tact must be used in bringing up such a subject because most people have the same feelings in regard to talking about ending a relationship as they do about death. Parting is a taboo subject that just isn't discussed. Most act as if they believe that if you don't talk about it, it won't happen. Though you have to sense just when and how to introduce the subject, when a relationship becomes an important one, it needs to be discussed. Believe it or not, thinking about it, discussing it and even planning what you will do should it become necessary can add a great deal to your sense of security and to your trust of and regard for one another.

There are three points in relationships when it is imperative to discuss the possibility of parting: (1) when you make an exclusive commitment, (2) when you move in with someone and (3) when you decide to get married. At these relationship levels, people are investing considerable energy and emotion and giving one another priority in their non-working time. In addition, they are acknowledging that this is an important relationship, and important relationships deserve to be treated with respect and consideration.

Most business contracts include termination clauses specifying under what conditions a relationship will end. Certainly a personal relationship is at least as important as a business one and deserves the same sort of forethought. And a couple who make a termination agreement are not saying they *will* part any more than an employer and an employee are saying they *will* part just because they promise to give one another two weeks' notice. A discussion of parting is an act of caring, for what it does is to remind both parties that separation is a common occurrence and to give them an opportunity to pledge themselves that in case it should happen to them, they will show one another courtesy and cause each other as little discomfort as possible.

A discussion of termination need not be lengthy. The most important point to agree upon is not to end the relationship in anger. This doesn't mean you won't get angry with each other; it simply means you will not end the relationship at this point. One may leave the room or leave the house, but he will agree to come back and to discuss what is bothering him. He will not leave the relationship arbitrarily. It is an agreement to hang in there and work on the issues that are causing the problems until they can be worked through and understood even if the problems cannot be solved.

An agreement not to part in anger can make your present relationship more dynamic—yet more secure. A lot of relationships get static because one or the other is afraid to bring up things he suspects or knows will make the other angry. A person fears an angry partner will abandon him rather than work on problem areas in the relationship. Knowing a person may get angry but won't leave for good at that time leaves people freer to work on issues in a relationship and to thoroughly discuss many options before deciding to part. The decision to separate is a vital one that needs to be made calmly and rationally—not in the heat of anger. Besides, when one has taken a stand in anger, saying, "I'll never sleep with you again," or "I'm moving out," he sometimes feels it is a loss of face to change his mind. Pride can thus make a person live up to a hasty declaration even though later he wishes he hadn't said it. However, an agreement not to part in anger can circumvent pride, for it is a good excuse to back down when a person wants to.

A second thing a couple who are willing to talk about the possibility of termination can do, is to figure out ways of making it as easy as possible should it occur. Just as people, when they organize a business, do certain things to protect themselves against legal and tax hassles, so a couple can, with foresight and planning, protect themselves against personal hassles in case they should ever part. For example, they can label their important possessions his, hers and ours. They can do the same with money, keeping it in separate accounts, commingling very little or even none at all. They can agree to give each a certain amount of advance notice if they should ever decide they want to break up. There are hundreds of ways couples can make it possible to end a relationship graciously, and it is up to each couple to find the best ways for them—those that suit their temperaments and situations.

Six months ago, Bart and Fay, who had been dating for over a year, decided to live together. Fay's daughter had just left for college, and for the first time in her life, Fay was going to live alone —a somewhat frightening prospect for her. Since Bart and Fay had been in the habit of spending weekends together, it seemed only logical to move in together. But, being realists, they both knew there might be problems. Neither had lived with a member of the opposite sex since their divorces many years before, and they were quite aware of differences in personality and interests that had already caused some conflict in their relationship.

Bart and Fay looked on living together as a "loving experiment" and hoped it would work out well for them, but whatever happened, they wanted to remain good friends. Thus they made careful plans for making it work but, at the same time, also made plans for a possible termination. They were determined to avoid the sort of traumas they had seen other live-in friends go through upon parting.

Enthusiastically, they rented a beautiful apartment and jointly bought several thousand dollars' worth of furniture. In addition, each moved in some furniture and personal possessions of his own. Their termination agreement, carefully written out, provided for the disposition of these material possessions as well as a way for one to let the other know if he or she wanted out. Here are the terms agreed upon:

Whoever wanted to terminate was to give the other written notice with the idea that between the time the written notice was received and the final parting, there would be a minimum of forty-five days for one or both to find another place to live, to handle any money transactions between them and to bring their emotional relationship to satisfactory closure. Fay was to have the option to keep the apartment and was to reimburse Bart for 50 percent of the furniture purchased jointly. Each was to keep the possessions he had brought into the arrangement, which were carefully recorded. Being very practical and businesslike, they not

only made their agreement as specific as they could, they had it
notarized—just in case they ended up in court.

After about six months, it gradually dawned on Fay that this
living together just wasn't working out for her. She realized she
needed some time to live by herself, to be totally on her own, and
besides, the kind of traditional relationship that Bart wanted
didn't suit her. At first, she vacillated—deciding one day to leave,
the next, to stay. And whenever she discussed the matter with
Bart, he would talk her into staying. Finally, when she was sure of
her own feelings and wanted to make him see she really meant it,
she sent him a termination letter. However, although their agreement was businesslike and impersonal, the letter wasn't. It was
very loving and personal, glowing with references to the good
times they had shared, the many qualities she admired in Bart and
what she had gained through knowing him.

That letter signaled the beginning of their forty-five-day termination process and they used this time to help each other through
the pain and problems of separating. Because they felt the need
for physical contact and reassurance, they agreed to sleep in the
same bed but, by mutual choice, ended their sexual relationship.
In addition to showing concern for one another, they realized
they had to reconstruct their own separate lives, so they decided
to use this time to start re-establishing old friendships, forming
new ones and dating other people. However, since this was a
loving closure, they were careful to do these things in ways that
wouldn't be hurtful. Together, they made these ground rules:
(1) they would not stay out overnight; (2) they could talk about
their experiences in dating others but would avoid specific details
that might hurt the person hearing them; and (3) if one planned
to be out for the evening he would have the courtesy to let the
other know.

During this transition period, they helped one another in numerous practical ways. She went with him to look at apartments
he was considering when he was having difficulty making a selection. He gave her a lead and smoothed the way for her to get a
new and better job. And there was no blaming all throughout this
time. As Fay says, "We operated in a clean and clear manner."

There was one thing they had not planned for in advance nor
had they discussed it during their termination period. That was
whether or not they would continue to see each other after they

had stopped living together. Bart brought up this matter when, shortly after he had moved out, they met to settle up some last-minute bills. He said he would very much like to date her but she declined. For her, the goodbye was final, and she told him this. Though he was very disappointed, because of the caring way they had gone about their ending he was able to say a final farewell also, and with grace and dignity.

Preparation for being alone

To have a friendly parting you must keep yourself prepared to get along well on your own. If you know you are adequately prepared to face a whole new phase in your life alone, if your relationship does turn sour or you outgrow it, you won't be as apt to stay together too long, thus building up resentments and bad feelings you may never get over. Continuing to stay together because one or the other is afraid or doesn't know how to get along alone is one of the major deterrents to, not just a successful ending, but to subsequent successful adjustment. Feelings and habit patterns developed by a couple in a non-nourishing relationship can greatly impede the development of new and good ones.

Whether you have one partner, many or none, there are many things you can do to minimize the pain of a parting that might someday occur. There are some basic skills that every person must develop for his own safety, to make certain that he or she can function well as a single. For example, a woman who wants nothing more than to be a housewife and mother must realize that she is running the risk of living much of her life trapped in a poor relationship or ending it with unnecessary pain and stress if she doesn't develop some skills for supporting herself financially should it become necessary. A man who doesn't want to be bothered learning homemaking tasks but thinks concentrating on business matters is the way to independence must realize that what he is doing is trading both freedom and peace of mind for clean socks and a home-cooked meal. And it isn't enough that you prepare yourself to function without a mate; you must insist that your mate prepare himself or herself, too. If you don't, someday your concern for his well-being may cause you to stay with him when you don't want to. Being prepared to live alone is one kind of insurance no couple can afford to be without.

In addition, as we recommended in Chapter 10, everyone should maintain a supportive network whether or not he is involved in a sexual relationship. One of the reasons so many people feel lost and alone after their sexual relationships end (even one that wasn't particularly good) is that they have spent most of their time with their lover and lost contact with their friends. Having an ongoing supportive network not only adds continuity to your life but also helps provide a buffer against loneliness when a relationship does end.

WHAT TO DO WHEN THE RELATIONSHIP IS OVER: UNDERSTANDING THE GRIEF PROCESS

It's over and no matter who you think is to blame, no matter who makes the decision to part, no matter how you part and no matter how you may have prepared for it in advance, the ending of a significant relationship is painful. You have suffered a loss; you grieve.

Unfortunately, most men and women don't know how to cope with the grief that accompanies the loss of an important relationship because they have never learned how to grieve. Our society considers grief an "unacceptable" emotion—unless a person has lost someone important to him through death. Even then, it is not considered "acceptable" to grieve too long or too publicly. The mourner who continues long after the funeral to show signs of sorrow is criticized and eventually shunned while the mourner who doesn't make a public "display" of his grief is considered to be "taking it well." Everyone praises him for his ability to adjust and it is assumed he is on the road to recovery.

But because the partings of people who have been sexual partners are so often accompanied by anger and bad feelings, the partners themselves as well as friends and relatives tend to overlook the very real grief that underlies the loss of the relationship—even though one or both wanted it to end. And friends and family discount the grief of men or women who do seem to be suffering from a breakup by saying, "You're lucky. He wasn't really your type anyhow," or "There are better things to do with your time than grieve. Forget the past and get on with your life." Or they give flippant and sometimes hurtful advice: "Men are like street-cars. There's always another one coming along," or "The best way to forget a woman is to find another."

Thus, because they are encouraged to ignore their feelings of grief, many people who have supposedly ended a relationship really carry it around with them like an albatross. They are unable to heal their wounds much less grow from their pain.

Today, some behavioral scientists are studying grief—what it is and how people can deal with it. However, since our Puritan ethic blinds us to the need to study the process of grief as it applies to people who have ended relationships by choice, the first studies have come about because of the fact that recent wars have left many widows. In fact, the U.S. Army hired Dr. Leonard Zunin, psychiatrist and author, to help war widows cope with the loss of their mates. Dr. Zunin found that the widows went through four distinct stages of grieving: (1) denial, (2) depression, (3) anger and (4) re-evaluation and readjustment. Healing will be quicker and more complete if a person will allow himself to fully experience his feelings in each stage and does not get stuck anyplace in the process. When a person can feel and express his grief, whether the end of his relationship has been brought about by accident or design, he has the opportunity to find new facets of himself, to learn, to stretch, to grow—to make new beginnings.

In this section and the next, our purpose is to help you understand the natural grief process experienced at the end of an important relationship and also to give suggestions for action to take at this time that will enrich your life and make you capable of having even better relationships in the future. Although our tips are geared to those who have suffered a significant loss, you can adapt some to the ending of relationships that are less significant.

The best way to benefit from our suggestions is to let yourself be the judge of how much or how little you need to grieve. Only you know how important the relationship was to you; only you know the loss you feel. But it may not be easy to allow yourself to take the amount of time you need for your wounds to heal, especially if it is more than a few weeks or a few months. Your friends may get tired of your grief. It will make them uncomfortable. Because they are uncomfortable and because they care and don't want you to suffer, they'll try to rush you through your stages of grief by saying, "When are you ever going to forget her?" or

"Stop feeling sorry for yourself. Think of all the people in the world who have real troubles."

And you'll get tired of your own grief and want to skip over this uncomfortable period as rapidly as possible. But give yourself all the time you need. This period is not only a necessary healing time for you but it is the foundation of what will happen next in your life. If you grieve properly, you'll be ready to trust again and love again in the future.

Following is what to expect if you grieve properly.

Denial

The first stage after any loss is denial. You just can't believe it has happened. If it is a watch you have lost, you may say to yourself: "I always put it right here on the nightstand. It must be around here someplace. Maybe it fell off onto the floor. Or maybe I left it in the bathroom." If you are told of a death, you may say, "That just can't be. I just saw him an hour ago," or "That isn't possible. We were going to have dinner together tonight." If it is a relationship that is withering away and you are not being treated as well as you used to be, your reaction may be: "He doesn't mean the nasty things he is saying. He is just tired. I must have done something to annoy him. It will be better tomorrow." Many times people go through years of discomfort, sometimes the greater part of a lifetime, rather than face the fact that a relationship that once served them well no longer is doing that.

When a partner is repeatedly thoughtless or cruel or no fun to be with, when the evidence that a relationship is either toxic or dead is apparent to everyone else, a woman may still tell herself, "But he is good to the children," or "He brought me flowers last week," or "I love him"; a man may profess, "But our sex is good," or "She cooks what I like," or "She is a good woman"—all of which is irrelevant to the fact that the relationship is not doing its job. It is very difficult to see that a relationship is over, and the more important it is, the more difficult it can be to see the evidence before us. Many times, even after one partner has moved out to live with someone else or a couple has been divorced for several years, sometimes in spite of the fact that a mate has remarried, a person will tell himself the parting is not final, that eventually they will get together and things will be good again. It is as though we only let ourselves discover what we see as an awful truth gradually to keep from having to look at more than we can handle. Denial is an important protective device if it does not go on too long, and if we are good to ourselves during this period and have some friends around who care about us, we will, sooner or later, move to the next step.

Depression

The second step in recovering from a loss is depression. Denial is over. You see that you have lost a relationship—and maybe a life style, a home, a dream and a family besides. You don't like it at all. It is more than you can stand. The situation is hopeless. There is nothing you can do, nothing anyone can do. Or at least that's how it feels. This is the stage of recrimination. A person will say to himself, "If only I had . . ." or "If only I hadn't . . ." The message one keeps repeating is: "I had it. I blew it. Life will never be that good again."

It is important in this stage to let yourself wallow in self-pity for a while. Allow yourself to feel sorry for you. Cry. Cry a lot. And when you cry, allow yourself to moan and let out all of those deep sounds made by animals in pain. It will hasten the healing process. Cry by yourself most of the time because you will have more pain than your friends can stand. But also try to find a friend or two whom you can complain to, who will give you sympathy and let you cry on his or her shoulder. It is especially helpful if you can find a member of the opposite sex not easily upset by your tears, whom you can occasionally cry in front of. It can help you get over the idea that members of the opposite sex don't give a damn, a conception that all of us have from time to time after a separation.

However, just be careful that you don't let crying or pitying or beating yourself become the only way you get attention. You don't want depression to become a chronic state. It probably won't if you will let yourself feel it and take time to really give in to it for a while. You may have trouble convincing your friends that it is O.K. for you to be depressed for a while after a loss, but it is. Depression is a low-energy state and certain kinds of healing take place in this state. So send your friends away if they bother you too much, and moan and groan by yourself. However, if you find yourself drained of energy over a long period of time, or if your energy is erratic and you are super-high at times but at others feel as though someone had suddenly pulled out the plug and drained you, you might suspect you are staying in this stage too long. If so, try giving yourself a time limit. You might tell yourself, "I am going to thoroughly pity and rest myself for the next two weeks and then on such and such a date, I'm going to move on. Enough is enough." Then for the next two weeks or whatever time period you select, get into bed every chance that you get. Pull the covers up over your head, roll up into a ball and weep, wail, moan and every once in a while say out loud, "Poor _____ (your name). He has had a rough time of it. Poor _____ (your name)." If you hear that message often enough, you'll probably get sick of it and move on to the next stage.

Anger

Anger is the stage that follows depression. You know your recovery is progressing nicely when you find yourself getting goddamned mad at that mate you used to think you couldn't live without or at a world that mistreats a person as good as you are. If you are the type of person who has never used profanity and you find yourself swearing, that is a good sign. If you rant and roar and refuse to do even little things that your friends suggest might be good for you, that is very healthy. They won't like it but they'll live through it. And what you are doing is important. You are asserting your right to live as the person you are becoming, a person without the relationship that was previously so much a part of you. The way a person asserts himself in the anger stage, while not the most desirable way in the world, is a step in the right direction. And so you aren't perfect—who is?

The anger stage is one in which you are beginning to get in touch with some of the fire and energy that may have lain dormant in you for a long time. Try not to get angry at yourself for getting angry. This, too, shall pass in time. But again, you don't want to get stuck in this stage. The way to hasten your movement through this phase is to find ways to cleanse yourself of it without letting it splatter all over other people. Since anger and resentment permeate a person's body and mind, try to work it out of yourself both physically and mentally. Here are a couple of suggestions: Some day when you are feeling grouchy, get into the shower and turn the water on full force and then, instead of singing in the shower, yell. Scream as loud as you can. Call the person you have separated from all the nasty names you can think of. Tell him where to go and what to do. Tell him all of the horrible things he's done to you and all of the horrible things you would like to do to him. If you run out of things to say, repeat your favorites over and over. Make it gory, specific and obscene. Keep it up until you feel yourself beginning to get hoarse, and then wash yourself and get out. You will probably feel clean inside and out. Some other day try pounding on your mattress with your fists, once again yelling all of those things you would never say in person because they would be too hurtful and no useful purpose would be served by saying them. Another way some people find helpful is by writing a nasty letter but, of course, not mailing it. Your anger belongs to you. Nobody is to blame for it any more than they were to blame for your separation. Your anger is a source of power. Don't suppress it but don't lay it on others. Instead harness its power. When you are screaming or writing, pay attention to what you are saying and see if you can find out what you are so angry about. What is it that you have been made to do that you didn't want to do? What have you not been allowed to do that you'd like to do? Later when you are feeling more rational, you may take action to avoid similar injustices in the future, even to rectify some. However, don't do it when you feel like getting revenge. It is O.K. to feel like getting back at somebody, to want to do something to hurt him, to relish the thought of subjecting him to slow torture or cutting him up into little bits, but it is *not* O.K. to do it.

Incidentally, when you are in this stage, it is a good time to go into therapy, not because there is anything wrong with you for being angry but because many times some sessions with a good therapist can help you learn how to harness your anger, to use its power in creative and productive ways, a skill that will be helpful all your life. Actually, a person can usually benefit greatly from therapy (which is really a sophisticated form of private tutoring) anytime he suffers a great deal of pain in the loss of a loved one. It's just that in the denial stage people usually deny they could use any help and in the depressed stage they don't think they deserve it.

Re-evaluation and readjustment

This fourth and final stage in the process of grief is well worth the trouble you have had to go through to get there. However, don't expect to get to this stage quickly, in a week or two or even a few months. Though when some relationships end, recovery may be very fast, if the relationship has been a long or very significant one and particularly if the ending has been traumatic, the process may take a number of years. However, you don't have to wait until this fourth stage to feel good. If you realize what is happening to you and allow yourself to experience the various feelings you have as you are having them, if you allow yourself to learn from the different kinds of thoughts you are bound to have in a crisis like this and if you take constructive action (see the next section), as you go along you will learn a great deal about yourself and your world. Many people (including both authors) who have gone through a long and intense recovery period following a divorce, as well as the not so intense stages that followed other less traumatic separations, credit these experiences with helping them become more human. Because of experiencing new depths of emotion and trying things we had never tried before, we became both softer and stronger, more loving and more lovable.

It is the stages of grief that form the cocoon that must envelop you for a while to effect your transformation from chrysalis to butterfly, and in the re-evaluation and readjustment you emerge to try new wings. One of the advantages to having many relationships, to going through many endings and many beginnings, is that you get used to both and know that they follow one another as surely as the dawn follows the dusk and vice versa.

A word of caution: As you go through the stages of grief, you will not find them as clearly delineated as we have described. You may flip-flop from anger one day to depression the next. One day you may be convinced that he is entirely to blame for your breakup and the next day be just as certain that you'd still be together if you weren't such a terrible person. And two years after you have parted, you may imagine that you hear his key rattling in the lock some evening at the time he used to come home for dinner and expect him to walk in. Or you might find yourself thinking that she will mend the hole in your coat pocket, thus denying for a few moments that she has gone out of your life. What we have described are the emotional states most prevalent as you go through a sequence of stages in recovering from a loss.

A word of hope: Re-evaluation and readjustment is a stage in which you have the opportunity to look at your life and your relationships from a different perspective. Many times in this stage a person will be motivated to embark on a new career, go back to school, move to a different city or even a different country. He may discover that his values have changed considerably and he is ready to try a dramatically different life style. Or perhaps his external life doesn't change but he has a new slant on things. Make the most of this period. Throw caution to the wind. Take time and get help to discover what you want to do with your new life. Get help by reading, by going to adult education classes, by trying things you have never tried before, with others and alone—by changing your eating and exercise habits and learning to live a healthier life, by studying and learning how to develop better interpersonal relationships.

A butterfly sees things from a loftier position than a chrysalis but this stage, like all stages, has advantages and disadvantages. You will become aware of things you never noticed before and these can be frightening. You are apt to see things that need to be changed—in yourself and your world—and may not know just how to change them, but you will find a way, for this is a stage of new hope, new insight. It will help to follow some of the suggestions in the following section. One day you will see clearly what that relationship gave you, and that it was important for you to have it, but you will be glad that it ended, for that enabled you to get to the place you are now. And that is a good place to be!

SUGGESTIONS TO AID CARING CLOSURE

At the time a person goes through the stages of grief, there is much he can do to facilitate this healing process. But what is even more important, he can take advantage of his loss and make it give him something.

The loss of a partner leaves a void. Some will try to fill it as quickly as possible, often by hurriedly seeking a new romance to replace the old. Others, thinking it can never be filled or that in time it will fill itself, will sit back and do nothing. But there is another way. Admit that there is a void. And that it hurts. And that you are upset. After all, a part of you has been removed. However, this void can be seen as a gift of space that you have been given. You now have the opportunity to look inside yourself and to fill that void with what you would like to have there. This is the time to explore, to experiment, to grow—to think about things you've never thought about before, to express yourself in new ways, to try new things, to meet new people and to use old friends in new ways.

In addition to working on your own caring closure, however, you should also do what you can do to help your former partner become more comfortable with his loss, too. Making it easy for a former partner to achieve caring closure is a way of helping yourself that is frequently overlooked. Following are some suggestions to help you profit from a relationship loss:

1. *Develop a close relationship with a friend of the same sex.*

Although a common reaction to the loss of a romantic partner is to immediately seek a replacement, this is not a good idea. What a person needs most at this time is not a serious sexual relationship but a good friend. Especially a friend of the same sex. Especially a friend who is going through or who has recently gone through the breakup of an important intimate relationship. You need a member of the same sex because you need to be reminded that not all the important people in this world are members of the opposite sex. You need to hear him talk about his reactions to his loss because, as he does, you will learn how members of your sex react and thus you'll learn about you. It doesn't matter whether he has just separated, is trying to decide whether or not to divorce or got a divorce three years ago. What matters is that he is in pain, has feelings he has difficulty coping with, is a bit confused in his thinking—and that he really wants two things: (1) to improve himself and his relationships and (2) to have you for a friend.

Make a pact with this person that you will listen to one another talk about your lost relationship as a way of learning to understand yourself and getting to know each other. Take turns talking about the good times and the bad, about your feelings and fears. But also agree that you will each ask the other to stop when the stories become boring. Or when the topic becomes too painful because it triggers memories in you. Ask your friend not to give you advice unless you ask for it. Not to tell you that you aren't being realistic and facing facts. Not to tell you that you shouldn't feel the way you feel. And not to tell you that you've got to do something in particular. Also ask him just to be with you without talking when you feel sad and lonely and to sometimes let you cry or swear or complain and complain and complain.

Unburden yourself with this one friend, or if one doesn't seem to be enough, work out a pact with another, but two is the maximum. Don't talk about your "ex" or load your miseries on everybody or you will send people away. In fact, don't *just* talk about the past every time you are with the friend, who, by listening, is helping you make sense out of your relationship. Take time to find some fun things to do with this friend, too. As you are doing all of this, you are learning to make use of and take care of people at the same time.

2. *Sort through your possessions.*

Possessions—furniture, pictures, knickknacks, even pots and pans—often have a symbolic meaning as well as a material function—particularly if they were shared with a love partner and especially if they were accumulated during a relationship. Thus, the period after a breakup is a good time for people to sort through their possessions with an eye to seeing what they want to keep, store or throw away. This can be an emotional housecleaning as well as a practical one.

To make this housecleaning more meaningful and facilitate your move toward closure, sometimes ask a close friend to be with you as you go through your possessions—many of which will be charged with memories. Let yourself experience your memories fully as you go through item after item. Tell your friend about the picnic the two of you had one summer night using that straw picnic basket. Recall how you shopped together for that couch and quarreled over where to hang that picture.

Then give away, sell or store possessions that have a negative emotional load. Do the same with those that don't affect you one way or the other. Surround yourself with those that make you feel happy and confident and that give you hope. You need all the strokes you can get.

As you go through your things, cry, swear, get angry, laugh—

express all that comes welling out of you. But afterwards, be sure to get closure with your friend. Thank him for the support and ask for some physical contact—a hug, a kiss, a massage. You've been through a catharsis and you want to be sure you are caring to yourself. Offer to help this friend sort through his possessions or find another friend to help. That will help you, too.

3. *Get actively involved with helping someone else who also has problems.*

Though going out of your way to help others is something everyone should fit into his life on a regular basis as a means of "paying his rent" for living on this planet, there are times when it becomes an urgent necessity. The period following the loss of an important relationship is one of those times. Then, deliberately seeking someone to help can be one of the best ways you can help yourself adjust to your loss and to achieve closure. After all, it is impossible to feel helpless or worthless for very long if you help someone who obviously enjoys being helped, someone who appreciates your concern and what you are doing. You are bound to get a sense of your own importance as you watch the impact you have on another person. Usually while engrossed in someone else's troubles, you keep your own lonely feelings at bay long enough for considerable healing to take place. And, in addition, when you contribute to another person's joy, some of it is bound to rub off on you.

There are a few precautions to take when your primary purpose is to help yourself feel important and appreciated while at the same time making somebody else feel good, too. These are:

a. Don't just contribute money to the heart fund or the community chest or spend one evening a week licking envelopes for your favorite political candidate and think that you are helping others in a way that will facilitate closure for you. These may be good things to do as a first step, but arm's-length involvement and menial tasks aren't going to help you feel important. To get the full benefit from helping as a "treatment" for your loss, you have to get caught up with the person or persons you are helping. You must talk with them, touch them, spend sufficient time so that you can get close enough to feel their pain and their joy. What you need is to give of yourself in a way that will allow you to gradually open up your heart again in a safe environment. With the loss of a significant relationship, the reaction is to close yourself up and wall yourself off from people—sometimes physically but always emotionally. Feelings of love are too painful and so you, either consciously or unconsciously, block them off and deaden yourself. It takes a while to open up again. There are two ways to get love flowing through your veins. One is to give it, to put yourself in another person's shoes, to do acts of personal service, to put yourself out to help. The other is to take love, to let others do for you, to take care of you sometimes and be appreciative even when they don't do exactly what you want, when and how you want it. It is much easier to give love than to take it, for you are less vulnerable. When you give, you are in the driver's seat. You can stop when you want to. You don't build up dependencies. You get thank-yous rather than having to give them.

b. Make certain the person or persons you help *want* your help. Although the primary reason for your helping someone else may be to help yourself (and there's nothing wrong with that), you must take the other's wishes into account, too. If you don't, you'll just be forcing your will on them instead of helping. Therefore, check it out to see if they want the help you want to give and in the way you want to give it. Don't be like the boy scout who was so intent on doing a good deed every day that he used to help little old ladies cross the street when they didn't even want to go that way.

c. Be sure to help only people that you really care about. Though there are times to put yourself out and help people you don't care about, this is not one of them. This is not the time to pick people to help that you look down on. For example, if you find cripples or the mentally defective repulsive, don't pick one of them to get personally involved with at this time. If you can't stand children or old people, don't make them your project. They will feel your distaste and be hurt by it. And you won't be able to open your heart up wide enough to do yourself some good. If you don't particularly care for your brother or your cousin, this is not the time to put yourself out to do them some favors just because they are needy and nearby. Pick some person you really enjoy being with, and both you and he will benefit more.

Although being a good "helper" does take some skill, don't let these cautions deter you. You'll become better at "selfish" helping —i.e., helping people you enjoy helping and in ways that are good for you—as you do it. The kind of stress that comes after losing a relationship requires that you find somebody to give love and help to—and as soon as possible. Though it may not feel like it at the time, you need to show somebody that you care about him much more than you need somebody to love you. Throwing yourself into helping another person or persons when you feel as if you are the one who needs help and love is like making yourself exercise when you feel tired and logy and believe you can't stay awake another minute. It doesn't sound logical that expending energy will give you more and will wake you up, but it will. And giving love to someone else by helping him will make you feel more loved, too, even though it doesn't seem to make sense. It's one of those psychological facts that doesn't fit in with the laws governing physical matter, and the fact is the more love you give away, the more you will feel.

4. *Change your image.*

No matter how much we like to think we are independent, our partners do influence the way we dress. And even though your relationship may have ended, your partner may still be hanging around—in your closet. Get rid of him by using this closure period as an opportunity to try out new ways of dressing. Create a new image—one that he might have kept you from developing when you were together. If he liked you in tailored things, try the provocative look. If she liked you in dark suits, go casual. Buy some colorful leisure suits. If you wore your partner's favorite color, now try wearing yours. Find ways to reveal facets of yourself that have not been allowed to show.

However, since a person doesn't always see himself as others see him, get some guidance as you develop your new image. Ask for help from a friend whose taste you admire and whose judgment you trust, but make certain that he won't try to keep you as you used to be but will encourage you to be daring. Invite your friend over and then go through your closet, trying on clothes and talking about the experiences you had while wearing those clothes. How did others react to you? How did you feel about yourself? How do you feel in these garments now? When clothes make you recall an unpleasant incident or even a pleasant incident that makes you feel sad, or when you don't feel good about yourself when wearing them, discard them, even if it means paring yourself down to a very limited wardrobe. Then gradually, again with your friend's advice and support, go out and buy some new clothes that represent a side of you that you want to project right now.

5. *Make new friends.*

There is no better time to take a good look at your friends than now. To begin with, many that were friends of both of you probably won't be available to you now. Some may feel they have to decide which of you to be friends with and they may choose him. Others may lead a life that is so couples-oriented that there is no place in it for you when you are without a partner. Don't let this bother you. Instead, seek out some people who are single or not involved with anyone. Pick as potential friends those who are making a success of being single—people who seem happy, who are absorbed in interesting jobs, who are interested in trying new things, who are available to do things with.

And make friends with new kinds of people. If you've always gone around with teachers because your husband was a teacher, seek out musicians or beach bums. If you always traveled in the "social set," seek out hippies. If your friends are mainly doctors, try artists or lawyers or stockbrokers. A way to learn about yourself and expand your horizons is to expose yourself to a wide variety of people, those with different values and interests, different customs. And most people involved in an intimate relationship simply don't do that. So take this opportunity to explore people.

And take a close look at your present friends. You want supportive non-judgmental people around you now—not people who have an emotional investment in keeping you the person they are familiar with. You need friends who will encourage you to express your feelings. You need friends who will encourage you to explore. You don't need friends who put you down, who tell you that you need to see a psychiatrist because you moved into a commune or opted for celibacy or quit your job. Many times, you can educate friends to help you during this transition period. Explain to them the ideas in this chapter and let them know you want to try new things, to make the most of this period in your life. If a friend simply can't understand that, stop seeing him for a while. You may be able to come together later but right now you especially need to surround yourself with people who are easy and comfortable to be with.

6. *Try a different home environment.*

This is an opportunity to try out a way of life you may always have wanted to try—a commune, a hippie pad, a singles complex, a trailer home, buying your own home or duplex. And if you have always lived just with your spouse or lover, try living alone, or with one other person you are not emotionally involved with or dependent upon. Ask yourself what are the basic minimum requirements you need in a home and find a place that has them but that is very different from what you are used to. After her divorce, Emily decided she needed a fireplace, a view of the ocean and to be within a few minutes' drive of one good friend. She moved from her posh waterfront home into another beach home but this one a hippie pad in an unfashionable area. Afraid that she would have no friends, she found to her amazement that despite the fact the house leaked in every room when it rained and her furnishings were far from elegant, she made so many friends she finally had to move because she couldn't get any work done. Betty moved from a suburban home to a large apartment complex because she wanted to experience a "slice of life." All her experiences weren't pleasant but she did find she could cope with problems on her own and without the protection of her husband.

7. *Explore your sexuality.*

Seek out courses and classes that will help you learn more about sex. Sex is like cooking. No matter how much or little you know, you can always learn more. Share sexual recipes with others.

Try having sex with people you have always passed up before— i.e., those who are considerably older or younger, those of a different race, those who are fatter or thinner than you like them to be.

If you have always been monogamous, try having several ongoing sexual relationships at the same time. However, be honest with your partners. Let each know he isn't the only one.

Deliberately try celibacy for a considerable period of time, not because you can't find a sexual partner but because you want to discover the advantages of it. Develop nonsexual close relationships with several members of the opposite sex.

8. *Create new rituals to help you adjust.*

There are many rituals that will help you let go of your old life and relationships and prepare you for the new. Some you can do by yourself; some you can share with one close friend; some you can do with a number of members of your supportive network; and some you can share with your ex-mate. Most you will have to create and develop for yourself, but we are going to suggest a few just to get you started.

Seriously consider sending out "divorce" announcements to let people know your new status. If divorce is nothing to be ashamed of—and it shouldn't be—why not let your friends know about this significant change in your life? It is a courtesy they deserve, and it may help you get back in circulation. In the same way, people who have been living together or dating exclusively can send out cards announcing a new "availability," whether or not they also have a change of address at this time. One woman sent out announcements printed on medium-sized cards like those that are used to spread the word of the opening of a law or medical practice or that a new partner has joined the firm. They read as follows: "Ms. Carole Haas would like it to be known that she is no longer living with Mr. Philip Driver and now has more time available for social contacts." Though you might want to have a different wording or a less formal tone, that is an idea of what you can do.

Suggest to some good friends that they give you a "breaking up" shower, or give one for yourself or for a friend. The idea is that people who have just broken up—especially those who have broken up housekeeping—i.e., married couples or live-in lovers—need and deserve a shower just as much as any bride or mother-to-be—maybe even more so. A shower, after all, is a ritual honoring the passage from single-womanhood to bride and from wife to mother. The gifts are to help in this transition, to celebrate and honor it and to give the bride- or mother-to-be things she'll need to fulfill her new status properly.

In the same way, men and women who have broken up need to be honored by a shower. Not only to commemorate their status change from half of a couple to an individual but to provide them with some practical necessities for reconstructing their lives. If more people would do this sort of thing, it could become a taken-for-granted ritual that would help people adjust more quickly. Not only would such a celebration help take some of the onus off partings, it would show people in stress their friends really care about them and want to help.

In gathering material for this book Emily and Betty decided that they would help a friend who had just broken up with a live-in lover of five years, by giving him a shower. They had to talk hard to get him to agree because he felt embarrassed by the idea, but finally he did. We sent out invitations to his friends—both men and women—inviting them to a "starting over" shower. We asked people to bring anything they thought would help Dick begin a new life on his own after all those years of togetherness. The shower was held on a Saturday night and instead of cake and punch we served a keg of beer and pretzels. And instead of party games everyone took a turn telling Dick what they liked about him and how they intended to support him during this difficult period.

Then we had the gift-opening ceremony. The gifts were creative and often unusual. One woman gave him a dine-out booklet which entitled him to two dinners at many nearby restaurants for the price of one. This was, she said, to help him get started on a new social life. A man friend gave him two tickets to a basketball game so he'd have an excuse to invite a friend to something as his guest. Some gifts were more practical—and needed—like pots and pans and sheets and dishes. However, the gift that made the biggest hit with Dick was an address book in which every guest had written the name, address and telephone number of an attractive and eligible woman!

9. *Explore your relationship.*

Taking an analytical look at your relationship can help you put it to rest in your mind. In fact, if people don't ask and answer some questions about the relationship that is over, they can never make sense of it. And for this particular experience to have any meaning they must fit it in with the other experiences that make up their life story.

Write out the answers to the following questions either in a notebook or on sheets of paper that you can save and reread from time to time when you feel confused and don't know quite what happened to you. It will take several hours at least, and if the relationship was a long and intense one, it could take days. And it will be painful at times. You will find all kinds of reasons for not doing it. However, you will find it well worth the time spent no matter how long it takes. And you don't have to do it all at once. You can spread it out over a period of several weeks or even months. Bite the bullet and do it. If it churns up uncomfortable emotions, let yourself express them using some of the suggestions given in the section on stages of grief. The questionnaire is written for a marriage partner but can be used to help you understand any significant relationship that you had and lost.

1. Why did you marry him/her?
   a. What qualities did you admire most?
   b. What did you want to do that you thought he/she could help you with?
2. Why did you get a divorce?
   a. At the time of your divorce, what qualities in him/her bothered you the most?
   b. What did you or he want to do that being married interfered with?
3. What were your most significant positive experiences in your relationship with your ex-mate?
   a. How have they affected your attitudes and your life?
4. What were your greatest sadnesses or failure experiences in your relationship with your ex-mate?
   a. How have they affected your attitudes and your life?
5. In what ways has this relationship added to your life? (E.g., what has it given you in the way of knowledge, experiences, material possessions, children, etc.?)
6. What could your ex-mate do for you now that he would like to do and that would make him feel good?
7. What could you do for your ex-partner that he would like to have you do and that would make you feel good?

10. *Validate your former partner.*

No matter how your former partner treated you in the past or is treating you now, you can be certain there are two questions that frequently go through his mind: What do you think of him? Do you appreciate him? He longs to know that he has been important to you and that you still think him worthwhile. If you can let him know that you appreciate him, not only will you help him feel good, you will advance yourself in your efforts to get emotional closure.

It isn't enough to just say to him the next time you see him, "I appreciate you," or even to phone him and say it. You must let him know in a more forceful way. Writing a letter of appreciation is a good way. In the letter you can say in your own words, "I've been thinking a lot about you lately, and I'd like you to know what I see as your good points and what I particularly enjoyed about our relationship, so I'm writing you this letter to tell you these things." Then list qualities and incidents in any way that you wish. Make certain that every incident you list is a positive one. Don't take a chance and put in any that could be interpreted in a negative way. (Remember, a parting has hurt him, too, and he has a lot of sensitive spots.) Make certain that the way you describe his qualities sounds positive even if you are aware that they have their negative aspects. (Every characteristic of a person is an asset at certain times and a liability at other times—e.g., a person who is good with words talks too much sometimes; a person who takes over and organizes things is also pushy sometimes.) This is a time to give strokes, not to point out shortcomings or to hint that changes are needed.

If writing a letter is too much trouble, send him a birthday card with a little note saying you are so glad he was born because he taught you so much or gave you so much pleasure or enriched your life so much or something like that. After Betty had been divorced for about a year, she sent her ex-husband a poem she had written about his importance in her life. Then later when her first book was published she sent him a copy inscribed, "In gratitude and appreciation for all the help and support you've given me with my writing during the years we spent together. A part of you is in everything I write." He phoned to thank her after receiving the book and his manner was soft and gentle, the way it used to be, and they shared a few moments of warm and caring contact.

Another way to validate your partner is to do something for him or her that you know he or she would appreciate and that will require that you put yourself out somewhat. Do it, not out of pity (or because you are trying to get your partner to do something for you), but out of gratitude, as a thank-you for what he or she has done for you in the past.

Don't be surprised if you are not able to follow this suggestion for validating your partner or if you find the thought of it offensive in some way. There is usually a time period in which you just don't appreciate an ex-mate or ex-lover. But wait a while. Maybe later the thought of validating an ex-mate won't bother you so much. While all our suggestions for caring closure will help you reach this point, completing the questionnaire presented in Suggestion 9 will be particularly useful. And there is a good reason for you to keep trying to build up as many good feelings as you can toward the person you are no longer with. A person who has been important to you will be part of you forever. Because of him or her, you became a different person—you tried behaviors that you had never tried before, you developed some new "roles" and you had to think about things you had never thought about before. You learned, you changed, you grew in some ways. And out of the time you spent together you have a storehouse of memories—some good and some not so good.

However, if you leave your relationship conscious only of the bad things, able to recall only bad memories, unable to think of any redeeming features about your mate, you will end up transferring some of these bad feelings to yourself. Since you will always carry that person around with you, if you hate him or her, you will also hate yourself. However, if you are able to take a more balanced view of the past relationship—remembering the good as well as the bad—and grateful for the good things you did have, these good feelings will become part of you and the way you feel about yourself.

By validating your partner you are also validating yourself. And you are giving him the best going-away present possible—a legacy of love he can carry around forever. And if you are able to give him some good feelings, he may be able to give some back to you. In fact, when you have validated your ex-mate a number of times and perhaps received some validation in return, you may want to contemplate taking the steps necessary to bring about an important new phase in your life—developing a new relationship with him or her.

15

A New Beginning with Your Ex-Mate:
Emily's story

Endings, painful as they are, often lead to new beginnings and sometimes even to new beginnings with a former spouse or romantic partner. However, many people, because of the myth that it is impossible for people to "go backwards"—i.e., to become "just friends" once they have been lovers—fail to see the possibility for starting a different kind of a relationship with an ex-mate once the romantic part of the relationship is over. Of course, there are cases where beginning a new relationship would be impossible or undesirable—e.g., where the relationship was bad before or where the ending left such scars no new beginning is possible. But some ex-partners have the potential to become friends on a new basis once the closure process is complete—many times very special friends.

It should not be surprising that this is possible. After all, as we discussed earlier, a sexual relationship builds up a special bond between two people. Those who have built up a strong bond have had to trust one another many times and in many ways, thus creating a reservoir of trust. Though many bonds are severed when a couple parts, memories of mutual pleasure and a sense of trust make a good foundation on which to begin anew.

It should not be surprising that this is desirable. Former intimates know each other in special ways. Sexual partners often share confidences not shared with others. They can acquire a tremendous storehouse of knowledge of each other, especially if the relationship is a long one. Thus when a relationship ends, one loss may be that of a confidant, of a person who has seen you at your best and your worst, of a person who knew you in a stage or at an age new friends will never know, a person to whom you can talk about things you may not be able to talk about with others. If partners can start a new relationship, though it will be different from the old, the storehouse of shared secrets need not go to waste. They can keep a part of themselves that would otherwise be lost.

Also, an ex-mate can be a good resource person. You know he has special talents, skills and knowledge. You know just how he can help you and how you can help him. Betty's ex-husband is a former navy corpsman who is now a pharmaceutical salesman. For all the years of their marriage she relied as much on him as on her doctor for medical advice. After her divorce, even when she still felt hurt and antagonistic, she found herself continuing to rely on his special knowledge when one of the kids got sick or when she needed advice or a discount on pills. But she wanted more. Though she wanted his knowledge and help, she wanted his friendship, too. She wanted their talks and meetings to be pleasant ones.

Developing a new relationship with an ex-mate (or long-time lover) not only is practical but also can make life more pleasant. When two people are deeply involved over a considerable period of time, they get entangled in ways that don't just dissolve when they part. They may have children, buy a house together, invest jointly in stocks, join the same health club or put money down on a future world cruise. After their breakup, they may have to meet to deal with financial matters, problems with the kids or decisions about property. Or they may find themselves on the same trip they signed up for the year before. If they can handle joint or parallel commitments as friends instead of as adversaries, it is to their best interest.

Before there can be a new relationship, the old one must be brought to closure. By following the suggestions in the preceding chapter, you can become a different person, able to see your former partner with new eyes, thus making a new relationship possible. When this happens, not only will you continue to appreciate the things you've always liked about him but the things you didn't like will seem different because you will see them from a different perspective.

Arnold, a friend, told us of taking his ex-wife out to dinner and starting to get annoyed when she couldn't make up her mind what to order. While the waiter stood there, she vacillated between the lamb, the shrimp, the lobster—or maybe just a salad. When they were married, her slower pace had led to many quarrels and sometimes even to their marching out of a restaurant with him berating her for being indecisive and her sobbing that he lacked patience. But now he says, "I suddenly realized it's not my problem. Instead of trying to force her to decide, or apologizing to the waiter, or blowing my top, I just sat back, sipped my drink and relaxed. Eventually she made up her mind and we had a delightful dinner."

But this seeing your partner through new eyes doesn't just happen overnight. It takes time—sometimes a lot of time. If the relationship was a long one—a two-decade one for example—it could take years for one or both to achieve the kind of closure necessary before a new beginning can occur. And the length of time isn't the only factor in achieving closure. Some relationships are so intense—even ones that may last only a few years or less—that it can take quite a while to get over the pangs of parting.

Emily, who was divorced after twenty-nine years of marriage, found that it took her approximately six years to achieve closure and another two to re-establish a new beginning with Roger, her ex-husband. Here is her story.

EMILY'S STORY

For more than two decades, things between Roger, my husband, and me had been good, very good. We had been inseparable. Not only were we husband and wife; we were each other's best friend, lover, teacher and business partner. And we had been everything to each other ever since college. Even there, we had more in common than most couples—our major, bacteriology.

And fortune had smiled on us. We had worked hard—very hard —and planned for the future. And it had paid off. We had two well-mannered sons with college degrees and a large waterfront home. We owned our own medical laboratory, a good-sized stock portfolio and two apartment houses. He had gotten a Ph.D. degree since our marriage and I, too, had continued my education. We admired each other, didn't play around and didn't quarrel. Not ever. Not for twenty-four years anyway. And then we started.

The last five years of our marriage were like some kind of crazy dream. Without there being any apparent major cause, our perfect marriage began to crumble. I felt the rug had been pulled out from under me. It was as though, for some reason I couldn't quite fathom, my best friend had turned against me. There were quarrels, days of hostile silence, pleading, long talks, short talks, and nasty acts of revenge. And mingled in between, short periods of ecstasy when I felt sure we had found one another again and all would be the way it used to be.

As I felt my world crumble, I did everything I could—including taking courses in psychology, sensitivity training and going into individual therapy—to help me understand what was happening. I remember weeping piteously that first day in my therapist's office and saying he had to help me save my marriage. He surprised me by saying that saving my marriage was not his job but that helping me become strong enough so that I could get along without Roger was. Though it shook me up, it made sense when he said that until I was strong enough to get along without Roger, I'd never be able to have a good relationship with him.

But with all my efforts to rid myself of emotional dependencies, the upsets at home did not abate. Finally, one night after a big quarrel, Roger left, subsequently getting his own apartment and moving his things out. I guess I was not able to see this for what it was—the ending of our relationship—and I spent a lot of time denying that it was really over. In fact, his moving out made me feel strangely calmer—as though now we could really work on our relationship without the stresses we had had living together. I talked him into taking a sabbatical from marriage, a year in which we would date other people as well as each other.

What I hoped was that by dating other women, he'd come to appreciate me more and then we'd get back together. And there was a part of me that wanted to date other men, to see what it was like to have sex with somebody else, to discover if other men found me attractive. I wanted to test the outside world so that I'd be ready—just in case.

The dates we had with each other during the months of our sabbatical were strange evenings when we both acted as if we were walking on eggs. But despite our care to be "nice" with each other the end result was usually the same—I'd cry, he'd become cold and withdrawn or else we'd argue.

Often, I would go home, get into bed, put a pillow over my head and moan and sob. Sometimes it was because spending an evening looking into his eyes and seeing such deep sadness there, sadness I believed I was causing and yet could do nothing about, was more than I could bear. Other times my tears were hot angry ones, the result of another argument over something of no importance. One time, the two of us, ordinarily pillars of decorum, were the center of attention in a fine French restaurant when our voices rose as we argued over whether or not women should be allowed to become jockeys. I insisted women were entitled to become jockeys if they were qualified. He insisted changes had to be made slowly, that it wasn't fair to allow women in races if their presence was emotionally upsetting to men and would keep them from doing their best. We never did resolve that one, but got up and left the restaurant, and he drove me home in stony silence.

My final effort to save my marriage was that old classic—taking a Caribbean cruise. I figured that maybe things would be better if I could somehow quit all this analyzing, probing, trying, and just have fun. When he agreed to go, I was elated. Surely, this would do it. I could feel that time was running out for us. And I think, now that I look back on it, that it did run out for good during that vacation.

Although there were some very good times, they were but a scattered few in a vast sea of concentrated and extended discomfort. In fact, our time together on that cruise was much like our dates had been. The good moments came when we had had a drink or two or when other people were around. Like dancing cheek to cheek on a ship that seemed as tipsy as we were, laughing and trying not to fall on other couples as the whole dance floor rocked from side to side. And giving a "come as you think you might be if the ship were to sink" party for twelve new friends in a stateroom that was crowded even when just two of us were in it.

However, the close quarters and the increased amount of time spent together were like a pressure cooker to our emotions. Both our coldness to one another and our quarrels intensified. After one particularly vicious quarrel, I walked the ship's decks at 3 A.M. planning to throw myself overboard. What caused me to decide against it was the realization that I'd not be there to revel in his pain when it dawned on him what I had done and that he might have prevented it. I went back to our stateroom hoping to find him awake and worried about me but not surprised to find him sleeping peacefully.

And then something happened that caused us to have one last, wonderful brief encounter before it was over—really over. Roger got the flu the last day at sea and when we got back to Long Beach, I invited him to come home and let me care for him. For three days, we locked ourselves in, not answering the doorbell or the telephone and I nursed him and loved him and felt loved by him. Something inside of me fell into place and I felt at peace.

And then he was well again and back at work and back at his apartment. Several months flew by without my hearing from him and I was confused by that. However, I was enjoying myself, coming and going when and where I pleased, not having to cook meals or be home when it was time for him to come home. And dating several men who treated me like a queen, who enjoyed my strong opinions and who were good in bed. I was having a fling I felt long overdue. I had been too "good" too long.

And then one day he called, not to ask me out but to say he wanted to come by and talk with me about something important. His voice sounded as if it was serious. And it was. He was in love with another woman and wanted a divorce.

I was stunned. It had never occurred to me that we would ever part for good. And certainly not that he would prefer another woman to me. My first thought was: "It's too soon. He hasn't given us a chance. Our year's leave of absence isn't up yet." Disbelief, disappointment and anger bubbled up in me but underneath was a layer of relief. I wouldn't have to be the one to take the blame for making the decision to part. If things didn't work out for him, it would be his own fault, not mine. I had tried everything I could think of to make *him* happy and now I would have the chance to make *me* happy. Some other woman could take care of him. I was free at last.

But this euphoria was short-lived. In a few days depression set in and I was calling him—pleading, begging, beseeching him to reconsider. At first he listened but when my pleadings turned into accusations he refused to see me anymore. And even when I sent friends as intermediaries to tell him I loved him and just had to talk with him, he still turned me down. I felt I reached the depths of loneliness and despair when he called and suggested that I select a lawyer to handle the divorce—one who would help us with the property settlement, one we could both talk with and one who would help us settle the whole thing amicably.

I picked a man we both had known, told him to just get me out as quickly and easily as possible, that I could support myself, and that since I loved my husband and wanted above all to have a good relationship with him after this was all over, I would not fight for anything. But for all my self-reliant speeches, I felt completely washed up. For five years, all of my energy had gone into trying to save my marriage, and now that had failed. To me, there was nothing left.

Somehow I got through the next year—one in which we drew up a property settlement (with some bitterness and fighting despite my brave and independent words to my lawyer) and one in which I became aware of how great my loss really was. I hadn't lost just a beloved husband—I had lost a whole way of life and a powerful illusion. At the time of our divorce we sold the spacious home I had lived in and had a love affair with for eighteen years. For all those years I had cleaned and polished and shopped and gardened and tended every inch of that house with loving care. But it was more than a house; it was a life style. The house was situated on a small strip of land, interlaced with narrow navigable canals, and the residents of our tiny sophisticated community spend a great deal of time out of doors—walking, boating, bicycling. They treated one another with the casual informality of vacationers at a fashionable resort. In the daytime, they sunned themselves on one another's floats, chattering, laughing and sipping martinis while watching their children swim, splash and squirt one another with water pistols. And at dusk, they strolled along waterfront walks, sometimes stopping to chat with friends barbecuing on their front-of-the-house patios. To give all this up was as painful as giving up my husband. But I knew I had to do it. Not only for financial reasons but for emotional ones. It represented my past and I had to move on to the future.

And at the same time I gave up my home and a whole way of life I also gave up a dream that had sustained me for twenty-nine years—the dream that I had a person I could depend upon—a person who would take care of me forever and whom I would take care of forever. With Roger I was secure—safe. I would never want, never know pain, poverty, suffering. I would not be lonely in my old age. And when I lost that dream I hadn't anything to replace it with—I felt helpless, lonely and afraid, and yet I had some crazy kind of hope that someday Roger and I would be together again—that we would grow old together.

I had taken to letter writing during this period to help me look at my thoughts and feelings and to try to sort out what was going on in me. My letters, of course, were usually, but not always, to Roger. Most of the time I didn't mail the letters I wrote but just threw them away or filed some in my journal, but sometimes I recopied parts and sent them out.

But one day I sent Roger a long letter telling him of some of the things I really liked about him and about our marriage so that he wouldn't feel guilty about breaking it off and so that I wouldn't feel guilty either. I told him I could see that it was one of those things that just had to be and I was glad he had called it off before we had hurt one another irrevocably. The letter took me a whole day to write because so much emotion churned up in me as I let my thoughts go backwards and allowed myself to feel the sadness, the anger, the joy of our years together.

After receiving that and several other letters from me, Roger asked me out for my birthday. That was the start of a post-divorce period of dating. However, our dating was not done with the idea of any reconciliation. It was just something we wanted to do. Even we weren't sure why except that we didn't want to completely lose touch. I see now we were working on closure.

Much as I sensed we needed these dates, I found out I couldn't let others know about them. My mother, who felt the divorce had been a mistake, let me know after every date that I had disappointed her—because we hadn't reconciled. Some friends would caution me as to what I should and shouldn't do to get him back; others told me I was crazy to keep on seeing him. I soon learned to keep our meetings secret.

Usually several months would go by between our dates and then they weren't like dates I had with other men. On the surface all was calm and slow and muted, while inside things were boiling and churning in turmoil as I tried to hang on and make sense of what was happening between us. All our get-togethers followed a very set pattern. We always went to some very nice, quiet, unhurried place for dinner, somewhere we had not been with each other when we were married. I think that unconsciously we both sought to avoid being swamped by old memories.

Dinner took a long time, for we lengthened it with a drink before, the careful selection of wine and a great deal of talking. We would talk about our children, who had heard what from them and our evaluation of how they were doing; we'd gossip about mutual friends; and then talk about our work. He'd brag; I'd brag. He'd complain how hard it was to make a buck or to cope with inefficient help or bureaucratic red tape; then I'd complain. If one or the other didn't brag or complain enough to even things out, the other would step in and help him out, saying how well he seemed to be doing or how hard things must be. It was as though we were both very anxious to make certain that everything stayed in balance. If the conversation touched on a sensitive chord or an awkward silence developed, he would jump in and tell a corny story or two, something just slightly off-color, and I would laugh more than was warranted and he would tell another until we had both regained our equilibrium. We made small talk but not contact.

I don't know what was going on in him but I suspect it was the same thing that was going on in me. I wanted him to know that my life was as good as his and in fact that I got along without him very well. Yet paradoxically, I wanted him to understand just how hard I had it. And I was trying to make some sense of the time we had spent together and our divorce. On our dates I looked him over—his features, his clothes, his mannerisms—trying to sort through clouds of memories and discover what he had really been like—this man I had lived with all those years, this man whose life had been more precious to me than my own, this man whose children I had borne and reared to manhood.

When I wasn't with him, I'd fantasize about him. Some of these fantasies were sexual although they weren't erotically detailed. One fantasy recurred frequently. In it, he'd ask me to go away with him for a weekend and I would go. He would be wildly enthusiastic about my body, and we'd spend the weekend making love and laughing, never leaving the room. And when the weekend was over, we would part. It was just that simple but it came to me time and time again.

I think what I really wanted was to know he still found me sexually attractive—not necessarily to have sex with him. But it was hard to know whether or not he was attracted to me sexually or even if I was to him. And, of course, we didn't discuss it. I tried to once but he was so obviously taken aback I quickly changed the subject. I laughed wryly to myself that the subject of sex was such an embarrassing one to us who had been married twenty-nine years.

And I had another recurring fantasy—one equally unrealistic. When I was alone, feeling lonely and needing comfort, I would imagine us together at some time in the distant future—our hair was white and thin, we were a bit crippled with arthritis, sitting alongside one another holding hands and talking about the past. I still believed we would get together again sometime in the future and grow old together.

And then he remarried. My fantasies vanished as suddenly as if they had been puffs of smoke. It was time to face reality—to get my life in order. I started working hard on my career as though I had just discovered I had to cope with life without Roger—right now and also in the future. I was not going to have him at my side when I was sick and dying. I got a sudden energy spurt and felt younger than ever. I became more creative, designing new programs and frequently going out of town to do them, experimenting in living in different places, under different conditions, with different people—trying to find the life style I liked.

For the next four years I saw very little of him because his new wife was very jealous and I was very busy. I wrote two books, had some affairs and developed a series of "families" throughout the country. These were people I loved and stayed with each time I visited their city when traveling around doing my programs. And at home, I worked on trying to free myself of old habit patterns that kept me attached to Roger. For one thing, I knew I had to learn to live alone, thoroughly enjoying it without feeling lonely and sorry for myself, before it would be safe to live with anyone else. And that took some doing because I had never lived alone, going as I had from my father's home to my husband's home when I married. And I knew I had to have several successful experiences living as an equal with one or more persons I was not dependent on, responsible for or sexually involved with before it would be safe for me to seek a new mate.

At about the time I had accomplished these objectives, an incident occurred that gave me another dollop of closure in my relationship with Roger. I found out through a friend that he was in a situation that could be harmful to him emotionally and financially. However, this information had been given to me in confidence and to reveal it would mean violating the trust of a friend. For a while I vacillated, torn by doubts. Should I tell Roger or not? After all, his life was no longer my business, and in fact, if I told him what I knew, he might doubt me, doubt my motives, and consider I was prying and interfering. And I had to ask myself if my motives were pure. Was I just trying to get one-up, to show him how dumb he had been to let himself get into such a situation, how smart I was to have access to information about such matters?

Finally I made my decision. The well-being of the man I had lived with and loved for so many years was extremely important to me. To protect him from even possible harm, I had to risk his anger and the loss of regard of a very dear friend. I told him. He didn't believe me, but he didn't get angry. And he appreciated my concern, and the risk I took.

This incident made me realize I had finally achieved a sort of closure to my relationship with Roger. It had taken six years but I now was at the point where I was over the longing, the bitterness, the anger and overconcern with his opinion of me. And perhaps he felt the same way, for after that he treated me differently. I think that, without our ever discussing it, we had made a new beginning.

We didn't date for more than a year, but we'd run into one another now and then. When we did, I noticed I didn't worry so much about what I looked like. I was calmer and didn't get a knot in my stomach the way I used to. And he seemed calmer, and sweeter, too—much softer and warmer. It was during that year that I began to look at men I went with in a different way, to fantasize how it would be to live with them, something I had never done before. It was as though I had had to cleanse myself of Roger before I could think of getting seriously involved with another man.

And then one came along who was just right for me—as both a business and romantic partner—and we moved in together. Keith Tombrink was fourteen years younger than I and the ideal living companion for me for several reasons. He believed in men and women sharing expenses, decision-making responsibilities and household chores; he was convinced that all people need not just a mate, but a supportive network of friends of both sexes, and he encouraged me to keep my friendships and continue to go out with other men; and what was particularly important, he understood my strong and loving feelings for my ex-mate, for he had such feelings for his, too.

With a man I loved at my side, a career as a group leader and author and a loving group of friends, I realized how rich my life had become through the years. It seemed ironic that I, who had been so afraid I couldn't get along without my husband, was now a symbol to many people of the "new woman"—a woman who not only dared try out new ways of living and loving but who also taught others to do the same thing.

It was shortly after Keith and I started living together that I got a chance to examine the course I was taking and to get a glimpse of the way my new relationship with Roger was going to go. One day he phoned and told me he was getting a divorce from his second wife. Of course, being Roger, he tried to play it cool, but I could hear the "don't give a damn" bravado he got in his voice when he was hurting. And I hurt for him. Knowing how proud he was and how difficult it must have been for him to call and tell me this—and suspecting he needed my help—I said in a light voice, "Well, there are some advantages to this. Now we can have dinner together. Let's do it." After we made plans to get together and I hung up the phone, I sat for quite a while trying to sort out my emotions, for I was shivering and sweating at the same time.

My first thought was: "Damn it, why did he have to wait until now to separate from her? If he had done it a few months ago before I got so involved with Keith, we might have had a chance to get together again. But what can I do now? Besides, I'm so busy with my work and so deep in this new relationship I don't know how I can possibly take care of him." And then I reminded myself that it was no longer my job to take care of him and that I wasn't tied to Keith, that I could do what I wanted—if I just knew what that was. And after thinking about it, I decided that even if I wasn't emotionally involved I wouldn't want to get romantically involved with Roger again. But I did want to be his friend. I knew the loneliness and lack of self-esteem that engulfs a person separated from a mate and wanted to help.

And helping him was very often a lot of fun for us both. When we talked on the phone a few days later, I suggested that we have a little celebration honoring the beginning of his new life and our reunion as friends. I knew he would appreciate a home-cooked meal and yet I didn't want to invite him to my place because Keith would be there. I thought it was important that we be alone for our reunion so we could talk and laugh and cry—or whatever it was we wanted to do.

So I suggested that we get together and shop, deciding what we wanted as we went along, and then return to his place and cook dinner. This was a whole new thing for us since we had never shopped or cooked together when we were married, but he agreed and we did it and had an absolutely delightful time. I had intended for us to split the cost of the food and had told him so in advance but he insisted on paying and it seemed important for him to do so. I let him. I suspect it kept him from feeling that I was just with him out of pity. In fact, he even gave me a bottle of wine to take home to Keith.

To help him get back into circulation, Keith and I subsequently sent him a free pass to a People Sampler, a program we give to help growth-oriented singles meet and get acquainted with many others and also improve their meeting skills. I also recommended him to the Sunday Supper Club, a small singles group started by some of my psychologically oriented friends.

We started seeing each other more often, but our dates presented some awkward situations for which there is no "etiquette." I'll never forget the first night he came to my apartment to pick me up to take me to dinner and Keith was there. Keith was dressed in old around-the-house type of clothes and Roger was all slicked up like a young boy on a first date. In a way, it was as though Keith were my father looking over Roger, a new boy friend. And in another way it was as though Roger were my father looking over Keith, my new boy friend. I could feel each appraising the other and finding him not good enough. And then as we went to leave, a problem I had not anticipated confronted me. Ordinarily, when I leave the house, either to go to work or to go out, I kiss Keith goodbye, and I felt it might seem that I didn't care about him if I didn't kiss him. Yet, if I did kiss him, I was afraid it would be like a slap in the face to Roger, reminding him of the little niceties of having a mate that he no longer had. I had to make a choice and I chose to kiss Keith good night. I wanted to say, "Don't wait up for us, Daddy," but resisted the impulse.

After our dinner was over, it was still early, so when Roger brought me home and Keith was still up, the three of us had a glass of wine and sat and talked for a little while. Then when Roger went to leave, the goodbye problem confronted me again, but this time in a different way. For a number of years Roger and I have been giving one another a kiss and a big hug when we leave each other. My problem was: "Is it O.K. for me to kiss my ex-husband in front of Keith?" Keith might feel bad if I do, but Roger will feel bad if I don't. I felt Roger needed reassurance more than Keith, and besides I could explain it all to Keith after Roger left, so I gave him a big kiss and a hug and he gave me one, too, even though Keith was looking right at us.

And I even felt that I was a sort of indirect matchmaker when Roger began dating a woman he had met at the Sunday Supper Club, which I had helped him join. I didn't see him or hear from him for a month or two and then one night he showed up at one of my Friday-night People Samplers with his new woman friend as his guest. I was dumbfounded because Roger had never before come to see me perform, or give a speech, or participate in any of my programs. In a way it seemed like a mark of acceptance that he could now not only come to see his ex-wife in a completely new role, but also bring a woman he was in love with. I think that he also wanted acceptance—for me to meet and approve of her.

In spite of the fact that he quickly became very involved with Lee, his new woman, and that she felt a bit threatened by our relationship, he still took time to occasionally get together with me alone. Then one day when we were having lunch, he told me he was going to marry her. Although I realized it would undoubtedly mean that we'd see less of one another, I was utterly delighted. I thought she was just what he needed. I suggested we set a time to sit down and talk about what we'd like the terms of our relationship to be now that he was remarrying and I was even more committed to Keith. I told him about the "We Process" and later sent him a copy of it to read.

Subsequently, although we didn't go through it formally, step by step, we used it as a basis to tell each other some important things. Roger said that while he wanted a relationship with me he didn't want it to be a source of worry to his future wife. I made it clear that while it had taken me a long time to get adjusted to getting along without him and while for a long time I had had fantasies of getting together again, I no longer had them. I made it clear that I still cared about him but not in the way I used to. And I told him I wanted to do what I could to make Lee realize I was no threat to her.

And taking his hand, I took the opportunity to tell him some of the things I particularly liked about him. Although he seemed to like hearing those things, he started telling some jokes. I asked him why he did that and his face got serious. "It's real hard," he said softly, "for some people to take compliments, you know."

As a result of that discussion it became clear that we really wanted the same thing from each other at this time—to be able to ask for each other's help and advice. And that is the way it is working out. Recently, when Keith needed some medical tests, I called Roger and asked—not just if he could do them (he owns a medical laboratory)—but if he would give us a discount on them. This wasn't easy—to ask an ex-husband for a favor for a new man friend. But I guess I felt I deserved it because I had helped build up the laboratory, and I guess I wanted Roger to want to do it. He very graciously did the tests and never charged us a cent. He also has been helpful to me with my mother, recommending just the right doctor and rest home, filling out her Medicare and income-tax forms. And I loaned him a rug and some furniture before he moved in with Lee.

Undoubtedly, our alliance will change its form many times in the future. There may be "deserts" when we don't see each other as much, "oases" when we spend a good deal of time together, but whatever happens, I can't imagine either of us turning our back on the other—ever.

But, of course, one can only live in the present and right now I am enjoying the "new beginning" Roger and I have made in our own lives and in our relationship together. I got a sense of the change that has occurred in our feelings about ourselves and each other and the real happiness we both have achieved through long years of pain and struggle when Roger and Lee gave a reception at

Christmas honoring their engagement. They invited Keith and me, but I wanted to go alone. This was an important occasion for me, and I wanted to give it all of my attention. I felt that somehow it was a rite of passage. And it turned out that it was.

What happened was that I saw him comfortably ensconced in a spacious, immaculate suburban home where everything was in its proper place and in good repair. The buffet was lavish and I could see it must have taken Lee days of preparation to get everything ready. She was the perfect hostess who introduced everybody to everybody else in a way that made each person feel important, and she never forgot a name or stammered even the least little bit. Though many people came and went and platters on the buffet were emptied, they seemed to get refilled somehow. She and Roger worked together so smoothly in their host and hostess duties that neither ever seemed to hurry, and every once in a while, they looked at one another with affection. Everything there was calm and low-key. All the guests were smiling and polite and I knew that Lee would never say anything that would upset either the guests or Roger in the least. Even the color scheme in the house reflected their serenity. Everything was blue—blue carpet, blue drapes, blue bedspreads, blue walls, even blue artificial flowers in the bathroom. This was not surprising, for blue had always been Roger's favorite color. And for years I had lived with his cool colors and had done all the things Lee was now doing— and I had loved it. But my favorite colors now are the hot ones— oranges and yellows and reds. And I have become like my colors— a bubbling mass of enthusiasm, all effervescent and impulsive. I have tapped into my fiery core.

Both Roger and Lee treated me with respect and so did the other guests, many of whom were people Roger and I had known when we were married. People I had not seen for years seemed genuinely glad to see me. Some told me they had read about me in newspapers and magazines and others inquired eagerly as to what I'd been doing in the years since my divorce. As I told of my adventures and my chaotic life, others eagerly gathered around to hear, and then, not wanting to upstage Roger and Lee, I toned myself down and gradually stopped talking. And suddenly, it dawned upon me how many times I must have done that to him, robbed him of the limelight when it was his turn to be paid attention to.

Looking at the kind of life Roger had and seeing that he had a good woman to be his partner, I felt content. I had somehow through the years since our divorce carried around a sense of guilt —guilt that I had promised once to give him the things he wanted and had failed to keep that promise. Now Lee had undertaken that responsibility; he would have a good home, delicious meals, clean clothes; he would be taken care of. At that moment I loved them both very much. We all hugged each other goodbye and I could feel the warmth and caring emanating from both of them.

When I walked into my own apartment after that reception— an apartment filled with the clutter of manuscripts and files—all the paraphernalia connected with my writing and the Man-Woman Institute—I felt such happiness I could hardly bear it. I looked at the mismatched furniture, at Keith busily dictating a letter into the Dictaphone, and I knew that I, too, had what I wanted. Roger and I had taken different paths and there was no way I could have kept on giving him what he wanted and needed and become the person I now am. My house will never be photographed for a homemaking magazine; my elaborate dinner parties are a thing of the past; and sometimes you could write a letter in the dust on my furniture. But I am leading a life of creativity and fulfillment. Roger is now happily involved in his new marriage and I in my new book. We both have what we want.

Suggested Reading List

We have chosen these books to supplement what we have said in
Brief Encounters about new ways to relate to others. While we don't
endorse every idea in every book, we believe that these provocative
books will stimulate, enrich and/or clarify your thinking about relationships. Whether you have a brief encounter, a short-term alliance
or a long-term relationship with one or some of these books, we hope
you'll receive both enjoyment and knowledge from reading them.

Allen, Gina, and Martin, Clement G. *Intimacy: Sensitivity, Sex, and
    the Art of Love*. Chicago: Cowles Book Company, 1971.
Bach, George R., and Deutsch, Ronald M. *Pairing: How to Achieve
    Genuine Intimacy*. New York: Peter H. Wyden, 1970.
Bach, George R., and Wyden, Peter. *The Intimate Enemy: How to
    Fight Fair in Love and Marriage*. New York: William Morrow and
    Company, 1969.
Brain, Robert. *Friends and Lovers*. New York: Basic Books, 1976.
Brenton, Myron. *Friendship*. New York: Stein and Day, 1974.
Burger, Robert E. *The Love Contract: Handbook for a Liberated
    Marriage*. New York: Van Nostrand Reinhold Company, 1973.
Buscaglia, Leo. *Love*. Thorofare, N.J.: Charles B. Slack, 1972.
Carson, Gerald. *The Polite Americans: A Wide-Angle View of Our
    More or Less Good Manners Over 300 Years*. New York: William
    Morrow and Company, 1966.
Casler, Lawrence. *Is Marriage Necessary?* New York: Human Sciences
    Press, 1974.
Coleman, Emily. *Making Friends with the Opposite Sex*. Los An-
    geles: Nash Publishing Corporation, 1972.
Colgrove, Melba; Bloomfield, Harold H.; and McWilliams, Peter.
    *How to Survive the Loss of a Love: 58 Things to Do When There
    Is Nothing to Be Done*. New York: Leo Press, 1976.

Colton, Helen. *Sex After the Sexual Revolution.* New York: Association Press, 1972.

DeLora, Joann S. and Jack R., editors. *Intimate Life Styles: Marriage and Its Alternatives.* Pacific Palisades, Calif.: Goodyear Publishing Company, 1972.

Edwards, Lawrence. *Lover: The Confessions of a One-Night Stand.* New York: Farrar, Straus & Giroux, 1976.

Epstein, Joseph. *Divorced in America: Marriage in an Age of Possibility.* New York: E. P. Dutton & Co., 1974.

Fast, Julius. *Body Language.* New York: M. Evans and Company, 1970.

Francoeur, Robert T. *Eve's New Rib: Twenty Faces of Sex, Marriage, and Family.* New York: Harcourt Brace Jovanovich, 1972.

Fromme, Allan. *The Ability to Love.* New York: Farrar, Straus & Giroux, 1965.

Gettleman, Susan, and Markowitz, Janet. *The Courage to Divorce.* New York: Ballantine Books, 1974.

Gillies, Jerry. *Friends—The Power and Potential of the Company You Keep.* New York: Coward, 1976.

Glasser, William. *The Identity Society.* Revised edition; New York: Harper & Row, 1975.

Godwin, John. *The Mating Trade.* Garden City, N.Y.: Doubleday & Company, 1973.

Goffman, Erving. *Relations in Public: Microstudies of the Public Order.* New York: Basic Books, 1971.

Howard, Jane. *Please Touch: A Guided Tour of the Human Potential Movement.* New York: McGraw-Hill Book Company, 1970.

Hunt, Morton M. *The World of the Formerly Married.* New York: McGraw-Hill Book Company, 1966.

———. *Sexual Behavior in the 1970s.* Chicago: Playboy Press, 1974.

Johnson, Stephen. *First Person Singular: Living the Good Life Alone.* Philadelphia and New York: J. B. Lippincott Company, 1977.

Keyes, Ralph. *We, the Lonely People: Searching for Community.* New York: Harper & Row, 1973.

Klapp, Orrin E. *Collective Search for Identity.* New York: Holt, Rinehart and Winston, 1969.

Lerner, Max. *America as a Civilization: Life and Thought in the U.S. Today.* New York: Simon and Schuster, 1957.

Levison, Teddi, and Faber, Stuart J. *The Upside Downs of Jealousy, Possessiveness & Insecurity.* Hollywood: Good Life Press, 1975.

Luthman, Shirley Gehrke. *Intimacy.* Los Angeles: Nash Publishing Corporation, 1972.

McDonald, Paula and Dick. *Loving Free.* New York: Ballantine Books, 1973.

Megan, Terry. *Couplings and Groupings.* New York: Pantheon Books, 1972.

Miller, Sherod; Nunnally, Elam W.; and Wackman, Daniel B. *Alive and Aware.* Minneapolis: Interpersonal Communication Programs, 1975.

Narciso, John, and Burkett, David. *Declare Yourself: Discovering the ME in Relationships.* Englewood Cliffs, N.J.: Prentice-Hall, 1975.

O'Neill, Nena. *The Marriage Premise.* New York: M. Evans and Company, 1977.

O'Neill, Nena and George. *Open Marriage: A New Life Style for Couples.* New York: M. Evans and Company, 1972.

———. *Shifting Gears: Finding Security in a Changing World.* New York: M. Evans and Company, 1974.

Otto, Herbert A., editor. *The New Sexuality.* Palo Alto, Calif.: Science and Behavior Books, 1971.

———. *Love Today.* New York: Association Press, 1972.

Packard, Vance. *A Nation of Strangers.* New York: David McKay Co., 1972.

Paul, Jordan and Margaret. *Free to Love: Creating and Sustaining Intimacy in Marriage.* Los Angeles: J. P. Tarcher, 1975.

Ramey, James W. *Intimate Friendships.* Englewood Cliffs, N.J.: Prentice-Hall, 1976.

Reid, Clyde. *Celebrate the Temporary.* New York: Harper & Row, 1972.

Ryan, Bryce F. *Social and Cultural Change.* New York: The Ronald Press Company, 1969.

Samuel, Dorothy. *Safe Passage in City Streets.* Nashville: Abingdon Press, 1975.

Satir, Virginia. *Conjoint Family Therapy.* Revised edition; Palo Alto, Calif.: Science and Behavior Books, 1967.

———. *Peoplemaking.* Palo Alto, Calif.: Science and Behavior Books, 1972.

Shain, Merle. *Some Men Are More Perfect Than Others: A Book about Men, and Hence about Women and Love and Dreams.* New York: Charterhouse, 1973.

Slater, Philip E. *The Pursuit of Loneliness: American Culture at the Breaking Point.* Boston: Beacon Press, 1970.

Smith, Gerald Walker, with Phillips, Alice I. *Me and You and Us.* New York: Peter H. Wyden, 1971.

Smith, Manuel J. *When I Say No, I Feel Guilty: How to Cope,*

Using the Skills of Systematic Assertive Therapy. New York: Dial Press, 1975.

Somers, Suzanne. *Touch Me.* Los Angeles: Nash Publishing Corporation, 1973.

Tanner, Ira J. *Loneliness: The Fear of Love.* New York: Harper & Row, 1973.

Toffler, Alvin. *Future Shock.* New York: Random House, 1970.

Van Deusen, Edmund L. *Contract Cohabitation: An Alternative to Marriage.* New York: Grove Press, 1974.

Walters, Barbara. *How to Talk with Practically Anybody about Practically Anything.* Garden City, N.Y.: Doubleday & Company, 1970.

Ziskin, Jay and Mae. *The Extramarital Sex Contract.* Los Angeles: Nash Publishing Corporation, 1973.

Zunin, Leonard, with Natalie Zunin. *Contact: The First Four Minutes.* Los Angeles: Nash Publishing Corporation, 1972.